Till J. Nesta Woerfel
Encoding Motion Events

Studies on Language Acquisition

Edited by
Peter Jordens

Volume 58

Till J. Nesta Woerfel

Encoding Motion Events

The Impact of Language-Specific Patterns and
Language Dominance in Bilingual Children

DE GRUYTER
MOUTON

ISBN 978-1-5015-2141-6
e-ISBN (PDF) 978-1-5015-0797-7
e-ISBN (EPUB) 978-1-5015-0791-5
ISSN 1861-4248

Bibliographic information published by the Deutsche Nationalbibliothek
The Deutsche Nationalbibliothek lists this publication in the Deutsche Nationalbibliografie;
detailed bibliographic data are available on the Internet at http://dnb.dnb.de.

© 2020 Walter de Gruyter, Inc., Boston/Berlin
This volume is text- and page-identical with the hardback published in 2018.
Typesetting: Integra Software Services Pvt. Ltd.
Printing and binding: CPI books GmbH, Leck

www.degruyter.com

Acknowledgments

The present volume is a version of my inaugural dissertation which was carried out from 2011–2016 at the "Graduate School Language and Literature Munich", Ludwig-Maximilians-Universität München. First of all I'd like to thank the children and their parents who have participated in this study. Without you this study could not have been carried out. I am also grateful for the assistance of all the teachers who supported me with the data collection in Germany, France and Turkey. In this context, I want to thank particularly Prof. Dr. Mehmet-Ali Akıncı and his students. It was his connections in France and his exceptional commitment to my project that made the data collection in France possible.

For the supervision during the past years I am very grateful to my supervisors, Prof. Dr. Wolfgang Schulze and PD Dr. Katrin Lindner as well as Prof. Dr. Christoph Schroeder, who continuously helped me, each in his or her own way.

For advices, corrections and encouragement I'd like to express my appreciation to Prof. Dr. Juliana Goschler, Dr. Anne-Katharina Harr, Prof. Dr. Peter Jordens, Dr. Nikolas Koch, Kathleen Rabl, Prof. Dr. Claudia Riehl, Dr. Charles Stewart, Dr. Nicole Weidinger and Seda Yilmaz Woerfel. Thank you for having shared your ideas with me!

And finally, I could not have finished this project without the support of my family (Ulf, Ute, Paula, Şenel, Durmuş) – I am particularly thankful to my sons Mats and Wim and my wife Seda, who supported me all along the way and, especially, gave me time to relax and enjoy non-academic life.

Contents

List of Figures —— XI

List of Tables —— XIII

Abbreviations —— XIX

1 Introduction —— 1
1.1 Why research on early second language acquisition matters —— 1
1.2 Why the domain of motion event encoding is a fruitful field for early second language acquisition research —— 1
1.2.1 Linguistic interactions —— 5
1.2.2 Communicative function of language —— 6
1.2.3 The relation between language knowledge and thought —— 6
1.3 Why the domain of early second language acquisition is a fruitful field for motion event research —— 7
1.4 The goal of the investigation —— 7
1.5 The organisation of the book —— 8

2 Multicompetence in child bilingualism —— 10
2.1 The interplay of two languages in child bilingualism: Exploring the factors of variation —— 10
2.1.1 Defining child bilingualism —— 10
2.1.2 Language dominance —— 11
2.1.3 The role of socio-economic status and linguistic input —— 16
2.2 Multicompetence —— 21
2.2.1 Nonmonolingual likeness —— 21
2.2.2 The relationship between L1 and L2: cross-linguistic (bidirectional) influence —— 23
2.3 The case of Turkish as a heritage language in second and third generation child bilinguals in Germany and France —— 29
2.3.1 Turkish immigration in Germany and France —— 29
2.3.2 Language use and maintenance of Turkish in the immigration context —— 32
2.3.3 Social factors and education —— 34
2.3.4 Successive language acquisition, attrition and language shift —— 34
2.3.5 Characteristics in L1 —— 36
2.3.6 Characteristics in L2 —— 37
2.4 Summary —— 40

3	**Motion events in language and cognition —— 42**
3.1	Spatial language and cognition —— 42
3.2	The study of motion events —— 42
3.2.1	General considerations —— 42
3.2.2	Defining motion events —— 45
3.2.3	Defining motion event conceptualisation —— 47
3.2.4	Motion event expressions —— 48
3.2.5	Typological approaches towards motion event expressions —— 54
3.2.6	Empirical implications of motion event encoding in German, Turkish, and French —— 61
3.2.7	General structural differences between German, French and Turkish —— 88
3.3	The impact of language-specific properties on cognition —— 91
3.3.1	Relativistic consequences in spontaneous speech —— 91
3.3.2	Conceptual transfer in the domain of motion —— 95
3.4	Summary and considerations for the current study —— 96
4	**Motion events in first and bilingual language acquisition —— 101**
4.1	The impact of language-specific properties in monolingual first language acquisition of German, Turkish and French —— 101
4.1.1	German —— 101
4.1.2	Turkish —— 102
4.1.3	French —— 104
4.2	The interaction of language-specific properties in bilingual language acquisition —— 105
4.2.1	Turkish-German in multilingual settings —— 107
4.2.2	Turkish-French in multilingual settings —— 108
4.3	Summary and considerations for the current study —— 109
5	**Implications and general assumptions —— 111**
5.1	Implications for the study —— 111
5.1.1	Language pairs —— 111
5.1.2	Participants —— 111
5.1.3	Stimuli —— 112
5.1.4	Criteria of analysis —— 112
5.2	Research questions and hypotheses —— 113
6	**Methodology —— 117**
6.1	Participants —— 117
6.1.1	Age, sex and residence —— 117

6.1.2	Migration context —— 118	
6.1.3	Acquisition context —— 119	
6.1.4	Educational background —— 121	
6.2	Design —— 122	
6.2.1	Manner Verb Control Task —— 122	
6.2.2	Voluntary Motion Task —— 122	
6.2.3	Sociolinguistic questionnaires —— 125	
6.3	Data collection procedure —— 125	
6.4	Transcription —— 126	
6.5	Coding and analysis —— 128	
6.5.1	Voluntary Motion Task —— 128	
6.5.2	Manner Verb Control Task —— 135	
6.5.3	Parental questionnaires —— 136	
6.5.4	Child questionnaire —— 137	
6.5.5	Statistical analysis —— 138	

7 Study on language dominance patterns and motion encoding by Turkish-German and Turkish-French bilinguals —— 143

7.1	Study 1: Language dominance —— 143
7.1.1	Results domain —— 144
7.1.2	Results dimension —— 150
7.1.3	The relation of domain and dimension —— 168
7.1.4	Summary and discussion —— 172
7.2	Study 2: Voluntary Motion —— 175
7.2.1	Results of Manner Verb Control Task —— 178
7.2.2	Results of motion verb choices —— 192
7.2.3	Results of other linguistic devices —— 220
7.2.4	Results of Path elaboration —— 228
7.2.5	Results of motion verb constructions —— 237
7.2.6	Results of locative and telic Path phrases —— 253
7.2.7	Quantification of cross-linguistic influence and the (in)significance of language dominance —— 294
7.2.8	Summary and discussion —— 297

8 General discussion and future directions —— 307

8.1	Contribution to second language acquisition research —— 307
8.1.1	Language use and language dominance —— 307
8.1.2	The nature of variation in bilinguals —— 308
8.2	Contribution to perspectives on motion event research —— 311
8.2 1	Motion encoding in multilingual settings —— 311

8.2.2	Multilingual variation —— 311	
8.2.3	Intra-typological variation —— 312	
8.3	Contribution to methodological implications —— 314	
8.3.1	Language dominance —— 314	
8.3.2	Motion encoding —— 315	
8.4	Limitations and future directions —— 315	
8.4.1	Limitations in language dominance and early second language acquisition and future directions —— 315	
8.4.2	Limitations in motion encoding and future directions —— 316	

Appendix
A. Questionnaires —— 319
B. Methodology —— 332
C. Results —— 343

References —— 357

Index —— 377

List of Figures

Figure 1	Encoding schema of a motion event situation (a) —— 44	
Figure 2	Types of motion event situations —— 46	
Figure 3	Conceptual structure of the macro-event (adapted from Talmy 20003:221) —— 47	
Figure 4	Conceptual structure of the framing event (adapted from Talmy 20003:221) —— 47	
Figure 5	Possible syntactic mapping: Manner-in-verb pattern (adapted from Talmy 20003:223) —— 49	
Figure 6	Possible syntactic mapping: Path-in-verb pattern in French (adapted from Talmy 20003:223) —— 49	
Figure 7	Possible syntactic mapping: Path-in-verb pattern in Turkish (adapted from Talmy 20003:223) —— 50	
Figure 8	Intransitive motion construction (adapted from Goldberg 1995:78) —— 51	
Figure 9	Intransitive motion construction with sein (adapted from Berthele 2007:245) —— 52	
Figure 10	Encoding schema of a motion event situation (b) —— 53	
Figure 11	Motion verb frequency in German oral text corpora (in tokens) —— 63	
Figure 12	Motion verb frequency in Turkish National Corpus (in token per million entries) —— 66	
Figure 13	frequency in CLAPI (in tokens) Motion verb. —— 68	
Figure 14	Encoding schema of a motion event situation (c) —— 90	
Figure 15	Internal structure of Path and Manner in German and Turkish —— 93	
Figure 16	Annotation of utterances and hesitation disfluency in EXMARaLDA —— 130	
Figure 17	Annotation of code-mixing/switching in EXMARaLDA —— 130	
Figure 18	Annotation of specific motion event categories in EXMARaLDA —— 134	
Figure 19	Analysis of (multiple) annotation tiers with EXAKT —— 135	
Figure 20	Transcription and annotation of the lexical control task with EXMARaLDA —— 136	
Figure 21	Individual difference-values of verbal fluency in L1 and L2 and individual dominance-score (*ds*) for Turkish-German bilinguals —— 151	
Figure 22	Individual difference-values of verbal fluency in L1 and L2 and individual dominance-score (ds) for Turkish-French bilinguals —— 152	
Figure 23	Individual difference-values of lexical repertoire in L1 and L2 and individual dominance-scores (ds) for Turkish-German bilinguals (in numbers) —— 154	
Figure 24	Given and expected lemmas in Turkish of Turkish-German bilinguals —— 155	
Figure 25	Given and expected lemmas in German of Turkish-German bilinguals —— 155	
Figure 26	Individual difference-values of lexical repertoire in L1 and L2 and individual dominance-scores (ds) for Turkish-French bilinguals (in numbers) —— 156	

Figure 27	Given and expected lemmas in Turkish of Turkish-French bilinguals —— 157
Figure 28	Given and expected lemmas in French of Turkish-French bilinguals —— 157
Figure 29	Correlation coefficients in both groups —— 168
Figure 30	Correlation coefficients in the Turkish-German group —— 169
Figure 31	Correlation coefficients in the Turkish-French group —— 170
Figure 32	Amount of combinations of dominance profiles (domain and dimension) —— 171
Figure 33	Inter-group differences in motion verb choices Turkish (in %) —— 180
Figure 34	Numbers of Turkish Manner verb choices in target events —— 181
Figure 35	Numbers of Turkish Path verb choices in test items —— 182
Figure 36	Inter-group differences in motion verb choices German (in %) —— 184
Figure 37	Numbers of German Manner verb choices in target items —— 185
Figure 38	Inter-group differences in motion verb choices French (in %) —— 187
Figure 39	Numbers of French Manner verb choices in target items —— 189
Figure 40	Numbers of French Path verb choices in target items —— 190
Figure 41	Inter-group differences in motion verb choices Turkish (in %) —— 210
Figure 42	Inter-group differences in motion verb choices German (in %) —— 212
Figure 43	Inter-group differences in motion verb choices French (in %) —— 213
Figure 44	Mean difference of the particular analytical levels motion verb choices (VCONF), Path elaboration (ELAB), motion verb construction (VCONST), locative (LOC) and telic Path phrases (TEL) between bilingual (TURGER, TURFRE) and minimal bilingual speakers (GER, FRE) in the respective L1 and L2 (based on %) —— 302

List of Tables

Table 1	Wälchli's cardinal kinds of displacement and Berthele's modifications —— 61
Table 2	Total frequency of Generic, Path, Manner and Manner-Path verbs and distribution of everyday and expressive Manner/Manner-Path verbs in oral corpora of German —— 64
Table 3	Total frequency of Generic, Path, Manner and Manner-Path verbs and distribution of everyday and expressive Manner/Manner-Path verbs in the Turkish National Corpus —— 66
Table 4	Total frequency of Generic, Path, Manner and Manner-Path verbs and distribution of everyday and expressive Manner/Manner-Path verbs in spoken corpora of French —— 69
Table 5	Adnominal and adverbal encoding in German —— 71
Table 6	Adverbal and adnominal encoding in Turkish —— 73
Table 7	Adverbal and adnominal encoding in French —— 75
Table 8	Combinations of Manner verbs with adverbial directionals (ADV_DIR) and postpositions (POSTPOS) in the Turkish National Corpus —— 78
Table 9	Schematisation of locative and telic Path phrases —— 82
Table 10	Verbal, adnominal and adverbal encoding in German, Turkish and French —— 97
Table 11	Number, sex, and age (mean (M), standard deviation (SD), and range (R)) of Turkish-German and Turkish-French bilinguals as well as German, Turkish and French minimal bilingual participants —— 118
Table 12	Birthplace and migration information of Turkish-German, Turkish-French bilinguals, German, Turkish, and French minimal bilinguals —— 119
Table 13	Acquisition background information of Turkish-German and Turkish-French bilinguals —— 120
Table 14	Mean (M) and numbers of parental educational levels —— 121
Table 15	Test items and target events of the Manner Verb Control Task —— 123
Table 16	Types of elicited motion event situations —— 124
Table 17	Levels of education among the International Standard Classification of Education (ISCED-2011) —— 138
Table 18	Language dominance patterns (domain) of Turkish-German bilinguals (intra-group comparison) —— 145
Table 19	Language dominance patterns (domain) of Turkish-German bilinguals (individual results) —— 145
Table 20	Language dominance patterns (domain) by Turkish-French bilinguals (intra-group comparison) —— 147
Table 21	Language dominance pattern domain by Turkish-French bilinguals (individual results) —— 148
Table 22	Amount of language dominance patterns (domain) by Turkish-German and Turkish-French bilinguals (in numbers) —— 149
Table 23	Amount of L1-, L2-dominance, no dominance and mixed patterns (domain) per group (in numbers) —— 150
Table 24	Summary of L1-, L2-dominance, and no dominance (verbal fluency) per group —— 152

https://doi.org/10.1515/9781501507977-203

Table 25	Amount of L1-, L2-dominance, and no dominance (lexical repertoire) per group (in numbers) —— 158
Table 26	Amount of code-mixing utterances and direction of mixing in Turkish-German and Turkish French bilinguals —— 163
Table 27	Amount of L1-, L2-dominance, and no dominance (code-mixing) per group (in numbers) —— 164
Table 28	Summarised results (dimension) for Turkish-German bilinguals —— 165
Table 29	Summarised results (dimension) for Turkish French bilinguals —— 166
Table 30	Summary of L1, L2-dominance, no dominance and mixed patterns (dimension) per group —— 167
Table 31	Encoded motion verbs in MVC-Task Turkish (in %); diversity of motion verbs (in numbers) —— 179
Table 32	Manner verb usage according to the TNC classification (in %) —— 182
Table 33	Encoded motion verbs in MVC-Task German (in %); diversity of motion verbs (in numbers) —— 183
Table 34	Manner verb usage in German according to DGD 2-classification (in %) —— 186
Table 35	Encoded motion verbs in MVC-Task French (in %) and diversity of motion verbs (in numbers) —— 187
Table 36	Manner verb usage in French according to CLAPI-classification —— 189
Table 37	Motion verb choices in motion descriptions of all participants (in %) —— 192
Table 38	Means (M), Standard deviations (SD) and ranges (R) of motion verb choices in Turkish motion descriptions of Turkish-German (TURGER) and Turkish-French bilinguals (TURFRE) as well as Turkish minimal bilinguals (TUR) (in %) —— 194
Table 39	Turkish-German bilinguals with a distance of one or more standard deviations (SD) in Manner verb (VM), Manner-Path verb (VMP), Path verb (VP) and Generic verb (VGEN) usage in Turkish, their educational background (SES) and standard deviation in types per lemma (TpL) —— 196
Table 40	Turkish-French bilinguals with a distance of one or more standard deviations (SD) in Manner verb (VM), Manner-Path verb (VMP), Path verb (VP) and Generic verb (VGEN) usage in Turkish —— 197
Table 41	Means, Standard deviations (SD) and ranges (R) of motion verb choices in German (in %) —— 199
Table 42	Z-scores of Generic/no motion verbs in German, Manner/Manner-Path repertoire in German, z-scores of tokens per lemma (TpL) in German and educational background profiles of Turkish-German bilinguals —— 201
Table 43	Turkish-German bilinguals with a distance of one or more standard deviations (SD) in Manner verb (VM), Manner-Path verb (VMP), and Generic verb (VGEN) usage in German —— 203
Table 44	Means (M), Standard deviations (SD) and ranges (R) of motion verb choices in French (in %) —— 205
Table 45	Proportion of motion verb choices in Turkish and French (in %) —— 206

List of Tables — **XV**

Table 46	Turkish-French bilinguals with a distance of one or more standard deviations (SD) in Manner verb (vm), Manner-Path verb (vmp), Path verb (vp) and Generic verb (vgen) usage in French, their standard deviation of tokens per lemma (TpL) in French as well as educational background (ses) profiles —— **208**
Table 47	Means (M) and ranges (R) of Motion, Manner/Manner-Path and Path verb diversity Turkish (in numbers) —— **214**
Table 48	Means (M) and ranges (R) of everyday and expressive Manner verbs Turkish (in %) —— **214**
Table 49	Means (M) and ranges (R) of Motion, Manner and Path verb diversity German (in numbers) —— **216**
Table 50	Means (M) and ranges (R) of everyday and expressive Manner verbs German (in %) —— **217**
Table 51	Means and ranges Motion, Manner and Path verb diversity French (in numbers) —— **217**
Table 52	Means (M) and ranges (R) of everyday and expressive Manner verbs French (in %) —— **218**
Table 53	Manner and Path devices Turkish (in %) —— **221**
Table 54	Manner and Path devices German (in %) —— **223**
Table 55	Manner and Path devices French (in %) —— **224**
Table 56	Verbal (V), adnominal (AN) and adverbal (AV) Path encoding of all participants (in %) —— **226**
Table 57	Means (M) and ranges (R) of Path elaboration Turkish (in %) —— **229**
Table 58	Turkish-German and Turkish-French bilinguals with a distance of one or more standard deviations (SD) in expressing no, one or two (or more) directional Path elements in Turkish —— **230**
Table 59	Means (M) and Ranges (R) of Path elaboration German (in %) —— **231**
Table 60	Turkish-German bilinguals with a distance of one or more standard deviations (SD) in expressing no, one or two (or more) directional Path elements in German —— **232**
Table 61	Means (M) and ranges (R) of Path elaboration French (in %) —— **234**
Table 62	Turkish-French bilinguals with a distance of one or more standard deviations (SD) in expressing no or one directional Path elements in French —— **235**
Table 63	Path elaboration in Turkish, German and French of all participants (in %) —— **237**
Table 64	Means (M) and ranges (R) of motion verb constructions Turkish (in %) —— **238**
Table 65	V- and S-constructions Turkish (in %) —— **240**
Table 66	Syntactic constructions in Turkish (in %) —— **241**
Table 67	Turkish-German and Turkish-French bilinguals with a distance of one or more standard deviations (SD) in vp_p, vm_0, vgen_p, vm_p and vmp_p constructions in Turkish —— **242**
Table 68	Means (M) and ranges (R) of motion verb constructions German (in %) —— **243**
Table 69	Syntactic constructions in German (in %) —— **245**
Table 70	Turkish-German bilinguals with a distance of one or more standard deviations (SD) in vm_p, vgen_p, vm_0, and vmp_p constructions in German —— **246**

XVI — List of Tables

Table 71	Means (*M*) and ranges (*R*) of motion verb constructions French (in %) —— 248
Table 72	V- and S-constructions French (in %) —— 249
Table 73	Syntactic constructions in French (in %) —— 249
Table 74	Turkish-French bilinguals with a distance of one or more standard deviations (*SD*) in VP_P, VM_0, VP_0, VGEN_P and VM_P constructions in French —— 251
Table 75	Means (*M*) and ranges (*R*) of motion verb choices in locative Path phrases Turkish (in %) —— 254
Table 76	Motion verb choices per motion event type with Path focus Turkish (in %) —— 255
Table 77	Turkish-German and Turkish-French bilinguals with a distance of one or more standard deviations (*SD*) in Manner verb (VM), Manner-Path verb (VMP), Path verb (VP), and Generic verb (VGEN) usage in Turkish locative Path phrases —— 257
Table 78	Means (*M*) and ranges (*R*) of motion verb choices in locative Path phrases German (in %) —— 259
Table 79	Motion verb choices per motion event type with Path focus German (in %) —— 260
Table 80	Turkish-German bilinguals with a distance of one or more standard deviations (*SD*) in Manner verb (VM), Manner-Path verb (VMP) and Generic verb (VGEN) usage in German locative Path phrases —— 262
Table 81	Turkish-German bilinguals with highest standard deviations (SD) in Manner-Path verb (VMP) and Generic verb (VGEN) usage in SUPER events in German, Path verb (VP) usage in SUPER events in Turkish, Generic verb (VGEN) usage in AD-events in German and Turkish as well as in overall German and Turkish locative Path phrases —— 263
Table 82	Means (*M*) and ranges (*R*) of motion verb choices in locative Path phrases French (in %) —— 266
Table 83	Motion verb choices per motion event type with Path focus French (in %) —— 267
Table 84	Turkish-French bilinguals with a distance of one or more standard deviations (*SD*) in Manner verb (VM), Manner-Path verb (VMP), Path verb (VP) and Generic verb (VGEN) usage in French locative Path phrases —— 269
Table 85	Turkish-French bilinguals with highest standard deviations (SD) in Manner verb (VM) usage in GENERALIS-events, in Generic verb (VGEN) usage in AD-events and Path verb (VP) usage in SUPER events in Turkish and French —— 270
Table 86	Means (*M*) and ranges (*R*) of motion verb choices in telic Path phrases Turkish (in %) —— 273
Table 87	Motion verb choices per motion event type with boundary focus Turkish (in %) —— 274
Table 88	Summary of boundary crossing constraint violations (in numbers) —— 277
Table 89	Turkish-German and Turkish-French bilinguals with a distance of one or more standard deviations (*SD*) in Path verb (VP) usage in Turkish telic Path phrases —— 278
Table 90	Means (*M*) and ranges (*R*) of motion verb choices in telic Path phrases German (in %) —— 280

Table 91	Motion verb choices with total telic Path phrases as a reference point (in %) —— 281
Table 92	Motion verb choices per motion event type with boundary focus German (in %) —— 281
Table 93	Turkish-German bilinguals with highest standard deviations (SD) in Manner verb (VM) and Generic verb (VGEN) usage in German telic Path phrases —— 283
Table 94	Generic/no motion verbs and Manner/Manner-Path repertoire among Turkish-German bilinguals —— 284
Table 95	Individual Manner verb usage in telic Path phrases in German and Turkish (in %) —— 285
Table 96	Means (M) and ranges (R) of motion verb choices in telic Path phrases French (in %) —— 286
Table 97	Motion verb choices per motion event type with boundary focus French (in %) —— 287
Table 98	Summary of boundary crossing constraint violations in French (number of occurrences) —— 290
Table 99	Turkish-French bilinguals' individual use of Manner and Manner-Path verbs in telic Path phrases in Turkish and French (in %) —— 291
Table 100	Turkish-French bilinguals with highest standard deviations (SD) in Path verb (VP) usage in Turkish and French telic Path phrases —— 291
Table 101	Unidirectional L1>L2 influence on analytical levels motion verb choices (VCONF), Path elaboration (ELAB), motion verb construction (VCONST), locative (LOC) and telic (TEL) Path phrases of Turkish-German and Turkish-French bilinguals and their language dominance profiles —— 295
Table 102	Unidirectional L2>L1 influence on analytical levels motion verb choices (VCONF), Path elaboration (ELAB), motion verb construction (VCONST), locative (LOC) and telic (TEL) Path phrases of Turkish German and Turkish-French bilinguals and their language dominance profiles —— 296
Table 103	Bidirectional influence on analytical levels motion verb choices (VCONF), Path elaboration (ELAB), motion verb construction (VCONST), locative (LOC) and telic (TEL) Path phrases of Turkish-German and Turkish-French bilinguals and their language dominance profiles —— 297
Table 104	Turkish-German and Turkish-French bilinguals with no influence and their language dominance profiles —— 297
Table 105	Summary of observed influence on the analytical levels motion verb choices (VCONF), Path elaboration (ELAB), verb construction (VCONST), locative Path phrases (LOC) and telic Path phrases (TEL) of Turkish-German and Turkish-French bilinguals (in numbers) —— 298
Table 106	Annotation specifics for coding the Voluntary Motion Task —— 335
Table 107	Coding method of questionnaires for parents of bilingual participants —— 339
Table 108	Summary of combinations of fine "L1-dominance" (3), "L2-dominance" (1), "no dominance" (2) patterns in domain and dimension of Turkish-German (TURGER) and Turkish-French (TURFRE) bilinguals —— 343
Table 109	Summary of combinations of global "L1-dominance" (L1), "L2-dominance" (L2), "no dominance" (no) and mixed dominance (mixed) patterns in domain and dimension of Turkish-German (TURGER) and Turkish-French (TURFRE) bilinguals —— 344

Table 110	Proportion of Turkish motion verb lemmas in Manner Verb Control Task of Turkish-German (TURGER), Turkish-French (TURFRE) bilinguals and Turkish minimal bilinguals (TUR) (in %) —— 344
Table 111	Proportion of German motion verb lemmas in Manner Verb Control Task of Turkish-German (TURGER) and German minimal bilinguals (GER) (in %) —— 345
Table 112	Proportion of French motion verb lemmas in Manner Verb Control Task of Turkish-French (TURFRE) and French minimal bilinguals (FRE) (in %) —— 346
Table 113	Proportion of Turkish motion verb lemmas in Voluntary Motion Task of Turkish-German (TURGER), Turkish-French (TURFRE) bilinguals and Turkish minimal bilinguals (TUR) (in %) —— 347
Table 114	Proportion of German motion verb lemmas in Voluntary Motion Task of Turkish-German (TURGER) and German minimal bilinguals (GER) (in %) —— 348
Table 115	Proportion of French motion verb lemmas in Voluntary Motion Task of Turkish-French (TURFRE) and French minimal bilinguals (FRE) (in %) —— 350
Table 116	Turkish motion verb constructions (VCONST) and the syntactic patterns (SYNPAT) in Voluntary Motion Task of Turkish-German (TURGER), Turkish-French (TURFRE) bilinguals and Turkish minimal bilinguals (TUR) (in %) —— 351
Table 117	German motion verb constructions (VCONST) and the syntactic patterns (SYNPAT) in Voluntary Motion Task of Turkish-German (TURGER) and German minimal bilinguals (GER) (in %) —— 353
Table 118	French motion verb constructions (VCONST) and the syntactic patterns (SYNPAT) in Voluntary Motion Task of Turkish-French (TURFRE) and French minimal bilinguals (FRE) (in %) —— 355

Abbreviations

1	first person
2	second person
3	third person
ABL	ablative case
ACC	accusative case
ADV_DIR	directional adverbials
ADV_M	Manner adverbs
ADV_P	directional adverbs/double particles
AOR	aorist
AUX	auxiliary verb
CONV_M	Manner/Manner-Path converb
CONV_P	Path converb
CVB	converb
DAT	dative case
DET	determiner
FRE	French minimal bilinguals
FOC	Focus particle
FUT	future tense
GEN	genitive
GER	German minimal bilinguals
GERUND_M	Manner/Manner-Path participles/gerunds
GERUND_P	Path participles/gerunds
IMP	imperative
INDF	indefinite
INF	infinitive
INST	instrumental case
LOC	locative case
MC	main clause
NEG	negation, negative
NMLZ	nominaliser/nominalisation
OTHER_M	other Manner device
OTHER_P	other Path device
PART	(separable) Path particle
PL	plural
POSS	possessive marker
POSTCASE	postpositional case marking
POSTPOS	postposition
PP	prepositional phrase
PREF	inseparable Path prefix
PRESP	present participle
PROG	progressive aspect
PST	past tense
PST.IPFV	past imperfective
PTCP	participle

https://doi.org/10.1515/9781501507977-204

QBIL	child bilingual questionnaire
QBILPAR	parental questionnaire (child bilinguals)
QMONO	parental questionnaire (minimal bilinguals)
REFL	reflexive
SBJV	subjunctive
SG	singular
TUR	Turkish minimal bilinguals
TURFRE	Turkish-French bilinguals
TURGER	Turkish-German bilinguals
VAUX	(non-motion) auxiliary verb used in a motion construction
VAUX_P	auxiliary verb construction with Path device
VAUX_P_M	auxiliary verb construction with directional Path and Manner device
VCONV	converbial clause
VGEN	Generic verb
VGEN_0	bare Generic verb construction without Manner/Path device
VGEN_M	Generic verb construction with Manner device
VGEN_P	Generic verb construction with Path device
VGEN_P_M	Generic verb construction with directional Path and Manner device
VLV	semantically weak verb used in a motion construction
VM	Manner verb
VM_0	bare Manner verb construction without Manner/Path device
VM_M	Manner verb construction with Manner device
VM_P	Manner verb construction with Path device
VM_P_M	Manner verb construction with Path and Manner device
VMOD	(non-motion) modal verb used in a motion construction
VMOD_P	modal verb construction with directional Path device
VMP	Manner-Path verb
VMP_0	bare Manner-Path verb construction without Manner/Path device
VMP_P	Manner-Path verb construction with Path device
VP	Path verb
VP_0	bare Path verb construction without Manner/Path device
VP_M	Path verb construction with Manner device
VP_P	Path verb construction with Path device
VP_P_P	Path verb construction with directional Path device and Path converb
VSC	subordinate clause

1 Introduction

1.1 Why research on early second language acquisition matters

Immigration to western Europe in the 20th century has brought new issues to (socio) linguistic research. Today, as a result of family reunification, marriage and birth, speakers with a Turkish immigration background in the first, second and third generation represent one of the most important ethno-linguistic groups in Europe. The linguistic practices of the individual speakers (second language acquisition), family languages (maintenance and development of minority languages), and speech communities (co-existence of minority languages and the dominant majority language), as well as mixed languages and varieties which have occurred as a result of language contact, have been in the focus of linguistic research over the past forty years or so.

In this context, early second language acquisition has become a focus within linguistic and educational research. The particular interest is on child second language learners, who have already begun acquiring one first language before they begin learning the second language. Children who grow up in a second or third immigrant generation in a second language environment typically acquire and speak the minority language (e.g. Turkish) at home and acquire and speak the majority language (e.g. German, French) at kindergarten or at school. Speakers with an acquisition background like those described have repeatedly been subject to controversial public debates about their linguistic abilities and educational success. Often such debates fail to recognise bilingual characteristics such as inter-individual linguistic development as well as varying linguistic performances as a result of the influences of one language on another. In this context, it becomes clear that an examination of characteristics in bilinguals' first and second language should focus on the nature of variation.

Moreover, research on second or third generation immigrant Turkish-German and Turkish-French bilingual children is also a fruitful field for investigating the language maintenance, language shift, attrition, and variation of the Turkish variety spoken in Germany and France, since the conditions of first language acquisition and maintenance may be favoured by the fact that the Turkish minorities in Germany and France are vital linguistic communities.

1.2 Why the domain of motion event encoding is a fruitful field for early second language acquisition research

Whereas phonological, grammatical, orthographical, or lexical "errors" are easily detectable in a speakers' linguistic output, it is much more difficult to recognise and understand lexical-semantic variation. The following examples,[1] taken from oral descriptions of an animated cartoon sequence which was elicited within the scope of the current study, illustrate the spectrum of different strategies by monolingual and bilingual speakers of German (their ages are presented in parentheses). The sequence presented to the participants to which we refer here shows a cat who swallowed a bowling ball and is rolling down a street into a bowling centre. The speaker has to use different lexical items (e.g. verbs, nouns) and grammatical structures (e.g. prepositional phrases) to express what she or he has "imagined" from the presented sequence.

(1) *dann   hat   er   bowling-zimmer   rein-gang
    then   has   he   bowling-room   =inside-went[2]
    'Then he went into the bowling room' (Burhan, 10;7)

(2) [sie]   rollt   in   ein   bowlingladen   rein
    she   roll.PR   in   INDF   bowling.magasin   inside
    'She rolls into a bowling centre' (Christian, 9;8)

(3) und   danach   ist   die   katze   in   bowlingcenter   rein-geflogn
    and   then   AUX.PR   DET   cat   in   bowling centre   =inside-fly.PTCP
    'Later, the cat flew into the bowling centre' (Ozan, 9;5)

(4) und   dann   ja   is   der   zu-m   bowlingladen   gegangen
    and   then   yes   AUX.PR   he   to-DET.DAT   bowling.magasin   go.PTCP
    'And then he went to the bowling centre' (Esna, 9;3)

(5) dann   is   der   gerollt   gerollt   und
    then   AUX.PR   he   roll.PTCP   roll.PTCP   and
    zu nem   bowling   rein-gegangen
    to =INDF.DAT   bowling   inside-go.PTCP
    'Then he rolled rolled and went to the bowling inside' (Tuana, 10;8)

---

[1] For further details of the transcription conventions see §6.4.
[2] The glossing conventions used are based on the "Leipzig Glossing Rules: Conventions for interlinear morpheme-by-morpheme glosses", see http://www.eva.mpg.de/lingua/resources/glossing-rules.php [accessed 2018-01-15].

(6) | und | ist | bis | zu-m | bowling | also | bis
    | and | AUX.PR | as far as | to-DET.DAT | bowling | well | as far as
    | zum | bowlinghaus | also | da | zu-m
    | to.DET.DAT | bowling.house | well | there | to-DET.DAT
    | stadium | wo | die | da | spiel
    | stadium | where | they | there | =play.PR
    | is | bis | dahin | gerollt
    | AUX.PR | as far as | there.hither | roll.PTCP

'And [she] is to the bowling...well there to the bowling house, where they play she rolled as far as there' (Taylan, 9;8)

(7) | und danach | ist | die | katze | mit | dem
    | and then | AUX.PR | DET | cat | with | DET.DAT
    | bowlingkugl | zu | eine | bowlingbahn | gerollt | danach
    | =bowling.bowl | to | INDF | bowling.alley | roll.PTCP | then
    | isses | auf | der | bowlingbahn | gerollt
    | =AUX.PR.it | on | DET | bowling.alley | roll.PTCP

'And later the cat rolled with the bowling ball to a bowling alley...later it rolled on the bowling alley' (Kurt, 10;3)

The variation in example (1) is obviously "visible" in terms of forming the present perfect tense deviantly. On the other hand, examples (3)–(7) are rather acceptable and in oral discourse grammatically correct. In contrast to the target utterance of a monolingual German child in example (2), we observe a "hidden variation" (Bryant 2012) in the target language of the bilingual speakers. In example (2), the speaker used an expressive verb which specifies the Manner[3] of motion (*rollen* 'to roll') and encodes the change of the location of the cat (from an external to an internal space) with a prepositional phrase (*in einen bowlingladen* 'into a bowling centre') and a verb particle (*rein* 'in'). As we will see later in detail, he follows the typical pattern of his first language, German. In comparison with the prototypical pattern described, three types of variation can be observed in the output of the bilingual speakers, who were all born in Germany and acquired Turkish as their family language and German as an early second language: i) the use of a neutral verb (*gehen* 'to go', see examples (4) and (5)) instead of an expressive verb (e.g. *rollen* 'to roll'); ii) the strategy to encode the Manner of motion ('to roll') and the change of location of the cat ('go inside') separately in a para-tactic construction (5); or iii) the avoidance of encoding the Endpoint in (6) and (7), when using an

---

3 Semantic components are emphasised with a capital letter.

expressive verb; instead both speakers describe only the direction towards the bowling centre.

Compared with the monolingual speakers, for the bilingual children, encoding both Manner and Path of motion together in one clause seems to be a challenge. Furthermore, the self-corrections in example (8) seem to reflect this challenge. Nevertheless, this example indicates that the speaker acquired the typical German pattern, however, she seems to use it differently.

(8) issa   da   rein-gerollt   und hat   und is   ja
    =AUX.PR.he there   inside-roll.PTCP   and AUX.PR   and =AUX.PR   yes
    und   is   rein-gegangen   rein-gerollt
    and   AUX.PR inside-go.PTCP   inside-roll.PTCP
    'He rolled inside and, well...he went inside...rolled inside' (Gamze, 10;8)

For a better understanding of the hidden variation observed in the target language, it is helpful to look at the typical pattern of the bilingual speakers' first language, Turkish. Contrary to German, Turkish speakers typically use verbs which specify the Path of motion (*gir-* 'enter') to express the change of location, and express the Manner of motion in a non-finite verb (*yuvarlanarak* 'rolling', (9)), or, when using a finite expressive verb (*yuvarlandı* 'she/he rolled'), express the change of location in another clause (10). Thus the speaker in example (5) seems to restructure the typical Turkish structure in her German description. This would not be surprising, since it is claimed that bilinguals' languages generally interact with each other.

(9) yuvarlan-arak bol / bovling   şey-in-e   gir-di
    roll-CVB   bowling   thing-POSS-DAT   enter-PST.3SG
    'It entered the bowling thing rolling' (Melis, 9;7)

(10) yuvarlan-dı,   or-da   bovling   oynan-acak   [[em]] salon   var-dı
     roll-PST.3SG   place-LOC   bowling   play-NMLZ   room   exist-PST
     oray-a   gir-di
     place-DAT   enter-PST.3SG
     'It rolled ....there was a saloon to play bowling, it entered there' (Ela, 9;10)

The difference of these preferences in German and in Turkish, by expressing Manner or Path in the verb stem and Path or Manner outside the main verb, is well documented in linguistic typology. All languages provide linguistic properties to express Manner and Path of motion linguistically. However, they differ in their syntactic organisation and how they encode and elaborate the Path of motion. According to Talmy's typological framework (Talmy 1985; Talmy 2003; Talmy 2008), languages differ either between satellite or verb-framed motion encoding. German, on the one hand, is classified as a satellite-framed-language, Turkish, on the other hand, is classified as a verb-framed-language. In this context, the question arises of whether the encoding of motion events is less challenging when the first (e.g. Turkish) and second language (e.g. French) display similarities in their typical motion encoding pattern.

Such typological differences between languages can serve to explain sources of individual differences. Otherwise, how can we explain the bilingual speakers' target-like productions as in example (3)? Limiting the described variation in the target language (German) to the impact of the preferred structure of the L1 (Turkish) would be an over-simplification. The direction of transferring linguistic elements or structures from one language to another or converging structures of both languages is often strong in relation to language dominance and usage preferences for certain linguistic structures in one language, overlapping structures in both languages, or conflicting linguistic and non-linguistic constraints of the languages acquired. Taking recent developmental research on motion event encoding into account, it is not merely the question of whether language-specific properties have an impact on language acquisition, but rather what the nature of this impact (Engemann, Harr & Hickmann 2012) and the variation in the output is. Therefore, when analysing motion event descriptions by bilingual speakers, the following aspects should be taken into account.

1.2.1 Linguistic interactions

Since the language production of bilinguals is a focus of this study, various influencing variables in language development, as well as language proficiency, need to be taken into account. Recent research on bilingualism confirms what Grosjean mentioned almost 25 years ago: "[t]he bilingual is NOT the sum of two complete or incomplete monolinguals; rather, he or she has a unique and specific linguistic configuration" (Grosjean 1989:6; emphasis in the original). If we consider language acquisition as dynamic in nature, we can assume that language-specific properties (such as language-specific patterns of motion event encoding), which were acquired successively, interact and have an impact on the encoding of motion events in both languages of bilinguals. The resulting variation in L1 and

L2 is a bilingual phenomenon in its own right, and can generally be understood as "multicompetence" (Cook 1992).

1.2.2 Communicative function of language

The language skills of bilinguals are distributed between languages (Pearson 2009:383). Bilinguals use their languages for different purposes or different domains/registers. Consequently, variation can occur in relation to the linguistic and social context of the interaction (first, second, or bilingual context). Often one language is dominant and the other non-dominant or weaker (irrespective of how the languages are acquired simultaneously or successively) (Pearson 2009:380). Language dominance can change over time at any point with new experience or new needs for one or the other language (Pearson 2009:380). As a result of the extensive use of one language over the other, language abilities can even be lost permanently.

Other influencing factors such as the age of acquisition, quantity and quality of the linguistic input or language use, may be distributed differently among speakers and also have a different impact on their language production.

1.2.3 The relation between language knowledge and thought

The observed differences across languages in motion event encoding raise the question of the extent to which a speaker's mental representation is influenced by the language which was acquired as first language, and what is, on the other hand, the impact on lexical and grammatical decisions. Among scholars, three positions can be distinguished: conceptual processes (i) are language free, universal and operate on the basis of conceptual primitives; (ii) are language-based in nature (Whorfian hypothesis); (iii) inter-dependent between conceptualisation and language knowledge (neo-Whorfian view). The lattermost, more moderate position, presumes that language users' conceptualisation of a motion event is influenced by the particular language that they speak (Cadierno 2008:146). When children acquire a native language, they might learn particular ways of thinking (Slobin 1996a:76). Slobin's "thinking for speaking hypothesis" claims that the language trains speakers to pay attention to particular details of events and situations when talking about them. The crucial question which arises in the context of bilingualism is, whether the acquisition of a second language involves a new way of thinking and, in that case, if the first way of thinking can be affected.

1.3 Why the domain of early second language acquisition is a fruitful field for motion event research

Based on the framework proposed by Talmy, a number of empirical studies investigated the field of motion encoding across a large variety of languages over the past three decades. Recent research has begun to question Talmy's clear dichotomous typology (Beavers, Levin & Wei Tham 2010; Croft et al. 2010; Filipović 2007; Goschler & Stefanowitsch 2013a; Berthele 2009; Slobin 2004a; Wälchli 2001). If we look more closely at the possible motion event encoding within languages, there seems to be more variation than Talmy assumes. Intra-typological patterns beyond the satellite/verb-framed-typology have already been demonstrated in different languages. Some languages are considered as V-languages (e.g. Aragones, Italian, Basque, French, Turkish) but also include "(pseudo)-satellite constructions" (Ibarretxe-Antuñano & Hijazo-Gascón 2012:351). Verb-framed languages with more complex morphological resources for spatial expression (e.g. Turkish or Basque) produce more elaborated Path descriptions than speakers of "prototypical" verb-framed-languages such as Spanish (Cadierno 2008:256). Moreover, diatopical variation has been observed in regional dialects (e.g. the Moutathal dialect in Switzerland or the local dialect in Bergamo in Italy) (Berthele 2006; Bernini, Spreafico & Valentini 2006). And finally, preferences of motion event encoding are influenced by multilingual settings, when speakers of one language type acquire a language of another type as a second or foreign language (Goschler & Stefanowitsch 2013b:2). The influence of language-specific properties in foreign language acquisition, for speakers who acquired two typologically different languages from birth on, have been investigated in several studies. Whereas, only a few studies have been carried out in bilingual and early second language acquisition as well as in the acquisition of two languages with similar motion encoding patterns. If we consider that languages provide structures beyond the satellite/verb-framed-pattern, it is merely the question of whether bilingual speakers make use of overlapping patterns and/or encoding strategies, or invent new structures which are not canonically used by monolingual speakers of the respective language. Thus, future research on early second language acquisition contributes to necessary "extensions and refinements" (Goschler & Stefanowitsch 2013b:10) in the domain of motion event encoding by investigating multilingual characteristics as a further aspect of variation.

1.4 The goal of the investigation

This empirical study attempts to provide insights into bilingual language usage and language dominance, as well as the nature of variation in the encoding of motion events, by evaluating the impact of language-specific properties (satellite- and verb-framed pattern) and language dominance patterns.

In order to examine linguistic interactions between two typologically different languages (in terms of motion event encoding), the transition from a verb-framed (Turkish) to a satellite-language (German) is a focus of the current study. Moreover, to evaluate the impact of language-specific properties (the verb-framed-pattern) and intra-typological variation within a language type, a transition from a verb-framed language (Turkish) to a verb-framed language (French) is within scope of the study as well. A total of 74 children (9–10 years) were tested: Turkish-French (n=15) and Turkish-German bilinguals (n=15) as well as Turkish (n=15), German (n=15) and French (n=14) monolinguals. On the basis of the research background illustrated above, the following research questions are included in the scope of the current study:

1. Are there intra- and inter-group differences among Turkish-German and Turkish-French bilinguals according to language dominance patterns?
2. Are language skills and language knowledge in bilinguals' first language interconnected with the language use of the minority language in second language environments?
3. Are there inter- and intra-group differences in the encoding of motion events in the first and second language between the groups tested?
4. What is the variation in bilinguals' speech when comparing them to monolingual children?
5. What is the nature of possible variation and how can this be explained within second language acquisition phenomena?
6. How does the performance in Turkish of both bilingual groups vary when comparing them with monolingual speakers and with each other?
7. Does L1/L2-dominance support the direction of L1/L2 influence in motion event encoding?

1.5 The organisation of the book

This book is divided into seven chapters: in Chapter 2, the concepts of bilingualism and language dominance (§2.1) as well as the theoretical background on cross-linguistic influence (§2.2) are introduced. A specific focus will be on the classification of second generation Turkish-German and Turkish-French bilinguals in the Turkish diaspora in Germany and France in terms of language use and maintenance, social factors and education, acquisition background as well as characteristics in their linguistic development in L1 and L2 (§2.3).

Chapter 3 sets up the testing case for the empirical study. First, the relation of spatial language and cognition (§3.1), as well as basic considerations regarding motion events, are introduced (§3.2.2–3.2.4). Section 3.2.5 presents typological approaches towards motion event encoding. Talmy's study of the systematic relation between meaning and form within a cognitive framework and the characteristics of his dichotomous typology is summarised in §3.2.5.1; variation in motion encoding (§3.2.5.2) and an alternative typology of Path salience are discussed subsequently (§3.2.5.3). Building on the typological approaches, §3.2.6 presents an empirical investigation, in terms of demonstrating lexical and syntactical patterns for motion encoding provided by German, Turkish and French. Furthermore, the investigation highlights speakers' usage preferences as well as cognitive and linguistic constraints in motion event encoding in the three languages under study.

Based on the question of whether differences across languages in motion event encoding are related to how speakers process motion events non-linguistically, Slobin's "thinking for speaking hypothesis" is presented in §3.3.1. Slobin's approach is further discussed by setting the focus on conceptualisation transfer in the domain of Motion in §3.3.2.

A final aspect among the theoretical considerations is discussed in Chapter 4, where the focus is on the acquisition of motion encoding patterns in German, Turkish and French in monolingual settings (§4.1) as well as on interactions in Turkish-German and Turkish-French multilingual settings (§4.2).

On the basis of Chapters 2–4, implications and general assumptions are discussed in Chapter 5. The discussion of methodology in Chapter 6 provides detailed background information on the participants (§6.1), information on the design (§6.2), the data collection procedure (§6.3), the transcription (§6.4), as well as the coding conventions, the analytical procedure and the statistical analysis (§6.5).

As regards the different aspects of this project, the illustration of the empirical investigation is divided into two studies and presented in §7.1 (Study 1) and §7.2 (Study 2): study 1 addresses the research questions 1 and 2 by determining language dominance patterns of Turkish-German and Turkish-French bilinguals and examining the relation of language use in different situations/contexts, as well as language skills and language knowledge in the speakers' first and second language. Study 2 addresses research questions 3–7; the focus is on crosslinguistic influence in oral motion event descriptions by Turkish-German and Turkish-French bilinguals, in order to evaluate the impact of language-specific properties in the context of early second language acquisition. Individual findings of cross-linguistic influence are further examined with respect to the language dominance patterns established in Study 1 and are summarised in §7.2.7.

Finally, the overall findings of each study will be presented and discussed with regard to limitations and future directions in Chapter 8.

2 Multicompetence in child bilingualism

2.1 The interplay of two languages in child bilingualism: Exploring the factors of variation

2.1.1 Defining child bilingualism

Depending on the age of onset (AoO), when children are exposed to their first (hereafter L1) and second languages (hereafter L2), there are different aspects for terminological classification. On the one hand, children who learn two languages from birth or during the first two years of life are called "simultaneous/balanced bilinguals" (Ruberg (2013: 182) suggests an AoO from 0 to 1;11). In contrast, children who have already begun establishing one first language before they start learning the second language by age three to nine, are considered as "L1 minority L2 learners" (Paradis 2007: 388), "child L2 (cL2) learners" (Meisel 2009: 6), or "successive bilingual children" (Schönenberger, Rothweiler & Sterner 2012: 3). Among others, Ruberg (2013: 182) sub-divides this type of acquisition into even finer steps. He differentiates between successive bilinguals (AoO 2;0–3;11) and child bilinguals (AoO 4;00–9;11). In contrast, children who learn the second language through immersion schooling or foreign language instruction are most commonly termed late bilinguals or foreign language learners.

In language acquisition research, simultaneous L1-acquisition is generally limited to speakers who are exposed to two or more languages from birth on; this is true for situations when for instance one parent speaks language A, and another parent language B to the child (and possibly the parent's language of interaction is another language C). However, successive/child bilinguals whose parents interact with their child both in only one language different than the surrounding (majority) language, may also be exposed to the L2 at a very early age, for instance, on a playground with other children and their parents or in a daycare centre before age 2;0. Within the scope of this study, this refers to children who grow up in a second or third immigrant generation in Germany and France and typically acquire the minority language (e.g. Turkish) at home and acquire the majority language (e.g. German, French) at kindergarten or at school.

Whilst it is commonly believed that simultaneous and successive/child bilinguals acquire a second language quickly and with monolingual speakers ultimate attainment (Paradis 2007: 404), it has barely been studied whether, and if so in which aspects, successive/child bilinguals' second language acquisition differs from simultaneous first language acquisition. Although it is still controversially discussed among researchers, the AoO is seen as an important factor. This circumstance is mainly related to the "critical period hypothesis" (Lenneberg 1967). This originally postulates that, due to brain maturation constraints, second language acquisition becomes more difficult after puberty. In the meantime, a number of researchers suggest that the line should be drawn earlier and assume that L1-like mechanisms of acquiring distinct linguistic domains are related to different critical periods. For phonology, it is assumed to end first, then for morphology and syntax, whereas the lexicon is less affected (Keim 2012: 181–182; Köpke & Schmid 2004: 20; Pearson 2009: 397). However, no consensus for or against the existence of such critical periods has been reached so far.

In fact there are various multifaceted variables which can have an impact on L1 and L2 development and linguistic proficiencies. This view also includes different proficiencies and dominance patterns in successive/child bilingual language production. Bilinguals, as is assumed in this study, display individual and characteristic variation in both their L1- and L2-knowledge system, irrespective of whether they were exposed to two languages from birth or to the L2 in early childhood. Furthermore, the search for balanced bilingualism is not promising, because it is "an ideal one, which is largely an artefact of a theoretical perspective which takes the monolingual as its point of reference" (Romaine 1995: 18) (we will turn to this point in greater detail in §2.2).

In this study we set a range of AoO of L2 by age ≤ 6 as a criterion for successive/child bilingualism. Furthermore, we will use the term *child bilinguals* in the following when referring to children with an AoO of L2 ≤ 6. Moreover, we define AoO as a dramatic change of L1 to L2-environment (for instance when entering kindergarten). Thus, we can assume that child bilinguals develop their languages as parallels. Although it is not clear at what age a language system is established, we can presume that when the AoO of L2 is determined by age ≤ 6, the L1-acquisition process is not completed. This is supported by empirical research which has shown that the establishment of a speaker's L1 takes a certain number of years (among others Nicoladis & Grabois 2002; Pallier et al. 2003).

In order to trace the nature of variation in a bilingual speaker's linguistic performance, the following section focuses, as a first step, on the assessment of L1-L2-dominance shifts and language attrition.

2.1.2 Language dominance

2.1.2.1 Defining and measuring language dominance

Research on second or third generation immigrant children's language performance needs to account for possible asymmetries of language skills in one language or the use of one language over the other (Birdsong 2014: 1). According to Birdsong, a Turkish-German bilingual speaker, who produces German more easily than Turkish, accesses lexical items faster in German than in Turkish, and uses German more often on a daily basis than Turkish, is generally considered dominant in German. Nevertheless, a bilingual person is not simply dominant in one language. For instance, when comparing two German dominant Turkish-German bilinguals with each other, they may not be dominant in German to the same degree. In order to quantify speakers' language dominance to a measurable degree, we first need to differentiate between (i) dimensions and (ii) domains of language dominance.

Dimensions relate to "linguistic competence, production, and processing" (Birdsong 2014: 2) among others: fluency of speech, lexical diversity, morpho-syntactic knowledge, length of utterances, parsing speed, accuracy, whereas domains refer to "situations and contexts of language use" (Birdsong 2014: 2) e.g. by comparing the two languages including counting, conversation with elder siblings or relatives, child directed speech, watching television, interactions at school etc. (see also Birdsong 2016; Grosjean 2016; Treffers-Daller & Korybski 2016). On the one hand, bilinguals' language dominance may then be measurable with respect to one or several domains, and, on the other hand with respect to language abilities. When measuring language dominance, research needs to account for this distinction, in order to establish for any bilingual a dominant pattern which is specific for him or her.

With respect to domains, generally questionnaire surveys are considered when investigating the amount of language used in various languages, different situations and contexts. Situations can be related to the interlocutor (e.g. "with the mother", "with siblings", "with peers") or a medium (e.g. "when using a personal computer", "when reading books", "when listening to music"). Moreover, such situations can differ with respect to contexts (for instance, "at home", "in the store", "in school" etc.).

When quantifying dimension, different criteria have been taken into account in language dominance research, and they are mainly related to a specific norm. The best known and most adopted criterion is measuring the Mean Length of Utterances (MLU) as well as the standard deviation (*SD*) of the MLU. The MLU was originally developed for investigating the development of younger children (<48 month) in order to determine the mean length of words or morphemes in an utterance, whereas *SD* measures the dispersion of a high MLU value and the mean. A high MLU, as well as a high *SD* value, can indicate a more advanced stage of language development in one language (Cantone et al. 2008: 317). However, this criterion has been criticised, because it turned out to be highly problematic when comparing languages with structural differences. For instance, the agglutinating structure of Turkish leads to longer but fewer word tokens than occur in German or French when the same content is expressed. Furthermore, it might not be an appropriate criterion for the assessing language development of older children.

Another measurement is the upper bound (UB), which denotes the longest utterance (e.g. in a transcript of elicited data) and can indicate a speaker's capacity to produce syntactically complex utterances. Even if this criterion may be more accurate for older children compared to MLU, it is again problematic in the case of typologically different languages (Cantone et al. 2008: 318).[4] Note that both, MLU and UB, are generally related to a norm (e.g. of a standard language which is based on written language) and thus can not provide (bilingual) variation.

The amount of mixed utterances and the direction of mixing from one language into another has also been applied in language dominance research (Genesee, Nicoladis & Paradis 1995). The same authors take verb types into account as well, a criterion which has also been combined with the total amount of tokens in developmental studies on assessing the lexical repertoire in both languages (among others Kupisch 2006). Daller et al. (2011) argue that a ratio (word token per second of a transcript) is a good index of language dominance.

De Houwer (1990) includes hesitations (pauses or sounds) by assuming that the dominant language contains fewer hesitations when determining language dominance. However, this criteria has been criticised; Cantone et al. (2008: 119) note that it is important "to clearly make a distinction between pauses and proto-syntactic fillers". Hesitations are also included when determining language dominance on the basis of verbal fluency (speech rate, articulation rate, number of words per second) (among others Daller et al. 2011)

Along with the question of an appropriate metric, quantitative research on linguistic abilities, however, raises the question of the interdependence of language dominance and language proficiency. According to Birdsong (2014: 4), proficiency and dominance are separable constructs; language dominance in one language does not necessarily determine the degree of proficiency in that language, only a lower proficiency in the other language, nor does a high level of proficiency in one language imply high language dominance in that language (except for considerable differences between the proficiency levels of both languages).

---

4 Daller et al. (2011) are faced with the problem of structural differences when comparing Turkish and German. In their study, they solve the problem by adjusting the token of elicited German texts according to a ratio which they gathered from parallel texts. These were translations from one language into the other, which had further been judged for equity by a Turkish-German bilingual. It turned out that Turkish texts were nearly ten per cent lower (ratio 0.8957) than the German parallel texts.

After having introduced common methodological measurements in language dominance research for quantifying language dominance within different domains and dimensions at a given time, we now turn to possible factors which have an impact on L1-L2-dominance shifts up to L1 attrition and point out L1 attrition resistance.

2.1.2.2 Language dominance shift and attrition

In §2.1.1, we defined AoO as the moment when the L2 is routinely used in interactions with speakers of that language. With respect to AoO and language dominance, Birdsong (2014) argues that the two are associable as well as dissociable with each other. This argument indirectly contradicts the assumption that the L2 is not and will never be the dominant language. This derives from common beliefs in second language acquisition research that late AoO is negatively correlated with ultimate levels of L2 proficiency.

On the one hand, Birdsong (2014: 14) claims that AoO is associable with dominance "in the sense that it is predictive of the timing and degree of L1 attrition, which in turn promotes the L2 to the dominant language". This assumption mainly originated with language attrition research (see the contributions in Schmid et al. 2004; Köpke et al. 2007; Schmid 2011). A few studies suggest that the younger the child is when the language of her or his environment changes (as noted above for instance when entering kindergarten), the higher the probability, that L1 attrition takes place (Ammerlaan 1996; Pelc 2001; for a discussion see Köpke & Schmid 2004: 10).[5] However, other studies did not find an age effect (Köpke 1999; Schmid 2002).[6] One possibility of an age related impact might be that attrition is influenced by the same factors which define the critical period hypothesis: "With respect to attrition, the sensitive period hypothesis would imply that the easier it is for the child to learn L2, the more likely is it that she will forget her L1" (Köpke & Schmid 2004: 20).

On the other hand, the AoO "is dissociable from dominance insofar as the L1 language is not necessarily the dominant language" (Birdsong 2014: 14). This is the case for adults who grow up bilingually from birth, but who are not balanced bilinguals, as well as for the context of multiple dominance shifts during the life span, for instance as a result of individual immigration history. Further-

---

[5] Ammerlaan examined Dutch-English bilinguals (range of age at departure 6–29 years); Pelc examined Greek-English bilinguals (range of age at departure 8–32 years).
[6] Köpke examined German-English/German-French bilinguals (range of age at departure 14–36 years); Schmid examined German-Jewish bilinguals (range of age at departure group 1: 11–16 years, group 2: 17–29 years).

more, domains and language use (talking with family members) are independent with respect to AoO and language dominance. The disassociation of AoO and language dominance also accounts for the context of L1-L2 shifts in immigrant child bilinguals, who are generally exposed to the majority language from early age onwards (≤ 6 years of age). It can be assumed that an L1-L2-dominance shift "occurs as individual transition from the home language to the school or community language" (Birdsong 2014: 5).

Consequently, research designs examining L1-L2-dominance shift and language attrition have to take time variables into account, in order to trace possible changes in the L1/L2 performance: these mainly concern (i) the age of onset of bilingualism, (ii) the age at the onset of attrition, as well as (iii) the length of time since the onset of attrition.

Note that it is not clear to what extent the variable language use (domain) would prevent L1 attrition. Nevertheless, with Schmid (2007), we can hypothesise a link between the amount of L1 contact (in the sense of frequency and settings of L1 use) and L1 attrition as well as – to some degree – protection against L1 attrition. In addition to language use, Köpke & Schmid (2004: 12) assess attitude to be more influential than length of time. Attitude comprises affective factors with respect to what a person feels or believes about language in general, and the L1 and the L2 in particular (including emotional factors).

Due to the limitations of the current study, we will adopt some specific situations and contexts of language use (domain), operationalised through language use with parents, siblings and peers (in and outside home), language use when reading as well as when watching television and/or videos in the internet. Furthermore, we will adopt linguistic processing (operationalised through verbal fluency and code-mixing) and language knowledge (operationalised through the combination of verb types (lemma) and token) as dimensions. Both methodological measurements serve to specify dominance patterns for each bilingual participant in this study (see methodological aspects in §6.5). The frequency and settings of L1 use are also taken into account in order to discuss a possible protection against L1 attrition of the speakers under study. However, since attrition is not within the focus of the current study, we will not examine this aspect in greater detail. Furthermore, attitude will not be included, since the degree of influence of attitude on L1 contact is often impossible to determine (Köpke & Schmid 2004: 14).

As a result of the bidirectional influences of two languages in a bilingual speakers' mind, we cannot expect equal levels when comparing proficiencies in the dominant language of bilinguals with monolinguals in that language. Thus, in this study, L1-/L2-knowledge will not be compared with respect to a norm (such as "monolingual", or "standard language") but in relation to each other (that is, the performance in a bilingual speaker's L1 and L2). When taking questionnaires and elicitation into account for assessing language dominance in domain and dimension – as we do in the current study (see §6.2) – we have to bear in mind that the significance of these measurements is generally limited. First, questionnaires as a type of method are largely based on self-reports by the speakers themselves or by persons in close proximity to the examined population. Such data then may be determined by "how a person wishes to view herself [or someone else] than by an accurate assessment of her linguistic behaviour" (Schmid 2002: 23). Second, the assessment of L1/L2 proficiency on the basis of elicitation methods might also indicate less significance than naturalistic observations.

The factors established in this section serve to assess language dominance, shift and attrition in the children under study. In addition, predictions with respect to language developmental patterns and skills cannot be made without considering the amount as well as the quality of linguistic input, which can be influenced by different socio-economic status.

2.1.3 The role of socio-economic status and linguistic input

Developmental patterns and language skills are influenced by families' socio-economic status and attitudes towards education (Thordardottir 2014: 142). Socio-economic status is conceptually "a compound variable, usually comprising education level, occupational prestige, and income" (Hoff 2006: 60).

Low socio-economic status has generally been found to be one of the most influential factors creating educational disadvantage. This, in turn, has an impact on the language proficiencies in school. Note that this is consistent across all language acquisition types, including those of monolingual children (Reich 2009a). As a consequence, and particularly in absence of additive support, children with a low socio-economic status background often fail within the educational system (Dirim, Hauenschild & Lütje-Klose 2008).

According to cognitive and functionalist approaches, the linguistic input and communicative functions of language play an important role in the language acquisition process. Thus, a speakers' lexical repertoire is influenced by the quantity and quality of the linguistic input, which is often lower in families with a low educational background and correlates with a low socio-economic status (Gathercole & Hoff 2007; Hoff 2006; Noble et al. 2006). Hart & Risley (1995) found in their longitudinal study on monolingual English-speaking families and their children (of age 0;9 to 2;6) in the US, that higher socio-economic status mothers talk more to their children compared to middle-socio-economic status mothers as well as lower socio-economic status mothers. In the course of one week, the results indicate that children with high socio-economic status parents hear about 215,000 tokens, children with middle socio-economic status parents hear about 125,000 tokens and children with low socio-economic status parents hear about 62,000 tokens. Furthermore, the input of children with high socio-economic status parents differed not only with respect to the quantity, but also to the quality of linguistic input.

The relation between the quantity and the quality of linguistic input and socio-economic status background across cultures has been documented in several other studies (see Hoff, Laursen & Tardif (2002) for an overview). However, Song, Spier & Tamis-Lemonda (2014) demonstrate considerable maternal input variation in low socio-economic status families. Furthermore, we need to bear in mind, that even if socio-economic status might be related to higher academic performance levels (Oller & Eilers 2002), it is not necessarily a predictor for the respective educational and occupational levels. Parents with low or middle socio-economic status may have a higher educational standard, and vice versa, parents with high socio-economic status may have lower levels of education. Note that this issue has not yet been researched in detail. However, the results of a few studies indicate similar input patterns in families with higher and with lower educational levels (irrespective of socio-economic status) which have been documented for high and low socio-economic status families (Hoff-Ginsberg 1991; Hoff-Ginsberg 1998). In this context, socio-economic status alone does not seem to be a reliable predictor of a child's linguistic input.

With respect to bilingual children, it is generally assumed that they receive less input in each of their languages compared to monolingual children (Genesee 2010), since they have to divide their time on tasks in two languages. In order to test this assumption, the focus of research in bilingual contexts is therefore rather on the absolute and relative input in bilingual families in comparison with monolingual families, than on determining the association of socio-economic status and input. Research, however, consistently displays a high variation in bilingual children's exposure to their languages (Allen 2007; de Houwer 2014; Hoff et al. 2012). This is not surprising, since input variation has also been documented in monolingual contexts, and bilinguals' input varies with respect to multiple possible parental input patterns and strategies (one person, one language; home language with/without community support, mixed languages etc., see Romaine (1995), de Houwer (2007)).

On average, children who are exposed to two languages on a daily basis are still likely to have less input in each language than children who are exposed to only one language (Hoff et al. 2012: 4). By contrast, de Houwer (2014) found no evidence for a reduced maternal input in bilingual Dutch-French children (with middle- to upper middle socio-economic status). The study is limited only to Dutch, but it further indicates that several children in the bilingual group had a lot more input in Dutch than some children of the monolingual group. Due to a lack of empirical investigations in successive second language acquisition, we can only assume that the amount of L1 input is not dramatically different from monolingual contexts – given the fact that socio-economic status and/or educational backgrounds are identical.

In regards to the relation of bilingual input patterns and language, development research provides evidence for links between the absolute input in each of the languages and the respective lexical and grammatical development. The study by Hoff et al. (2012) indicates that Spanish-English bilinguals' different home input pattern (dominant exposure in the minority language, dominant exposure in the majority language, equal exposure in both languages) has an impact on the lexical and grammatical development in both languages at age 1;10, 2;1 and 2;6. The more dominant the exposure in language A was, the lesser difference was found compared to monolingual children of that language, but vice versa, the greater the difference from monolinguals of the other language B was. The results clearly indicate that, irrespective of the input pattern, bilinguals do not acquire their languages at the same rate as monolinguals and display some (but statistically not consistently significant) variation in their languages. This finding has been proven to apply to older English-French bilingual speakers (mean 4;11) in the study by Thordardottir (2011). The results clearly indicate that speakers with a higher relative amount of exposure in English or in French also scored higher in receptive and expressive vocabulary tests in English or respectively in French.

Let us turn now to the associations between socio-economic status-related input and children's linguistic development in infancy. On the one hand, research in this field provides evidence that children with a high socio-economic status background develop more advanced language skills than lower socio-economic status children of the same age (Hart & Risley 1995). In their longitudinal study of children with different socio-economic status backgrounds in Germany, Weinert, Ebert & Dubowy (2010) found similar results. Irrespective of the participants acquisition background,[7] differences in language knowledge and production (receptive and productive vocabulary, receptive and productive syntactic processing, production of morphological forms) are significantly related to the mother's education. Children with highly educated mothers scored significantly higher in the respective tests than children with less educated mothers. This finding is partly proved by Czinglar et al. (2015) who found a significant relationship

---

[7] The children indicated three different acquisition backgrounds: (i) monolingual German parents, (ii) bilingual parents of which one spoke a language other than German and (iii) parents of which both did not speak German.

between high socio-economic status and more highly receptive vocabulary scores in German by monolingual children (mean age 3;1). On the other hand, the study indicates no significant relation between low and high socio-economic status and receptive vocabulary in L1 Turkish and L2 German among Turkish-German bilingual children (mean age L1 3;5, L2 3;3). In contrast, the difference is evident in grammatical features in both L1 and L2. Bilingual Turkish-German children with a high socio-economic status have indications of a faster and more diverse development of the Turkish nominal morphology and produced more complex determiner phrases and plural marking in German as compared to low socio-economic status Turkish-German bilinguals.

Although the effects of socio-economic status on language development tend to be stronger in early childhood, the study by Weinert, Ebert & Dubowy (2010) further shows that the disparity of language knowledge and production and a mother's educational background persists over time (until age five). When examining the results of receptive vocabulary individually, the differences even increase. With respect to the linguistic demands across the school curriculum, this has dramatic consequences for children, particularly when low socio-economic status and low levels of education persist simultaneously.

Methodologically, research on input generally takes detailed parent questionnaires or parent diary reports into account, surveying the relative amount of a child's exposure to the respective language(s) over a certain period (language(s) spoken at home, by whom and how many hours per week, spoken in daycare, and other contexts of interaction with relatives and friends) and accumulating the time on tasks of each language with respect to waking hours and residing in environments in which the interlocutors used that language (Thordardottir 2014: 144). Although it is possible to calculate a percentage exposure rate in relation to each language, the ratio can only display an approximate quantity of the input (and is also affected by the same problems of inaccurate values which can occur in self reports, as mentioned in §2.1.2.1).

Studies measuring socio-economic status generally use parent questionnaires and take maternal or parental education and/or family income as an index. Additionally, variables determining attitude towards education (for instance home literacy activities such as reading, narrating, writing) are included, in order to disentangle levels of socio-economic status and education.

For the purpose and because of limitations of the current study, parental input patterns are only limited to language use with their children. This primarily serves to assessing bilinguals' language dominance (domain), but it is not within the scope of this study to provide information about the total amount of exposure in L1 and L2. In order to determine appropriately the absolute quantity and also the quality of linguistic input, a research design would have to include methods which allow us trace the exact amount of input as well as proficiency levels (e.g. lexical and syntactical diversity) of all interlocutors. It is worth saying that this is a challenging and difficult undertaking, which has been, until now, limited to studies based on repetitive (but often only dyadic) recordings of mother/adult-child interactions[8] at home (Allen 2007; de Houwer 2014; Song, Spier & Tamis-Lemonda 2014). A more detailed assessment of language use and input patterns could be provided by the "Traceback method", which has recently been used to investigate the emergence of language within a usage-based perspective (among others Dąbrowska & Lieven 2005; Lieven, Salomo & Tomasello 2009; Koch in prep.; for adult speakers see also Dąbrowska 2014). This method comprises recordings of typical interactions which are made by the caregivers themselves one hour per day, five days per week over a period of six weeks.

The assessment of socio-economic status should be based instead on both parents' educational background (operationalised as the highest level of education of one of the parents), since it is believed to be a better indicator than income or occupational prestige. Moreover, an assessment of educational background needs to account for possible differences of educational systems (e.g. Germany, France, Turkey). Information on the bilingual's educational background are not examined in detail in this study, but serve to describe the different groups that are considered as qualitative variables when interpreting the performance of the speakers under study in L1 and L2.

A first step towards accounting for varying language skills in one language or the use of one language over the other has been established in §2.1. We can state that variation in bilingual speakers' performances can be related to dominance in different domains and/or dimensions as well as being associated with the received quantity and quality of linguistic input. As a consequence, a speaker can also be more proficient in one language than in another and display different language skills (in terms of language knowledge and processing) compared to other speakers of the same age. Furthermore, when bilingual speakers grow up in an L2 environment, and are exposed to the L2 in early childhood ($\leq$ age 6) they are expected to some degree to lose L1 monolikeness proficiency. This assumption, however, challenges common beliefs in second language acquisition and theoretical linguistics

---

[8] In relation to the assumption that "the main adult to regularly and continuously interact with a child, regardless of work status, continues to be the child's mother" (de Houwer 2014: 53), a vast amount of input studies exclusively focus on mother-child interactions. Although the importance of a mother's initial input can not be denied, we should bear in mind that in most of the societies, where the reported studies have been conducted, the traditional role of the mother has already been subject to change. As a consequence, parental input should be the basic input variable in early language acquisition research.

about L1 skills, which have generally been treated as stable, "such that once a speaker's language system has maturated, his or her linguistic competence is no longer subject to change" (Jarvis & Pavlenko 2010: 17). We will adopt the opposite perspective in the current study. When assuming that child bilinguals display variation in both, L1 and L2, there is need for further explanations of the characteristics of bilingual performances in both languages. According to the framework proposed by Cook (1991; 1992; 1997; 2003), these characteristics are termed "multicompetence", which is discussed in the following section, in particular by taking bidirectional cross-linguistic influences between the languages of bilinguals into account. We will argue that variation in bilinguals' performances is not only evidence for dominance shift or L1 attrition, but a phenomenon in its own right.

2.2 Multicompetence

2.2.1 Nonmonolingual likeness

The concept of multicompetence contrasts, in line with Grosjean's approach (Grosjean 1989; 1998), the long tradition of a monolingual bias in second language acquisition research by treating a speakers' L2 system as an approximation of a monolingual speaker's L1 system. Grosjean (1989: 6; emphasis in the original) argues, that "[t]he bilingual is NOT the sum of two complete or incomplete monolinguals; rather, he or she has a unique and specific linguistic configuration". The term multicompetence refers to the knowledge of two or more languages in one mind, or as originally introduced by Cook (1991: 112) "the compound state of a mind with two grammars". The multicompetence framework, however, not only fills a gap within the interlanguage theory (first proposed by Selinker 1972) by introducing a concept which goes beyond a speakers' knowledge of the L2, but it also "allows us to theorize the interaction between multiple languages in the speaker's mind as a natural and ongoing process and to understand why multilinguals may perform differently from monolinguals in all of their languages, including the L1" (Jarvis & Pavlenko 2010: 17).

The idea, by also including effects of the L2 on the L1, is not new (sometimes called reverse transfer) and it is in a diachronic perspective similar to language attrition studies, introduced in §2.1.2.2. However, within the multicompetence perspective, bilinguals are seen rather as "unique combinations" (Cook 1992: 557) than equivalent or comparable to two monolingual speakers. Their linguistic and conceptual repertoires (e.g. L2 effects on the L1) are "influenced both by their interlocutors and the linguistic and social context of the interaction" (Pavlenko 2004: 48). In situations where only one language can be used (when interacting with speakers in L1 or L2 contexts) bilinguals have to select elements of that language which is needed for the interaction and inhibit elements of the other language (Treffers-Daller & Sakel 2012: 3). The fact that bilinguals have to "control attention to the target system in the context of an activated and competing system is the single feature that makes bilingual speech production most different from that of monolinguals" (Bialystok 2009: 3–4). According to Bialystok, this has consequences for both the cognitive and linguistic behaviour of bilinguals and contributes to the unique perspective of bilingual speakers.

The inhibition (or deactivation) of one language, while using the other for interaction does not always succeed, and bilinguals have to (re)activate the other language (over a varying period of time). As a consequence, bilinguals cannot always completely separate their languages "and features of the deactivated language regularly appear in the language the speaker intended to use" (Treffers-Daller & Sakel 2012: 3) (which we referred to as *variation* above). Such variation in the speech of bilinguals can occur in all contexts, probably most obviously in bilingual contexts, where bilingual speakers of the same languages interact with each other (for instance code-mixing and code-switching), and also (but to a lower degree) in monolingual L1 or L2 contexts. Note that, in a broader definition of multilingualism, this refers also to diastratic (e.g. sociolects) and diatopic (e.g. dialects) contexts in one diasystem (e.g. German) (Wandruszka 1979).

When studying child bilinguals[9] within the multicompetence framework, the research interest lies in discovering the characteristics of bilingual performances rather than deficiencies compared with monolingual L1 speakers (Cook 2003: 5), which is perfectly in line with the goals of the current study. Cook (2002: 4–8; 2003: 5) defines the characteristics of multicompetent speakers as following: They have different uses for language than monolinguals; their knowledge of the L2 is not identical to that of an L1 speaker of the respective language; their knowledge of the L1 is not the same as that of monolingual speakers of that language; and they have different minds (conceptualisations) from those of monolinguals.

Such characteristics may vary with respect to the grade of bilingualism (minimal vs. maximal bilingualism)[10] and inter-related variables such as language use, dominance and attitude as well as to the time or intervals at which

---

9 Cook consequently uses the term "L2 user" in order to account for all kinds of language acquisition types other than monolingualism: "An L2 user is any person who uses another language than his or her first language (L1)" (Cook 2002: 1). We keep the term child bilingual on purpose for the focus of the current study.
10 They are for instance speakers with the least possible exposure to another language, such as acquiring the L2 as a foreign language versus speakers with double exposure to two languages on a daily basis from an early stage on, see Cook (2003: 14).

the (linguistic, cognitive) measurement takes place. Nevertheless, with respect to child bilinguals, we can assume variation in both L1 and L2 as a result of bidirectional influences in language and cognition.

When following the view of a multicompetent speaker in this study, we have to abandon adopting the monolingual speaker as a norm and to rethink the terms used above such as "native speaker ultimate attainment" (§2.1.1), "ultimate levels of L2 proficiencies", or "L1 monolikeness proficiency" (§2.1.2.2). When talking of bilingual language performances, we instead take bilingual speakers as the norm and only include monolingual speakers when identifying the nature of variation (e.g. because of structural or typological differences between L1 and L2). Furthermore, in order to take into account the fact that true monolingualism hardly exists, speakers, who are commonly termed "monolinguals", are termed in the current study "minimal bilinguals".

Up to now, we have used the term variation in a broader sense when, for example, referring to the appearance of features of one language in another. In second language acquisition theory, this is traditionally referred to as "interference", "transfer" or "cross-linguistic influence". Let us now deal with this issue in greater detail, by emphasizing the linguistic processes of interactions between two languages acquired in early childhood.

2.2.2 The relationship between L1 and L2: cross-linguistic (bidirectional) influence

Interactions between two languages are often referred to as "language transfer" or "cross-linguistic influence" (two notions which we will use interchangeably in the following). Odlin (1989: 27) defines language transfer as "resulting from the similarities and differences between the target language and any other language that has been previously (and imperfectly) acquired". When taking the multicompetence framework into account, the investigation of interactions between two language knowledge systems always includes bidirectionality of transferred linguistic material and conceptual repertoires. This means that the traditional understanding of transfer in second language acquisition research as a "use of native language [...] knowledge [...] in the acquisition of a second (or additional) language" (Gass & Selinker 1992: 234) is expanded to include the reverse, from a L2- to a L1-knowledge system. Thus, Odlin's definition of language transfer should be expanded to "resulting from the similarities and differences between [a] target language and any other language that has been previously [or subsequently](and imperfectly) acquired". Research shows that transfer affects all linguistic subsystems (morphology, orthography, phonology, phonetics, pragmatics, rhetoric, semantics, syntax) (Odlin 2011).

The assessment of the relationship of L1- and L2-knowledge systems, as well as the direction of transfer, has been debated for a long time in language acquisition research. The two models of separated languages (Weinreich 1953) and integrated languages cannot both be absolutely true. When assuming that both languages are in the same mind, total separation is impossible, and "total integration is impossible since L2 users can keep their languages apart" (Cook 2003: 7). Interconnection models assume different degrees and types of interconnection within these two positions of total separation and total integration. They generally account for how the development of the interlanguage has an impact on the L1. The Revised Hierarchical Model (Kroll & Stewart 1994) for instance "assigns unequal strengths to the links between L1 and L2 according to direction and stage of acquisition" (Cook 2003: 8). Other interconnection models such as the Bilingual Interactive Model (Dijkstra & van Heuven 2002) take a partial overlapping of L1 and L2 systems into account. By taking these models as a whole, Cook (2002: 11) proposes an "integration continuum", which is characterised by "complete separation for the two languages at one end and complete integration at the other" (Cook 2002: 11). He argues that the continuum applies across the different areas of language (phonology, morphology, syntax, lexicon etc.), whereas, again, neither total separation nor total integration can be completely true. This would explain why balanced bilingualism in the sense of displaying equated abilities in two languages is the exception rather than the norm.

The idea of the integrated continuum is also provided for in the "dynamic model of multilingualism" (de Bot, Lowie & Verspoor 2007; Herdina & Jessner 2002; Jessner 2003; Verspoor, de Bot & Lowie 2011). Within this model, "bilingual knowledge, competence and proficiency are not made up of separate or separable subsystems (L1, L2...) but consist of one holistic and dynamic system within which every change has ramifications throughout all subsystems" (Riehl 2013: 256). Matras (2007) also presents an integrated approach. In his view, bilingual speakers acquire, maintain and reset so-called "demarcation boundaries" between different linguistic components within their bilingual repertoires. However, it is rather normal for bilingual speakers not to constantly preserve boundaries. Depending on the linguistic and social context of an interaction, demarcation boundaries can instantaneously or temporally collapse, or even get lost: "[T]he maintenance of demarcation boundaries, within the repertoire, and their partial lifting or even longer term-removal around specific structures, are functional to communication in multilingual settings" (Matras 2007: 52). Therefore, a collapse of demarcation boundaries has ramifications on L1 and L2 and language contact phenomena. In addition, Rehbein, Herkenrath & Karakoç (2009) claim that in multilingual settings, the L1 is catalysed by the contact language (L2), since bilingual repertoires are simultaneously active. This leads bilingual speakers to prefer structures in their L1 which also exist in the L2 – and which have a functional correspondence (Rehbein, Herkenrath & Karakoç 2009: 178).

According to Cook (2002: 12) ramifications of L1 and L2 can apply to different areas of language. "An L2 user might have an interconnected vocabulary but entirely separate grammars, or use grammatical structures independently but depend on the first language for L2 pragmatic functions […]". Furthermore, the relationship between L1 and L2 can change with respect to the stage of development or of language attrition: "At the early stages of L2 acquisition the languages might be tightly linked by translation and transfer, at later stages unified into one system" (Cook 2002: 12).

Another aspect which can have an impact on the relationship is the closeness of languages: "For various historical reasons the first language and the second language can be related to each other (like English and Dutch), or totally unrelated to each other (like Japanese and Spanish)" (Cook 2002: 12). Additionally, the relationship between L1 and L2 can vary from one person to another: "Some individuals keep the languages predominantly separate, others integrate them massively. Every mind does not necessarily relate two languages in the same way; there is no single final state of L2 use common to everybody […]" (Cook 2002: 13).

In coming back to the definition of language transfer, to which we referred to as a bidirectional influence of one language over another, our considerations do not, however, provide details on the constitution and the process of influence. In establishing processes of interactions between two languages we follow Pavlenko and Jarvis (Pavlenko 2000; Pavlenko & Jarvis 2002; Pavlenko 2004; Jarvis & Pavlenko 2010), who established a "cross-linguistic influence-framework". They adopt the multicompetence perspective by taking into account that "[bilingual] speakers' use of their linguistic and conceptual repertoires is influenced both by their interlocutors and the linguistic and social context of the interaction" (Pavlenko 2004: 48). In the following, five processes of interactions are distinguished (of which (4) and (5) have already been discussed above):

1. borrowing
2. restructuring
3. convergence
4. shift
5. attrition

Borrowing

The borrowing of new elements occurs most characteristically in the lexicon ("lexical borrowing", "lexical transfer"), but can also be visible in pragmatics or in rhetoric. The process of borrowing is often a result of "the need to name new objects and new types of relationships, or recognise new conceptual distinctions" (Pavlenko 2004: 48). Borrowing can also be evident in loan translations, idioms, and lexical collocations from one language into the other, which typically occur in immigrant contexts, "in which new L1 forms and expressions appear to reflect new social and conceptual reality" (Pavlenko 2000: 185). As an example, Edwards (2006: 18) refers to lexical transfer, in cases where a Brussels French speaker uses the Dutch word *vogelpik* (for a game of darts), rather than the French word *fléchettes*. In this context, the Dutch word can be seen as a loan word, "since it is an 'intrusion' regularly used in unchanged form" (Edwards 2006: 18). Lexical transfer is also visible in loan translation (which is also called calque) such as the copy of the word "skyscraper" into German (*Wolkenkratzer*) or French (*gratte-ciel*). Loan translations can also occur in quite complex forms. The utterance *Lustum yok kitap okumağa* 'I don't feel like reading books' (Boeschoten 1998: 19) by a Turkish-German bilingual illustrates a more complex form of loan translation.[11] The speaker morphologically integrates the German word *Lust* 'pleasure' (here literally "to feel like") into his Turkish and reproduces the typical L2 order main sentence (*Ich habe keine Lust* > *Lustum yok* 'I don't feel like') – subordinate clause (*zum Bücherlesen* > *kitap okumağa* 'reading books').

Pavlenko (2004: 48–49) argues that if the lexical item does not have an equivalent translation in the L1, borrowing cannot be seen as a predictor for L1 attrition. Even if an equivalent form exists in the other language, a speaker may display particular conceptual distinctions during the process of borrowing. Moreover, "it signifies an enrichment of the bilingual's linguistic and conceptual repertoire" (Pavlenko 2004: 47) within a multicompetent perspective.

Restructuring
The process of restructuring "typically involves a deletion of certain L1 elements and/or addition of L2 elements into L1 [or vice versa]" (Pavlenko 2004: 50). Consequently, restructuring results in "some changes or substitutions, or a partial shift" (Pavlenko 2000: 179). Mostly restructuring occurs in morphosyntax (e.g. case-, gender-, number-marking, use of prepositions or word order), but it can also be visible in the lexicon, where meanings of translation equivalents in one language are incorporated into the L1/L2 word (semantic extension) (Pavlenko 2004: 50–51). Boeschoten (1994: 255) brings in the replacement of the word *ders* 'lesson' by *saat* 'hour' in Turkish by Turkish-German bilinguals. Here the

---

11 Boeschoten (1998: 19), however, refers to an instantaneous syntactic change of a drift from SOV to SVO order. In addition, Backus (2006: 715) suggests that syntactic change "may have been jump started by full and mixed loan translations of particular phrases".

meaning of the L2 word *Stunde* 'hour' is semantically extended in L1 Turkish (*saat* 'hour'). Riehl (2014: 105) observes semantic restructuring in speakers of the relict variety of Barossa-German, who extended the use of English "take" to German *nehmen* (e.g. *ein Foto nehmen* 'to take a photo', *die Gelegenheit nehmen* 'to take the opportunity').

Convergence
Convergence is seen as a contact-induced effect on a linguistic system, which may involve "L1 and L2 values, distinctions, or boundaries" (Pavlenko 2004: 52), often observed in phonology and conceptual representation. The type of transfer is not unidirectional from one language into another. This means that the resulting convergent structures cannot be traced back to a single source. Thomason (2001: 89) notes that such structures may be "already present, but less prominent, in both languages, or they resemble both languages in part but do not match either one completely". As an example, she refers to Turkish-German bilinguals who learned two phonetically different phrase final intonation patterns in Turkish and German (monolingual Turkish and German speakers only have one pattern in each language). The bilingual speakers kept both patterns in Turkish and German and indicated a semantic differentiation. In this context, these patterns can not be traced back to a single (Turkish or German) source, since neither Turkish nor German provides the two different functions (Thomason 2001: 90).[12] Matras (2007) also counts pattern replication as part of the phenomenon of convergence, e.g. as a result of the influence of the dominant language. Such pattern replications can also be considered as the fusion (or convergence) of a construction from language A and a construction from language B (in the sense of Goldberg's Construction Grammar, cf. Goldberg 1995).

Language shift
Language shift, which has been characterised in §2.1.2.2 as a move away from L1 to L2 skills in language dominance change over time, often occurs in phonology or the mental lexicon (Pavlenko 2004: 53). In the process of shift, L1 structures, boundaries or values typically shift towards approximate L2 structures or values. For instance, in the context of loan shift (semantic extension), lexical items in the L1 are "vested" with the meanings of the translation equivalents of the L2

---

12 See also Queen (2001; 2006) who discusses this observation in details. In contrast to convergence, she refers to this phenomenon as 'fusion', "because [fusion] does not rely on the tendency to utilise what is common to the two languages; instead, it depends critically on exploiting the formal differences between them" (Queen 2001: 57).

(Pavlenko 2000: 179). Language shift can also concern a group as a whole who shifts from its language to another language (over multiple generations) (Thomason 2001: 22).

Attrition
As stated above, attrition is also seen as a process – or rather a permanent result – of cross-linguistic influence. It refers to the loss of some L1 elements "seen in inability to produce, perceive, or recognise particular rules, lexical item, concepts, or categorical distinctions" (Pavlenko 2004: 47) due to the dominating influence of another language. In the multicompetence view of the CI framework, L2 influence on the L1 (processes 1–4) is seen as a "temporary or permanent phenomenon which is exhibited predominantly in the L2 and bilingual contexts or in the presence of bilingual interlocutors" (Pavlenko 2004: 54). As an example, Riehl (2015) observed the loss of dative case markers by speakers of the relict variety of Barossa-German (see above). As a consequence, Barossa-German "is on its way to arriving at a system of pronominal case marking" (Riehl 2015: 282), which, again, is the result of restructuring.

However, cross-linguistic influence does not imply that corresponding rules, lexical items, concepts, or categorical distinctions are permanently lost in the respective language. In contrast, attrition involves a permanent cross-linguistic influence – borrowing, restructuring, convergence, shift – or loss of previously acquired elements in one language "exhibited not only in the L2 but also in a monolingual L1 context, and not only in production but also in perception and comprehension" (Pavlenko 2004: 54).

In addition to these processes of interactions, cross-linguistic influence is also evident in the avoidance and simplification of L1- or L2-elements (Jarvis & Odlin 2000: 537). Pfaff (1994: 85), for instance, found that German dominant Turkish-German bilinguals tend to avoid expressing evidential modality (-*miş*)[13] in Turkish. The influence seems to be L2-based, since German does not provide this grammatical category which, in turn, leads to avoidance in L1. Alternative strategies which are caused by avoidance of linguistic categories, structures etc. are sometimes referred to as simplification (Jarvis & Pavlenko 2010: 192). Pfaff (1991), for instance, observed the avoidance of synthetic clause linkage devices, such as non-finite verb forms, in Turkish by Turkish-German bilinguals, who used conjunctions instead. From a morphological perspective, the use of conjunctions instead of non-finite

---

[13] Evidential modality "consists of statements based upon knowledge acquired indirectly" (Göksel & Kerslake 2005: 309).

verb forms in Turkish can be interpreted as simplification, since non-finite verb forms are seen as syntactically more complex than conjunctions.

In this study, we adopt the dynamic view of an integrated continuum by assuming that ramifications of L1 and L2 can apply to all sub-systems. When referring to cross-linguistic influence in the current study, we will generally refer to the direction of influence. When any influence is determined as an L1 influence on L2 we will use the term "L1>L2 influence" and, vice versa, "L2>L1 influence" when L2 properties have an impact on the L1. Further possible processes of influence will be discussed. However, since younger child bilinguals (around ten years of age), who use both of their languages in various situations and contexts, are within the scope of this study, it is hypothesised that cross-linguistic influence will not account for processes (4) (shift) and (5) (attrition). Cross-linguistic influence is expected rather in avoidance, alternative structures,[14] borrowing, restructuring and convergence.

We now have established the crucial aspects of child bilingualism within a multicompetence and cross-linguistic influence framework which serves as theoretical background of the current study. Since we set the focus of the investigation on children who grow up with Turkish as a heritage language in an L2 environment (German in Germany and French in France), we introduce in the following background information with respect to the immigration context of Turkish minority speakers in Germany and France. As a priority, the factors established in the previous sections are included successively, in order to make general assumptions on the acquisition context of Turkish-German and Turkish-French child bilinguals.The case of Turkish as a heritage language in second and third generation child bilinguals in Germany and France.

2.3 The case of Turkish as a heritage language in second and third generation child bilinguals in Germany and France

2.3.1 Turkish immigration in Germany and France

Today, as a result of family reunification, marriage and birth, nearly three million[15] speakers of Turkish origin live in first, second and third generations in Germany.

---

[14] The notion of simplification is negatively connoted since it refers to some kind of deficiency. Thus, we keep the term 'alternative strategy' in the following.
[15] The number is estimated. The Mikrozensus (Statistisches Bundesamt 2015: 75) counts 2,706,000 persons with a so-called *Migrationshintergrund im engeren Sinn* 'immigrant back-

Whereas the Turkish speakers[16] represent the most important ethno-linguistic group in Germany, they vary in France, but their absolute numbers are impressive (almost half a million speakers[17]). Reports on the Turkish diaspora in Europe indicate that the majority of Turkish immigrants in Europe are actually living in Germany and France.

As a result of Turkey's labor force agreements with various European destination countries, the Turkish immigrant community started in the early 1960s in Germany, when (mainly male) workers for factory work were recruited from rural areas of Turkey, especially Central and Southwestern Anatolia, and the Black Sea area (Backus 2006: 689). Subsequently, also female workers were recruited, in particular mainly for the textile industry. The labor migration ended in Germany with the oil crisis in 1973. In contrast, the influx of workers in France only started at the end of the 1960s. Nevertheless, in both countries the Turkish population increased subsequently due to family reunification, birth and in-group marriage. Although the plan was to return to the destination countries, the opposite trend could be observed. The Turkish minorities were joined into immigrant communities in both countries (Backus 2006: 690). This trend was favoured by the fact that birth rates in the immigration context were, and are still, higher than in the host society as well as the endogamous marriage pattern, which is typical and displays a similar rating for both immigrant groups in France and Germany (Yağmur 2011: 114). These circumstances contributed to establishing a paradigm in German integration policies by considering Germany as a country of immigration in the 2000s.

The huge difference in populations of Turkish minority speakers in Germany and France is also evident in the amount and diversity of available empirical data. In Germany, research has been carried out in quite different disciplines, domains

---

ground stricto sensu'. The definition refers to (i) persons with a Turkish citizenship who have immigrated to Germany; (ii) persons who are born in Germany and have a Turkish citizenship; as well as to (iii) German citizens of Turkish origin (which means that one of the parents has an immigration background and that the person is living in the same household) (Statistisches Bundesamt 2015: 6).

16 Note that the statistics given also include other persons who have a different first language (e.g. Kurdish). The notion 'Turkish speakers' therefore is inaccurate.

17 In 2010 the *Çalışma ve Sosyal Güvenlik Bakanı* 'Ministry of labor and social security' counts 459,611 Turkish citizens living in France http://www.sp.gov.tr/upload/xSP Rapor/files/tHvTk+Calisma_ve_Sosyal_Guvenlik_Bakanligi_2009_yili_Faaliyet_Raporu.pdf [accessed 2018-01-15]. However, the number does not include French citizens of Turkish origin. Among the Turkish consulates the total number of persons with Turkish citizenship and French citizenship of Turkish origin is today 650,000 http://paris.emb.mfa.gov.tr/Mission/Message [accessed 2018-01-15].

2.3 The case of Turkish as a heritage language in second and third generation

and various empirical settings. We could assume that this is due to the substantial importance of Turkish (as the most spoken minority language) in the societal and educational context, but also to pragmatic factors, since a vast amount of speakers of several generations are much easier to come by compared to other much smaller minority groups. The reverse situation holds true for France. Research on Turkish minority speakers in the French setting is limited to a few research groups carried out by projects mainly in the regions of Lyon, Rouen and Strasbourg as well as by European studies on minority communities. As a consequence, available data is much more restricted compared to the German setting. This is particularly the case for psycholinguistic and developmental studies which investigate the characteristics of Turkish as a heritage language and the successive acquisition of German and French.

Furthermore, we have to be aware that the notion Turkish in this context can not be generalised. According to the region of origin, as well as the time of immigration (first generation of Turkish immigrants in the 70ies, or first generation of Turkish immigrants in the 90ies), different Turkish dialects and styles coexist in both countries. Simultaneously, Turkish in Europe is subject to change due to language contact with the majority languages but probably also to the intergenerational contact of different dialects and styles in Turkish families and communities. There is an ongoing discussion on the existence of a diaspora variety of Turkish (e.g. a "Turcia Germanica", see Johanson (1991)) in sociolinguistic and language contact research. Research in this field mainly focuses on systematic language change of the second and third generation of Turkish minority speakers (Backus & Boeschoten 1998; Bommes et al. 2011; Cindark & Aslan 2004; Johanson 1991; Keim 2004; Rehbein & Karakoç 2004; Rehbein, Herkenrath & Karakoç 2009; Schroeder & Şimşek 2010).

In the literature, the notions of first, second and third generation commonly refer to speakers of the labor migration in the early 1960s (first), their children (second) and grandchildren (third). When looking closer into the marriage patterns of the present day Turkish communities in Germany and France, two tendencies can be observed: First, due to renewed migration from Turkey to Europe, there is continually a (new) first generation of Turkish minority speakers, whose fashion of speaking Turkish is quite likely different from that spoken by labor migrants of the 70ies first generation. Secondly, due to the endogamous marriage pattern, it happens that one parent was born in Turkey, the other in Germany/France. Consequently, there are two intermediate generations, which we will term in the following "1.5 generation" when referring to parents, and "2.5 generation" when referring to their children who are born in Germany/France and are exposed to different varieties of Turkish spoken at home. Note, that this differentiation of Turkish minority generations has been neglected so far in language contact research. Thus, a review of studies on second or third generation bilingual speakers generally can not provide such a differentiation. Although we will not examine this issue in greater detail in this study, the questions arise of how the family language is subject to change when a Turkey-Turkish and a Germany-Turkish variety is spoken by the parents, and what is the influence on a child's L1 development when comparing his or her fashion of speaking Turkish with children of first or third generation parents.

Being aware of the limitations raised in this section concerning (varieties of) Turkish in Germany and France, in some cases only tendencies can be observed. Nevertheless, we focus in the following on research findings with an emphasis on the second generation of Turkish-German and Turkish-French bilinguals who are of special interest for the current study.

2.3.2 Language use and maintenance of Turkish in the immigration context

Today, the Turkish minority in Germany is a vital linguistic community. The language loyalty of Turkish immigrant communities in Germany seems to be above average (Gogolin & Reich 2001: 198). Akıncı & de Ruiter (2004: 266) also report a high ethno-linguistic vitality of Turkish in France. Tribalat (1998) notes a strong sense of solidarity among Turkish immigrants in France, which enables them to use Turkish in everyday life (Yağmur & Akıncı 2003). However, there are also differences in the use of Turkish with respect to the interlocutor. Second generation adolescent Turkish-German and Turkish-French bilingual speakers report speaking mainly Turkish to their parents, but much less with siblings and peers (Akıncı 2008: 68; Yağmur & Akıncı 2003: 116; Yağmur 2004: 135).

A high ethno-linguistic vitality and solidarity is not necessarily self-evident in immigration contexts. Generally, immigrant minorities "are forced to shift away from their ethnic language towards a national language, by national education policies and various social pressures" (Appel & Muysken 2005: 102). Often the languages of immigrants are perceived as non-prestigious and therefore are not maintained adequately, and are "'subtracted' from bilingual proficiency" (Appel & Muysken 2005: 102). This assumption might account for languages with both a non-prestigious perception and a weak language vitality, which generally tend to be replaced within generations by the majority language.

Due to the reported high language vitality of Turkish in Germany and France it can be assumed that Turkish has a good chance of intergenerational language maintenance. Turkish immigrants in Germany and France have great resources, domains and facilities for first language use, which provide a wide social network for Turkish immigrants and contribute to language maintenance (Yağmur & Akıncı 2003: 111). First, the geographical proximity to Turkey favours visiting their homeland or the homeland of their (grand-)parents regularly. Second, Turkish language media are, today, readily accessible in various fashions via internet, but also, for a long, time Turkish television channels have been received by cable or satellite dish. The major Turkish newspapers have European editions, and public libraries (particularly in main Turkish concentration areas) provide Turkish books. Both contribute to the access of (classic) written media (Yağmur & Akıncı 2003: 111). Third, due to bilateral agreements between the governments of Germany and Turkey, as well as France and Turkey, L1 education is provided for children of Turkish origin. Although L1 education is the subject of controversial debates (in particular in Germany, see Woerfel 2014), the opportunity of learning and teaching Turkish contributes to language maintenance and the development of Turkish as a first language among the younger generations. Whereas in France mother tongue education is governed by *ELCO* (*enseignement des langues et cultures d'origine* 'instruction of heritage languages and cultures'), the organisation is much more diverse in Germany: Some *Bundesländer* provide *Muttersprachlicher Ergänzungsunterricht* 'additive mother tongue instruction' within and outside the school curriculum, whereas others do not (Löser & Woerfel 2017). In such cases, the Turkish consulates or private associations provide equivalent offerings (for more details see Küppers, Schroeder & Gülbeyaz 2014). However, it seems that instruction in Turkish does not have a significant impact on the linguistic development in Turkish (Woerfel & Yılmaz 2011; Tunç 2012), nor can it prevent a dominance shift towards the L2 (Akıncı 2001).

In general, the reported factors can have positive effects with respect to language attitude. When studying intergenerational differences among first and second generation Turkish immigrants in France, Yağmur & Akıncı (2003) found that the younger generation registers much higher ratings for the importance of Turkish (acceptance in the Turkish community, maintenance of identity, cultural survival, family, and importance of Turkish in parenting) compared to the older generation. In the German context as well, attitudes towards Turkish are generally high among members of the second generation (e.g. with respect to the value of the Turkish language for childrearing, communication with family, friends, and the community as well as for travel, see Yağmur (2004)).

The Turkish language use of second generation Turkish-German and Turkish-French bilinguals provides great resources which can promote resistance to a permanent shift or loss of L1-competences. However, since research on second generation Turkish use in the German and French diasporas is limited to adolescent speakers, we can only hypothesise that the findings also account for younger speakers. Furthermore, the context of L1 education (type, frequency, content) is a factor which should be considered when examining differences in Turkish-German and Turkish-French L1 performances.

2.3.3 Social factors and education

With respect to the Turkish minority groups in Germany and France, Yağmur (2011: 114) states that they "are usually portrayed as a low status and an economically disadvantaged group in the media". This portrait may be, on the one hand, stimulated by the (socio-) demographic and educational background of the first generation of Turkish immigrants in the early 1970s, as well as their status as blue-collar workers in the host countries, as described above. On the other hand, the educational profile of the second and third generation in Europe is not very good either (Backus 2006: 691). Particularly in Germany, immigrant families are affected by educational disadvantages more frequently, compared to families without immigration background. This is the case especially for the Turkish minority group. According to the National Report on Education in Germany (Autorengruppe Bildungsberichterstattung 2014: 23), about 50% of the children of Turkish origin risk being educationally disadvantaged. Note that this is the highest rate among immigrant groups in Germany. With respect to Turkish minority children and adolescents in Western Europe, Backus (2006: 691) notes that they "suffer worrisome, though falling, rates of educational failure, Turks tend to be concentrated in cheap housing districts, and they have minimal clout as a political pressure group".

It is worth emphasising that problems within the education systems are not the result of the bilingual acquisition background, but are linked to the educational disadvantage of low socio-economic status and educational background (and a failure of the education systems to provide adequate language support within the school curriculum). We will keep this issue in mind, but are not going to discuss it in greater detail in the current study.

2.3.4 Successive language acquisition, attrition and language shift

If we make (generalised) assumptions with respect to the variables (i) age of onset of bilingualism, (ii) age at the onset of attrition, as well as (iii) length of time since the onset of attrition (indicated in §2.1.2.2), the following picture emerges for children of Turkish origin in Germany and France.

With respect to (i), surveys on language use and the practices of speakers of the second generation and their children (the third or hypothetically the 2.5

generation) indicate that they generally grow up bilingually (Akıncı 1996; Akıncı 2008; Akıncı 2006). Turkish-German and French-Turkish bilinguals usually grow up as child bilinguals, since they start acquiring Turkish monolingually or dominantly, and continue acquiring the L2 in early childhood (mostly by age three or earlier). From then on, most likely when they are exposed to the L2 on a regular basis (when attending kindergarten or between five (France) and six (Germany) when starting school) there is a dramatic change in their language environment, a stage where the acquisition of Turkish might be incomplete to some degree and subsequently develops parallel with the respective L2.

With respect to (ii), the possible age of onset of language attrition can be determined in early childhood, which in turn should favour L1 attrition in Turkish and L2 gain in German and French.

With respect to (iii), de Bot, Gommans and Rossing (1991) suggest that the length of time only has an effect when there is little or no contact with the L1. In this context, we should bear in mind that the conditions of first language acquisition and maintenance may be favoured by the fact that the minorities of (diaspora varieties of) Turkish in Germany and France are vital language communities. In this context we pursued the question of whether strong ethno-linguistic vitality would prevent L1 attrition in the context of child bilinguals who are exposed to language environment change in early childhood. Taking the reviewed studies on language use and practice of young Turkish minority speakers in Germany and France into account, we can assume that there is a great likelihood that child bilinguals have contact with different varieties of Turkish on a daily basis and in various settings (use with parents, siblings, relatives and peers at home, and/or in Turkey, via various media, through language instruction at or outside school, in the mosque). Nevertheless, there is a general consensus among researchers that language dominance shifts after the age of eight from Turkish towards the surrounding majority language (Akıncı, Jisa & Kern 2001). This dominance shift is probably strongly related to a decrease of Turkish input as a result of schooling and moving into an L2-dominated world (Backus 2006: 696). However, we can hypothesise that Turkish-German and Turkish-French bilingual speakers are unlikely to lose the L1-element even when an L2-dominance shift can be observed. However, language use and dominance patterns can vary strongly when, for instance, a child grows up in an area with no Turkish community, or if the child attends a kindergarten or not, and, if so, whether there is an opportunity to speak Turkish regularly or not.

We should bear in mind that, dependent on the generation, Turkish-German and French-Turkish bilinguals are exposed to a diaspora variety of Turkish, which contains differences to Turkish varieties in Turkey (see §2.3.1).

Thus, for speakers of the second or third generation we can not assume that they acquire Turkish in a similar way to (monolingual) children in Turkey (not even in the first years, when they possibly grow up monolingually or dominantly Turkish).

2.3.5 Characteristics in L1

Studies which investigated the language production of second generation child bilinguals (primarily morphosyntax) with L1 Turkish (for instance the Berlin and Tilburg projects, Pfaff 1991; 1994; 1999; van der Heijden & Verhoeven 1994) found similarities and differences to the monolingual acquisition of Turkish. Within a developmental perspective, research indicates that bilinguals need more time to acquire the more complex syntactic structures in Turkish, and also exhibit a slower lexical development – a phenomenon which is well known in bilingual research and not surprising within the multicompetence perspective. Furthermore, the studies report considerable inter-individual variation in different domains,[18] which strongly correlates with the respective dominance pattern. However, variation in bilinguals, who become dominant in the L2 at an earlier stage, does not show up in errors, but in the avoidance or overuse of certain structures (Backus 2006: 697). Some studies in this context found that bilinguals often avoid more complex syntactic structures in everyday conversation as well as certain vocabulary or rely on structures which are typically used in colloquial monolingual Turkish (Schaufeli 1994). Note that this is in any case an indication of a reduced proficiency, since this also can be observed in monolingual contexts. Provided that bilinguals have Turkish exposure on a daily basis and in various fashions (as described above), more complex syntactic structures (e.g. clause linkage by multiple converbial clauses) seems to be well acquired by age twelve (Backus 2006: 700). Building on spoken data of the LAS-project (Bommes et al. 2011), Şimşek & Schroeder (2011: 217) report alternative strategies among younger Turkish-German child bilinguals (first graders) with respect to syntactic structures in Turkish. With increasing age however, bilinguals use more complex syntactic structures (seventh graders). Despite inter-group heterogeneity among the bilinguals, the use of alternative structures might not be a matter of cross-linguistic influence, but an age-appropriate circumstance in the case of the younger speakers, because simple structures are also found in the speech of younger Turkish

---

18 Note, that these cannot be described in detail here, since we always need to include the respective language pair, and consequently take structural differences into account. Furthermore, the results reported here, are exclusively limited to spoken data of young speakers.

monolinguals. The same picture concerning a delayed use of complex structures in Turkish is found in Turkish-French bilinguals in the study by Akıncı (2001). He reports that until nine to ten years of age, simple structures (coordination, juxtaposition) dominate in the speech. Only from then on do bilinguals begin to use more complex structures, whereas these are already more dominantly present in the speech of monolinguals.

The lexicon, however, does generally developing with regard to different domains and registers. Difficulties among Turkish-German child bilinguals occur with respect to their semantic and lexical knowledge in Turkish in specific (for instance school-based) domains, (Şimşek & Schroeder 2011: 217). Problems related to the access of lexical items are often accompanied with verbal fluency in online use and entail a shift to the dominant language. Equivalent and available lexical items in L2 are then often incorporated into the L1 syntax.

Given these findings, the deficit hypothesis cannot be supported. Variation in the speech of bilinguals is usually not linked to incomplete acquisition or attrition. Moreover, as a result of cross-linguistic influence and language dominance, it is most evident in the preference (and overuse) or avoidance of certain structures and elements as well as the convergence of linguistic structures (see examples in §2.2.2). It has to be noted that variation in bilingual speakers' Turkish is generally based on comparisons with speakers who acquire (another variety of) Turkish in monolingual contexts. Furthermore, the differences found are mainly related to written language requirements (such as complex sentence structures), which reflect a monolingual bias in second language acquisition research as mentioned above. Similarly, there is still need for distinguishing (individual) cross-linguistic influence, age-related constraints, and the role of linguistic input, which is a considerable challenge when discovering the nature of variation in the speech of young child bilinguals.

2.3.6 Characteristics in L2

The case studies which investigated the acquisition and development of L2 German demonstrate that child bilinguals with L1 Turkish who begin acquiring German around age three generally pass the different milestones of German syntax in a relatively short period of time and behave like L1 learners of German (Kroffke & Rothweiler 2006; Rothweiler 2006; Thoma & Tracy 2006; Tracy & Lemke 2012). Other studies, in contrast, report much more variation with respect to syntax acquisition (Haberzettl 2005; Jeuk 2011). Haberzettl's longitudinal study on the acquisition of verbal placement in German by Turkish-German bilinguals (age 6–8) further suggests that the varying word order in Turkish helps bilingual speakers to acquire the typical L2 word order more quickly. In addition, Ahrenholz (2006) suggests that the basic verbal placement in German by Turkish-German bilinguals (AoO mainly around age three or earlier) is mastered by age eight to nine. However, the acquisition and mastery of complex sentence structures, which are central to the norms of written language, occurs after elementary school age (Reich 2009: 73). The study by Schönenberger, Rothweiler & Sterner (2012) on the acquisition of case marking in German by Turkish-German bilinguals (age 4;0–6;6) indicates no difference from monolingual German speakers' performance. However, the study further specifies that bilingual and monolingual performances are strongly related to the data collection method. Both groups produced many more structural case errors in experimental than in spontaneous data.

In French, the use of basic sentence structures is reported by Akıncı (2001) to be predominant until the age of seven by Turkish-French bilinguals, but the use of more complex structures (such as subordination) develops with increasing age. At the stage of nine to ten years, major differences between bilinguals and monolinguals no longer exist.

Variation, however, has also been reported by several studies in terms of lexical development. At primary school age, the German lexicon of Turkish-German bilinguals varies between simple basic and elementary school-like vocabularies (Reich 2009b). This variation may be linked to the children's different prior knowledge of German when they started kindergarten. The same is observed for Turkish-French bilinguals, who lag behind the monolingual lexical development when starting elementary school (Gagneux 2013; Le Coz & Lhoste-Lassus 2011). However, due to the dramatic input change, the L2 lexicon develops quickly after starting elementary school; similarly a slowdown of the Turkish lexicon gain can be observed both in the Turkish-German (Karasu 1995) and Turkish-French context (Crutzen & Manço 2003; Hamurcu 2014).

Using naturalistic observations, Keim (2012: 149–156) illustrates how interactions with nursery teachers and playmates in the German kindergarten built the basis of the first code-switching incidences, which reflect the two different linguistic (and pragmatic) environments (Turkish at home, German at kindergarten with nurseries and playmates as well as Turkish with playmates of the same origin). Code-switching strategies and complexity develop increasingly with age and constitute a consistent and a characteristic feature of Turkish-German bilingual speech. This fact may also be supported by the observation that code-switching is often prominent in the input in early stages of acquisition (Pfaff 1999) and that the usage is "not frowned upon by parents" (Backus 2006: 698).

In the Turkish-French context, limited research in this domain indicates that code-switching is much less prominent among second generation bilinguals compared to available data from Germany or the Netherlands (Akıncı & Backus 2004).

On the basis of the reviewed empirical studies on the Turkish-German and Turkish-French acquisition context, we can conclude that (a variety of) Turkish is dominantly acquired until schooling. As a consequence of the dramatic change of exposure to the dominant languages, it slows down in favour of a developmental progress in L2. Bilinguals, however, lag somewhat behind monolingual speakers of the respective language: while some features of German and French are considered unproblematic, others are not – they require much more time to be mastered. This primarily concerns domains where Turkish and German/French display considerable (structural) differences and which are generally required in a written language context. With respect to the Turkish-German pair, this is the case with relative clauses, passive constructions, indirect questions, and gender (see Reich (2009a:74) for an overview). For Turkish-French bilinguals determiner, copula, gender, and prepositions are seen as a challenge in the acquisition of French (Akıncı 2002). Generally, deviations in the L2 of bilinguals concerning these domains decrease with age and are also detectable in the German and French of monolinguals. However, such deviations can be observed more frequently in bilinguals and some of them tend to persist for a longer time.

Such persistence can also vary between Turkish-German and Turkish-French bilinguals, when lexical-semantic differences and similarities of the verb typology in German, French and Turkish are considered. It is hypothesised that such differences causes difficulties within the Turkish-German, but not within the Turkish-French acquisition context. Bryant (2011; 2012), for instance, refers to the acquisition of the German locative system. Due to structural and semantic differences of the two languages in this domain, Turkish-German bilinguals require more time to establish the adequate patterns compared to bilinguals, whose languages' locative system share some basic features (in her study Russian-German, but the same applies to Turkish-French). Her studies indicate that, after ten years of intensive contact with German, Turkish-German bilinguals still vary with respect to the expression of semantic (spatial) categories in German. These categories primarily concern the adequate use of positional verbs (such as *stehen* 'to stand' or *liegen* 'to lay' as well as expressive motion verbs (such as *schleichen* 'to creep' or *hüpfen* 'to bounce') (Bryant 2011; 2012). With respect to the latter domain, Schroeder (2009: 191) argues that the variation observed in Turkish-German bilinguals' usage and (syntactic) construction of motion verbs (in his study expressive and Generic motion verbs) in German is a stylistic phenomenon which can be traced back to the typical patterns acquired in Turkish. By contrast, Turkish-French bilinguals should not have difficulties in this domain, since their languages share lexical-semantic characteristics concerning the verb typology (for more details see Chapters 2 and 3).

As in the context of characteristics in L1 Turkish above, the reviewed studies on L2 German/French indicate a monolingual bias in second language acquisition research. Furthermore, deviations in bilinguals' L2 which tend to persist for a longer time, again, mainly refer to written language requirements. As mentioned above, in this study we do not compare language skills in bilinguals' L2 in relation to monolingual norms. There are, however, exceptions that are particularly related to lexical-semantic differences between Turkish and German. For the current study it is hypothesised that a varying usage of expressive verbs in German by Turkish-German bilinguals is not related to (bilingual) developmental constraints but rather to an L1-influence. In such contexts, a comparison with monolingual control groups is required.

2.4 Summary

In §2.1–2.3 we established the multicompetence perspective inasmuch as bilinguals develop their language skills differently compared to monolinguals of the respective languages. An equal language development in childhood cannot be provided, nor can it for bilinguals when comparing them with each other, and in any case when comparing them with monolinguals. The reasons for this are multifaceted. According to their L1 and L2, bilinguals display different dominance patterns concerning domains and dimensions. Furthermore, language skills in each language can vary according to dominance patterns in different domains and might be related to language use and the amount and quality of linguistic input. Furthermore, speakers' language skills in L1 are interconnected with the language vitality of and the attitude towards the minority language in L2 environments.

On the one hand, variation in monolinguals L1, as well as in bilinguals L1 and L2, can be influenced by the quantity and quality of linguistic input, which is strongly related to educational levels and attitudes in the family. On the other hand, variation in bilinguals' L1 and L2 can similarly be a result of cross-linguistic (bidirectional) influence of one language on the other.

In later acquisition stages, child bilinguals' variation is sometimes only obvious in subtle differences. Its detection involves the need of quantitative and qualitative research. In the case of child bilinguals who might not yet have completed the acquisition process, it is necessary to consider developmental constraints (that is for instance the use of more economic linguistic structures, which can also be found in monolingual contexts) when determining the nature of variation as a result of cross-linguistic influence. In order to do so, investigations focus on domains where the L1 and L2 display considerable conceptual and linguistic differences but also similarities (for instance concepts or linguistic structures which are present in both languages, but which are more prominent in one than in another).

Chapter 3 establishes the testing ground for discovering the characteristics and the nature of variation in the speech of Turkish-German and Turkish-French child bilinguals. The focus is on the encoding of motion events, a domain which has been a topic of special interest particularly in psycho-linguistics during the past thirty years. For the aim of our study, the domain of motion events is promising for multiple reasons. On the one hand, differences between the languages tested with respect to characteristic patterns of motion event encoding are expected to be a considerable challenge within the bilingual acquisition context and apparent in variations in both L1 and L2. Similarities in L1 and L2, on the other hand, may also be a case for differences in the frequency and overuse of certain structures. Variation in L1 is then expected to be dependent on the degree of differences and similarities of the L2. In addition, it is assumed that the relative dominance of the two languages of bilinguals has an impact on the direction of cross-linguistic influence. Furthermore, the domain of motion events can also serve for the interrelation of language and thought. It is argued that the acquisition of different motion encoding patterns in the context of early second language acquisition can lead to differences of conceptual categories in this domain and can have an impact on how bilingual speakers encode motion events. The investigation of this domain can produce a better understanding of the above-mentioned circumstance that difficulties related to lexical-semantic categories in German and Turkish among Turkish-German bilinguals persist longer, whereas syntactic categories are mastered relatively quickly. In the following, a specific focus is on linguistic devices and structures provided by the three languages involved and how speakers of these languages typically express motion events (§3.2.6). The findings are adopted in our methodological implications and serve as an additional theoretical framework in the study of child bilingualism.

3 Motion events in language and cognition

3.1 Spatial language and cognition

A number of different scientific traditions and various disciplines have studied the domain of space. This is due to the fact that, in the Kantian tradition, space can be seen as an "a priori form of intuition", a cognitive primitive which constitutes the existence of a human being. Moreover, language "provides a unique and powerful symbolic system that constitutes one of the means whereby we construct and categorize space" (Hendriks, Hickmann & Lindner 2010: 182). All languages of the world provide linguistic properties that categorise and map spatial and temporal images, which a speaker represents mentally (for further details see next section). Furthermore, spatial organisation and spatial language are considered to be fundamental for thinking (Miller & Johnson-Laird 1976). This fact has led to the crucial question in cognitive linguistics of whether spatial cognition is indifferent to spatial language or if distinct linguistic properties of languages constrain speakers' mental motion event representation.

In cognitive linguistics, the study of linguistic symbolisation of mental motion representation is a topic of special interest. Linguistic research of the past thirty years indicates differences in the spatial systems of various languages (e.g. grammaticalisation and lexicalisation patterns for encoding location and motion). The results of a growing number of psycholinguistic studies revived the Whorfian hypothesis by postulating that speakers' cross-linguistic differences in the expression of spatial information are constrained by the way languages "filter" and "channel" this information (Hendriks, Hickmann & Lindner 2010: 184). It is argued that some of this information is more salient and thereby accessible to cognitive functioning. The opposite approach claims that language-specific properties do not affect the cognitive organisation: cross-linguistic differences are only apparent in speech and do not affect underlying cognitive representations (Hendriks, Hickmann & Lindner 2010: 184).

3.2 The study of motion events

3.2.1 General considerations

Let us begin with some general considerations with respect to the overriding research question of how bilingual speakers of Turkish and German as well as Turkish and French linguistically encode a motion representation and whether language-specific properties have an impact on motion representation in the different languages. When, for instance, a speaker says "The cat rolled down the street into a bowling centre", they have verbalised their "mind's eye" – a mental representation of a motion event situation which takes place in the external world. The linguistic symbolisation of a motion event situation requires a perceptual (what the speaker perceives), conceptual (mental representation) and a subsequent linguistic symbolisation (which linguistic elements the speaker selects) process. Let us explore this issue in greater details. In a first attempt we assume that the perception of a motion event situation underlies a universal process: Goldstein (2010: 8) counts eight steps which are involved in such a perceptual process:

1. the presence of an environment;
2. a person's attention to the environmental stimulus;
3. the reception of energy from the stimulus by the person's neural receptors (e.g. light);
4. the transduction of that energy into electrical signals within the person's nervous system;
5. the neural processing of those signals by organised and interconnected neural pathways;
6. the person's conscious perception of the stimulus;
7. the person's recognition of the stimulus (what is generally termed in cognitive psychology mental categorisation or mental imagery);
8. the person's physiological action response to his or her recognition of the stimulus.

Steps 1 to 7 are central here to our concerns: 1–6 refer to what we have introduced as "what a speaker perceives". The perceptual conglomeration of visual, auditory, haptic, motoric, olfactory, and gustatory experiences are represented in what is generally termed concepts (Oakley 2007: 216). Furthermore, Jarvis (2009: 100–101) defines concepts as a reflection of "the level of thought and experiential knowledge [...] they consist of various types of mental images, image schemas, mental scripts and forms of knowledge that are organized into structured categories of thought and categories of meaning". This means that speakers provide conceptual knowledge in their long-term memory which is fundamental to perceive the different parts of a given stimulus as motion event components (for further details, see next section). Usually, a healthy person is able to "place an object, event, relationship, and so forth, into a conceptual category" (Jarvis 2007: 51). Concepts generally derive from human interaction with the physical-social world and crucially involve sensory mental imagery (Tyler 2012: 42). This refers to what we have termed above "mental motion representation" or "a person's mind eye";

when referring to motional contexts we will use the term "motion image" in the following). Oakley (2007: 216) states that "immediate perceptions form the basis of mental imagery, the images themselves are abstractions in which the individual can fill in details as he or she frames new experience". With respect to the mental motion representation, this means that in the seventh step the person has recognised the stimulus of the external world as "a motion event", and further has built up mental imagery, which is a central part of human conceptualisation. Conceptualisation is understood as "the process of selecting specific concepts from long term-memory, calling them up into working memory, and combining them dynamically in various orders, structures, and configurations in order to construct temporary representations of various types of phenomena [...]" (Jarvis 2007: 54).

Recognition is, as Jarvis (2007: 51) points out, "a matter of conceptual categorization". Let us turn back to our example above. The processes of the resulting linguistic symbolisation are generalised in the schema in Figure 1, which is by no means exhaustive, but should provide an initial illustration of a possible encoding process. The required substantial components and further explanations are successively added and discussed in greater detail in the following sections.

When speakers talk about something, we need, first, to consider that generally one of possibly multiple languages is activated (for communication). For instance, in everyday communication the speaker and the listener share a

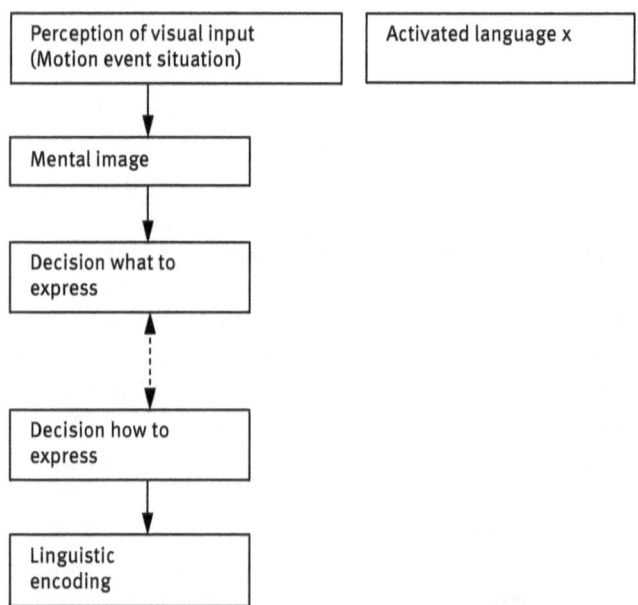

Figure 1: Encoding schema of a motion event situation (a).

common language which is activated and used for communication. In linguistic experiments a speaker may also be forced to use a certain language. This language may be the speaker's or listener's first, second or foreign language, or have become a speaker's dominant language. As pointed out in §2.2.2, the languages of multilingual speakers generally interact with each other: In the case of child bilinguals this means that the L1 is to some degree "present" when using the L2 as well as is the L2 to some degree present when using the L1.

We assume that from a given visual input (e.g. a situation to which a speaker is exposed to in reality or through a video stimulus in an experiment) a speaker perceives various information on which they build their motion image. Furthermore, they have to decide what of this information is relevant for the linguistic symbolisation. On the one hand, this decision process may be constrained by the complexity of the visual input. The more complex a motion event situation, the higher the processing cost in a speaker's working memory (which is, from a developmental perspective, generally more constrained the younger a speaker is). On the other hand, it is hypothesised that the "decision-what-to-express-process" is influenced, as mentioned above, by language-specific properties.

In order to linguistically encode a motion image, the speaker can use different lexical items and grammatical structures of the language in use. This "decision-how-to-express-process" is also seen to be constrained by specific properties of the language in use. Moreover, we assume that linguistic properties, again, interact with distinct properties of the speaker's other language(s) and are influenced by the speaker's language knowledge, proficiency and dominance in the language in use.

After having introduced some basic considerations, we will now turn to the different aspects of motion events, motion event conceptualisation and motion event expression.

3.2.2 Defining motion events

In cognitive science the different elements, which constitute a speaker's motion image, are generally analysed as semantic domains. According to the Gestalt theory, the object is often denoted Figure, the location with respect to which the Figure moves Ground (e.g. a physical (un)bounded plane), the fact of physical action Motion, the initial position Source and the final position Goal (or more specifically, the Endpoint of a Goal or Endstate of the Figure's directed Motion). The course followed by the Figure with respect to the Ground is denoted Path, the way in which it moves Manner and the motive for the Motion Cause. In addition, the Path can be subdivided into three main components: The Vector (the arrival, transversal or departure of the Figure), the Conformation (details about the geometric complex of the Ground, e.g. vertical or horizontal) and the Deixis (the perspective of the speaker) (Talmy 2003: 56).

A speaker perceives a motion event situation as a Figure's change of location from an initial spatial position A over intermediate spatial positions $B_{1,2,3}$ etc. (in direction or until a possible final position C). Thus, a speaker's motion image is construed by the Figure's changing relationship with its Ground (Schulze 2015: 176).

Furthermore, Motion can be carried out by an agent voluntarily (agentive or voluntary motion), or involuntarily (caused motion), whereby Motion can take place at a location or is directed. At that point, Motion has to be distinguished from Movement, since the latter is seen as the state of Motion at a location, "rather than change of location which is the defining feature of motion" (Filipović & Ibarretxe-Antuñano 2015: 527). For the purpose of this study the focus has to be limited to one particular event type, because it constitutes the basis of the theoretical considerations, namely directed agentive motion.

Agentive motion event situations, in turn, can cover different event types (see Figure 2): (i) the Figure (F) displaces on a Ground with no defined Source (S) or Goal (G) (a), with a direction towards a Goal (without explicitly reaching the Goal) (b), or until a defined Endpoint (EP) with a proximity to another Ground (c); (ii) the Figure displaces from an external into an internal bounded space or vice versa (d), or crosses over a plane to the other side of a threshold (e) (which is termed boundary crossing; for more details see §3.6.4).

With respect to the recognition of such motion event situations we referred to above, this is a matter of conceptual categorisation. Let us now turn to the underlying conceptual categorisation of language in motion contexts.

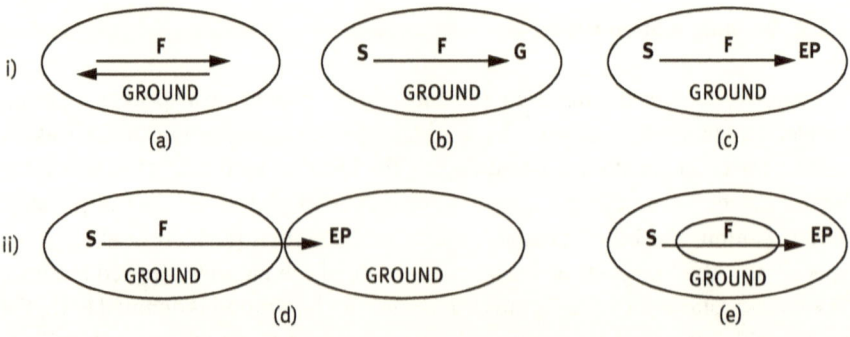

Figure 2: Types of motion event situations.

3.2.3 Defining motion event conceptualisation

In Talmy (2003: 213) there is a certain type of event complex in the underlying conceptual categorisation of language which he terms "macro-event". With respect to Motion, such a complex event is composed of (i) a framing event, (ii) a co-event and (iii) "the support relation that the co-event bears to the framing event" (Talmy 2003: 220; see Figure 3). According to Talmy, the conceptualisation of a motion event integrates a series of different conceptual components, which constitute the "main event": the (physical) figural entity which is going to be located or moved (Figure), the activating process (Transition, in this context Motion), and the association function which relates the Figure to the spatial ground and the spatial environment in respect to which the Figure moves (Ground). The association function alone or together with the ground entity constitutes the Path and is seen as the core schema of the motion event conceptualisation (Talmy 2003: 219). Together, the three conceptual components of the main event have a "framing function" of the motion event; Talmy (2003: 219) therefore uses the term "framing event" (i) (see Figure 4). Furthermore, the framing event can be supported by a subordinate event which "can be seen to fill in, elaborate, add to, or motivate the framing event" (Talmy 2003: 220). Talmy (2003: 220) terms this event type "co-event" (ii). The co-event, however, has a support relation (iii) which frequently bears the semantic information Cause and Manner of motion to the framing event. In sum, the macro-event is composed of a framing event, a co-event, and the support relation, and may, additionally, include an "[a]gent-initiated clausal chain", that is,

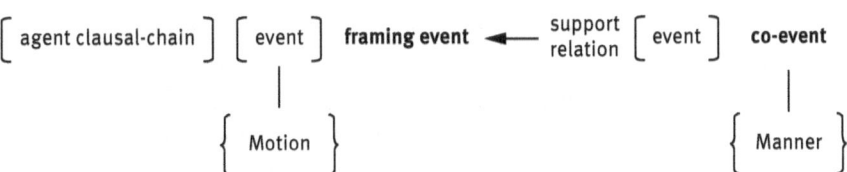

Figure 3: Conceptual structure of the macro-event (adapted from Talmy 2003: 221).

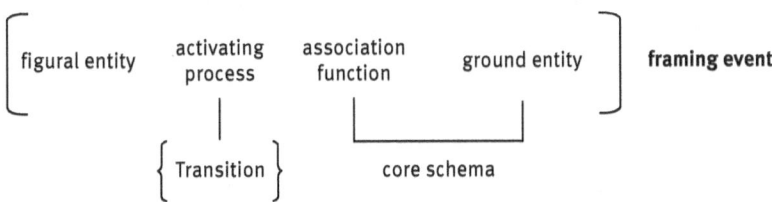

Figure 4: Conceptual structure of the framing event (adapted from Talmy 2003: 221).

when the agent "has volitionally performed the initiating action and has a scope of intention that extends over the whole sequence" (Talmy 2003: 216), which may "causes either or both of the framing event and the co-event" (Talmy 2003: 221).

We now have elaborated the conceptualisation of a motion event, but it has to be stressed that there is a great deal that is yet unknown about conceptualisation. With respect to the linguistic symbolisation of a given stimulus, there seems at least to be a consensus, by dividing conceptualisation into three levels (grounded in Levelt's model of language processing, Levelt 1989; see also Jarvis 2007: 50):
- general, non-linguistic thought and cognition;
- preverbal thought that has been macro-planned in relation to the conceptual material that will be communicated (what we have termed "decision what to express");
- preverbal thought that has been micro-planned for speaking in terms of how that conceptual material will be packaged for linguistic symbolisation (what we have termed "decision how to express").

Having elaborated motion event situations (external world), motion event conceptualisation (human cognition), we turn now to the linguistic symbolisation of motion events. We return to the question of what level of conceptualisation language may be involved and influence the way speakers conceptualise motion events differently in §3.3.

3.2.4 Motion event expressions

Generally all languages provide linguistic properties which serve to express a motion event linguistically. First, when looking into the linguistic symbolisation (or in Talmy's term "syntactic mapping") of the framing event, the Figure is typically expressed by the subject nominal phrase, and the activating function (Motion) by a verb. The verb, however, can carry besides the conceptual component Motion further additional components, for instance, the association function (Path) or the co-event (Manner). Consequently, two possible patterns emerge which add further information to the activating function in the verbal root: "Manner-in-verb" (see Figure 5) and "Path-in-verb" (see Figures 6 and 7). Following Talmy (2003: 27–28), when the verb slot conflates Motion and Manner, the Path has to be expressed by another linguistic device,[19] in German and French,

---

[19] Linguistic devices, which serve to express Path, are examined in §3.2.5.1. Note, that Talmy does not count prepositional phrases among these devices, as the examples a) and c) in Figure 5 indicate; this problem is also discussed in greater detail in §3.2.5.

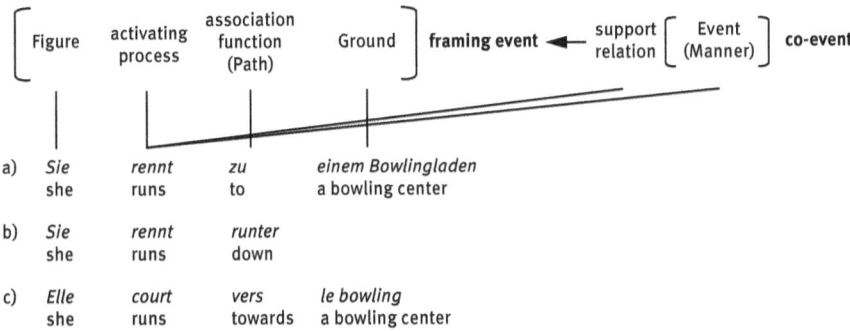

Figure 5: Possible syntactic mapping: Manner-in-verb pattern (adapted from Talmy 2003: 223).

for instance, by a preposition (see examples a) and c) in Figure 5). The Ground is expressed by a dative prepositional phrase in the German example (a) and constitutes together with the association function the Path, whereas in example (b) the Path is constituted by the association function alone (by a verb particle).

In the second pattern, Motion and Path are conflated in the verb slot (Talmy 2003: 58), consequently the co-event is either expressed by another linguistic device or not at all: In the German (a) and French (b) example in Figure 6, Manner is expressed by a subordinated non-finite construction (a gerund or present participle).

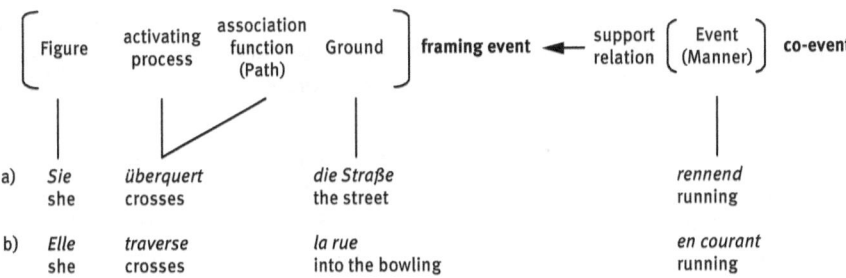

Figure 6: Possible syntactic mapping: Path-in-verb pattern in French (adapted from Talmy 2003: 223).

Note that in pro-drop languages, such as Turkish, it is not obligatory to express the Figure by a single linguistic device. In the Turkish example in Figure 7, Manner is also expressed by a subordinated non-finite construction (here a converb).

Talmy's analytic procedure of syntactic mapping is sometimes problematic. In his view, semantic elements correspond to one surface element (e.g. Motion

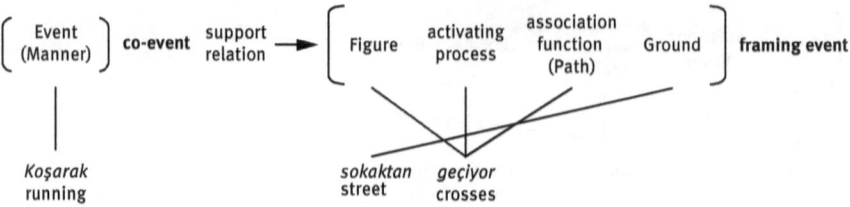

Figure 7: Possible syntactic mapping: Path-in-verb pattern in Turkish (adapted from Talmy 2003: 223).

and Manner correspond to a verb, and Path to a verb particle as illustrated in example b) in Figure 5). Berthele (2006: 45), for instance, points out that in German it is also possible to express motion events without using a motion verb. Example (11) demonstrates that the motion verb is missing; instead, an auxiliary verb (*sein* 'to be') is used in combination with a prepositional phrase and a directional adverbial.

(11) *Danach ist er eben auf diesen Baum rauf.*
then AUX.PR he just on this tree up
'Then he was just up on the tree.' (Berthele 2006: 45)

We can assume that the speaker (and the listener) conceptualise this utterance as a motion event – but the question here is which linguistic element corresponds to the semantic component of Motion, when the motion verb is missing? On the one hand, we can consider this example as an elliptic construction, where a part of the verbal phrase is omitted (e.g. *geklettert* 'climbed') by the speaker and is added by the hearer. However, Berthele (2006: 46) claims that, even an integration of elliptic constructions into the syntactic mapping procedure, would not be exhaustive for determining the conceptual structure of such an utterance. He further notes, that the adverbial (*rauf* 'up') and the accusative (the indefinite article in the prepositional phrase *auf den Baum* 'on the tree') contributes to the semantic component Motion. Talmy's analytic procedure of syntactic mapping is not exhaustive here for explaining the semantic meaning of such an utterance. The semantics of any utterance like (11) is not primarily produced by the verb but by the construction itself. This aspect constitutes the basic idea of Construction Grammar by assuming constructions to be conventionalised form-meaning pairs which already carry semantic features (Goldberg 1995; Goldberg 2006).

As a first step, it is necessary to illustrate the intransitive motion construction (see Figure 8a). Like Talmy, Goldberg (1995) proposes a pairing between the semantic and syntactic level. The semantic level encompasses two semantic roles:

the theme (in our context, this is the Figure) and the goal (the Path(+Ground)), which have corresponding argument roles on the syntactic level. The first argument role refers to the subject nominal phrase and the second to the directional Path component. PRED represents a variable that is filled by the motion verb when it is integrated into the construction (as an illustration, the motion verb *klettern* 'climb' is filled into the construction in Figure 8b).

The construction, however, "specifies which roles of the construction are obligatorily fused with roles of the verb" (Goldberg 1995: 51). In Goldberg's term, these "participant roles" fuse, on the one hand, obligatorily with the verb's array (in Figure 8 indicated by a solid line). On the other hand, roles, which are not obligatorily fused with roles of the verb, can be contributed by the construction (indicated by a dashed line) (Goldberg 1995: 51). In the case of the intransitive motion construction, such contributions refer to the Path components (such as directional prepositional phrases, adverbs or verb particles in German, for more details see §3.2.6.2), which in turn contribute to the inherent part of the motion construction. Goldberg (1995: 160) notes that the intransitive motion construction "can also add a motion interpretation to verbs that do not lexically code motion". Since the semantic component Motion is already an inherent part of the motion construction (expressed by the case and the adverb), it is then not necessary to express this component in the verbal root. Consequently, we need to add a third pattern which is characterised by the lack of a motion verb, but consists of semantic features which

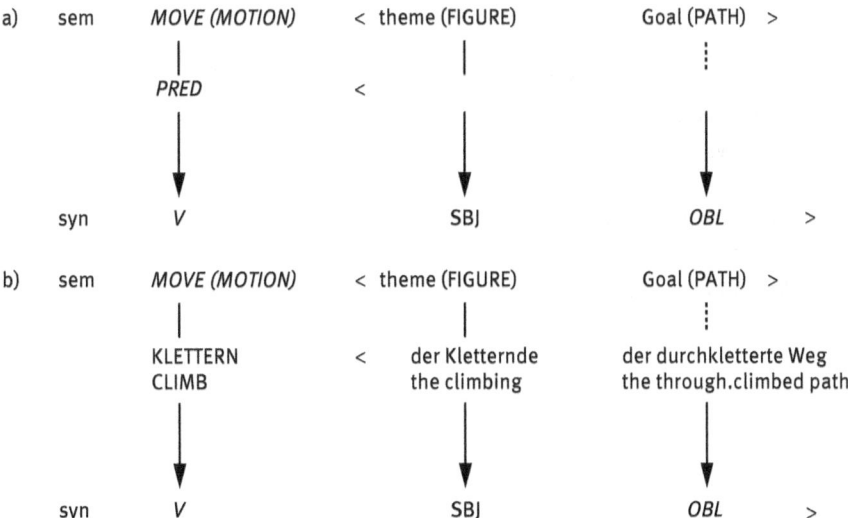

Figure 8: Intransitive motion construction (adapted from Goldberg 1995: 78).

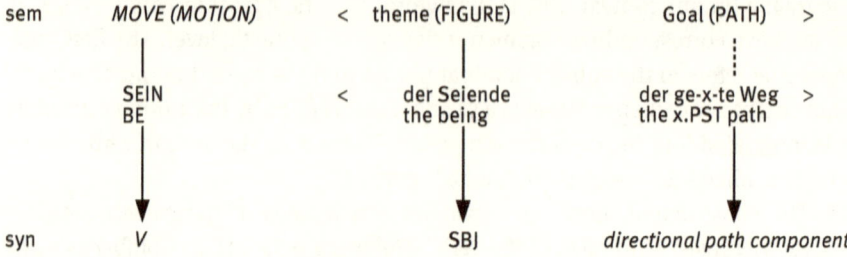

Figure 9: Intransitive motion construction with sein (adapted from Berthele 2007: 245).

can be conceptualised as motion event. In order to do so, we establish in the following a variant of the intransitive motion construction (which has been suggested previously by Berthele (2006, 2007) for the case of (Switzer-)German.

In Figure 9 the verb *sein* is integrated into the intransitive motion construction and introduces two argument roles (the Subject nominal phrase and the complement which denotes Path). The latter is the attribute which is assigned to the subject nominal phrase (Berthele 2007: 245). In the case of utterances such as illustrated in example (12) this assignment does not simply concern the subject nominal phrase, but a motional reading. With Goldberg, we can argue that this additive information (the integration of the different concepts, Figure, Path, Motion) are stored, defined and attributed by the motion construction itself (Berthele 2007: 245). Furthermore, utterances with modal verbs can be explained within the constructional approach as well (see example (12)).

(12) Sie   will   rüber/hoch/rein.
     she   want.PR   over there/up/inside
     'She wants over there/up/inside.'

Note, that the *sein*-construction seems exclusively to concern German varieties (which may occur mostly in south Germany and Switzerland, see Berthele 2007: 231–232) and do not occur in a motional context in French[20] and Turkish.[21]

---

[20] A corpus research of French written and spoken data (the FRANTEXT corpus consists of 14,700,000 tokens taken from 214 different novels from 1950–2000 (accessible online http://www.lexique.org, version Lexique 3.8 [accessed 2014-10-01]) (New et al. 2001); the *Corpus de Langue Parlée en Interaction* (CLAPI) 'corpus of spoken language in interaction' consists of 2,400,000 tokens (Balthasar & Bert 2005)) did not reveal any results of the type AUX+Path device with a motional reading (constructions such as *Elle est à travers/en haut/en bas/à la maison/sur l'arbre* only have a locative reading, whereas constructions such as *Elle est vers la maison* are grammatically incorrect).

In sum, the first pattern ("Manner-in-verb") integrates more than one event into one single clause, namely the framing event and the co-event, since the verb slot conflates Motion and Manner; the second pattern ("Path-in-verb") integrates the framing event into one single clause and the co-event in a subordinate clause, since the verb conflates Motion and Path. The third pattern ("Non-motion-verb") integrates the framing event into one single clause; the motion semantic is, however, contributed by the inherent part of the motion construction. Thus, speakers have different options as to how they linguistically encode a motion image (what we have termed the "selection-of-linguistic-properties") by either integrating only one event or multiple events into a single clause. From a cross-linguistic perspective, it is claimed that speakers differ in how they typically make use of these options when encoding motion events. In order to identify differences of language-specific patterns in German, Turkish and French, the following section focuses on typological approaches towards motion event encoding. Before turning to the linguistic material and cross-linguistic differences, we can elaborate the encoding schema introduced at the beginning, by adding the further information established in §3.2.2, 3.2.3 and 3.2.4 in Figure 10.

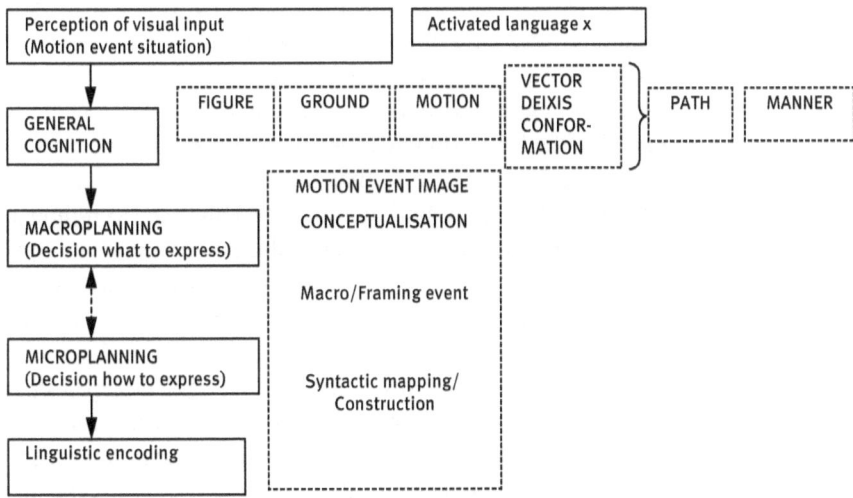

Figure 10: Encoding schema of a motion event situation (b).

---

21 In Turkish the auxiliary verbs *olmak* (to be) or *etmek/yapmak* (to do) can serve for different construction types. A corpus analysis of the Turkish National Corpus (see https://www.tnc.org.tr/) which consists of 47,641,688 tokens) did not reveal any results of the type AUX+Path device in motional contexts (e.g. *yukarı/dışarı oldu/yaptı/etti* 'she/he did/made up/out').

3.2.5 Typological approaches towards motion event expressions

The study of motion events has a long tradition in linguistic research. Much of the early research already focused on motion verbs (Tesnière 1959) by categorizing two different types: extrinsic verbs, such as "to enter" or "to exit" which encode information about the Ground on which the Motion takes place (corresponding to the "Path-in-verb" pattern; in Tesnière's terms *déplacement* 'displacement', where we will use the term "Path verb" in the following which is predominantly used in motion literature) and intrinsic verbs, such as "to run" or "to falter" which encode "somatic conditions" (corresponding to the Manner-in-verb pattern, in Tesnière's terms *mouvement* 'movement'; we will use the term "Manner verb" in the following). However, we need to add here at this point that these categories (the classification of two verb types) are radial categorisations (Berthele 2006: 57). According to Berthele (2006: 57–58), each motion verb category comprises typical and atypical verbs and is characterised by fuzzy boundaries. Additionally, we can add a third pattern which refers to overlaps between both categories, that is, when a verb encodes both semantic components, Manner and Path. For instance the verb "to climb" can incorporate the activating process (Motion), the surmounting of an obstacle (Manner) and the Conformation (a vertical Path)[22] (Berthele 2006: 54–55). The verb "to fall" encodes, besides Motion, a downward directed Path per se; however, some basic Manner components are encoded as well (immediateness or velocity). Following recent motion verb analysis (among others Berthele (2006), Harr (2012), Tschander (1999)), such verbs are classified in the following as "Manner-Path-verbs".

Furthermore, we add a fourth category that refers to verbs which neither express specific Manner nor Path information but general Motion. Even though the verbs "to go" and "to come" display some deictic information, these verbs are classified as "Generic motion verbs" in the following. Since the semantic degree of Path of these verbs is so weak (Goschler et al. 2013: 244) they generally require additive directional Path information (e.g. "go to X").

A phenomenon which has been of special interest in linguistic typology is that the languages of the world differ with respect to their use and the diversity of Path and Manner verbs. Among scholars studying cross-linguistic differences in this domain, the work by Talmy (Talmy 1985; Talmy 2003; Talmy 2009) probably "yielded the most prolific further research and novel theoretical and methodological developments in this field" (Filipović & Ibarretxe-Antuñano 2015: 527);

---

[22] Note that the equivalent verbs in Turkish (*tırmanmak*) and French (*grimper*) only encode, beside Motion and Manner, an upwards directed Path. A construction with a Path device expressing downwards directed motion (e.g. *aşağı* or *en bas* 'downwards') is not possible, whereas in German constructions of this type are normal (*Sie kletterte herunter* 'She climbed down').

this work has set the agenda for the study of motion events across a wide range of languages (in particular Slobin and colleagues) within an interdisciplinary research and for challenging typological approaches (e.g. Croft et al. 2010). Other researchers focused on static and dynamic prepositional meanings (Herskovits 1986; Vandeloise 1991) or took, as indicated above, a constructional approach into account (Goldberg 1995).

Approaches which serve as theoretical background for the current study are discussed in the following sections: Talmy's theory of lexicalisation patterns is discussed in §3.2.5.1. Furthermore, an alternative typological approach revising Talmy's framework by analysing languages with respect to a cline of Path salience is presented in §3.2.5.3.

3.2.5.1 Lexicalisation patterns

As introduced in §3.2.4, Talmy's main interest is the study of the systematic relation between meaning and form within a cognitive framework. Focusing on lexicalisation patterns in motion event expressions, he examines which semantic element (Figure, Ground, Path, Cause, Manner) is typically expressed by which linguistic surface elements (verb root, other linguistic devices) (Talmy 2008: 66).

The systematic analysis of the relation between mapping semantic elements on the surface structure indicates that languages differ in how they typically encode the Path of motion which typologically is the "most diagnostic component" (Talmy 2008: 153), since it frames and structures the whole motion event. As mentioned above, Talmy proposes two main conflation patterns with respect to the first surface form (the verbal root[23]): Motion+Path (e.g. "to enter") and Motion+Co-Event (e.g. "to run").[24] With respect to the second surface form Talmy (2003: 102) defines other linguistic devices, encoding Path, as "satellites":

> It is the grammatical category of any constituent other than a noun-phrase or prepositional-phrase complement that is in a sister relation to the verb root. It relates to the verb root as a dependent to a head. The satellite, which can be either a bound affix or a free word, is thus intended to encompass all of the following grammatical forms which traditionally have been largely treated independently of each other: English verb particles, German separable and inseparable verb prefixes, Latin or Russian verb prefixes [...]. A set of forms that can function as satellites in a language often overlaps partially, but not wholly, with a set of forms in another grammatical category in that language, generally the category of prepositions, verbs, or nouns (Talmy 2003: 102).

---

[23] Talmy focuses on the verbal root alone, allowing comparisons of typologically very different languages (Harr 2012:88).
[24] A third conflation pattern proposed by Talmy includes Motion+Figure (e.g. 'to spit') which will not further specified, since it is not of interest in the current study.

This definition is more strict compared with what we have termed "other linguistic devices", since it excludes for instance prepositional phrases or adverbs; in the following this analysis is therefore termed satellites "stricto sensu" (Fortis & Fagard 2010). Talmy (2008: 139) argues that the recognition of satellites as a grammatical category can be justified by the fact that "the semantics of a motion event seems to be comprised of those components encoded in verb roots and those expressed in satellites" (Harr 2012: 91).

Building on this deductive reasoning, Talmy proposes a dichotomous typology of motion event encoding: languages following the "Path-in-verb" pattern are considered "verb-framed languages" (hereafter V-languages), since Path is characteristically expressed by the main verb of a clause (in example (13) by the verb *sortir* 'exit'); in "satellite-framed languages" (hereafter S-languages), which follow the "Manner-in-verb" pattern, Path is expressed by an element (a satellite) associated with the main verb (in example (14) by the particle "out"). As the obligate element of a motion event, the Path, is expressed outside the main verb in S-languages, the verb slot stays free to encode besides Motion the Co-Event (Manner). It is claimed that in V-languages Manner is usually expressed in subordinate or adverbial clauses or it is not encoded at all (when it is not foregrounded; see example (13)).

(13) D'   un   trou   de   l'   arbre sort   un   hibou.
     from   INDF   hole   of   DET   tree   exit.PR   INDF owl
     'An owl exits from a hole in the tree.' (Slobin 2004b:224)

(14) *An owl popped out.* (Slobin 2004a:224)

Talmy (2003: 27) claims that the proposed lexicalisation patterns are exhaustive and that the languages of the world use only one of these types in their most characteristic expression of motion events. Talmy means by "most characteristic" that the type is colloquial in style, frequent in speech and pervasive in its extension in the lexicon (in line with Filipović & Ibarretxe-Antuñano 2015: 528, it should be added that the proposed patterns are commonly employed by young and adult native speakers of standard varieties). Building on this dichotomous distinction, Romance, Greek, Semitic, Turkic, Basque, Korean and Japanese languages are categorised as V-languages, and Germanic, Slavic, Celtic and Finno-Ugric languages as S-languages (Slobin 2006: 62).

Following this binary categorisation, German would be an S-language and French and Turkish both a V-language. Nevertheless, in §3.2.4 we have seen that, at least in German and French, the use of both patterns is possible. In Talmy, this circumstance is explained by the assumption that one pattern is more characteristic than the other, which, in turn, would not exclude the use of the less characteristic pattern. Talmy (2003: 64–65) is also aware of this problem, which emerges from his dichotomous distinction when pointing out the existence of "split", "parallel" and "intermixed" systems of conflation within languages. Languages have a split system, when different conflation types for different types of motion events are used. A parallel system can only account for languages which use S- and V-pattern to a comparable degree: languages such as Greek "can use different conflation types with roughly comparable colloquiality in the representation of the *same* type of Motion event" (Talmy 2003: 66, emphasis in the original). The intermixed system is rather hypothetical in nature and might account for languages which "exhibit no consistent pattern of conflation for some type of Motion event, but rather intermix different forms of conflation for the various members of that Motion event type" (Talmy 2003: 67). Nevertheless, in Talmy, the predominant pattern within a language determines the categorisation of V- or S-language. This point of view is, at least from a typological perspective, still highly problematic and has led to criticism and revisions of the Talmian typology.

3.2.5.2 Beyond conflation patterns

When looking more closely into the possible verbalisation of motion events within languages, there seems indeed to be more variation than assumed by Talmy's dichotomous typology (Wälchli 2001). Moreover, Talmy's typology has been criticised for not accounting for all language types (among others Berthele 2009; Croft et al. 2010; Filipović 2007), which goes beyond the problem of split systems. Languages such as Mandarin do not have a clear finite verb and consistently use both S- and V-patterns. Slobin suggests another third type, so called "equipollently framed languages" (Slobin 2003; Slobin 2006). In addition, Croft et al. (2010) propose "double framing" languages, which denote patterns in which Path is redundantly expressed. Examples (15) and (16) illustrate that in Turkish and French, Path verbs can be combined with Path devices:

(15) *Adam aşağıy-a in-iyor.*
 man down-DAT descend-PROG.3SG
 'The man is descending down.' (Daller, Treffers-Daller & Furman 2011: 109)

(16) *Elle descend en bas.*
 she descend.PR down
 'She descends down.'

(17) La   botella entr-ò   a   la   cueva.
     DET   bottle   enter-PST   in   DET   cave
     'The bottle entered in the cave.'

Talmy, however, recognises some of the double-framing constructions with respect to Spanish prepositions (see example (17)) which express Path. However, he considers these constructions, in which a Path device is dependent on the Path verb, as verb-framed. Again, this assumption is problematic, because the preposition *a* 'to' in the Spanish example is clearly Goal oriented; the same also applies to French prepositions, such as *à* 'to', *de* 'from', or *dans* 'inside', when they are used in a motional context. According to Talmy's definition, a satellite construction such as *Sie rennt zum Bowlingladen* 'She runs to the bowling centre' or *Elle court vers le bowling* 'She runs towards the bowling centre' (see Figure 5 in §3.2.4) would be neither V- nor S-framed, because the prepositional phrase is not a satellite stricto sensu. However, the particle *runter* 'down' in *Sie rennt runter* 'She runs down', is a satellite stricto sensu, because it is in a sister relation to the verb root (see the discussion in Fortis & Fagard 2010). As with German, many S- (but also V-) languages provide constructions of the type [motion verb+prepositional phrase]. As a consequence, several studies (among others Berthele 2006; Harr 2012; Ochsenbauer & Hickmann 2010; Haggblade 1995) analysed Path expressions outside the verb as satellite and therefore do not distinguish satellites stricto sensu and prepositional phrases. Furthermore, Beavers, Levin & Tham (2010: 337–338) argue that satellites are not proper constituents, but prepositional phrases are. Consequently, the authors also do not distinguish between satellites stricto sensu and prepositional phrases, and employ satellites even in a broader sense as "any constituent that is sister to or adjoined to the verb (root)" (Beavers, Levin & Wei Tham 2010: 339). This broader definition is also advocated in the current study which means that a prepositional phrase expressing a Goal or a Source such as presented in Figure 5, as well as the directional adverb *aşağı* 'down' in example (15) and *en bas* 'down' in example (16), are considered as linguistic devices which encode direction equal to Talmy's satellites stricto sensu. In fact Talmy later changed his definition slightly by adding prepositions to the category of satellites (Talmy 2009: 390). However, advocating this broader definition of a satellite has consequences for analysing languages from a typological perspective, in particular for languages which are considered V-framed. The studies by Özçaliskan & Slobin (1999; 2000a), Engberg-Pedersen & Trondhjem (2004) and Ibarretxe-Antuñano (2004), for instance, observed that speakers of V-languages with more complex morphological resources for spatial expression (here Turkish, Basque, and West-Greenlandic) produce more elaborated Path descriptions than speakers of "prototypical" V-languages such as Spanish (Cadierno 2008: 256). Ibarretxe-Antuñano & Hijazo-Gascón (2012: 351) point out that some languages are considered V-languages but also include "(pseudo)-satellite constructions" (Aragones, Hijazo-Gascón & Ibarretxe-Antuñano 2010; Italian, Hijazo-Gascón & Ibarretxe-Antuñano 2013; Basque, Ibarretxe-Antuñano 2004; Chantyal, Noonan 2003). Generally, the observance of such split systems are also considered as an intra-typological variation within a given type of language. In order to identify such patterns, one needs to analyse satellites in a rather broader sense and less stricto sensu, as well as focus on Path-constructions outside the main verb. We turn to this point in the following section, by presenting additive and alternative typological approaches of Path expressions.

3.2.5.3 Clines of Path salience

On the one hand, Slobin (2004b: 251) argues that "a tripartite typology with regard to Path expression (verb-framed language, equipollently-framed language, satellite-framed language) does not seem to be necessary in accounting for the relative attention to manner in a language". He criticises Talmy for not focusing sufficiently on the semantic component Manner and suggests a "cline/continuum of Manner salience".[25] On the other hand, since Path is typologically the "most diagnostic component", it seems to be more natural to analyse languages with respect to a "cline/continuum of Path salience" when comparing them on the basis of the number of Path devices accompanying the main verb (Ibarretxe-Antuñano 2009; Ibarretxe-Antuñano & Hijazo-Gascón 2012). The analysis of a falling scene in the Frog story sample of 21 different languages shows that languages considered as V-languages (Chantyal and Basque) are high-Path-salient languages, while other V-languages such as Turkish and French fall in the middle of the cline, close to German, an S-language (Ibarretxe-Antuñano & Hijazo-Gascón 2012: 354). A more detailed comparison of Frog Story descriptions provides evidence of intra-typological variation within the Romance language family. The three languages analysed in the study of Hijazo-Gascón & Ibarretxe-Antuñano (2013) are situated on a cline of Path salience as follows: Italian > Spanish > French. Italian speakers clearly prefer plus-ground constructions compared with Spanish and French speakers (Hijazo-Gascón & Ibarretxe-Antuñano 2013: 47–48).

---

25 Compared with speakers of V-languages, the Frog story studies (Berman & Slobin 1994) show that speakers of S-languages more frequently use Manner verbs in their descriptions as well as display a greater lexical diversity; on the other hand the results also display a great variance of Manner verb usage within S-languages (Slobin 2004b).

A more fine-grained typology of "basic intransitive motion" events[26] focusing on the encoding of Path is proposed by Wälchli (Wälchli 2001; Wälchli & Zúñiga 2006; Wälchli 2009). Wälchli criticises Talmy and Tesnière for only focusing on verbs. He points out that [Motion+Path] "is a semantic domain that is expressed in all languages, but not exclusively by verbs" (Wälchli 2001: 300). Aside from verbal encoding, Path can be expressed adnominally by prepositions, postpositions or case marking, or adverbially by verb affixes, verb particles or adverbs. A crucial factor in his assumption is, that most languages of the world combine verbal, adnominal and adverbal slots (Wälchli 2001: 300). He distinguishes three different encoding patterns of Path (in his terms displacement): (i) verbal encoding; (ii) adnominal encoding and (iii) adverbal encoding. While (i) is like the assumed lexicalisation pattern in V-languages, (ii) and (iii) refer to the assumed encoding patterns of S-languages. Furthermore, Wälchli (2001: 300) sub-categorises Path (Goal and Source) into six "cardinal kinds of displacement": AD, IN, SUPER (Goal), and AB, EX, DE (Source) (see Table 1). By doing so, this more finely grained approach allows a more adequate analysis of the locus of expressions of Path (Berthele 2004: 99). Berthele (2004) modificates Wälchli's categorisation with respect to two aspects: first, he considers an unnecessary constraint with respect to vertical direction (away or towards a Goal); downward directed motion (DE) coincides with Motion away from a Source (AB). In French, for instance, a Manner-Path verb such as *tomber* 'to fall' "can open a slot for either the source [le garçon tombe de l'arbre 'the boy falls from the tree'] or the goal [le garçon tombe sur le sol 'the boy falls on the ground'] or even both source and ground objects [le garçon tombe de l'arbre sur le sol 'the boy falls from the tree on the ground']" (Berthele 2004: 99). Furthermore, Berthele (2004: 100) proposes to disregard deixis as well, "since the deictic center taken depends on the deictic stance taken in a particular narrative". He points out that a Path such as "F come into G" is perfectly possible. With respect to the analysis of the languages involved in the current study, these modifications are adapted for the motion event analysis. Furthermore, three transition types (PRAETER, PRO, TRANS) are added, in order to match the needs of the current study (presented in Table 1).

The following sections emphasise the options which the three languages, German, Turkish and French provide for their speakers and examines native speakers' preferences of motion event encoding in the respective language. Furthermore, it is of special interest whether, within a split system, linguistic

---

[26] "'Basic' means that the kind of movement involved is prototypically the normal motion of humans (not animals or objects) moving without special haste and without vehicles [...]" (Wälchli 2001:300).

Table 1: Wälchli's cardinal kinds of displacement and Berthele's modifications.

	Wälchli (2001)	Berthele (2004)	This study
AD	"F go to G"	"F displaces to G"	"F displaces to G"
IN	"F enter/go into G"	"F displaces into G"	"F displaces into G"
SUPER	"F go onto G"	"F displaces up"	"F displaces up"
AB	"F come from G"	"F displaces away from G"	"F displaces away from G"
EX	"F come out of G"	"F displaces out of G"	"F displaces out of G"
DE	"F come down from G"	"F displaces down"	"F displaces down"
PRAETER			"F displaces by G"
PRO			"F displaces through G"
TRANS			"F displaces over G"

constraints lead speakers to encode different types of motion events by a consistent pattern. Within a variational perspective, Talmy's lexicalisation theory serves as a theoretical framework, in particular with respect to the possible and preferred motion verb choices (§3.2.6.1). Moreover, the analysis also includes other linguistic devices encoding Manner and Path (adverbal and adnominal encoding; §3.2.6.2) and the syntactic organisation of motion events as well as the productivity of motion verb constructions (§3.2.6.3), in order to obtain a supplementary perspective beyond the verbal conflation patterns. The encoding of boundary crossing events is a focus as well, in order to shed some light on linguistic constraints within languages that lead a speaker to encode motion event types differently.

Since typological classifications of motion event encoding, such as Talmy's lexicalisation theory, "is based largely on deductive reasoning and less on corpus analysis" (Berthele 2013: 56), the empirical research has become an important contribution to this field. In order to obtain a contrastive and usage-based perspective, the following analysis of the linguistic material provided by the three languages is, as far as possible, based on recent empirical findings and corpus analysis.

3.2.6 Empirical implications of motion event encoding in German, Turkish, and French

3.2.6.1 Motion verb choices

It is generally claimed that compared with V-languages, S-languages have a greater lexicon of Manner verbs with semantically fine distinctions. On the basis of his empirical contribution to the study of motion events from a cross-linguistic perspective (among others Berman & Slobin 1994; Slobin 2000; Slobin 2003;

Slobin 2004a; Slobin 2006), Slobin demonstrates that the different conflation patterns in S- and V-languages have an impact on the size and diversity of a language's verbal lexicon. In language use, speakers of S-languages can easily access the Manner lexicon; as a result, various Manner verbs are used in natural everyday conversation as well as in elicited oral narratives (Slobin 2003; Slobin 2006: 70).

German

Since in S-languages, Path is encoded in the verbal periphery, the main verb slot stays free to encode Manner. It is assumed that the vast majority of German motion verbs encode Motion and Manner (Weber 1983), so that German provides a large lexicon of Manner verbs with fine semantic distinctions.

An analysis of the corpus-based frequency list, DeReRO (2012)[27] indicates that around 10% of the 500 most frequent verbs in written texts can be used in a motional context (58 types). These contain Generic motion verbs (*kommen* 'to come', *gehen* 'to go'), Manner verbs (*laufen* 'to walk', *fahren* 'to drive', *drehen* 'to turn', *landen* 'to land', *fliegen* 'to fly', *verfolgen* 'to chase', *stürzen* 'to overthrow'), one Manner-Path verb (*fallen* 'to fall'), and Path verbs (*verlassen* 'to leave', *gelangen* 'to proceed'). This analysis can only be seen as a first tendency, but it is not exhaustive. First, the list of verbs also includes verbs which can be used in a non-motional context (*es kommt darauf an* 'that depends', *es lief gut bei ihr* 'it went well for her'; *sie stürzte sich in die Arbeit* 'She started working immediately'), second, the frequency list is based exclusively on written texts. In order to match the purpose of the current study, an analysis of the motion verb inventory of the respective language should only comprise "true" motion verbs which are used in oral conversation. Figure 11 gives an extended overview of the German motion verb inventory, including the amount of Manner, Path, Manner-Path and Generic verbs in oral corpora of German.[28]

---

[27] The frequency list contains 326,946 tokens and is based on the *DEUTSCHE REFERENZKORPUS* (German reference corpus of written texts) (DeReKo 2012).
[28] The analysis is based on a corpus research of various oral corpora (Forschungs- u. Lehrkorpus für gesprochenes Deutsch, Freiburger Korpus, König-Korpus, Pfeffer-Korpus) of the *Datenbank für gesprochenes Deutsch DGD-2* 'Database of spoken German' (Institut für deutsche Sprache 2014) which contain 1,856,044 tokens [version 2.2, accessed 2014-10-01]. Instances of non-motional context were eliminated by manually coding all occurrences with respect to motional and non-motional contexts. The total amount of motion verbs, which occur with a high frequency in the corpora (*kommen* 'to come', *gehen* 'to go', *fahren* 'to drive', *schwimmen* 'to swim'), is estimated: as a first step the percentage of verbs with motional context was calculated by coding a random sample of each verb type (10% of the whole sample); as a second step the total amount of a verb type occurring in the whole sample was divided by the calculated percentage of the random sample (e.g. *kommen* has 7165 instances in the selected corpora; 716 instances have

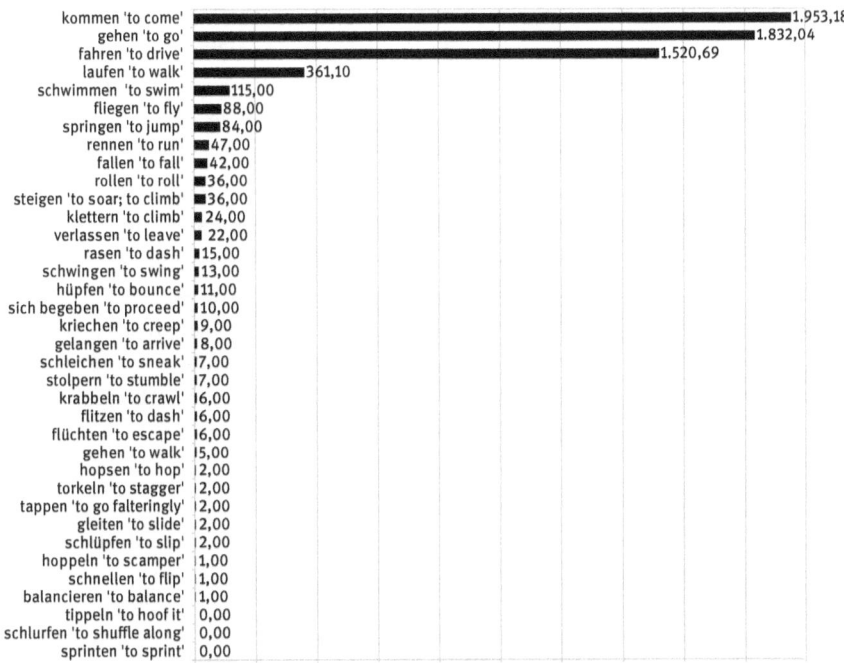

Figure 11: Motion verb frequency in German oral text corpora (in tokens).

The analysis indicates that the polysemous verbs *kommen* 'to come' and *gehen* 'to go' are most frequently used in oral texts. Note that *gehen* can also express Manner which, however, needs to be highlighted by adding further information (e.g. *zu Fuß* 'by foot'). There are only a few verbs encoding Motion and Path in German: *verlassen* 'to leave', *sich begeben* 'to proceed' or *gelangen* 'to arrive'. Thus, with respect to the cardinal kinds of displacement, German provides three distinctions in the locus of verbal encoding, however, these verbs are used less frequently. Moreover, German provides, beyond the Manner verbs of the top 500 motion verbs (as listed above) and analogous to other S-languages, several hundreds of other Manner verbs (Slobin 2006: 71). The Manner verbs listed in Figure 11 therefore only give an overview of the semantic diversity and their usage frequency. In some cases, there is even no monolexematic equivalent in other S-languages, such as English (e.g. *tappen* 'to go falteringly'; Ochsenbauer & Hickmann 2010:

---

been randomly selected, of which 196 were used in a motional context (36.68%); when adding this percentage up to the total amount of instances found in the corpora, we can estimate that *kommen* occurs 1953.18 times in motional contexts.

220). Whereas the Manner-Path verb *fallen* 'to fall' and the Manner verbs *laufen* 'to walk', *fahren* 'to drive', *fliegen* 'to fly', *schwimmen* 'to swim', and *springen* 'to jump' are highly frequent, other Manner verbs such as *kriechen* 'to creep', *flitzen* 'to dash', *hopsen* 'to hop', or *balancieren* 'to balance' were less frequently found in the oral corpora. Other Manner verbs such as *schlurfen* 'to shuffle along' or *tippeln* 'to hoof it' are not found at all. It can be expected that the latter and the less frequent Manner verbs are also semantically more expressive compared with the more frequently used Manner verbs. This finding is consistent with Slobin's assumption of a "two-tiered" lexicon (Slobin 1997: 459). There are neutral, everyday Manner verbs which are used more frequently and more expressive Manner verbs, which are used less frequently. When setting a 1% threshold for expressive Manner verbs on the basis of all analysed Manner and Manner-Path verbs in the DGD-2 corpora, the following picture emerges (see Table 2).

Table 2: Total frequency of Generic, Path, Manner and Manner-Path verbs and distribution of everyday and expressive Manner/Manner-Path verbs in oral corpora of German.

Motion verb category	Token	%	everyday	%	expressive	%
VP	40.00	0.64				
VM	2.349.79	37.41	2251.79	95.83	98.00	4.17
VMP	102.00	1.63	102.00	100	/	/
VGEN	3.785.22	60.32				

There are sixteen Manner lemmas which fall under the 1% threshold. However, as regards their frequency, they only cover 4.17% of the total amount of analysed Manner verbs. Moreover, there are seven Manner lemmas which can be classified as everyday Manner verbs. The numbers show that these few lemmas cover about 96% of all analysed Manner verbs in the DGD 2. The three Manner-Path lemmas, which were analysed in the corpora, are frequently used and are classified as everyday Manner-Path verbs.

In addition, Manner can also be expressed by other motion constructions, for instance by the semantically weak verb *machen* 'to make' and a Manner device (e.g. *einen Sprung machen* 'to make a jump'), which is often referred to as *Funktionsverbgefüge* in German. It can be used as opposed to a near synonym Manner verb (here *springen* 'to jump') (Abraham 2010: 20).

Overall, the figures reveal that Manner verbs occur predominantly in oral corpora compared to Path verbs. This finding confirms the prediction that in German Manner is typically encoded in the verb stem and most frequently used.

However, the high amount of Generic verbs found in oral discourse indicates that a neutral expression of motion events in German is commonly employed.

Turkish

It is assumed that Turkish, as a V-language, frequently provides motion verbs which typically encode Path. Figure 12 gives an overview of the motion verb inventory and its frequency in a written text corpus of Turkish (Turkish National Corpus, hereafter TNC; Aksan et al. 2012). The verb selection corresponds to the motion verb inventory in German (see Figure 11).[29]

Overall, the corpus analysis comprises eight verb types which do not encode Manner at all (Generic and Path verbs) and twenty three verb types which encode Manner (and Path). There are verbs which specify i) general Motion (*gitmek* 'to go'; *gelmek* 'to come'), (ii) a change of location (*girmek* 'enter'; *çıkmak* 'exit'; *geçmek* 'to pass'/'cross', (iii) vertical Motion (*inmek* 'descend'; *çıkmak* 'ascend') and the Endpoint of a Path (*ulaşmak* 'to arrive'). Thus, with respect to the cardinal kinds of displacement, Turkish provides six unambiguous Path distinctions in the locus of verbal encoding. Furthermore, Turkish provides three Manner-Path verbs (*düşmek* 'to fall', *yükselmek* 'to soar (ascend)' and *tırmanmak* 'to climb').

The corpus analysis indicates that Generic and Path verbs are predominantly used; analogous to oral corpora of German, the Generic verbs *gelmek* 'to come' and *gitmek* 'to go' were most frequently found. Path verbs were found approximately three times as frequently as Manner verbs in the corpus (see Table 3), whilst some Manner and Manner-Path verbs occur more frequently.[30] When setting a 1% threshold for expressive Manner verbs on the basis of all analysed Manner and Manner-Path verbs in the TNC, it can be expected that verbs such as *düşmek* 'to fall', *yürümek* 'to walk' and *koşmak* 'to run' are semantically less salient in con-

---

29 Due to the lack of representative oral corpora of Turkish as well as technical limitations at the present moment (last access 2017-08-15) of the TNC (see https://www.tnc.org.tr/) the analysis exclusively comprises written text types (books, periodicals, and (un)published documents from a period of 20 years, 1990–2009; 47,641688 tokens) and only includes finite verbs in the present, future and the past tense (since a lemma-based frequency analysis is not available at the time of the corpus access). Instances of non-motional context were eliminated by manually coding occurrences with respect to motional and non-motional contexts. Due to the different size of the TNC, the amount of motion verb tokens are estimated by following the same procedure as described for the DGD-2 in footnote 28 and indicated per million tokens.
30 The number of tokens of polysemous verbs is higher, since the verbs were not further subdivided. This is, for instance, the case for the verb *sürmek* which denotes also 'to push' or 'to spread (something) on/over (something)'.

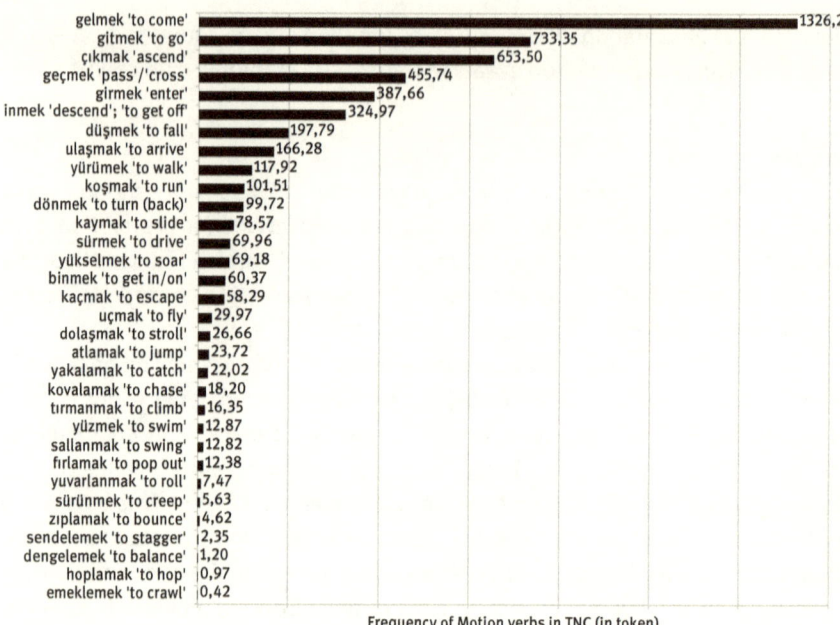

Figure 12: Motion verb frequency in Turkish National Corpus (in token per million entries).

trast to the less frequent and more expressive Manner verbs *yuvarlanmak* 'to roll', *sürünmek* 'to creep', *zıplamak* 'to bounce', *sendelemek* 'to stagger', *dengelemek* 'to balance', *hoplamak* 'to hop' and *emeklemek* 'to crawl'.

Table 3: Total frequency of Generic, Path, Manner and Manner-Path verbs and distribution of everyday and expressive Manner/Manner-Path verbs in the Turkish National Corpus.

Motion verb category	Token	%	Token everyday	%	Token expressive	%
VP	2048.52	40.18				
VM	707.26	13.87	684.61	96.80	22.65	3.20
VMP	283.32	5.56	283.32	100.00	/	/
VGEN	2059.60	40.39				

Note that Turkish also provides constructions with semantically weak verbs (mostly *etmek* 'to do', *yapmak* 'to make') which can serve for encoding Manner (e.g. *takip etmek* 'to do/make pursuit [to follow]').

Although the analysis of Turkish motion lemmas is based on a written text corpus, the results suggest that the Turkish Manner verb lexicon – in particular the inventory of expressive Manner lemmas – is much smaller and semantically less specific compared to German (oral corpora). Some of the German Manner lemmas do not have a corresponding equivalent in the Turkish lexicon. Where German provides different verbs to describe the specific Manner with semantically fine distinctions (e.g. *torkeln* 'to stagger', *wanken* 'to stumble', *taumeln* 'to tumble', *straucheln, stolpern* 'to trip'), Turkish provides only two verb types for these kinds of Manners (*sendelemek; tökezlemek*). Aksu-Koç (1994: 354) points out, that "Turkish compensates for the lack of lexical richness characteristic of English and German verbs of Manner by the use of productive verb morphology that allows for packaging of events in different ways". We will come back to this phenomenon in the following section.

French

A corpus analysis[31] of the 500 most frequent verbs in written texts indicates that, analogous to German, around 10% are motion verbs (57 lemmas). These contain Generic verbs (*aller* 'to go'; *venir* 'to come'), Path verbs (e.g. *passer* 'to pass by', *arriver* 'to arrive', *sortir* 'to exit', *partir* 'to leave', *monter* 'to ascend', *entrer* 'to enter'), Manner verbs (*marcher* 'to walk', *courir* 'to run', *glisser* 'to slide', *rouler* 'to roll', *conduire* 'to drive', *sauter* 'to jump'), and Manner-Path verbs (*tomber* 'to fall', *grimper* 'to climb', *dévaler* 'to rush down'). For the methodological reasons that were introduced in the context of German above, Figure 13 gives an overview of the motion verb frequency in oral corpora of French.[32]

The results indicate that, analogous to German and Turkish, the Generic verbs *aller* and *(re)venir* are used predominantly in spoken corpora. Similar to Turkish, Path verbs are most frequently used (*partir* 'to leave', *sortir* 'to exit', *monter* 'to ascend', *arriver* 'to arrive', *rentrer* 'to come in/back', *entrer* 'to enter', *descendre*

---

31 The corpus (version Lexique 3.8, accessed 2014-10-01) consists of 14,700,000 tokens, taken from FRANTEXT (214 different novels from 1950–2000) and is accessible online (http://www.lexique.org) (New et al. 2001).

32 The analysis is based on various smaller oral corpora (2,400,000 tokens) which are accessible via the *Corpus de Langue Parlée en Interaction* (CLAPI) 'corpus of spoken language in interaction' (Balthasar & Bert 2005). Instances of non-motional context have been eliminated (e.g. *on va manger* 'we will eat'; *elle vient de manger* 'she is eating'; *ça marche* 'this works'; *ça sort souvent marron* 'this often ends up ridiculous') by manually coding all occurrences with respect to motional and non-motional contexts. The total amount of motion verbs, which occur with a high frequency in the corpora (*aller, tomber, (re)venir, partir, sortir, monter, arriver, rentrer*), is estimated by applying the same procedure as explained in footnote 28. In contrast to the DGD 2, CLAPI displays some problems due to incorrect annotations; e.g. instances of the lemma *entrer* 'to enter' also include the adverb *entre* 'between'. Such instances were extracted before selecting a random sample.

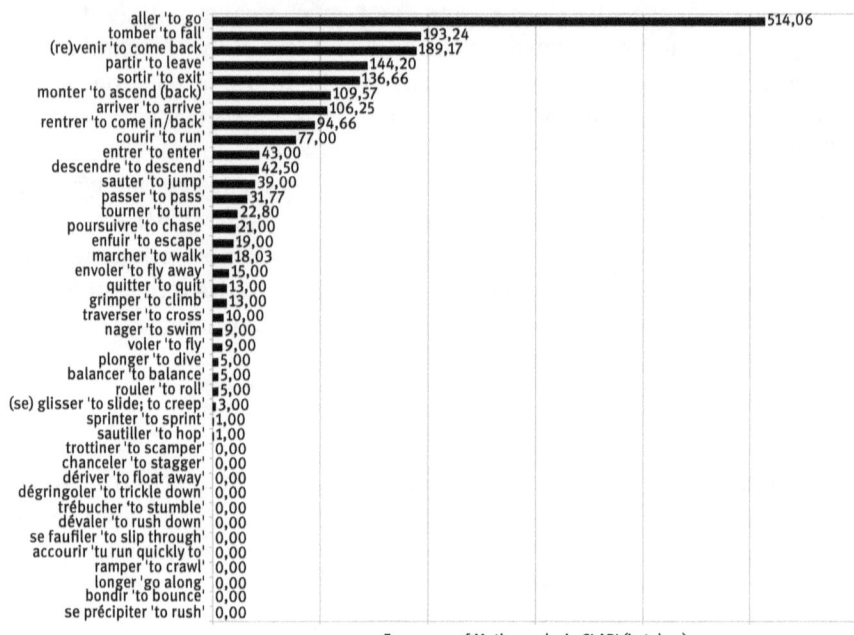

Figure 13: frequency in CLAPI (in tokens) Motion verb.

'to ascend', *passer* 'to pass', *quitter* 'to leave'; with respect to the cardinal kinds of displacement, French provides seven distinctions in the locus of verbal encoding (when including revenir 'to come back' as AD). Some Manner (-Path) verbs occur more frequently (e.g. *tomber* 'to fall', *courir* 'to run', *sauter* 'jump'), others were found less frequently (*voler* 'to fly', *nager* 'to swim', *rouler* 'to roll', or not at all (among those *chanceler* 'to stagger', *trottiner* 'to scamper', *se faufiler* 'to slip through', *dégringoler* 'to trickle down'). In comparison with (written texts of) Turkish, the analysis shows that French provides a richer set of verbs which encode Motion and Manner, but they were hardly used in oral discourse.

Table 4 indicates that verbs, which do not conflate Manner, are predominant in French. This seems to confirm the prediction of preferring to encode Path in the main verb. However, the amount of verbs that encode Motion and Manner is substantial but seems to be restricted to some single Manner verbs, which can be classified as expressive Manner verbs. The figures include, again, a classification with a 1% threshold for expressive Manner/Manner-Path verbs on the basis of all analysed Manner and Manner-Path verbs in CLAPI. The figures show that there are eighteen expressive Manner verbs (of which twelve were not found at all) and eleven everyday Manner(-Path) verbs.

Table 4: Total frequency of Generic, Path, Manner and Manner-Path verbs and distribution of everyday and expressive Manner/Manner-Path verbs in spoken corpora of French.

Motion verb category	Total amount	%	everyday	%	expressive	%
VP	731.61	38.69				
VM	249.83	13.21	251.91	91.99	20	8.70
VMP	206.24	10.90	206.24	100	/	/
VGEN	703.23	37.19				

Interestingly, two verbs (*envoler* 'to fly away', *enfuir* 'to escape'), which were included in the analysis are beyond the V-pattern suggested by Talmy. Kopecka's research indicates a diachronic shift from an S-pattern (Old French) to a V-pattern (contemporary French) (Kopecka 2004; Kopecka 2006; Kopecka 2009; Kopecka 2013). As a result, contemporary French provides about 22 prefixes, inherited from Latin and Greek which play a role in the derivation of verbs (Kopecka 2006: 86). Kopecka (2006: 88) divides the prefixes with respect to their spatio-temporal semantics into three phases: initial phase or source (***em-/en-*** 'away, off' (AB); ***dé(s)-*** (from, off, apart) (AB); ***é-/ex*** 'out of' (EX)), medial phase or journey (***tra-/trans-*** 'across, through' (TRANS); ***par-*** 'by' (TRANS) and final phase or goal (***a(d)-*** 'to, toward' (AD); ***entre-/inter-*** 'between, among' (***em-/en-*** 'in, into' (IN); *re-* 'back' (AB); ***sur-*** 'on, on top of' (SUPER)). These prefixes occur as hybrid monomorphematic units (e.g. ***dégringoler*** 'to trickle down', ***dériver*** 'to float away', ***dévaler*** 'to rush down' as well as satellite prefix verbs (see example (18)) in the verbal lexicon. Note that the type of lexical hybrid verbs are no longer perceived as morphologically composite (Kopecka to appear), since they can no longer be de-prefixed. Thus, this kind of S-pattern in French is no longer productive in contemporary French (Kopecka 2006: 93).

(18) L'   oiseau s'   est   en-volé   du   nid.
     DET   bird   REFL   AUX.PR   away-fly.PTCP   from the nest
     'The bird flew away from the nest.' (Kopecka 2006: 88)

Moreover, Harr (2012: 126) notes that French contains a large set of so called *constructions à verbe support* corresponding to German *Funktionsverbgefüge* or Turkish constructions with semantically weak verbs to express Manner (e.g. *faire de la natation* 'to swim'; *faire du patinage* 'to ice-skate'). However, these examples are rather used to refer to habitual actions, but not to describe (directed) motion (*J'ai fait de la natation pendant trois ans* 'I swam [for the period of] three years' vs. *Je suis nagée dans l'eau* 'I swam in the water').

3.2.6.2 Other linguistic devices

German

The corpus analysis in the last section emphasises that in German the verb slot is mainly occupied by the semantic components Motion and Manner. Consequently, Path should be largely encoded outside the verb stem. German provides a large set of Path satellites. Following Haggblade (1995), four types of Path satellites are predominant in German: separable (see example (19)) and inseparable verb prefixes (see example (20)) (both adverbal encoding), prepositional phrases (adnominal encoding, see example (21)) and adverbs (adverbal encoding, see example (22)).

(19) Der   Linguist   setzt   über.
     DET   linguist   ferrie.PR   over.
     'The linguist ferries over.'

(20) Der   Linguist   über-quert   die   Brücke.
     DET   linguist   across-traverse.PR   DET   bridge
     'The linguist crosses the bridge.'

(21) Der   Linguist   hinkt   aus   der   Bibliothek.
     DET   linguist   hobble.PR   out   DET   library
     'The linguist hobbles out of the library'

(22) Der   Linguist   läuft   hinüber.
     DET   linguist   walk.PR   over.
     'The linguist walks over.' (all examples from Berthele 2006: 24)

Whilst the class of inseparable verb prefixes are more restricted within their combinability (e.g. a combination of *über-* and *balancieren* 'to balance' is unusable), separable verb prefixes allow in particular to make the Path information more precise. They encode deictic (*hin-* 'towards' (AD), *her-* 'from there' (AB), *weg-* 'away' (AB)) and vertical (*runter-* 'down' (DE), *hoch-* 'up' (SUPER)) information, as well as the trajectory (*entlang-* 'along' (PRAETER), *über-* 'over' (TRANS), *vorbei-* 'past' (PRAETER), *herum-* 'around'), and the course (*los-* 'start', *weiter-* 'further'). Furthermore, German provides adverbial double particles (Altmann & Kemmerling 2005: 88–89) which add a deictic (and/or local) information to the directionality. The double particle *darauf* 'up there' encodes a local (*da* 'there') and a vertical information (*rauf* 'up' (SUPER)), whereas *hinüber* 'towards over (across)' encodes a deictic (*hin-* 'towards' (AD)) and a vertical (*-über* 'over' (TRANS)) information. Often these adverbial double markers are expressed by using short forms: *rein* (*her-/hin-ein* (AB/DE-IN)), *raus* (*her-/hin-aus* (AB/DE-EX)), *runter* (*her-/hin-unter* (AB/DE-DE)), *rauf* (*her-/hin-auf* (AB/DE-SUPER)), *rüber* (*her-/hin-über* (AB/DE-TRANS)). Note, that this device does not exist in other S-languages such as English and consequently allows to encode directionality more precisely in German (Bamberg 1994: 219).

When encoding Path by using prepositional phrases, the preposition determines the Path information. They can encode the source (*von* 'from' (AB)), a general direction (*nach Hause* 'towards home', *zu der Schule* 'to the school' (AD)), an entry into a bounded space (*in das Haus* 'into the house' (IN)), an exit out of a bounded space (*aus dem Haus* 'out of the house' (EX)), a traversal over a bounded space (*über die Straße* 'across the street' (TRANS)), a trajectory (*zwischen den Stühlen* 'between the chairs' (PRAETER), *durch die Menge* 'through the crowds' (PRO)). When analysing prepositions and their following (etymologically determined) dative or accusative case, Carroll (2000: 100–101) argues that the dative generally points to a trajectory or within boundaries and/or relates to the source (e.g. *von* 'from' (AB), *aus* 'out of' (EX)), and destination of a path (e.g. *zu* 'to' (AD), see example (23)). Prepositions with accusative case marking specify a target state or a change of location (*in* 'in(to)' (IN); see example (24))

(23) *Sie rennt vom Hof-tor zu-m Haus.*
 she run.PR from.INDF yard-gate.DAT towards-INDF house.DAT
 'She runs from the yard gate towards the house.'

(24) *Sie rennt in das Haus.*
 she run.PR into DET house.ACC
 'She runs into the house.'

In sum, German provides one adnominal (seven types) and two adverbal slots (eleven types) for expressing Path outside the main verb (see Table 5).

Table 5: Adnominal and adverbal encoding in German.

	adnominal slots: 1 (7 types)	adverbal slots: 3 (11 types)
German	prepositional phrase (7)	Separable (6) and inseparable verb prefixes (/¹), adverbs (5)

Note:
1 Due the restriction with regard to the combination of inseparable verb prefixes, types are not counted.

However, Manner can also be expressed outside the main verb by instrumental prepositional phrases (*mit dem Fahrrad* 'by bike'), adverbials (*schnell* 'fast') or present participles (*schwimmend* '(by) swimming'). Note that the last is part of a more elaborated narrative style in written discourse. The use of a present participle can highlight the semantic component Manner (in example (25) and (26) by the use of additional present participles).

(25) *Sportliche   können   den   wenige   hundert Meter*
     sporty.humans   can.PR   DET.ACC   slightly   hundre   meter
     breiten   See   schwimmen-d durch-queren.
     broad   lake   swim-PRESP   through-cross.INF
     'Sporty humans can cross the lake, which is only a few hundred metres wide, by swimming.' (Süddeutsche Zeitung: Der Pilsensee[33])

(26) *[Er]   lief   die   Treppe   zu-m   Schloss Bellevue*
     he   walk.PST   DET   stair   to-DET.DAT castle   Bellevue
     eher   stolpern-d   als   schreiten-d   hinauf.
     rather   stumble-PRESP   than   stride-PRESP upwards
     'He ran up the stairway to the castle Bellevue rather stumbling than striding.' (Berliner Zeitung, 20.10.2010:4)

Turkish

In Turkish, Path and Manner can also be expressed by other linguistic devices. Turkish Path verbs are often accompanied by disambiguating directional adverbs (*dışarı* 'out' (EX); *içeri* 'inside' (IN); *yukarı* 'up' (SUPER); *aşağı* 'down' (DE); *ileri* 'forward' (AD), *geri* 'backwards' (AD)) which elaborate the Path. As stated by Deni (1921: 244), directional adverbs are considered to be fixed postpositional phrases. They are composed by using a spatial noun, the dative and the directional postposition *-ri/-rı*. Schroeder (2001: 328) notes that only *dış* 'outside' and *iç* 'inside' are still used as spatial nouns. However, neither *dışarı* nor *içeri* can be decomposed anymore into its original morphological units.

Furthermore, spatial postpositions (*doğru* 'towards' (AD); *kadar* 'as far as' (AD); *kenar* 'to' (AD)) can specify the direction or the Endpoint (Aksu-Koç 1994: 351–352). Often the use of these elements seems to be dependent on the valence and semantic of the verb (Schroeder 2001: 332).

In Turkish, most often case marking serves as an indication of Goal and Source. The Goal of a Figure's motion is indicated by dative (*-E*) (AD) and the Source or the space through which the Figure moves by ablative case markers (*-dEn*) (AB). Note that also spatial nouns, such as *dışar* are combined with case markers (e.g. *dışardan* 'from its exterior', *içine* '(in)to its interior', *önüne* 'to the upper'), which are also

---

33 http://www.sueddeutsche.de/muenchen/seen-in-muenchen-und-umland-unbekannte-badebuchten-1.1116293-8 [accessed 2017-08-15]

considered possessive postpositions (Johanson 1998: 63). For the purpose of this study we will classify spatial nouns+case in the category case marking, whereas adverbial directionals with the spatial nouns *dış and iç* are considered separately.

In sum, Turkish provides two adnominal slots (five types) and one adverbal slot (six types) for expressing Path outside the main verb (see Table 6).

Table 6: Adverbal and adnominal encoding in Turkish.

	adnominal slots: 2 (types 5)	adverbal slots: 1 (types 6)
Turkish	Postpositions (3), Case marking (2)	Directional adverbials (6)

When the main verb slot is occupied by a Path verb, information about Manner can only be expressed by an associated non-finite verb, an adverb (*yavaş yavaş/ yavaşça* 'slowly'), a phrase or is omitted (Aksu-Koç 1994: 350; Küntay & Slobin 1999: 177). At that point, Turkish contrasts to the typical motion encoding pattern of German, as indicated above. Otherwise, Turkish differs from the typical V-pattern proposed by Talmy, since Turkish has "a high degree of grammaticalisation of morphologically differentiated forms according to their semantic orientation" (Schroeder 2008: 352). Event internal adjuncts carry the "main load of the expression of Manner" (Schroeder 2008: 356). There are non-finite verbs such as converbs (*-Ince; -Erken; -Ip; -ErEk;* see example (27)) "which function as adverbials and take their temporal specification from the tense of the main verb" (Aksu-Koç 1994: 346). In this way, Path and Manner information can be subordinated to the main (motion) verb. Redublictive converbs (*-E -E;* see example (28)) and *-ErEk-*clauses can be interpreted as Manner adverbials (Schroeder 2008: 249–250). Both forms "express manner directly, in terms of an accompanying action or state" (Göksel & Kerslake 2005: 411). However, in contrast to *-ErEk, -E -E* can occur with identical or different verb stems and its use "is less widespread […] and its meaning is more emphatic, stressing the continuous or repeated nature of the action it expresses" (Göksel & Kerslake 2005: 411). We will return to this issue when discussing structural differences between the languages involved in the current study in §3.2.7.

(27) *Yürüy-erek   uzaklaş-tı-lar.*
    walk-CVB   move.away-PST-3PL
    'They moved away walking.' (Schroeder 2008: 350)

(28) *Üçgen   döne döne   çık-tı.*
    triangle turn.CVB   ascend-PST.3SG
    'The triangle ascended by turning.' (Allen et al. 2007: 31)

French

In French Manner and Path can also be expressed by other linguistic devices. When the verb slot is occupied by the semantic element Path, Manner is typically expressed in prepositional phrases (*sur la pointe des pieds* 'on tiptoes'), adverbial phrases (*rapidement* 'fast'), in gerund phrases (*en courant* 'running') or simply is omitted. Path can be expressed outside the main verb by prepositional phrases (*à la maison* 'towards the house'), gerund phrases (*en traversant* '(by) crossing'), and relative clauses (*La fille qui traverse la rue, court* 'The girl, who crosses the road, is running'). As indicated in the last section, French also provides Path prefixes which, however, occur as hybrid monomorphematic units.

With respect to Path expressions, Harr (2012: 128) points out that *à* + nominal phrase ('to') or *jusque* + other preposition + nominal phrase ('as far as') can be used to express the Goal (AD) of a motion event. Whereas *à/en* + nominal phrase (AD) and *dans* + nominal phrase (IN) also encodes a general location, only *jusque* (AD) indicates the Endpoint of a Path (see example (31)).[34] In example (29) the preposition + nominal phrase denotes Motion towards a Goal, whereas in example (30) the preposition + nominal phrase expresses the location. Such unambiguous prepositions are generally interpreted by context (Harr 2012: 128).

(29) La   fille   cour-t   [de l'autre côté]   à   l'   hôpital.
DET   girl   run-PR   [from the other side]   to   DET   hospital
'The girl runs from the other side to the hospital.'

(30) La   fille   cour-t   à   l'   hôpital
DET   girl   run-PR   to   DET   hospital
[bien que c'est interdit à courir dans le bâtiment].
[even it is forbidden to run inside the building]
'The girl runs inside the hospital [even if it is forbidden].'

(31) La   fille   cour-t   jusqu'à   l'   hôpital.
DET   girl   run-PR   as far as   DET   hospital
'The girl runs as far as the hospital.'

French satellites for Path can also take a verb particle type (which are less frequent than prefixes and also no longer productive in contemporary French) (Pourcel & Kopecka 2005): *dehors* 'outside' (EX); *dedans* 'inside' (IN); *(par)dessus* 'above' (SUPER); *à travers* 'through/over' (TRANS). Furthermore, Path can be expressed by adverbs such as *derrière/à l'arrière* 'behind' (AD), *en haut* 'up' (SUPER), *en bas* 'down' (DE).

---

[34] Other prepositions with spatial relation are *sur* 'onto' (SUPER) or *de* 'from' (AB).

Based on this illustration, French provides one adnominal slot (four types) and three adverbal slots (seven types) for expressing Path outside the main verb (see Table 7).

Table 7: Adverbal and adnominal encoding in French.

	adnominal slots: 1 (4 types)	adverbal slots: 3 (7 types)
French	prepositional phrase (4)	Verb particles (4), inseparable verb affixes (/¹), adverbs (3 types)

Note:
1 Due to the fact that French Path prefixes occur as hybrid monomorphematic units, types are not counted.

3.2.6.3 Syntactic organisation

When studying the development and complexity of the syntactic organisation of motion events, Allen et al. (2007) propose three different types of syntactic packaging: (i) Tight; (ii) Semi-Tight; (iii) Loose. Type (i) refers to a compact construction in which both semantic elements, Manner and Path are packaged within one matrix clause (e.g. a finite Manner-verb, followed by a Path-particle or a prepositional phrase, see example (32)). This type seems to be typical for S-languages. The construction type also occurs in V-languages, although a rare use is assumed (see example (33)). Type (ii) refers to a construction in which Manner and Path are expressed in one sentence by a separate verbal element (e.g. a finite Path verb, and a subordinated non-finite element encoding Manner; see example (34)). This type seems to be typical for V-languages. Type (iii) refers to constructions in which Path and Manner are each expressed in one separate clause (which may be coordinated or juxtaposed; see example (35)). This construction type occurs in all language types.

(32) *He rolled up the hill.*

(33) *Domates adam aşağı yuvarlan-ıyor tepe-den.*
tomato man down roll-PROG.3SG hill-ABL
'Tomato Man is rolling down the hill.'

(34) *Domates adam yuvarlan-arak yokuş-u in-di.*
tomato man roll-CVB hill-ACC descend-PST.3SG
'Tomato man descended the hill while rolling.'

(35) *Sonra yukarı çık-tı.*
then up ascend-PST.3SG
'Then (he/she/it) ascended up.' (Allen et al. 2007: 30–31)

Another observation on the constructional level refers to Path elaboration. Since S-languages typically express Path outside the verb stem in satellites which can frequently be combined with other Path satellites, Path elaboration is generally higher compared to V-languages. Furthermore, Slobin (1996b) distinguishes between "Minus-Ground" and "Plus-Ground" constructions. Minus-Ground constructions comprise bare motion verb constructions such as "he ran", where the main verb is alone, or combined with only one satellite ("he ran inside"), whereas Plus-ground constructions consist of a main verb, a satellite and an additional Path element such as "he ran from the other side over the street into the house". Due to the typical pattern of V- and S-languages, V-languages are expected to use Minus-Ground constructions more frequently than Plus-Ground constructions. Slobin (1996b) also notes, that in cases where speakers of V-languages use a main verb and an additional Path element, they usually mention just one piece of extra information, whereas speakers of S-languages frequently use more than one additional Path element. This assumption needs further support, since, as shown in the last section, all three languages provide linguistic devices to elaborate Path information outside the main verb. What is then of special interest is whether, compared with German, the frequency and combination of motion verb+Path device in Turkish and French is restricted in some way.

German

The combination of Manner verbs with different Path devices in German enables speakers to use detailed descriptions of the Manner and Path of motion (Bamberg 1979: 220). With regard to Path complexity, on the syntactic level, German speakers tend to package a number of Path components in one single clause (Slobin 2004b: 240). The analysis of re-narrations of a Frog Story scene (see example (36)) indicates that the majority of German speakers use at least three event segments per phrase:

(36) *Plötzlich fällt der Hund aus dem Fenster von dem*
    suddenly fall.PR DET dog out DET window from DET.DAT
    Fensterbrett herunter.
    windowsill down
    'Suddenly the dog falls down out of the window from the windowsill.'

The prototypical syntactic structure of a motion event construction in German includes a Manner verb followed by one or more directional Path satellites. Such combinations are generally highly productive and the encoding of both, Path and Manner in one single clause (Tight), is seen as the typical syntactic pattern of S-languages (Allen et al. 2007: 29; Özyürek et al. 2005: 228).

Turkish

In Turkish, Path and Manner verbs require in some cases a directional specification. They can be expressed by case (dative, ablative), spatial postpositions and directional adverbials.

Schroeder (2001: 332) classifies different verb groups which require a directional specification:
1. verbs encoding a vertical downwards direction (*inmek* 'to descend') or verbs which encode a vertical downwards direction where the Cause of Movement is unintentional (*yuvarlanmak* 'to roll');
2. verbs encoding direction without specifying the vertical direction (*atmak* 'to throw'; *gitmek* 'to go'; *koşmak* 'to run').

Furthermore, ambiguous verbs such as *çıkmak* ('descend'/'to exit') are, in some discourse contexts, necessarily accompanied by disambiguating adverbs (Aksu-Koç 1994: 352). Note that in some cases directional adverbials are considered redundant or pleonastic, when for instance they represent a Vector component of the Path and the verb represents a Vector too (Daller, Treffers-Daller & Furman 2011: 109; see example (37)).

Interestingly, the construction type Path verb/Manner(-Path)verb + directional specification is typical for S-languages, notably it is similar to German separable verb constructions, when Manner verbs are combined with Path satellites (Aksu-Koç 1994: 354; Daller, Treffers-Daller & Furman 2011: 109). Furthermore, this type of construction also exists in other V-languages (Italian, Basque), which are considered high-Path salient languages (Hijazo-Gascón & Ibarretxe-Antuñano 2013: 49). Reverse framing patterns can occur as well (see (38)).

(37) *Adam   aşağıy-a   in-iyor.*
     man   down-DAT   descend-PROG.3SG
     'The man is descending down.' (Daller, Treffers-Daller & Furman 2011: 109)

(38) *Kurbağa   kavanoz-dan   çık-arak   kaç-tı.*
     frog   glass-ABL   exit-CVB   escape-PST.3SG
     'The frog escaped from the glass (by) exiting.' (Aksu-Koç 1994: 356)

The combination of Manner verbs, which are used as a predicate of a main sentence, with Path devices, nevertheless seems to be restricted. Schroeder (2009: 184) claims that Turkish Manner verbs are generally intransitive and cannot be combined with linguistic devices which specify the Path or direction (except for those verb groups specified above). Otherwise, a tendency that such constructions occur typically with more frequently used Manner verbs has been observed in other V-languages (Goschler 2013: 121). In order to test possible restrictions in Turkish, a constructional analysis of a corpus sample,[35] including frequent and infrequent Manner verbs as well as Manner verbs which require directional specifications, has been conducted. The results indicate that the combination of Manner verbs with adverbial directionals and spatial postpositions is indeed extremely infrequent in written Turkish (see Table 8). Moreover, the Path elaboration of Manner verbs that require a directional specification seems to be restricted to certain constructional patterns: The combination of *koşmak* 'to run' is limited to the spatial postposition *doğru* 'straight'. *Kaymak* 'to slide' and *yuvarlanmak* 'to roll' are combined with different adverbial directionals and spatial postpositions. On the other hand, the linguistic devices *aşağı(ya)* 'down(towards)' and *doğru* occur predominantly with these verbs compared to the other linguistic devices.

Table 8: Combinations of Manner verbs with adverbial directionals (ADV_DIR) and postpositions (POSTPOS) in the Turkish National Corpus.

	Linguistic device	Manner verbs					Total
		koşmak	yürümek	kaymak	yuvarlanmak	hoplamak	
ADV_DIR	aşağı(ya)	0	5	6	11	0	22
	dışarı	0	0	0	0	0	0
	geri	0	0	2	0	0	2
	içeri	0	0	2	0	0	2
	içine	0	0	0	8	0	8
	yukarı	0	0	1	0	0	1
POSTPOS	doğru	14	0	34	8	0	56
	kadar	0	0	2	2	0	4
	kenar	0	0	0	0	0	0

The tendency that combinations of Manner verb and Path devices occur typically with more frequently used Manner verbs cannot fully account for these results. The construction of *yürümek* 'to walk', a Manner verb which occurs frequently in the TNC (see results above), is restricted to the adverbial directional *aşağı* 'down', whereas *yuvarlanmak* 'to roll', which occurs less frequently in the corpus, is combined with different Path devices. However, the Manner verb *hoplamak* 'to hop', which does not require a directional specification and occurs infrequently in the corpus, is never combined with any Path device.

---

[35] The analysis is based on a random sample of 2,500 entries in the TNC and includes only finite verbs in the present and the past tense.

On the basis of these results, it can be assumed that in Turkish, Manner verbs can be combined with Path devices; the construction is, however, limited to Manner verbs which require a directional specification and to preferred constructional patterns.

Both directional adverbs and spatial postpositions can, however, be combined when specifying the trajectory of motion: *dışarı-a* 'outside-to'; *üstün-e* 'top-to'; *kenarın-a* 'edge-to'; *için-den* 'inside-from' (see example (39)). In some cases the motivation of combining directional adverbs and postpositions is quite weak and may be dependent on the verb classification proposed above (for a more detailed corpus analysis see Schroeder 2001).

(39) *İçin-den   arı-lar   çık-ıyor.*
   inside-ABL   bee-PL   exit-PROG.3SG
   'The bees are exiting from inside.' (Aksu-Koç 1994: 352)

The possibility (and for certain verbs the requirement of) Path specification in Turkish seems to contradict Slobin's assumption. However, in comparison with e.g. German, Path elaboration is much more restricted in terms of frequency and combination.

Regarding the syntactic organisation of motion events, it is assumed that Turkish speakers typically use separate clauses to express Manner and Path (Özyürek & Kita 1999) and prefer a "Semi-Tight"-construction, in which Path is encoded in the main verb and Manner in subordinate elements (Allen et al. 2007).

French
It is assumed that when linguistically encoding motion images, French speakers typically follow the V-pattern (40), encoding Path in the main verb and Manner in adverbial phrases or gerunds.

(40) *Elle   entre   en courant.*
   She   enter-PR   run.PTCP
   'She enters (by) running.'

Interestingly, in oral French, Path satellites occur in combination with Manner verbs (*Il court dehors* 'he run out'), which is syntactically comparable to S-languages (Porquier 2001; Porquier 2003). However, this construction seems to be much more restricted in the standard (written) language.

The existence of S-patterns is also observed in other Romance languages (Aske 1989; Hijazo-Gascón & Ibarretxe-Antuñano 2013; Slobin 1997). The pattern variability in French goes even further and challenges the assumption that French cannot be seen as a typical V-language. Pourcel & Kopecka's (2005) study of usage patterns in French claims that French is a "hybrid language" and reports four usage patterns beyond the V-pattern, suggested by Talmy's typology (in order of usage preference): a juxtaposed pattern, a hybrid pattern, a satellite pattern and a reverse pattern.

In the juxtaposed pattern (see example (41)), Manner is encoded in the first verb phrase followed with a possible locative prepositional phrase, while Path is encoded alone in the second verb phrase. This pattern seems to be common in French. The hybrid pattern involves the monomorphematic units discussed above (such as *dériver* 'float away') and Path-Manner verbs conflating both items of semantic information in one lexical unit (see example (42)) (Ochsenbauer & Hickmann 2010). The reverse pattern type (Pourcel 2004) displays constructions in which Manner information is encoded in the main verb and Path information in an adjunct (see example (43)). This pattern "upset[s] the Talmyan verb-framing pattern so that the prototypical syntactic slots for Path and Manner information are swapped round" (Pourcel & Kopecka 2005: 145).

(41) Il cour-t dans une rue puis rentre dans une maison.
he run-PR in DET street then enter.PR in DET house
'He runs in a street and then enters in a house.'

(42) Il plong-e.
he dive-PR
'He dives (in).'

(43) Il cour-t en traversant la route.
he run-PR cross.PRESP the street
'He is running while crossing the street.' (all examples from Pourcel & Kopecka 2005: 145–146)

Note that the classification of French as a hybrid language is controversial, since French prefixes have their counterparts in other Romance languages, and they are all scarcely productive or frequent in motion event descriptions (Hijazo-Gascón & Ibarretxe-Antuñano 2013: 49). Furthermore, Hijazo-Gascón (2018) found that French speakers rather tend to express no or only one Path element in the verbal periphery in French and thus displaying a difference from Italian and Spanish speakers. This fact, again, emphasises the need for building a typological classification rather on usage-based observations instead of on the patterns which a language provides.

In contrast with the assumption that V-language speakers prefer a semi-tight pattern, Harr (2012: 196) found that French speakers mainly prefer single constructions without any subordinate element, but with prepositional or adverbial phrases (for further details see §4.1 below). Therefore, Harr (2012) proposes a "Tight-simple" construction for this type.

3.2.6.4 Boundary crossing

In order to fully account for the encoding of motion events in the three languages involved in the current study, the expression of boundary crossing events needs to be taken into account as well. The reason for this is that several studies observed a specific constraint in V-languages when expressing a Figure's traversal of a spatial boundary ("boundary crossing constraint" Slobin & Hoiting 1994). According to Aske (1989: 6), a boundary crossing is defined as a Path expression with "an end-of-Path location/state". It appears that in V-languages that crossing a spatial boundary is conceived of as a change of location which requires an independent predicate (Slobin 1997: 441). Consequently when expressing this type of motion event in V-languages, it is characteristic to use a main verb encoding Path, rather than any other linguistic device. In S-languages, on the other hand, Manner is expressed in the main verb and the change of location is typically expressed by Path satellites. Özçalışkan (2013: 2) argues that this type of motion event therefore imposes "the tightest linguistic constraints in the expression of motion events" in V-languages.

However, Aske (1989) has further noted the possibility of using an S-pattern (Manner verb with Path complement) in V-languages and distinguishes two types of Path expressions to explain the variable use of V- and S-patterns. Specifying the endstate of the Path, in Aske's terms "telic path phrases" (Aske 1989: 6), are overtly directional and/or resultative (see (44)), while "mere locative path phrases" (Aske 1989: 6; see example (45)) only specify the median Path trajectory (the location in which the activity takes place). The former type necessarily requires a Path verb in order to express the change of location, whereas the use of Manner verbs is possible in the latter type.

However, Slobin & Hoiting (1994) noted that the use of Manner verbs in various V-languages is acceptable, even when the motion event has a definite endstate (and are in Aske's terms telic), but do not predicate "a specific locative endstate except for proximity to a ground" (Slobin & Hoiting 1994: 495); see examples (46) and (47). In order to account for the usage licence of Manner verbs in V-languages, they suggest the terms "path focus" and "boundary focus" (Slobin & Hoiting 1994: 498).

(44) *Koş-arak* ev-e *gir-di.*
 run-CVB house-DAT enter-PST.3SG
 'She/he entered in the house (by) running.'

(45) Il   marche   le   long   de la   route.
     he   walk.PR   DET   along   of DET   road
     'He walks along the road.' (Pourcel & Kopecka 2005: 145)

(46) Salih'-in   ayak-lar-ı-nın   dibin-e   kadar   yuvarlan-dı.
     Salih-GEN   foot-PL-POSS-GEN   down-DAT   as far as   roll-PST.3SG
     'It rolled down as war as Salih's feet.' (Turkish National Corpus 886CA16B2A-0159G1li)

(47) Valiz-in-i   al-ıp   köy-e   doğru   yürü-dü.
     suitcase-POSS-ACC   take-CVB   village-DAT   towards   walk-PST.3SG
     'She/he took his/her suitcase and walked towards the village.' (Turkish National Corpus RA16B2A-3329)

In order to account for these empirical observations, three different types of telic Path phrases with boundary focus can be distinguished (which were introduced in Figure 2d) and e), see §3.2.2): (i) an entry into a bounded space; (ii) an exit out of a bounded space and (iii) a traversal over a plane to the other side of a threshold. In addition, the types of motion events may then involve three-dimensional enclosed boundaries (which are traversed by going into or out of, e.g. a house) and unenclosed two-dimensional boundaries (e.g. a carpet that is crossed over) (Özçalışkan 2013: 11). The "maximum" of Goal orientation in locative Path phrases with Path focus is a Figures' proximity to the Ground. The orientation can cover a non defined endpoint ("along a plane"), a direction ("towards a goal") and a proximity to a ground ("up to an endpoint") (see Figure 2). Table 9 summarises the empirical observations in S- and V-languages with respect to the possible verb choices in the two types proposed.

Table 9: Schematisation of locative and telic Path phrases.

		Cardinal kinds		German	Turkish & French
Locative Path phrases [+ Path focus]	Median Path trajectory	(AD)	"along a plane"	Path & Manner verbs	Path & Manner verbs
	Goal oriented	AD, AB, DE	"towards a goal"		
	Endpoint oriented	AD, SUPER	"up to an endpoint"		
Telic Path phrases [+ boundary focus]	Traversal	IN, EX, PRO, TRANS, PRAETER	"in(to)"/"out of" a bounded space; "over a plane"	Path & Manner verbs	Path verbs

On the other hand, some research findings give rise to doubts about the validity of this constraint. Naigles et al. (1998) show that a certain use of Manner verbs in boundary crossing events is possible or quite normal. In their data Spanish speakers used Manner verbs such as *saltar* 'to jump', *resbalar* 'to slip', *deslizar* 'to slide' or *desplazar* 'to splash' to describe the Motion of a Figure jumping into a swimming pool. Such events, where the Figure performs an "uncontrolled motion" (Naigles et al. 1998: 543), might not be seen as a "true" boundary crossing. Slobin (2004b: 226) argues, that "[t]he only exception seems to be verbs that encode particular force dynamics – high energy motor patterns that are more like punctual acts than activities, such as equivalents of 'throw oneself' and 'plunge'". Also other verbs, such as "to dive" or "to leap", involve instantaneous motion and highlight the duration of motion (Özçalışkan 2013: 17). Slobin (2006: 67) points out that this type of Manner verb is "not readily conceived of as activities, but, rather, as 'instantaneous' acts".

In summary, a possible conceptional distinction between the locative and telic Path in V-languages can generate a different linguistic symbolisation of motion images (Aske 1989). As a result, V-languages can use the S-pattern in locative motion events, while in telic motion events, where the Path involves crossing from an external space to an internal space (and vice versa), Manner cannot be conflated in the main verb. Only when the Figure performs a sudden boundary crossing can this obviously be conceptualised as a change of location and be expressed by a restricted set of Manner verbs. The boundary crossing constraint leads speakers of V-languages to conflate Path in the main verb and to express Manner additionally to obtain a telic reading.

German

Since Path satellites constitute the most productive linguistic device to encode Path in German, they are typically used to express a Figure's traversal of a spatial boundary. Moreover, there seems to be no restrictions on using a Manner verb in boundary crossing events (see example (48)). As shown above the Path information can be specified by multiple Path satellites. Note that constructions such as in (48) are considered pleonastic, since the particle and the preposition denote the same semantic context; here they double-mark the Goal (but see Carroll 2000: 102 for an alternative analysis).

(48) *Sie läuf-t/renn-t/krabbel-t/hops-t   in   das   Haus   (hinein).*
      she walk-PR/run-PR/crawl-PR/hop-PR into DET house (hither.in)
      'She walks/runs/crawls/hops into the house.'

The use of Path verbs in boundary crossing events is, though relatively infrequent, nevertheless totally acceptable. Note that in example (49), the change of location is expressed by the prepositional phrase, not by the verb. This, again, emphasises the lower semantic differentiation of Path in the verbal root in German in comparison with, e.g. Turkish and French.

(49) Zu   diesem   Zweck   begab   sich   ein   Techniker
     for   this   purpose   proceed.PST   REFL   INDF   technician
     in   den   Kontroll-raum.
     in   DET.ACC controll-room.
     'For this purpose, a technician went into the control room.' (COSMAS 2 NUN00/JUL.00886)

Turkish
When expressing spatial boundaries in Turkish, the dative and ablative do not encode the Figure's change of location. In example (50), the ablative (*ev-den* 'house-from') expresses the Figure's departure which refers to a proximity to the Ground, but not to a traversal from an internal to an external bounded space; the dative (*arabay-a* 'car-to') expresses the Figure's direction to a Ground, but not a traversal from an external to an internal bounded space. In order to express a Figure's traversal of a spatial boundary, an independent predicate is required in both event types (see example (51)). Consequently, Manner can only be expressed by a non-finite clause (here by a converb). In locative motion events, when no boundary is crossed, it is, however, acceptable to express both elements in one verbal clause (52).

(50) Ev-den   arabay-a   hopla-dı.
     House-ABL   car-DAT   hop-PST.3SG
     'She/he hopped from the house to the car.'

(51) Ev-den   cık-tı   hopl-arak   ve
     House-ABL   exit-PST.3SG   hop-CVB   and
     yine   hoplay-arak   arabay-a   bin-di.
     again   hop-CVB   car-DAT   enter-PST.3SG
     'She/he exited the house hopping and again entered in the car hopping.'

(52) Yokuş   aşağı   kayı-yor.
     hill   down   slide-PROG.3SG
     'She/he is sliding down the hill.' (Özyürek & Kita 1999: 510)

Özçalışkan (2013: 12–14) observed that Turkish speakers display a varied pattern of verb choices in boundary crossing events and violate the Path verb requirement in a boundary crossing event when the Figure performs some physically very rapid ("to flip", "to jump", "to dash") or instantaneous motion ("to dive", "to leap") as described above. The former is particularly present in two-dimensional unenclosed boundaries. When the Figure performs a sudden boundary crossing, this can obviously be conceptualised as a change of location (see example (53)). However, verbs which encode temporally extended motion types (e.g. "crawling into a house"), are not present (Özçalışkan 2013: 14).

(53) *Bir   top   cam-dan   dışarı   fırla-dı   ve   zıplaya zıplaya*
     a   ball   glass-ABL   outwards   pop-PST.3SG   and   bounce.CVB
    yokuş   aşağı   yuvarlan-dı.
    hill   down   roll-PST.3SG
    'A ball popped out of the glass and bounced down the hill.' (Turkish National Corpus LA16B1A-1252)

Nevertheless, an analysis of the TNC indicates, in a few rare cases, a violation of the boundary crossing constraint: In example (54), a temporally extended motion is expressed; the construction follows the predicted pattern of S-languages. The directional adverb *içeri* encodes the Figure's traversal over a bounded space, *koş-* encodes Motion and Manner.

(54) *Eşik-te   yat-an   gelin-i   gör-ünce   bağır-arak*
    treshold-LOC   sleep-REL   bride-ACC   see-CVB   scream-CVB
    içeri   koş-tu.
    inside   run-PST.3SG
    'After he saw the bride, who was laying on the threshold, he ran inside screaming.' (Turkish National Corpus TA16B1A-0835)

In the current study, constructions of the type [Manner verb+linguistic device] are considered telic Path phrases, when the linguistic device encodes IN or EX. Being aware of the controversial issue, we consider *dışarı, içeri, içine* and *içinden* as linguistic devices which encode a traversal over a bounded space. Whenever it is necessary, we will discuss controversial cases in greater detail. Constructions in which a Manner verb is combined with atelic adverbials (*aşağı, yukarı, geri, ileri*), postpositions or Ground elements with case marking (*-dEn, -E*), are considered locative Path phrases.

Another observation with respect to the segmentation of boundary crossing events was made by Özçalışkan (2013): Turkish speakers usually tend to describe temporally extended types of boundary crossing events with multiple clausal segments, than in a compact way, by encoding Path in the main verb and Manner in a subordinate clause or in adjuncts (Özçalışkan 2013: 12): first, using Manner verbs to indicate the movement towards a boundary, second, marking the traversal of a boundary by a Path verb and finally, encoding the movement away from the boundary with a Manner verb (Cadierno 2010: 4; Özçalışkan 2013: 3). Furthermore, it seems to be a common strategy to convey boundary crossing implicitly by parsing the event into a series of sub-events (e.g. setting up the scene with a boundary, marking the location of the Figure on one side and then on the other side, describing each sub-event with a Manner verb, see example (56).

(55) *Ev-e   doğru   sürün-dü,   içeri   gir-di,   ve*
     house-DAT   towards   crawl-PST.3SG   inside   enter-PST.3SG   and
     sürün-mey-e   devam   et-ti.
     crawl-NMLZ-DAT continue   do-PST.3SG
     'He crawled toward the house, he entered, and continued crawling.'
     (Özçalışkan 2013: 4)

(56) *Emekl-iyor,   halı   var,   bebek   gibi*
     crawl-PROG.3SG   carpet   exists   baby   like
     emekl-iyor   halı-da   sonra   halın-ın   öbür
     crawl-PROG.3SG   carpet-LOC   then   carpet-GEN   other
     taraf-ın-da   devam   ed-iyor.
     side-POSS-LOC   continue   do-PROG.3SG
     'He is crawling, there is a carpet, he is crawling like a baby on the carpet, then he continues on the other side of the carpet.' (Özçalışkan 2013: 16)

These strategies lead to a more segmented description of spatial boundaries in Turkish (Özçalışkan 2013: 16), and may also contrast intra-typologically with other V-languages. In addition, differences in the grammatical structure could also play a role in the expression of subordinated Manner encoding in Turkish. Given the fact that Turkish is an agglutinative language, speakers have to decide in advance if they want to include a subordinated Manner verb, since the verb subordinated to the main verb must precede the main verb which is expressed at the end of a sentence. Other V-languages, such as Spanish or French, are free to add subordinated Manner ad hoc (Özçalışkan 2013: 18). This could be an explanation for a greater use of such subordinated Manner verb constructions (Özçalışkan & Slobin 1999).

French

When expressing the change of state of a Figure by using a prepositional phrase, which is typical for S-languages, the construction does not express Path, but Location (see example (57)). Its semantic differs from those in S-languages, where the change of location is typically expressed with a Path satellite. The use of a telic Path satellite in French (such as *dedans* 'inside') in combination with a Manner verb is not acceptable grammatically (see example (58), but recall the use of Path satellites in oral discourse, stated in §3.2.6.3). In addition, a combination of a preposition which does not encode the traversal and a prepositional phrase which denotes the endstate, remains questionable, whereas the use of Manner verbs in locative Path phrases such as (60) is unproblematic. However, in order to obtain a telic reading, speakers of V-languages are forced to use the V-pattern, by encoding the change of location with a predicate which encodes Path (see example (61)).

(57) Elle cour-t dans la maison.
　　　she walk-PR in DET house
　　　'She is walking within the house.'

(58) *Elle court dedans la maison.
　　　she run-PR inside DET house
　　　'She runs inside the house.'

(59) ?Elle court jusque dans la maison.
　　　she run-PR as far as in DET house
　　　'She runs just inside the house.'

(60) Elle court jusqu'à la maison.
　　　She run-PR as far as.the DET house
　　　'She runs as far as the house.'

(61) Elle entr-e dans la maison en courant.
　　　She enter-PR in DET house run.PRESP
　　　'She enters in the house (by) running.'

In some cases, it appears that Manner verbs are used in boundary crossing events. In example (62), the question is whether the activity is conceived of as a change of location. If we assume that the entire event is conceptualised as a single bounded space, the use of a Manner verb is possible. This would be a plausible explanation, because the Source is expressed (with proximity to a Ground), but there is no locative endstate – consequently no boundary is crossed ("away from" not "out of"). In example (63) the use of a Manner verb is acceptable in the sense of a Path focus, since no boundary is crossed. Also the use of *sauter* 'to jump', in example (64), is acceptable; as noted above, the activity can be conceived of as an instantaneous act. However, examples (65) and (66) obviously violate the boundary crossing constraint.

(62) L' oiseau s' est en-volé du nid.
　　　DET bird REFL AUX.PR away-fly.PTCP from.DET nest
　　　'The bird flew away from the nest.' (Kopecka 2006: 88)

(63) Grimpez   au   palmier.
     climb.IMP.3PL   on.DET   palm
     'Climb on the palm.' (Arias Oliveira 2012: 176)

(64) Ils   ont   saut-é   hors du   lit.
     they   AUX.PR   jump-PTCP   out   from.DET bed
     'They jumped out of the bed.'

(65) Je   cour-us   dans   la   chambre   de   Laurence   et
     I   run-PST   in   DET   room   of   Laurence   and
     la   réveill-ait.
     her   wake.up-PST
     'I ran into Laurence room and woke her up.' (Berthele 2006: 233–234)

(66) Gliss-ez   sous   la   grille.
     slide-IMP.3PL   under   DET   grid.
     'Slide under the grid.' (Arias Oliveira 2012: 249)

When analysing the FRANTEXT corpus of written French, Berthele (2006: 234) reports numerous other violations of the boundary crossing constraint. Nevertheless, he emphasises that due to the relative frequency of Path verbs in such events, there is a clear tendency towards a boundary crossing constraint in French.

3.2.7 General structural differences between German, French and Turkish

Since the German, French and Turkish languages involved in the current study display wide structural differences, some further details are required with respect to clause linkage. Whereas motion verbs in coordinate and subordinate clauses appear as finite verbs in German and French, they are in most cases non-finite in Turkish. For instance, in (67), the conjunction *und* 'and' coordinates two main clauses (the same applies for French with the conjunction *et* 'and', see example (68)). This typically requires a non-finite structure (with the converbial suffix *-Ip*) in Turkish (see (69)) or, alternatively, a segmentation into multiple main clauses.

(67) Sie   rennt   und   fällt   hin.
     she   run.PR   and   fall.PR   hither
     'She runs and falls (down).'

(68) Elle   court   et   elle   tombe.
     she   run-PR.3SG   and   she   fall.PR
     'She runs and she falls (down).'

(69) *Koş-up   düş-üyor.*
    run-CVB   fall-PROG.3SG
    'She/he runs and falls (down).'

The same applies for other subordinating subjunctions in German and French that introduce a subordinate clause (e.g. *damit, so dass/pour que* 'so/so that'; *da, weil/parce que* 'because'; *wenn, als/quand, lorsque.*'when'; *während/pendant que* 'while' *nachdem/après que* 'after'; *sobald/dès que* 'as soon as'. By contrast, Turkish makes use of non-finite converbial structures such as *-diye, -IncE, -Erken, -dIktEn sonra, -r mEz* (for a detailed comparative analysis of Turkish converbial structures and subordinate structures in German, see Schroeder 2004). Note that these converbs differ in their function from converbs which are used as Manner adverbials (such as *-ErEk* clauses in (27) or *-E -E* reduplications in (28), introduced in §3.2.6.2). For instance, in the context of motion events, the suffix *-Ip* is used to link two events (e.g. "She ran to the house and jumped in"), whereas *-ErEk* (as well as *-E -E*) are used to present "two situations [...] as part of one event" (Slobin 1995: 357) (e.g. "She entered the house jumping"). Consequently from a methodological point of view, a differentiation between these forms is necessary.

Another structural difference can be seen in Turkish non-finite noun clauses. They are marked by the suffixes *-dIk* or *-(y)AcAK* (in combination with a possessive suffix). Whereas in German and French relative or temporal clauses (see (70)) the motion verb appears as a finite verb, it does not in Turkish (see (71)).

(70) *Quand j'   arriv-ait   à   la   maison   les   porte-s   étaient*
    when   I   arrive-PST   at   DET   home   DET   door-PL   AUX.PST
    ouverte-s.
    open-PL
    'When I arrived home the doors were open.'

(71) *Ev-e   git-tiğ-im-de   kapı-lar   açık-tı.*
    home-DAT   go-NMLZ-POSS.1SG-LOC   door-PL   open-PST.3SG
    'When I arrived at home the doors were open.' (Göksel & Kerslake 2005: 240)

Infinitives with the preposition *zu* 'to' in German (see (72)) or with the preposition *à* or *de* 'to' in French (see (73)) can also be expressed by noun clauses in Turkish. In the Turkish example (74), the suffix *-mA* and a possessive suffix is attached to the verbal noun, literally meaning "my home returning".

(72) Es   war   nicht schwer für mich nach Hause zu kommen.
     it   AUX.PST NEG   difficult for me   at   home   to come
     'It wasn't difficult for me to return home.'

(73) Il ne   m'   était   pas difficile de rentrer   à   la
     he NEG REFL AUX.PST NEG difficult to return.INF to DET
     maison.
     home
     'It wasn't difficult for me to return home.'

(74) Ev-e   dön-me-m   zor   ol-ma-dı.
     home-DAT   return-NMLZ-POSS.1SG   difficult AUX-NEG-PST.3SG
     'It wasn't difficult for me to return home.' (Göksel & Kerslake 2005: 240)

Since Turkish display strong structural variations compared to German and French, these aspects have to be included into the methodology.

We can now add the observations established in §3.2.5–3.2.7 to our encoding schema (see Figure 14) by assuming that lexicalisation patterns are, from a cross-linguistic perspective, distinct with respect to the characteristic expression of certain event types.

We now turn back to the question pursued in §3.2.3: to what extent cross-linguistic differences in the expression of spatial information may have an impact on how speakers conceptualise a motion event (macro- and micro-planning) or

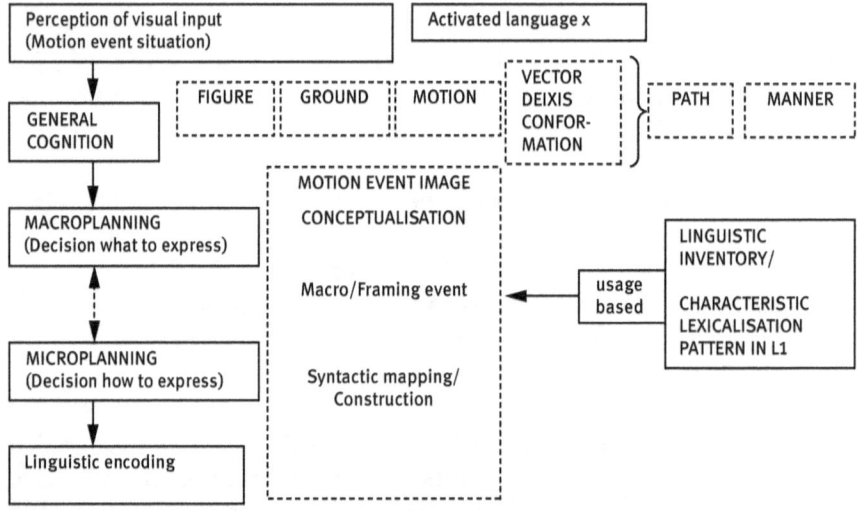

Figure 14: Encoding schema of a motion event situation (c).

3.3 The impact of language-specific properties on cognition

3.3.1 Relativistic consequences in spontaneous speech

Talmy (2003; 2008) argues that his motion event typology predicts (cognitive) consequences with respect to the amount (and the type) of information that can be expressed in either a foregrounded or a backgrounded way (Cadierno 2008: 245). Talmy (2008: 163) claims that semantic components are more or less salient, depending on the surface element in which a component is typically encoded. In this context, he suggests three principles of semantic fore- and backgrounding (Talmy 2003: 126–127): (i) principle of backgrounding according to constituent type, (ii) principle of ready expression under backgrounding and (iii) principle of low cognitive cost of extra information under backgrounding.

(i) If a semantic component is expressed in the main verb root or in a satellite, it is backgrounded, while if it is encoded elsewhere, it is foregrounded. As a consequence, it is assumed that speakers of S-languages encode more semantic components, expressing Manner typically in verb roots and Path in satellites. Speakers of V-languages typically foreground information about a co-event, since it is encoded peripherically.

(ii) Speakers tend to express a concept (or a category) more readily when it can be encoded in the background. "[They] tend to opt for its expression over its omission more often where it can be referred to in a backgrounded way than where it can only be referred to in a foregrounded way" (Talmy 2003: 129). Moreover, an expression tends to be stylistically more colloquial and less awkward when it can be expressed in a backgrounded way (Talmy 2003: 129). Furthermore, since the informational content of a backgrounded concept can be included in a sentence, the cognitive cost is lower.

(iii) As a consequence, Talmy (2003: 129) claims that languages can easily pack more information into a sentence "where [they] can express that information in a backgrounded fashion". Because of the predicted different lexicalisation patterns in S- and V-languages, speakers differ in the way they encode semantic information. Speakers of S-languages express the semantic components Manner and Path in backgrounding constituents (verb roots, satellites) more easily and more often than speakers of V-languages, who characteristically only express Path in backgrounding constituents (verb roots).

A central application of this assumption is that language user's conceptualisation of a motion event is influenced by the particular language that they speak (Cadierno 2008: 146). Slobin (1996a: 75) points out that "[...] [t]here is a special kind of thinking that is intimately tied to language – namely, the thinking that is carried out online, in the process of speaking". When children acquire a native language, they learn particular ways of thinking (Slobin 1996a: 76). This assumption has lead to the "thinking for speaking hypotheses" which claims that the first language trains speakers to pay different kinds of attention to particular details of events and situations when talking about them. For example "[s]peakers of S-languages have been trained by their languages, to make more distinctions of motor pattern, rate, affect, and evolution of Movement, in comparison with speakers of V-languages" (Slobin 2000: 113). Slobin assumes that this difference can be attributed to the language-specific pattern of the first language within the acquisition process: when acquiring an S-language, children learn to distinguish "expressive nuances of manner" (Slobin 2003: 169) from an early stage on, whereas children acquiring a V-language learn "broad categories of basic types of motor pattern" (Slobin 2003: 169). Furthermore, Slobin (2006: 71) points out that a semantic field saturated with a rich lexicon (e.g. the Manner verb lexicon of S-languages) might have psycholinguistic consequences, since "language user[s] must make a number of distinctions of manner of movement that might well be ignored by users of languages with less diverse vocabularies in the domain". As a consequence, S-language speakers construct a set of systematic semantic categories by learning distinct nuances of Manner. For instance, the category of MOVE FAST is lexicalised in German by verbs with fine-grained distinctions (*flitzen* 'to dash', *rasen* 'to rush', *sausen* 'to speed'), whereas Turkish only provides a broad category (*koşmak*) (see also the example of *sendelemek* 'to stagger, to stumble, to tumble, to trip, to falter' in §3.2.6.1). Figure 15 illustrates the possible internal structure of the semantic component Path (IN/TRANS) and Manner (MOVE FAST) and its possible encoding in Turkish and German.

With respect to Path, Turkish provides distinct verbs which encode the different semantic components of the category in backgrounded constituents. German lacks equivalent verbs, but can make use of distinct Path satellites (e.g. *hinein* 'hither.in', *rein* 'inside', *(hin)durch* '(hither)through') in order to encode the category in a backgrounded way as well. On the other hand, German provides distinct verbs which encode expressive nuances of Manner in a backgrounded way, whereas Turkish lacks equivalent verbs (here of the type MOVE FAST).[36] In Turkish,

---

[36] Turkish also provides verbs of the expressive Manner verb category such as *emeklemek* 'to crawl'. These verbs are, however, more limited compared with German as shown in §3.2.6.1.

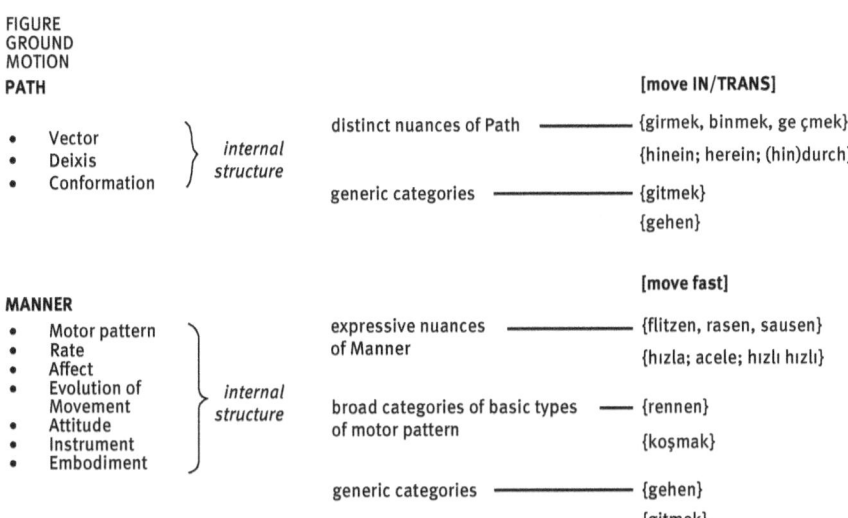

Figure 15: Internal structure of Path and Manner in German and Turkish.

it is only possible to encode expressive nuances of the type MOVE FAST in a foregrounded way by using Manner adverbs (e.g. *acele*, *hızlı hızlı*), or by making use of the broad category of basic types (to which we referred to an everyday Manner verb such as *koşmak* 'to run'). Note that it is also possible to make use of a generic category by using a Generic verb (*gehen*; *gitmek* 'to go'), which encodes neither Path nor Manner (and then requires a directional and an optional Manner specification, e.g. "go fast to X"). If we assume that the use of a Manner verb requires the same cognitive cost as using a Generic verb, Manner is, then, more accessible in German (and other S-languages) (Slobin 2003: 162), whereas it is less "codeable" in Turkish (and other V-languages) (Slobin 1996a). In other words, Manner is less routinely encoded in V-language discourse (Bohnemeyer, Eisenbeiss & Narasimhan 2006: 2).

Both Talmy's and Slobin's accounts provide explanations for the outcome of cross-linguistic research in this domain (Berman & Slobin 1994; Slobin 1996a; 1997; 2000; 2003; 2004b; 2006). S-language speakers are exposed to more frequent and distinct Manner information from an early acquisition stage on, easily provide frequent and distinct Manner information when linguistically encoding motion images, continue lexical innovation in this domain and have a rich mental imagery of manner of motion. It is argued that this habitual, online attention to

Manner "has made it especially salient in S-language speakers' conceptualizations of motion events" (Slobin 2003: 164).

V-language speakers are exposed to less frequent and distinct Manner information, express Manner less frequently, or rather when Manner has to be highlighted for some contextual reason, and make fewer semantic distinctions. On the one hand, the expression of Manner is, however, more restricted in V-languages (as shown in §3.2.5 and 3.2.6). It is assumed that the expression of Manner requires in some kinds of motion event types a higher cognitive processing cost (when, in Talmy's terms, it is expressed in a foregrounded way). This may lead to a more frequent omission of Manner by speakers of V-languages or by making use of a broad category of basic types. As a result, we can expect that speakers of V-languages differ with respect to the formation of systematic semantic categories of Manner which results in a semantically less distinct expression of Manner and a different conceptualisation of this domain. Moreover, speakers of V-languages are expected to focus on the Path, "the physical details of the surroundings, the protagonist's inner state, and his trajectory of movement" (Slobin 2000: 129).

However, the "thinking for speaking hypotheses" does not claim that language-specific properties affect the mental images that a person forms about the world, but that they can have an impact on which components of these mental images are selected for the linguistic symbolisation as well as on the organisation and elaboration of these components (Jarvis 2007: 48). With respect to the different levels of conceptualisation introduced in §3.2.3, the "thinking for speaking hypotheses" originally accounts for the fact that language-specific properties only have an impact on the macro-planning for speaking (which is in line with Levelt's assumption). The outcome of further research in this domain indicates that the "thinking for speaking hypotheses" also applies to the level of micro-planning (von Stutterheim & Nüse 2003). An application for cross-linguistic influence in general cognition is, however, overwhelmingly rejected by studies testing the "thinking for speaking hypotheses".

In contrast, Goldstein (2010: 8) assumes that a person's neural processing and conscious perception within the perception process (step five and six, see §3.2.1) are affected by their knowledge and past experiences. This brings us to the question of whether members of different cultures, who are also speakers of different languages with distinct linguistic preferences, perceive a same visual stimuli in different ways. A number of studies provide empirical evidence of differences existing in perception due to culture; it is, however, not clear to what extent the impact of language is involved (Jarvis 2007: 51). If the answer here is affirmative, this would mean that differences in the conceptualisation of motion events can be found, not only at the level of macro- and micro-planning, but in general cognition. This would challenge the existence of "a universal form of mental representation, independent of any particular language" (Slobin 1991: 8).

When the first language has an impact on how speakers attend to a particular semantic domain when using that language or in language-free tasks, the question arises of what happens when two language types and different conceptualisation patterns confront each other in the context of L2-acquisition. Slobin (1993: 245) argues that the characteristic pattern of a language acquired during L1-acquisition is exceptionally resistant to restructuring in adult L2 acquisition. However, this might not account for the case of child bilingualism, when both languages are acquired during early childhood. In §2.2 we have argued that within the multicompetence framework, the acquisition of any supplement language is seen as a dynamic process which can also affect language skills in L1. Consequently, L2 effects can appear in child language acquisition, but also in foreign language acquisition. As emphasised in this section, these effects can arise from a different conceptualisation due to cross-linguistic differences in a speakers' L1. In order to fully account for possible cross-linguistic influences within the domains of bilingual language acquisition and motion event conceptualisation and encoding, an additive theory of conceptual transfer is presented in the following section. By doing so, we focus on conceptualisation transfer which is produced by cross-linguistic differences "in the ways L2 users process conceptual knowledge and form temporary representations in their working memory" (Jarvis 2007: 53). This is in line with the scope of the current study, which asks if the successive acquisition process of L1 Turkish speakers is influenced by a different (German) or similar (French) conceptualisation in terms of learning a new or a similar way of "thinking for speaking".

3.3.2 Conceptual transfer in the domain of motion

The "conceptual transfer hypothesis" (set forth by Jarvis 2007; Jarvis 2000; Jarvis & Pavlenko 2010) overlaps with the "thinking for speaking hypotheses" with respect to the conceptualisation levels of macro- and micro-planning. In contrast, the "conceptual transfer hypothesis" research also focuses on conceptual transfer at the level of general cognition. Note that the notion "conceptual" refers to both, concepts and conceptualisation. Whereas concept transfer "results from the nature of a person's stored conceptual inventory, [...] conceptualization transfer occurs during the processing of that knowledge" (Jarvis 2007: 52). Even if in some cases it is difficult to distinguish between these two, they apply similarly to conceptual transfer which "can occur either because of differences in L2 user's conceptual inventories or because of differences in how they process their conceptual knowledge; it can also involve both of these at the same time" (Jarvis 2007: 53). Concept transfer, however, is a result of the "makeup of the inventory of concepts in a person's long-term memory" (Jarvis 2007: 54), whereas, as noted above, conceptualisation transfer takes place in temporary representations in the working memory.

With respect to Motion it has been argued that cross-linguistic differences in this domain involve the internal structure of the category, Path or Manner, which can lead to a different conceptualisation of that category. In the context of bilingual language acquisition, conceptual transfer is assumed when speakers are exposed to conflicting patterns in the two languages from an early stage on (e.g. Turkish-German bilinguals).

What makes the "conceptual transfer hypothesis" promising within the multicompetence framework is its assumption that the patterns which a speaker uses in one language can reflect the concepts and conceptualisation patterns that the speaker has acquired through another language, irrespective of whether this is the speaker's L1 or L2. The acquired conceptualisation patterns have an impact on how speakers use all of their languages. Furthermore, it is assumed within the "conceptual transfer hypothesis", that "all healthy humans have the necessary perceptual and cognitive abilities to attend to input, to form new conceptual categories, and to restructure existing representations, and that these abilities can be exercised throughout the lifetime, in schooling, in apprenticeship, and in foreign/second language learning" (Jarvis & Pavlenko 2010: 122). This assumption is also adopted in the current study.

In addition to types of transfer that are "purely linguistic in nature (e.g., phonological, syntactic, semantic transfer) [...] conceptual transfer appears to be more inherently bidirectional and convergent" (Daller, Treffers-Daller & Furman 2011: 101).

3.4 Summary and considerations for the current study

The corpus analysis has shown that in all three languages, Generic motion verbs are highly frequent in oral discourse. German, however, corresponds to the predicted typological assumptions by providing a diverse Manner verb lexicon and a frequent use of Manner verbs. Compared with German, Turkish and French, in contrast, display a greater lexicon of Path verbs which are dominantly used in the analysed corpora. Nevertheless, the corpus analysis indicates that there are Manner verbs in the corpus which are frequently used in all three languages and support Slobin's assumption of a "two-tiered" lexicon (Slobin 1997: 459). There are neutral, everyday Manner verbs, such as *fallen/düşmek/tomber* 'to fall', *laufen/yürümek/marcher* 'to walk', *rennen/koşmak/courir* 'to run' and more expressive (and less frequently used) Manner verbs such as *hopsen/hoplamak/sautiller* 'to hop' or *stolpern/sendelemek/chanceler* 'to stagger'. In German, such expressive Manner verbs are much more elaborated and distinct compared to Turkish and French, in which these verbs obviously play a minor role, although French displays marginally more Manner verbs than Turkish. Turkish, in turn, compensates for the lack of Manner verb richness with a productive verb morphology.

A further outcome of the results is that the traditional focus on the use of verb types is not sufficient to fully account for the encoding of motion events (Goschler 2013: 128). Table 10 summarises the analysis of Path encoding in German, Turkish and French. The results indicate that all languages provide different slots in each encoding type. In both Turkish and French, the locus of the highest differentiation of Path encoding is verbal and adverbal encoding, whereas in German it is adverbal and adnominal encoding. This result fits only for German into Talmy's assumed lexicalisation patterns; due to the more fine-grained analysis of Path expression, it appears that French is more similar to German with respect to the Path differentiation achieved by adverbal encoding. Moreover, Turkish provides a higher differentiation of Path in adnominal encoding compared to French. This finding emphasises the possibility of (pseudo-) satellite-constructions in V-languages. Moreover, the high differentiation of Path (including also the verbal slot) in Turkish and French allows patterns which are considered pleonastic or hybrid (see example (37). Nevertheless, the analysis of Manner verb combinations with directional Path devices in Turkish indicated that compared with satellites in German, they are much less frequent and more restricted with respect to their productivity and combination. The same holds true for French, in which the combination of motion verbs with (pseudo-) satellites seems to be even less frequent and harder to combine compared to Turkish (Filipović & Ibarretxe-Antuñano 2015: 531; Hijazo-Gascón 2018: 244).

Table 10: Verbal, adnominal and adverbal encoding in German, Turkish and French.

	verbal encoding slots (types)	adnominal encoding slots (types)	adverbal encoding slots (types)
German	1 (3)	1 (7)	3 (11)
Turkish	1 (6)	2 (5)	1 (6)
French	1 (7)	1 (4)	3 (7)

When considering the syntactic organisation, it can be assumed that Manner is not typically encoded in subordinated verbs, as predicted originally by Talmy. Turkish and French display different strategies; whereas French speakers prefer single constructions and encode Manner either in the main verb or in prepositional or adverbial phrases, Turkish speakers tend to separate clauses and display a higher segmentation of series of sub-paths. On a constructional level, the combination of Manner verbs with Path devices is possible but restricted in both languages. German speakers, on the other hand, prefer to express both semantic elements in a compact way, and elaborate Path with multiple Path devices outside the main verb by making use of a high frequency and ease of combination within this construction type.

According to the empirical findings, there is a clear tendency towards a boundary crossing constraint in Turkish and French, when speakers encode the change of location of a Figure in three-dimensional enclosed boundaries (telic Path phrases). In such boundary focus events, speakers of Turkish and French largely use Path verbs or verbs that encode force dynamics (Slobin 2003: 226). When using Manner verbs Turkish and French speakers express locative motion events along a plane, towards a Goal, or up to an Endpoint with proximity to a Ground, when the Figure does not cross a boundary. Furthermore, verbs which are considered to encode force dynamics, occur in a higher frequency in the analysed corpora of all three languages and therefore fall into the category of everyday Manner (-Path) verbs.

Nevertheless, further explanations are required, since violations of the boundary constraint beyond the exceptions discussed have been found in both V-languages. It may be hypothesised that, due to the relative frequency of a Manner verb (e.g. *koşmak, courir* 'to run'), the semantic information of this verb is conceived of as less expressive (in Slobin's terms they are (or became) neutral, everyday Manner verbs), which in turn may allow their use in boundary crossing events. Note that this hypothesis needs to be proven by studying boundary crossing constructions with other frequent Manner verbs cross-linguistically in large corpora and through experimental studies that test the acceptance level of such constructions by native speakers of the respective language. However, speakers of Turkish and French tend rather to omit Manner and express only Path in such event types. When Manner is highly salient, Turkish speakers express Manner in subordinate elements or adjuncts or make use of an implicit strategy, in parsing boundary crossing events into many sub-events, without encoding directly the change of location (Özçalışkan 2013: 17).

According to Talmy (2003), German is classified as an S-language. The corpus analysis in §3.2.6.1, as well as the reviewed empirical studies, confirm this assumption with respect to the German standard variety, since German speakers typically follow the S-pattern by making use of a high differentiation of adnominal and adverbal encoding.

Turkish is characterised by Talmy (2003) and several others (Aksu-Koç 1994; Özçalışkan & Slobin 1999; Özyürek & Kita 1999; Schroeder 2008; Schroeder 2009;

Slobin 1996b) as a V-language. However, the empirical observations indicate that Turkish displays numerous Path devices (adnominal and adverbal encoding) which can serve to express Path outside the verb stem and make it possible to encode motion events in an S-language-manner by elaborating the Path of motion and combining Manner verbs with Path devices.

In addition to Talmy (2003), a number of studies examining the expression of spatial relations in French, consider French a typical V-language (Aurnague 1995; Aurnague 1996; Borillo 1998; Hickmann 2006; Hickmann 2007; Hickmann, Hendriks & Champaud 2009; Hickmann & Hendriks 2006; Vandeloise 1991). Taking the results of naturalistic language data into account, French exhibits a great pattern variability, in particular with respect to Path distinctions by adnominal and adverbal encoding and cannot be considered a typical V-language.

However, exceptional and problematic cases, as discussed in §3.2.5 and 3.2.6, should not overlook the premise of Talmy's framework which accounts for speakers' "first/habitual/most frequent/preferred choices" (Filipović & Ibarretxe-Antuñano 2015: 528). Nevertheless, the usage-based observations established in §3.2.6, in particular with respect to French and Turkish, emphasise reconsidering Talmy's framework in terms of a discursive continuum (Slobin 2004b), which includes "a range of typological options, where the members of the typological category vary in the degree to which they follow the same typological pattern or somehow deviate from it" (Jovanovic & Martinovic-Zic 2004: 224).

This is in line with recent motion research which "show[s] that there is significant variation and change within individual languages and language families and that languages may fall along a cline of encoding strategies rather than into clear-cut categories" (Goschler & Stefanowitsch 2013b: 10–11). Harr (2012: 94) points out "that the typology of a given language cannot reliably predict the lexicalization pattern of that language." Berthele (2004: 118) identifies the reason for this in typological research where the diversity that exists within one language is usually simplified. For methodological reasons, typologists treat languages as "homogenized categories such as 'German', 'Spanish', 'French' etc." (Berthele 2004: 118). Goschler & Stefanowitsch (2013b: 3) claim that Talmy's dichotomous typology is too simple and that "there is by now substantial evidence" that the existence of "split", "parallel", and "intermixed framing patterns", as pointed out by Talmy (2003: 64–67), cannot be ignored. Such intra-typological patterns beyond the S/V-typology have also been demonstrated for the languages analysed in §3.2.6, in particular for Path elaboration in Turkish and the use of Manner verbs in different motion event types in French.

Berthele's studies (2004; 2006) demonstrate the importance of a diatopical approach. He observed more variation, when analysing varieties within one language which go beyond the S- and V-prototypes. The results show diatopical variation in a Swiss-German contact variety, the Moutathal dialect. A speaker's performance of this dialect is more similar to French than as assumed to German. The study by Bernini, Spreafico & Valentini (2006) comes to a similar finding in hybrid structures of the (Italian) local dialect of Bergamo.

In the context of bilingual speakers' multicompetence, the existence of a split system in Turkish and French (in the sense of the use of Manner verbs in atelic events and possible S-constructions), is an important observation, in so far as it suggests where to look for cross-linguistic influence. Furthermore, there is a need to look more closely at the motion event expression on a constructional level as well to analyse different kinds of motion event types (bounded vs. unbounded event types).

It is argued that language users' conceptualisation of a motion image is influenced by the documented language-specific pattern of a particular language. In the case of Turkish-German bilinguals who are confronted with distinct conceptualisation patterns, conceptual transfer is probably most perceptible in the preference for Path over Manner verbs (Jarvis & Pavlenko 2010: 147) or vice versa as well as in the linguistic symbolisation of boundary crossing events. Consequently, we can hypothesise that, due to simultaneous influences from L1 and L2 in a single domain (here conflation patterns or linguistic constraints), the performance of Turkish-German bilinguals in L1 and L2 falls somewhat between the patterns of monolinguals of the respective languages. In contrast, due to similar conceptualisation, Turkish-French bilinguals are expected to display positive conceptual transfer in these categories.

Keeping this hypothesis in mind we will now focus on motion event encoding in first and bilingual language acquisition, which further serves to establish general assumptions and the hypothesis for the current study.

4 Motion events in first and bilingual language acquisition

4.1 The impact of language-specific properties in monolingual first language acquisition of German, Turkish and French

Most of the empirical studies that explore the verbalisation of motion events have focused on standard varieties and/or monolingual language acquisition. The results largely provide evidence of Talmy's predicted lexicalisation patterns across a wide range of languages. Developmental research has shown that children's language production and comprehension is constrained by these typological properties from an early stage on (Hendriks & Hickmann 2010: 192). Based on an experiment measuring the visual fixation time for different Manner/Path scenarios, Pulverman et al. (2013) found that even seven month old children already distinguish between Path and Manner. The spatial categories provided by the native language play an important role in child language acquisition. Children "construct a spatial language that tightly fits the adult system and further tune into this system during language and cognitive development" (Hickmann 2006: 281). Monolingual children are tuned to the language-specific motion encoding patterns of their first languages. In addition, a number of studies have shown that the children's constraint in working memory limit their cognitive capacity in the beginning (Hickmann 2006; Hickmann, Hendriks & Champaud 2009). As a result, children produce fewer semantic components when they describe a motion event.

4.1.1 German

A few studies investigated how German children learn to verbalise motion events. Bamberg (1994) observed a large number of verb-satellite combinations used by three-year-old children and a broad use of different Manner verbs in all age groups (three-, five- and nine-year-old children). The study does not provide detailed information about the use of the spatial devices, whereas Ochsenbauer & Hickmann (2010) examined in detail the cognitive and linguistic development of children's spatial language in a pseudo-longitudinal study of German. They show, that children from three years on usually encode Manner in the verbal root and Path in other linguistic devices outside the verb and use a wide range of Manner verbs in all age groups (three-, four-, six-, and ten-year-old children were tested) (Ochsenbauer & Hickmann 2010: 231–232). With increasing age, German children clearly prefer Manner verbs. First Path verbs increase with age but sharply decrease around the age of ten (Ochsenbauer & Hickmann 2010: 227). With respect to the spatial information encoded outside the verb stem, children in all age groups frequently use particles; prepositional phrases decrease after the age of six. Other devices such as adverbs were used infrequently. With respect to the semantic information, Path devices were significantly more frequent than Manner devices (Ochsenbauer & Hickmann 2010: 228–229).

The observed patterns, expressing Manner in the main verb and Path in particles or other linguistic devices, suggest that German children linguistically encode motion images in accordance with the typical S-patterns of their L1. Ochsenbauer & Hickmann (2010: 226) and Harr (2012: 164–170) also report a frequent use of the Generic verb *gehen* 'to go' in combination with various other devices between the ages of three to six years (see (75)) which decreases sharply around the age of ten.

A preference for auxiliary verb constructions (*Sie tut rennen* 'She goes running') and semantically neutral verbs (*er geht hoch* 'he goes up') can generally be observed in motion descriptions of English and German speaking children. Harr (2012: 112–113) points out, that in language acquisition these preferences have three major functions: a lower degree of cognitive demand; familiarity as a result of a high frequency in children's input and lexicon, and ease of accessibility in oral speech.

With respect to the syntactic packaging of motion events the study by Harr (2012) demonstrates that German speakers clearly follow the typical S-pattern, expressing Manner and Path together in one single clause, irrespective of target items and age. Complex responses (with subordinate constructions) are very rare and occur primarily only in adult usage.

(75) *Der   geht   dahin   und   geh-t   da   hoch,   frisst*
     he   go.PR   there   and   go.PR   there   up   eat.PR
     den   ganzen   Honig,   wieder   runter   und   geht   dann   weiter.
     DET.ACC   all   honey   again   Down   and   go.PR   then   along
     'He goes there and goes there up, eats all the honey, again down and goes then along.' (Ochsenbauer & Hickmann 2010: 226)

4.1.2 Turkish

In contrast to German much less detailed information is known about the acquisition and the development of motion events in Turkish child language. Based on the Frog Story elicitations, Aksu-Koç (1994: 352) demonstrates that Path verbs such as *çıkmak* ('to exit; ascend') are acquired early and that the combination with locative adverbs or postpositions increases during the preschool years. Manner verbs are also acquired very early (children frequently use, from three years on, *atlamak* 'to jump'; *kaçmak* 'to escape'; *yüzmek* 'to swim'), but the lexical diversity remains limited in the children's lexical development (Aksu-Koç 1994: 335). Özçalışcan & Slobin's pseudo-longitudinal study indicates that the use of Path verbs in the development of child speech (ages three, five, seven, nine, ten) decreases with age, while the use of Manner-Path verbs increases (Özçalışkan & Slobin 2000a: 7). Moreover, when Turkish does not provide an option for encoding both Manner and Path in a single word, children at all ages greatly prefer Path verbs (Özçalışkan & Slobin 2000a: 9). The children's lexicon extends slowly until the age of ten but does not have the same diversity compared with adults. Overall the study points out that young Turkish speakers prefer less complex constructions, e.g. they prefer Manner-Path conflated verbs (e.g. *kovalamak* 'to chase') over subordinate constructions that express Manner outside the main verb. In a developmental perspective, Turkish speakers prefer clausal or phrasal descriptions of Manner (Aksu-Koç 1994: 356). Özçalışcan & Slobin (1999) discuss intra-typological differences in the use of Path verbs by Spanish and Turkish speakers in all age groups tested (three, four, five, six to eight, nine to eleven, adult) in the Frog Story sample. Turkish speakers display a greater use of Path verbs at the ages of nine to eleven and a more diverse Path lexicon compared to Spanish speakers (Özçalışkan & Slobin 1999: 549–550), whereas there is almost no difference with respect to the use of Manner verbs. Moreover, the expansion in the Manner and Path lexicon takes place much earlier in Turkish compared with Spanish (by age five). Surprisingly, Turkish speakers show no difference in the lexical diversity of Manner verbs during six and eleven years compared with English speakers which, however, disappears in adult age (Özçalışkan & Slobin 1999: 550–551).

In regard to the acquisition of event internal adjuncts, converbs are already present by the age of three and highly frequent by five years (e.g. converbs marking simultaneity -*ken*; and temporal overlap -*Ince*; sequenced clauses with -*Ip* develop slightly later) (Küntay & Slobin 1999: 172). By contrast, the converb -*ErEk* does not appear until age seven to nine. Since this converb "functions to treat two situations as constituent parts of a single superordinate event" (Küntay & Slobin 1999: 173) it is conceptually quite complex and appears late in child speech (Berman & Slobin 1994: 547–551). Moreover in the Frog Story sample, an elaboration of locative trajectories with age (three to nine years) can be observed. Postpositions, specifying the trajectory of motion, and locative adverbials increase (Aksu-Koç 1994: 353). In general, Aksu-Koç's study shows that children typically specify either the Source or the Goal, but rarely conflate both (Aksu-Koç 1994: 354).

When considering syntactic organisation, Allen et al. (2007: 34) found that Turkish-speaking children (three to four years of age) have difficulties producing complex syntactic constructions. Consequently they produce less complex constructions ("loose"), packaging the semantic elements, Path and Manner, in two separate clauses or "Manner-only" and/or "Path-only" sentences. However, the frequency of the typical construction type of V-languages (semi-tight) increases with age, while the loose-construction type decreases. Allen et al. (2007: 41) argue that children's avoidance of the typical semi-tight pattern, produced largely by Turkish adults, can be explained by the quite complex syntactic construction required, combining a main verb with non-finite (subordinate) elements. This is also in line with research findings of e.g. the later acquisition of converbs such as *Ince, -Ip, -ErEk* (see above). Instead, Turkish children, compared with adults, much more often use a tight-construction, e.g. combining a Manner verb with a spatial noun (*Onun etrafında zıpladı* 'It jumped around it') or a Path verb with onomatopoeia (*Tak tak indi* 'It tak tak descended') (Allen et al. 2007: 35).

4.1.3 French

During the past decade a couple of empirical studies investigated the acquisition and the linguistic development of motion events in French child language. The work of Hickmann and her colleagues (Harr 2012; Hickmann 2007; Hickmann & Hendriks 2006; Hickmann, Hendriks & Champaud 2009; Hickmann, Taranne & Bonnet 2009) provides an important empirical basis for the understanding of children's linguistic symbolisation of motion images and their cognitive development. In the following, the results of Harr's pseudo-longitudinal study will be focused on since they represent the most current and detailed findings within this research area. The results show that utterances encoding only one semantic component (Manner or Path) are frequent in all younger ages tested (four, six, eight, ten years of age), compared to utterances encoding more than one semantic component. With respect to the semantic components (Manner only, Path only, both, or none) encoded in speakers' descriptions, the results indicate that the expression of simultaneous Manner and Path increases with age, while Path responses are quite dominant (Harr 2012: 158). Moreover, the analysis of the linguistic devices used to encode Manner and Path indicates that French speakers mainly encode Path in the verb stem and Manner significantly less in the main verb or in other linguistic devices (Harr 2012: 178). From a developmental perspective, the use of Path verbs increases with age, while it decreases with Manner verbs. With respect to other linguistic devices, constructions combining Manner verb with Path devices and Path verbs with Manner devices increase with age which can be explained by a parallel increase of sentence complexity (Harr 2012: 226–227). However, in more than half of their motion descriptions, children do not use any Path or Manner device by age ten. When encoding Path outside the motion verb, they primarily use prepositional phrases. Adverbial or noun phrases were preferred to more complex subordinate clauses when encoding Manner in peripheral devices (Harr 2012: 228–229). This finding is also true for the analysis of syntactic complexity, which suggests that French speakers at all levels usually express all semantic information in single utterances without any subordinate element and rarely use constructions involving one or more subordinate elements (such as relative clauses or gerunds) or where information was spread over several clauses (juxtaposed or coordinated) (Harr 2012: 196).

As shown in this section, from about ten years on, monolingual children generally follow the specific linguistic pattern of adults speaking the same language. "[C]hildren are guided in constructing spatial semantic categories by the language they are exposed to" (Choi & Bowerman 1991: 110). Note that research in the field of motion event encoding and developmental implication has been largely carried out in first language acquisition. The investigation of bilingual or early second language acquisition has received much less attention. The following section briefly summarises studies in this field and provides a more detailed review of possible cross-linguistic interactions on the basis of research findings involving German, Turkish and French in multilingual settings.

4.2 The interaction of language-specific properties in bilingual language acquisition

When taking a dynamic view of language acquisition, we can expect different conceptualisation patterns to influence the linguistic symbolisation of motion images in both languages of bilinguals. However, it is not merely the question of whether language-specific properties have an impact on language acquisition, but rather what the nature of this impact is (Engemann, Harr & Hickmann 2012: 265).

It is only recently that research has investigated the linguistic symbolisation of motion images in the context of foreign, second and bilingual language acquisition. In this process a vast amount of empirical studies focused on foreign language learning (among others Bernini, Spreafico & Valentini 2006; Brown & Gullberg 2008; Brown & Gullberg 2010; Brown & Gullberg 2012; Cadierno 2004; Cadierno 2008; Cadierno & Robinson 2009; Cadierno & Ruiz 2006; Filipović 2010; Jessen 2014; Jessen 2013; Larrañaga et al. 2012; Reshöft 2011; Stam 2006). Only a few studies concentrated on motion event encoding in the domain of bilingual first language acquisition (Spanish-Swedish early (and late) bilinguals: Bylund & Jarvis 2011; English-Spanish bilinguals: Filipović 2011; English-French bilinguals: Ochsenbauer & Engemann 2011; English-Turkish bilinguals: Özçalışkan & Slobin 2000b; German-French bilinguals: Berthele & Stocker 2017; Berthele 2017) and in the domain of early second language acquisition (Turkish-German bilinguals: Daller, Treffers-Daller & Furman 2011; Goschler 2009; Goschler et al. 2013; Schroeder 2009; English-Spanish bilinguals: Hohenstein, Eisenberg & Naigles 2006). Note that studies in this field mainly investigated the interactions between L1 speakers of a V-language acquiring an S-language. This may be due to the fact that a transition from a V-language to an S-language "is more challenging than vice versa, because the learners have to acquire the habit of attending to Manner of motion and encoding it to speech" (Pavlenko 2014: 150). Interestingly, the vice versa transition, L1 speakers of S-languages acquiring a V-language, "can still be challenging because they need to restructure their lexicalization patterns by shifting Path expression from satellites to main verbs and by acquiring new rules, such as the boundary crossing constraint" (Pavlenko 2014: 152). However, only a few studies were devoted to the intra-typological distinction within S-languages which has been identified in the context of foreign (Danish learners of English: Cadierno & Robinson 2009; German and Russian learners of Danish: Cadierno 2010; German learners of Danish: Jessen & Cadierno 2013; Jessen 2014; Russian learners of English: Pavlenko 2010; English learners of Russian: Hasko 2010) or simultaneous L1/early L2 acquisition (Russian-English bilinguals, Gor et al. 2009; Volynsky 2012). A limited number of studies investigated the effect of acquiring a V-language as L1 and L2 (Italian learners of Spanish: Cadierno & Ruiz 2006; Italian and French learners of Spanish: Hijazo-Gascón 2011; Hijazo-Gascón 2018). Until now, to my knowledge, no research has been carried out in the context of simultaneous L1/early L2 acquisition.

The studies reported exhibit a wide range of interactions between S- and V-languages or within a given type. In the spectrum of different learner types (ranging from native to foreign language learners), the impact on L1, L2 and L3 is dependent on different factors and variables (age of onset, context of acquisition, linguistic input, length of exposure, length of instruction, length of resistance, language dominance, and language use). While the direction of cross-linguistic influence in foreign language acquisition is almost unidirectional (L1 influence on L2),[37] in the context of bilingual/early second language acquisition the results

---

[37] A few studies also observed that the first foreign language influences the L1 (see Brown & Gullberg 2008; Brown & Gullberg 2012 on late bilingual Japanese-English speakers).

are more diverse. Some studies found unidirectional cross-linguistic influence from the L1 on the L2 (Engemann, Harr & Hickmann 2012; Ochsenbauer & Engemann 2011), and from the L2 on the L1 (Daller, Treffers-Daller & Furman 2011; Hohenstein, Eisenberg & Naigles 2006). The study by Hohenstein, Eisenberg & Naigles (2006) also reports bidirectional cross-linguistic influence in the speech of bilinguals: Spanish-English bilinguals used more Manner verbs in Spanish than monolingual Spanish speakers and again more Path verbs in English than English monolinguals. Daller, Treffers-Daller & Furman (2011) found "in between performance" (Pavlenko 2014: 151) by German-Turkish bilinguals in both languages with regard to the lexicalisation of locative trajectories and the use of Path satellites; other studies observed convergence patterns and avoidance strategies (Goschler et al. 2013; Schroeder 2009). We will now focus on this aspect in more detail by reviewing empirical studies in Turkish-German and Turkish-French in multilingual settings.

4.2.1 Turkish-German in multilingual settings

Very recently, a few studies initiated research on German-Turkish bilinguals' motion event encoding. Schroeder (2009), Goschler (2009; 2013) and Goschler et al. (2013) only focus on speakers' L2-performance (German), whereas the study by Daller, Treffers-Daller & Furman (2011) investigates both languages, including Turkish. The study by Schroeder (2009) is based on elicited written narratives of Turkish-German bilinguals (eleven to thirteen years of age). He found a preference for constructions of Generic motion verbs (*kommen* 'to come'; *gehen* 'to go') with Path satellites and an avoidance of Path satellites in combination with Manner verbs (Schroeder 2009: 191–193). Moreover, the results indicate a tendency for paratactic organisation of motion events in German (Path and Manner are expressed in two separated or coordinated verbal phrases). This phenomenon can possibly be traced back to the typical oral pattern of L1 Turkish to which German-Turkish bilinguals are predominantly exposed in Germany (Schroeder 2009: 189). The study by Goschler et al. (2013) found similar preferences. On the basis of a naturalistic corpus (self recorded, informal, spoken conversation) of young speakers (14–17 years of age) of a multiethnic variety (Kiezdeutsch "neighbourhood German", Wiese 2009; Wiese 2012), mainly spoken in multilingual urban areas, the study analyses motion constructions of Turkish-German bilinguals. Their results are in line with the findings of Schroeder's study. Compared with monolingual German speakers, bilinguals use fewer Manner verbs with Path satellites and display a preference for Generic motion verbs (*kommen* 'to come' and *gehen* 'to go') (Goschler et al. 2013: 243–244). However, the latter are frequently combined with Path satellites, which supports the idea of a typologically motivated convergence of the (Turkish) V- and the (German) S-pattern (Goschler et al. 2013: 245).

The study by Daller, Treffers-Daller & Furman (2011) is based on elicited written narratives in German and Turkish and investigates the transfer of conceptualisation patterns of one resident group (Germany) and another returnee group (Turkey) of Turkish-German bilinguals, in order to determine the direction of transfer in terms of language dominance. Their analysis focuses on the selection of concepts (Vector, Conformation, and Deixis), the use of Path satellites, the linearisation of clauses (Action-Goal/Goal-Action) in two events involving a boundary crossing. Their results clearly show that speakers' performance, in both languages, is related to the dominant language surrounding them. Both groups of bilinguals fall between the two monolingual groups, whereas the resident group performance is closer to the monolingual German control group and the returnee group is closer to the monolingual Turkish control group, irrespective of the language they use. In comparison with monolingual Turkish speakers, bilinguals in Germany prefer encoding Motion with a Conformation and a Vector component (*gir-* 'to enter'), while the former clearly prefer encoding Motion without Conformation but with a Vector (*in-* 'to descend'), or neither with Conformation nor Vector (*git-* 'to go'). Since German monolinguals prefer encoding Motion with Conformation, by using a Path particle (*rein* 'into; *hinein* 'hither.in'), the choices of the bilingual resident group are closer to this group than to the others. However, bilingual returnees are closest to monolingual Turkish speakers which is evident in their not preferring to include a Conformation component (Daller, Treffers-Daller & Furman 2011: 108). The analysis of the usage of [Path verb+directional Path device]-constructions in Turkish texts and in German monolingual texts shows that the bilingual groups are again in between the two monolingual groups. Here, both bilingual groups are closer to the monolingual German group than to the monolingual Turkish group (Daller, Treffers-Daller & Furman 2011: 110). Furthermore, the study does not find any violation of the boundary crossing constraint in Turkish texts, since all three groups use no Manner verb when the Figure performs a change of location. The analysis of additive boundary crossing elicitations in German indicates, that both bilingual groups prefer other motion verbs such as *laufen* ('to walk') or *gehen* ('to go') over *rennen* ('to run'). The latter is clearly preferred by German monolinguals.

4.2.2 Turkish-French in multilingual settings

As noted in §2.3, the investigation of the Turkish diaspora in France has generally received less attention, compared to other European countries. In fact, no study, to my knowledge, has been carried out in the context of motion event encoding. As noted above, only one study, involving French, investigated the acquisition of another V-language (here Spanish as the foreign language) (Hijazo-Gascón 2011; Hijazo-Gascón 2018). Thus, we focus here on the general findings of these studies in order to derive possible consequences for the acquisition of French by bilingual Turkish-French speakers. The results indicate that there were no difference between the encoding of Manner and Path in the verbal root in L1 and L2 by Italian L1/L2 Spanish and French L1/L2 Spanish learners. Thus, the typological closeness of L1 and L2 (preference for encoding Path in main verbs) leads to a positive (conceptual) transfer from L1>L2. However, the study found differences in the Path elaboration in L2 Spanish. In comparison with French L1/L2 Spanish learners, Italian L1/L2 Spanish learners indicate a greater Path elaboration in terms of using more "Plus-Ground" constructions (see §3.2.6.3) in the verbal periphery in their Spanish narratives. However, the two groups do not differ significantly from L1 Spanish speakers. This finding is mainly due to intra-typological differences in terms of a greater usage of Plus-Ground constructions in Italian (Bernini, Spreafico & Valentini (2006), see also §3.4). Furthermore in Hijazo-Gascón's study, French L1 speakers also indicate a lower Path elaboration in their L1 narratives and contrast not only to Italian native speakers' L1 performance but also to Spanish native speakers' Path elaboration in L1. Thus, the argument can be put forward that, although French provides various devices which would enable the encoding of Path in the verbal periphery, native French speakers tend to avoid complex Path elaboration in their L1. For the scope of the current study, this is an important finding, since we can expect that bilingual Turkish-French speakers are confronted with different preferences for Path elaboration in L1 and L2 (see §3.2.6.3).

4.3 Summary and considerations for the current study

The review of empirical studies on the acquisition of language-specific properties of motion event encoding in monolingual settings indicates that young children of age ten already prefer patterns which are seen as typical for S- (German) and V-languages (Turkish, French). In multilingual settings, a transition from a V-language to an S-language seems to be more challenging. Research indicates that distinct conceptualisations and motion encoding patterns have an impact on Turkish-German bilinguals' motion descriptions in L1 and L2. Within the scope of the current study, we can assume that conceptual transfer is mainly visible in Manner encoding in German by Turkish-German bilinguals. Vice versa, due to possible conceptualisation restructuring, Manner and Path encoding in Turkish might be influenced by the L2 as well. Because of a research desideratum in multilingual Turkish-French settings, we can only hypothesise that similar Motion conceptualisation and encoding patterns in L1 and L2 lead to a positive (conceptual) transfer in motion event encoding in L1 and L2 by Turkish-French bilinguals. Thus, it is expected that speakers do not differ as regards their preference for conflation patterns. However, intra-typological differences between the two languages (see §3.4) might affect speakers' encoding patterns in L1 or L2, mainly visible on the level of motion constructions. Such influence might be an overuse of directional Path devices in French or, vice versa, an avoidance of such devices in Turkish. In both contexts (transition from a V-language to an S-language as well as from a V-language to a V-language), it is of special interest whether language dominance turns out to be a factor which determines the direction of influence as well as the degree of impact of one language on another.

Furthermore, the findings illustrated in §4.1 strongly suggest that the interpretation of motion event descriptions by younger speakers requires a consideration of developmental constraints. Furthermore, we have to bear in mind that in elicitation settings, such as oral re-narrations, speakers might generally tend to use simpler constructions due to their oral discourse mode; younger children might relate even more often to constructions which require a lower processing cost.

Let us now turn to methodological implications and establish the general assumptions and hypothesis which are tested in the current study.

5 Implications and general assumptions

The current study thus aims to provide insights into the nature of variation in bilingual children's motion event expression by evaluating the impact of language dominance patterns (domain and dimension) and language-specific properties (V- and S-patterns) as well as motion event conceptualisation in bilingual speakers' L1 and L2.

In this context, central issues which serve as theoretical background (multicompetence, lexicalisation patterns, adverbal and adnominal encoding, "thinking for speaking hypotheses", "conceptual transfer hypothesis"), as well as a usage-based analysis of linguistic devices provided by the respective languages, speaker's preferences and development in monolingual and bilingual language acquisition have been focused on in Chapters 1–3. In order to establish general assumptions and hypotheses based on the theoretical background, we first consider some implications that are relevant for the methodology.

5.1 Implications for the study

5.1.1 Language pairs

The transition from a V- (Turkish) to an S-language (German) is a focus of the current study, in order to examine bidirectional (conceptual) transfer on the basis of the cross-linguistic differences of two typologically different languages in terms of preference for motion encoding patterns. Moreover, in order to evaluate the impact of language-specific properties (V-pattern) and intra-typological variation within a language type (split systems), a transition from a V- (Turkish) to a V-language (French) is within the scope of the study as well.

As outlined in §2.2 and 3.3.2, research on child bilingualism has to investigate both languages that a speaker acquired during early childhood by reconsidering bidirectional transfer on the basis of conceptualisation patterns, which is hypothesised to be different from those of monolingual speakers of the respective languages.

5.1.2 Participants

For methodological reasons, the investigation focuses on bilingual speakers who attained a certain exposure to the L2. This allows identifying L2 effects on L1, as well as assumptions about language dominance patterns. It is assumed that this applies for children who are born in Germany and France, acquired Turkish as the family language and attended a kindergarten from at least three years on, where the dominant language is spoken. With respect to the children's language development, the current study aims to test children at the end of elementary school (by nine to ten years of age). Furthermore, by testing this age group, L3 effects are potentially minimised, provided that the participants have only started attending foreign language instruction. Since monolingual speakers are hard to come by, L1 speakers of German, Turkish and French with minimal exposure to an L2 and of similar age are included as well, in order to determine bilingual speakers' bidirectional influences and differences in the conceptualisation of motion events. In order to minimise inner- and intergroup heterogeneity, efforts should be made to equate the groups with respect to their educational background.

5.1.3 Stimuli

Possible language effects should be measured with verbal tasks. By eliciting motion events in the oral mode, it is assumed that the time available is much more limited and that speakers rely on the links between L1/L2 forms and L2/L1 equivalents, which also entails a reliance on L1/L2 mediated concepts. In cases where lexicalised and grammaticised concepts are distinct in L1 and L2, conceptual transfer is expected (Jarvis & Pavlenko 2010: 120). Furthermore, in order to identify lexical gaps and explain a possible avoidance of Manner verbs in the participants' performance (e.g. by the use of Generic verbs), an additional verbal task testing the participants specific Manner verb lexicon should be reconsidered as well.

5.1.4 Criteria of analysis

In §2.1.2.1 the argument was put forward that an assessment of language dominance should be subdivided into domain and dimension and comprise different measurements, in order to attain a more reliable dominance profile for each bilingual speaker.

As regards future motion research, §3.2.6 indicates the need of substantial extensions and refinements, since "the traditional distinction with the focus on the use of verb types is not sufficient" (Goschler 2013: 128). Therefore, the linguistic analysis should cover, besides verb conflation, the verbal periphery (adnominal and adverbal encoding), and resulting motion event constructions (combinations of motion verbs and other linguistic devices) which would also provide information about Path elaboration (Plus- vs. Minus-Ground) in greater detail. Furthermore, the analysis of specific motion event types (here Path focus vs. boundary focus) can cover language-specific constraints which lead to a speaker's different conceptualisation. Since bilingual speakers are under study, we can expect inter-individual performances. Thus, the methodical approach should provide in addition to quantitative, also qualitative statistical analyses (which have usually been neglected in empirical motion research).

5.2 Research questions and hypotheses

Two main implications were drawn from the research findings in the monolingual and bilingual acquisition of German, French and Turkish. According to these different aspects, the illustration of the empirical investigation is divided into two studies.

First, bilingual speakers develop their language skills differently compared to monolinguals of the respective languages. According to their L1 and L2, bilinguals are not only dominant in one language but may display different dominance patterns concerning domains and dimensions. However for Turkish-German and Turkish-French bilinguals, there is a consensus in the literature that language dominance shifts by age eight. Nevertheless, we assume that individual language use (domain) can prevent language dominance shift in dimension. This object of investigation is focused in Study 1 (6.1) by examining language dominance patterns (domain and dimension) among Turkish-German and Turkish French bilinguals. The first study addresses the following research questions:
1. Are there intra- and inter-group differences among Turkish-German and Turkish-French bilinguals according to language dominance patterns (domain, dimension)?
2. Does a dominance in L1 in domain prevent an L1>L2-dominance shift in dimension? Thus, is L1/L2 language use (with parents, siblings and peers as well as media/reading activity) interconnected with language skills (verbal fluency, code-mixing) and language knowledge (lemma diversity) in L1/L2?

Based on the theoretical background established in Chapter 1 the following hypotheses are tested in Study 1:

H_0	There is no differences between L1 and L2 with respect to language dominance in domain and dimension by Turkish-German and Turkish-French bilinguals.
H_1	Language dominance (domain) is related to the interlocutor.
$H_{1.1}$	Turkish-German and Turkish-French bilinguals are dominant in their L1 as regards language use with parents.
$H_{1.2}$	Turkish-German and Turkish-French bilinguals are dominant in their L2 as regards language use with siblings and peers.
H_2	Turkish-German and Turkish-French bilinguals with an "L1-dominance" in domain are L1-dominant in dimension
H_3	Turkish-German and Turkish-French bilinguals with L2-dominance in domain are also L2 dominant as regards verbal fluency, lemma diversity and code-mixing.

Second, when analysing the three languages with respect to language-specific patterns, it seems more beneficial to shift away from Talmy's bipartite distinction of a V- and an S-typology and to look more closely at the respective language profile – the structures provided by the respective language – for expressing motion events and speakers' usage-based preferences. As documented in §3.2.6 Turkish and French speakers display preferences for the V-pattern with some intra-typological exceptions, while German speakers clearly prefer the S-pattern. Taking a typological continuum into account, Turkish and French are farer from prototypical V-languages (such as Spanish) as regards encoding Manner in main verbs. Furthermore, both languages provide typical S-patterns which are also used in everyday speech. Since multiple "pseudo-satellite"-constructions (such as verb + case and/or Path adverb combinations) are more restricted in French, Turkish is considered more Path-salient than French.

It is predicted that young speakers follow the typical pattern of their native languages. However, they are generally restricted with respect to their cognitive capacities, which have an impact on the encoding process. Moreover, bilingual speakers acquiring two typologically different languages must learn both particular patterns provided by their native languages, which entails cross-linguistic transfer or convergence of the challenging patterns. This may also occur in a situation where speakers acquire two languages of the same type, given the fact that languages also vary intra-typologically. Furthermore, younger children frequently avoid the use of complex structures and use Generic verbs, which might be due to an age related language development or to lexical gaps. Study 2 (6.2) focuses on cross-linguistic influences in oral motion event descriptions by Turkish-German and Turkish-French child bilinguals, in order to evaluate the impact of language

5.2 Research questions and hypotheses

specific properties in the context of early second language acquisition. The study addresses the following research questions:

Are there inter- and intra-group differences in the encoding of motion events in L1 and L2 between the groups tested with regard to

- the proportion and diversity of Manner, Path, Manner-Path and Generic motion verbs?
- the proportion of expressing Manner and Path in other linguistic devices?
- the proportion of combining Manner, Path, Manner-Path and Generic verbs with other linguistic devices and the elaboration of Path?
- the proportion of expressing Manner and Path in verb roots in locative and telic Path phrases?
- the motion verb repertoire which can explain individual motion verb choices?

Based on the theoretical and empirical background established in Chapters 1–3 the following hypotheses are tested in Study 2:

H_0 Turkish-German and Turkish-French bilinguals do not differ when comparing the groups with each other and with minimal bilingual speakers;

H_1 Turkish-German and Turkish-French bilinguals exhibit an "in-between performance" in L1 and L2 inasmuch as they differ in their performance in comparison with minimal bilingual speakers of the respective languages;

$H_{1.1}$ Turkish-German bilinguals differ in their performance in German when comparing them with German minimal bilinguals;

$H_{1.2}$ Turkish-French bilinguals differ in their performance in French when comparing them with French minimal bilinguals;

$H_{1.3}$ Turkish-German and Turkish-French bilinguals differ in their performance in Turkish descriptions when comparing the groups with each other and with Turkish minimal bilinguals.

Furthermore, the findings of Study 1 are taken into account to further specify the possible direction of cross-linguistic influence in relation to the relative dominance of the bilinguals' two languages. The following research question and hypotheses are included in Study 2 as well:

Does L1/L2-dominance impact the direction of L1/L2 influence in motion event encoding?

H_0 Language dominance does not impact the direction of cross-linguistic influence in Turkish-German and Turkish-French bilinguals' motion expressions;

- **H₁** Language dominance impacts the direction of cross-linguistic influence in Turkish-German and Turkish-French bilinguals' motion expressions;
- **H₁.₁** Turkish-German and Turkish-French bilinguals display a higher degree of L2 influence on Turkish when they are L2 dominant in domain and dimension;
- **H₁.₂** Turkish-German and Turkish-French bilinguals display a higher degree of L1 influence on their L2 when they are L1 dominant in domain and dimension.

To summarise, the current study investigates language dominance patterns, the expression of voluntary motion in the transition from a V- (Turkish) to an S-language (German) and within a transition from a V- (Turkish) to a V-language (French). In addition, the study explores the relation of language dominance patterns (Study 1) and motion encoding strategies (Study 2).

6 Methodology

6.1 Participants

The following presentation is based on the parental questionnaires. For the questionnaires' coding procedure see §6.5.

6.1.1 Age, sex and residence

The studies on linguistic development in German, Turkish and French, mentioned above, indicate that children approach adult-like performance from ten years on (with some restrictions in French and Turkish with respect to complex sentence structure). In order to presume an equalised cognitive development and to minimise an effect of foreign language learning, participants recruited for the study were around ten years of age (M=9;8; SD=0.50, R=9;0–11;6). In total, there were 74 participants in the study: minimal bilingual speakers of German (N=15), minimal bilingual speakers of Turkish (N=15), minimal bilingual speakers of French (N=14[38]), bilingual speakers of Turkish and German (N=15) and bilingual speakers of Turkish and French (N=15) (see overview in Table 11).

Minimal bilinguals grew up with the respective majority language as first language (German, Turkish or French) and have had a minimal exposure to a second language (in this context English as an early first foreign language, see Table 13 below). Bilingual participants grew up with Turkish as first or family language and had exposure to the majority language on a daily basis before age six.

Turkish-French bilinguals were recruited from a suburban public primary school as well as from a Turkish cultural association which regularly offers afternoon and holiday activities to Turkish minority children, both situated in the suburban area Canteleu in Rouen/France.[39] Turkish-German bilinguals were recruited from a public primary school in Berlin/Germany[40] which is situated

---

[38] One participant was excluded afterwards from the minimal bilingual French group, since one of her parents spoke Arabic with her on a daily basis. One parent of the minimal bilingual German group is of Austrian origin, but the participant (Sophie) has not been excluded.
[39] I am very grateful for the help and assistance of Prof. Mehmet-Ali Akıncı (Université Rouen II), and all the teachers who have supported the data collection, in particular Ayşenur Catak and Marceau Privat.
[40] I am very grateful for the help and assistance of Prof. Christoph Schroeder (Universität Potsdam), and all the teachers who have supported the data collection, in particular Ursula Rasch, Ulrike Bruns and Susanne Löffler.

Table 11: Number, sex, and age (mean (*M*), standard deviation (*SD*), and range (*R*)) of Turkish-German and Turkish-French bilinguals as well as German, Turkish and French minimal bilingual participants.

Group	Total		Sex		Age		
	N	f	m	M		SD	R
TURGER	15	8	7	9;9		0.44	9;3–10;8
TURFRE	15	8	7	10;1		0.41	9;5–10;9
GER	15	6	9	9;9		0.60	9;0–11;6
TUR	15	9	6	9;5		0.46	9;0–10;2
FRE	14	8	6	9;5		0.31	9;0–9;8
Total	74	39	35				
mean				9;8		0.50	9;0–11;6

in a working-class district (Wedding). French minimal bilingual speakers were recruited from the school, which offers L1-instruction (*ELCO*) in Rouen/Canteleu. Nine German minimal bilingual speakers were recruited from the same school in Berlin/Wedding and six from a public primary school in a working-class district in Munich (Neu-Perlach). Turkish minimal bilingual speakers attended a public primary school in Adana/Turkey which is also situated in a working-class district.[41] All the participants were attending their fourth year in elementary school.

6.1.2 Migration context

The numbers in Table 12 show that the bilingual speakers were (almost) all born in Germany or France. Two participants were born in Turkey, but both moved to Germany/France before the age of six. The parents were all native speakers of Turkish of the first, intermediate 1.5 or second immigrant generation and reflect the endogamy pattern of Turkish minorities addressed in §2.3.1. Eight participants in each group belong to the second generation, since their parents were both born in Turkey, whereas only one participant (Dana) belongs to the third generation (both parents were born in Germany). Four Turkish-German and six Turkish-French participants belong to the intermediate 2.5 generation, since one

---

[41] I am very grateful for the help and assistance of Şenel Yılmaz and all the teachers who have supported the data collection.

parent was born in Turkey, the other in Germany/France. Despite some missing questionnaire responses, we can conclude that most of the immigrated parents have a long-term residency in Germany/France.

Table 12: Birthplace and migration information of Turkish-German, Turkish-French bilinguals, German, Turkish, and French minimal bilinguals.

	TURGER	TURFRE	GER	TUR	FRE
Quest. Total	13	14	13	15	5
Birth Children					
in GER/FR	12	13	15		14
in TUR	1	1		15	
Birth Parents					
Both in GER/FR	1	0			
one in GER/FR; one in TR	4	6			
both in TR	8	8			
immigrated parent live in Germany/France	20	22			
...longer than 20 years	8*	7*			
...longer than 10 years	7*	8*			
...less than 10 years	2*	2*			

* incomplete questionnaires

6.1.3 Acquisition context

All bilingual participants acquired Turkish as their family language and German/French as an early L2.[42] For most of the participants the age of acquisition can be determined by the age of three, since they all attended a kindergarten, where German or French was the instructed language. However, some bilinguals had

---

[42] Interestingly, in the (oral) child questionnaires four Turkish-French bilinguals considered French as their mother tongue, three both languages and eight Turkish, whereas all Turkish-German bilinguals indicated that Turkish was their mother tongue. One child (Esna) reported that her mother's origin was Greece, but that she never spoke Greek but only Turkish and German to her; another child (Tuana), who was excluded from the current study, reported that Kurdish and Turkish were her family languages (see Brizić 2006 for this case of "the secret life of languages").

Table 13: Acquisition background information of Turkish-German and Turkish-French bilinguals.

	TURGER	TURFRE	GER	TUR	FRE
Quest. Total	13	14	13	15	5
AoO L2 Children					
<3 years*	4	1			
≈3 years	8	11			
>3 ≤6 years	1* (3)	1* (2)			
>6 years			13* (15)	15	5* (14)
Language disorder					
attended logopedician	2	2	4	1	1
L1 instruction					
None	1	5*			
L1 instruction (in/outside school)	0	7*			
bilingual education	12	0			
Length of L2/L3 instruction					
<3 years	11* (15)	13* (15)	13* (15)	15	5* (14)

* incomplete questionnaires

extensive contact to German/French before entering kindergarten.[43] The AoO of the two bilinguals, who were born in Turkey, is determined later, by age five. Note that two parental questionnaires in the bilingual Turkish-German group, one in the bilingual Turkish-French group, two in the minimal bilingual German group and ten in the minimal bilingual French group, were incomplete. On the basis of the information by the respective children given in the (oral) child questionnaire,[44] as well as the respective school curricula, the missing values were added in parenthesis in Table 13. Based on the definition of child bilingualism in §2.1.1 all bilingual participants can be considered child bilinguals.

---

[43] Extensive contact was determined when answers in the parental questionnaires included at least three items of the following: Contact i) with German/French in family (and at least one parent was born in Germany/France or moved before ten years of age); ii) with acquaintance; iii) with other children; iv) in L2 speaking daycare (see questionnaire items QBILPAR9.2, QBILPAR14.1–15.2 in Appendix B.III.a).

[44] The bilingual children indicated that they were born in Germany/France. Therefore we can conclude that their AoO of German/French can be determined before age six. In the French school, where the data collection took place, English classes start in *CE2* (around age seven); in the German school in Berlin, where the data collection took place, English classes start in the third class (around age eight).

Two parents in each bilingual group, one parent in each, Turkish and French minimal bilingual group, and four parents in the minimal bilingual German group reported that their child attended a logopedician in earlier childhood because of language disorders. However, the participants were not excluded from the current study, since they do not differ from other speakers of the respective group as regards their grammatical errors produced in the different tasks.

Both bilingual groups receive additive instructions in Turkish, however, the picture is much more diverse. Whereas from the first grade on, almost all Turkish-German bilinguals attended a biliteracy program, in which instruction in Turkish and German is coordinated in regular classes (five hours a week and two hours "only-Turkish"-instruction), only seven Turkish-French bilinguals attended L1-instruction (*ELCO*, see §2.3.2), or private classes offered by Turkish cultural associations (in average two hours per week).

Both bilingual groups started learning English as a first foreign language (L3) in elementary school (mostly one to two hours per week). None of the participants have had exposure to English for more than three years.

6.1.4 Educational background

Table 14 summarises the individual (number of reached categories per group, see §6.5) and group mean scores (reached levels per group) of all available parental information (as noted above, some questionnaires were not completed or were incomplete). The mean educational level of bilinguals' and minimal bilinguals' Turkish parents is quite similar, whereas the mean of German minimal bilinguals'

Table 14: Mean (*M*) and numbers of parental educational levels.

	Questionnaire numbers		PARENTAL EDUCATION		
		M	*Low* (ISCED levels 0–2)	*Medium* (ISCED levels 3–5)	*High* (ISCED levels 6–8)
TURGER	13	3.5	5	5	3
TURFRE	14	2.9	3*	9*	0*
GER	13	5.3	3	1	9
TUR	15	3.1	6	7	3
FRE	5	3.8	0	4	1
mean		3.7			

* incomplete questionnaires

parents is much higher. Because of the high number of missing questionnaires, the results of the minimal bilinguals' French parents are of very little significance. In general, the individual results indicate a high heterogeneity across all groups. This fact implies some limitations for the current study, insofar as the educational variable can only be used for individual (qualitative) interpretations.

6.2 Design

The data of the study were gathered with different stimuli eliciting speakers' specific motion verbs and voluntary motion expressions. Furthermore, questionnaires were used in order to gather extra-linguistic information.

6.2.1 Manner Verb Control Task

A Manner Verb Control Task (hereafter MVC-Task) was designed for explicitly eliciting the speakers' encoding of Manner of motion. The task serves to controlling a speaker's Manner verb lexicon and identify lexical gaps in order to explain a possible avoidance of Manner verbs in the participants' performance. The MVC-Task consists of 30 short video clips (five to ten seconds), where a Figure performs different types of motion.[45] In eleven test items (target events), the Figure performs different kinds of Motion where Manner is focused on (see Table 15). The test items were randomised with 18 fillers, showing daily routine actions (to cut, to eat, to blow one's nose, to dress, to write, to fill, to pour in, to bind, to unlock, to sleep, to light, to screw the top on, to sit, to drink, to read, to wash one's hands).

6.2.2 Voluntary Motion Task

In order to elicit different types of voluntary motion events the Voluntary Motion Task (hereafter VM-Task) was adopted. The task comprises eight sequences of an animated cartoon ("Sylvester and Tweety"). Most of the selected sequences were drawn from the episode "Canary row", which has been used by several studies investigating the encoding of motion events (McNeill 2001). In addition, two sequences of other "Sylvester and Tweety" episodes were added. In the selected sequences the Figures (mostly a cat "Sylvester" and a bird "Tweety") perform

---

[45] I am very grateful for the help and assistance of Fabian Bross.

Table 15: Test items and target events of the Manner Verb Control Task.

Item no.	Description	Target event	Expected GERMAN	Expected TURKISH	Expected FRENCH
2b	A man climbing up a tree.	CLIMB (UP)	klettern	tırmanmak	Grimper
3b	A man running in front of a building.	RUN	rennen	koşmak	Courir
4b	A man rolling down a hill.	ROLL (DOWN)	rollen	yuvarlanmak	Rouler
5b	A bird flying in the sky.	FLY	fliegen	uçmak	Voler
6b	A man jumping from a tree.	JUMP (DOWN)	springen	atlamak	Sauter
7b	A man balancing on a bench.	BALANCE	balancieren	dengelemek	[faire l'équilibre]
8b	A man swinging with a rope into a lake.	SWING	schwingen	sallanmak	Enjamber
10b	A man hopping over a wall.	HOP	hüpfen	hoplamak	Sautiller
11b	A man sneaking across a corridor towards a door.	SNEAK	schleichen	-	[faufiler]
12b	A man creeping under a table.	CREEP	kriechen/ krabbeln	sürünmek	Ramper
14b	A child falling from a pole.	FALL	fallen	düşmek	Tomber

various actions (running, climbing, rolling, flying, swinging, jumping, balancing, falling, creeping, sneaking) in telic (e.g. runs into a house, rolls into a bowling alley, falls out of the drainpipe) locative (e.g. rolls down the street, runs along the wires etc.) and vertical (e.g. climbs up the drainpipe, falls down the wall) Motion. The task provides all types of motion situations whose encoding is in the cross-linguistic focus of the current study (see Table 16 for an overview of the different motion situations). Note that the task setting (oral retelling) is not suitable for a controlled test design (as is the MVC-Task). Speakers might not verbalise all motion event situations shown in the stimulus. They also might encode motion events which are not explicitly shown in the stimulus, but can be inferred or invented. In contrast to other motion studies, the focus of this task is on the speakers' encoding strategies.

Table 16: Types of elicited motion event situations.

Order of presentation	Task number	Type of motion event	Cardinals of displacement	Event description
1	1	OUT of a bounded space	EX	Sylvester runs out of the house.
2		OVER a plane	TRANS	Sylvester runs over the street.
3		INTO a bounded space	IN	Sylvester runs into the house.
4		INTO a bounded space	IN	Sylvester falls into trash.
5	2	UP	SUPER	Sylvester climbs up the drainpipe.
6		OUT of a bounded space	EX	Tweety flies out of the cage.
7		INTO a bounded space	IN	Tweety flies in the window.
8		INTO a bounded space	IN	Sylvester runs in the window.
9	3	INTO a bounded space	IN	Sylvester climbs into a drainpipe.
10		UP	SUPER	Sylvester climbs up the drainpipe.
11	4	OUT of a bounded space	EX	Sylvester falls out of the drainpipe
12		DOWN	DE	Sylvester rolls down the street.
13		INTO a bounded space	IN	Sylvester rolls into a bowling alley.
14	5	OVER a plane	TRANS	Sylvester swings across from his building to Tweety's building with a rope.
15		DOWN	DE	Sylvester falls down the wall.
16	6	UP	SUPER	Sylvester climbs up a pylon.
17		ALONG a plane	AD	Sylvester balances on the wires.
18		ALONG a plane	AD	Sylvester runs along the wires.
19	7	INTO a bounded space	IN	Sylvester sneaks into the garden.
20		PASS through a bounded space	PRO	Sylvester creeps through the dogs.
21	8	ALONG a plane	AD	Sylvester runs along the boardwalk.
22		DOWN	DE	Sylvester climbs down the wall.
23		INTO a bounded space	IN	Sylvester climbs into a boat.

6.2.3 Sociolinguistic questionnaires

In order to obtain information about bilingual speakers' linguistic input, language use and dominance, three questionnaires were designed. First, a questionnaire for parents of the bilingual participants provides information about the speakers' biographical (date and place of birth, length of resistance), linguistic (AoO of L2, foreign language acquisition, family language, language disorder, L1 instruction) and the parents' biographical and educational background. Second, a questionnaire for the bilingual participants provides information about the sociolinguistic background (language use and preferences at home and outside with family members and peers; language use and preferences with respect to literacy and digital media). A questionnaire for parents of the monolingual participants is limited to information about the speakers biographical (age, place of birth), linguistic (second/foreign language acquisition, language disorder) and the parents' biographical and educational background.

6.3 Data collection procedure

The data for this investigation were collected in separated classrooms in the participants' schools in Berlin (Germany), Adana (Turkey) and Rouen (France) as well as in a Turkish cultural association in Rouen (France). After bringing a letter of permission from their parents, each participant performed the different tasks individually with assistant investigators who were native speakers of the respective language[46] and instructed only to speak the language of the actual investigation. To ensure that the elicitation procedure was consistent, an instruction sheet in German, French and Turkish had been distributed beforehand and discussed with the assistant investigators (for more information see Appendix B.I).

The investigators started each interview with a small talk in the language of investigation, before introducing the first task. The aim was to create a comfortable environment and place the bilingual participants in a minimal bilingual mode. All tasks were performed on a laptop with colour screen and recorded with a digital voice recorder in the following order.

---

[46] I am very grateful for the help and assistance of Başak Akbıyık, Merve Düzgün, Kurt Bilgin Gürel, Büşra Hamurcu, Alican Kocabiyikoğlu, Merve Tekir, Anıl Türe, Eda Yilmaz, Seda Yilmaz Woerfel & Şenel Yılmaz (elicitation in Turkish); Mehmet-Ali Akıncı, Manon Anquetin, Katia Cauchois, Clementine Carlin, Jeanne Conseil, Marie Darcy, Amélie Jullien, Nolwenn Lacoume, Pauline van Poucke, Rüveyda Şentürk, Onur Üçler, Marine Verney (elicitation in French); Tamara Demberger (elicitation in German).

The first task was the VM-Task. The video was not shown at once, but in eight sequences. Participants were asked to retell what they saw in each video sequence. In order to get more detailed descriptions, it was made clear that the investigators acted as if they did not know the video at all ("When the video is finished, I'd like you to tell me what happened. Please watch carefully, since I don't know the videos and I am not going to watch with you."). In cases in which a participant did not remember the scene, they were asked to review the scene. In cases in which participants provided very poor descriptions, the investigator encouraged the participants to retell a scene ("I didn't understand exactly what happened, please would you tell me again"). In cases of lexical gaps, the investigator encouraged describing the missing word and/or gave assistance to them (only with specific nouns, such as "drainpipe", but never with verbs).

The second task was the MVC-Task. Participants were instructed to watch the videos carefully and tell after every video what the Figure was doing. In cases of lexical gaps, the investigators were instructed to act as they did in the first task.

In a third step, the investigator completed the sociolinguistic questionnaire together with the bilingual speakers in the L2 in a structured oral interview, which allow the gathering of some more detailed and further information. Additionally, the parents of each participant completed the parental questionnaire at home. All interviews with the bilingual participants were first done in the L2. Task 1 and 2 were repeated in the L1 at least a month later, in order to minimise translation effects.

6.4 Transcription

The system EXMARaLDA (Extensible Markup Language for Discourse Annotation)[47] was used for preparing and analysing the elicited spoken data (VM-Task and MVC-Task). It is a system of concepts, data formats and tools for the computer assisted transcription and annotation of spoken language, and for the construction and analysis of spoken language corpora (Schmidt & Wörner 2009). A transcription manual has been developed for all three languages adapting the transcription system HIAT (*Halbinterpretative Arbeitstranskriptionen* 'Semi-Interpretative

---

[47] EXMARaLDA is available free and was originally developed in the project "Computer assisted methods for the creation and analysis of multilingual data" at the Collaborative Research Centre "Multilingualism" (Sonderforschungsbereich "Mehrsprachigkeit" SFB 538) at the University of Hamburg. Since July 2011, the development of EXMARaLDA has been continued at the Hamburg Centre for Language Corpora, since November 2011 in cooperation with the Archive for Spoken German at the Institute for German Language in Mannheim. For further details see http://www.exmaralda.org/en_index.html [accessed 2018-01-15].

Working Transcriptions')[48] and the GAT (Gesprächsanalytisches Transkriptionssystem 2, Selting et al. 2009) convention for the analysis of prosody. The main features of the transcription convention and their notation symbols are summarised in the following:

- the speaker's speech (what they have actually said, including dialectal characteristics) was transcribed in lower case, but with specific German, French and Turkish orthography (normalised speech is transcribed in another supplement tier)
  Ex.: **sone**=so eine 'such a', **geklettat**=geklettert 'climbed'; **gadın**=kadın 'the woman', **aşağa**=aşağıya 'towards down'; **p'tit** = petit 'small', **i**=il 'he')
- repairs or word truncation are marked with a slash < / >
  Ex.: **rausgegeg / rausgegang** 'out.went')
- intonation patterns at the end of an utterance are marked with a question mark < ? > (rising intonation), a comma < , > (slight rising or slight falling intonation), or a dot < . > (falling intonation). Slight rises or falls in intonation that occur within utterances are not transcribed
  Ex.: tweety war am käfich , und hat sylvesta zugeschaut ,
  'tweety was in the cage , and he was watching sylvester ,'
- the speaker's speech (what she/he has actually said) is transcribed in lower case, but with specific German, French and Turkish orthography (normalised speech is transcribed in another supplement tier)
- Pauses within and between utterances are measured in seconds (s) and transcribed using the HIAT notation symbols: < • > (very short pause = 0.25 s), < • • > (short pause = 0.5 s), < • • • > (pause = 0.75s) and < ((_s)) > (measured pauses ≥ 1.0 s, e.g. ((1.8s))).
- Unfilled Pauses within a word are transcribed with a hyphen < - >
  Ex.: ge-laufen 'wal-ked'
- Filled pauses which denote hesitation disfluency are transcribed with < **em, mh, ee** >[49]
  Ex.: und ers dann **em** • • raufgeklettat 'and then he em climbed up'
- Completely incomprehensible words and utterances are transcribed with < **((incomprehensible))** >

---

[48] HIAT is used predominantly in functional-pragmatic discourse analysis. It was developed in the 1970s by Konrad Ehlich and Jochen Rehbein. The use of HIAT with EXMARaLDA is recommended in the EXMARaLDA manual (Rehbein et al. 2004), since it provides instructions for notation of typical spoken language phenomena and can be used for multilinguality in transcription and instructions.

[49] When using in-text examples taken from a transcription, we will use square brackets [[em]] for a better visual separation (e.g. und ers dann [[em]] • • raufgeklettat.

In the first step the data was transcribed with EXMARaLDA Partitur Editor which is a tool for inputting, editing and outputting transcriptions in partitur notation. Since the mastery of a native language is a basic requirement for transcribing linguistic data (Rehbein et al. 1993:104), all transcriptions were made by native speakers[50] of the respective language. All transcribers were trained in advance with respect to the specific requirements of the transcription tool and conventions.

6.5 Coding and analysis

6.5.1 Voluntary Motion Task

In the following step the transcriptions were manually annotated. The linguistic annotation of the VM-Task comprises nine annotation tiers, in order to analyse the data with respect to the specific hypotheses. For each category, annotation tags have been specified (see Table 106, Appendix B.II), which were tagged according to the respective event in the transcription. Tiers 1–4 serve to determine language dominance on the level of dimensions (see §2.1.2.1):

1. Task [TASK]
2. Utterances [UTTER]
3. Verbal fluency [LD_PAUSES]
4. Code-mixing [LD_CS]
5. Type of event [EVENT]
6. Motion verb choice [VCONF]
7. Linguistic device [LINGDEV]
8. Verb construction [VCONST]
9. Path elaboration [ELAB]

1. Task

The respective task (video sequence), which was re-narrated by a speaker, was tagged according to the task number indicated in Table 16. Tagging the different tasks serves for determining the amount of disfluency signals per utterance in a respective task and the statistical analysis.

---

[50] I am deeply grateful for the work of Vanessa Goetzendorff (German transcriptions), Sibylle Béchet and Katharina Scholtz (French transcriptions), as well as Arzu Batmaz and Elif Güney (Turkish transcriptions).

2. Utterances

For the current study, utterances are defined as a unit of talk, bounded by the speaker's silence or intonation pattern at the end of a complete or incomplete clause (rise, fall). Thus, utterances can include only one clause or more as well as repetitions, self-corrections and truncations and were tagged on the [UTTER]-tier.

3. Verbal fluency

In this study we include unfilled and filled pauses (as well as repairs or word truncation) as "hesitation and monitoring phenomena" (Hlavac 2011). Unfilled pauses are not necessarily markers of utterance boundaries, but can signal "how speakers search memory and monitor their search, displaying meta-cognitive states of lexical retrieval" (Hlavac 2011:3794; see also Brennan & Williams 1995). Most of the studies include shorter pauses (≤0.25 s) as disfluency signals (among others O'Connell & Kowal 2005). In this study, we only draw the line at the level of ≥1.0 s for unfilled pauses as a true sign of disfluency. Furthermore, we differentiate between protosyntactic unfilled pauses and disfluency. As an illustration, in example (76) the protosyntactic unfilled pause at the beginning and at the end of the utterance is not tagged as disfluency. Only unfilled pauses ≥1.0 s, which occur within utterances or after a truncation were tagged as hesitation disfluency on the [LD_PAUSES]-tier. Filled pauses that are sounds such as < mh, em, ee, bah >, which occur between words (see (77)), but not at the beginning or the end of an utterance (unfilled pauses frequently occur with expressions such as *und dann/ danach* 'and then/afterwards', see example (76)), were also tagged as hesitation disfluency.

(76) • *hat   das   seil   abgeschnittn* , ((1,5s)) *und* •   [[em]] •   *dann*
      AUX.PR   DET   rope   =off.cut.PTCP   and   then
      is   das • •   *kanu   gesunkn*
      AUX.PR   the   canoe   =sink.PTCP

'He cut off the rope and then the canoe sank' (Eda, TURGER, 1522–1537)[51]

---

[51] In examples, tables, figures as well as group specific percentages given in the text the following abbreviations are used: TURGER=Turkish-German bilinguals; TURFRE=Turkish-French bilinguals; GER = German minimal bilinguals; TUR = Turkish minimal bilinguals; FRE = French minimal bilinguals. In examples, the speakers' pseudonym as well as the tier numbers within the respective transcription are further indicated.

(77) un   danach   is   [[ee]]   aus   dem   käfisch [[em]] • •
      =and   then   =AUX.PR   from   DET.DAT   =cage
      käfisch [[ee]]((1,8s)) raus   geflogn
      =cage   out   =fly.PTCP

'And then he ... ee ... from the cage ... em ... cage ... ee ... flew out' (Sefar, TURGER, 248–261)

Figure 16 illustrates an extract of the transcription of the speaker Beren. The speech was transcribed at the transcription tier (Beren [v]) and normalised at the [%norm] tier. The respective task, which was re-narrated, was tagged on the [TASK]-tier. According to the intonation patterns < , > utterance boundaries were tagged on the [UTTER]-tier. The sound < em > followed by a pause < ((1.2s)) >, both were defined as disfluency and thus tagged on the [LD_PAUSES]-tier.

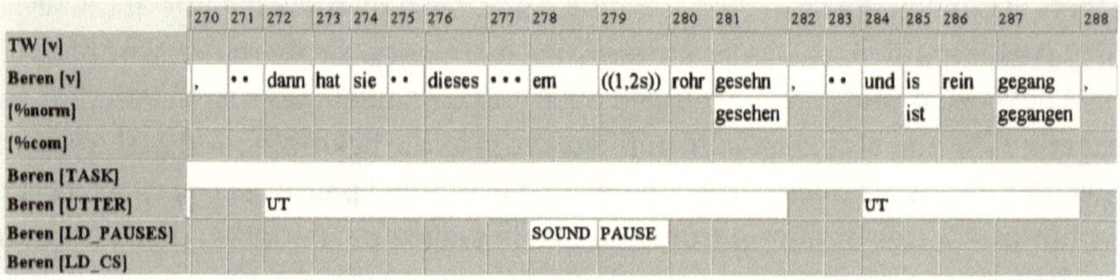

Figure 16: Annotation of utterances and hesitation disfluency in EXMARaLDA.

4. Code-mixing

In the current study, code-mixing in a transcript is defined as any detectable morpheme, word or utterance from the other language, which was not the language of investigation. Figure 17 shows an example of the speaker Nihal, who morphologically integrates the French noun *tuyau* 'pipe' within her Turkish re-narration. This type of insertion was tagged on the [LD_CS]-tier specifying also the direction of mixing (L2>L1).

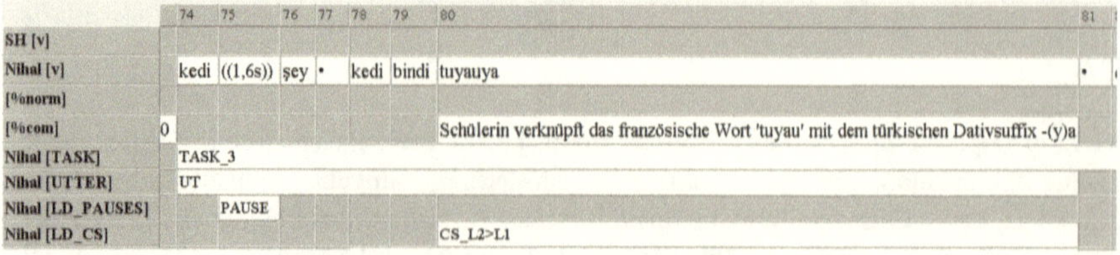

Figure 17: Annotation of code-mixing/switching in EXMARaLDA.

In regard to motion event descriptions, only voluntary motion expressions were considered for the analysis. These include motion verb constructions in main clauses and subordinate clauses.

Subsequent repetitions of motion events, such as in (78), were annotated once. Motion events, which have been expressed because of an intervention of the interlocutor, were only tagged when the event had not been expressed before. If the same event had been repeated by using a different motion verb, only the first description was tagged. Truncations were not tagged at all.

(78) un   danach   is   er   zu-m •   bowling   gegang , ((1,6s))
     and   then   AUX.3SG   he   =to-DET.DAT bowling   =go.PTCP
     ja .   nach   is   er   zu   bowling   gegang
     yes   =then   =AUX.3SG   he   to   bowling   =go.PTCP
     'Then he went to the bowling, ((1,6s)), yes then he went to the bowling'
     (Dana, TURGER 444–461)

Annotation tiers 5–9 serve for the specific analysis of motion event encoding, established in §3.2.6:

5. Type of event

On the basis of the expressed motion construction in a transcript, specific motion event types were tagged on the [EVENTTYPE]-tier by using cardinal kinds of displacement (see §3.2.5.3). Motion events, where Path was not specified in the verb or by another linguistic device (e.g. "(because) she ran"), were considered as GENERALIS event types. Only verbs, which do not require a Path device to specify the direction of motion because Path is unambiguously encoded in the verb stem, were tagged with the respective cardinal kinds (*girmek/entrer* 'to enter' (IN), *sortir* 'to exit' (EX), *monter* 'to ascend' (SUPER), *descendre* 'to descend' (DE)).[52]

This procedure allows an analysis of the overall expressed motion event types by a speaker or a group. Furthermore, individual and group specific preferences of motion verb choices in motion event types with boundary (telic Path phrases) and Path focus (locative Path phrases) can be determined.

---

[52] Although the verbs *kommen/gelmek/venir* 'to come' and *gehen/gitmek/aller* 'to go' have some deictic reading as well as Manner-Path verbs such as *fallen/düşmek/tomber* 'to fall', *klettern/ tırmanmak/grimper* 'to climb' encode Path in the verb stem, they are all tagged as GENERALIS in cases where the direction is not specified by another linguistic device.

6. Motion verb choice

In order to analyse individual and group specific preferences for motion verb choices, any expressed motion verb which was considered on the [EVENTTYPE]-tier was tagged on the [CONFPAT]-tier by using the following categories: Manner verb (VM), Manner-Path verb (VMP), Path verb (VP), Generic verb (VGEN). Additionally, modal verbs and other intentional non-motion verbs such as *versuchen*, *çalışmak*, *essayer* 'to try', *beginnen*, *başlamak*, *commencer* 'to begin', *aufhören*, *arrêter* 'to stop' were tagged as [VMOD] in cases when they were combined with Manner, Manner-Path, Path or Generic infinitives/nominalisations or with Path devices. Other motion infinitives with *um zu*, *pour* or *-mEk için* '(in order) to' were not further specified but also included in the analysis.

In order to consider motion event expressions without motion verb, auxiliary verbs (VAUX) were tagged in German, when they were combined with Path devices. Other motion constructions (VLV) with semantically weak verbs such as *machen*, *faire*, *yapmak* 'to make' were tagged in cases when they were combined with Manner devices.

Generally motion/modal/other verbs were reconsidered which were used as finite verbs in main and subordinate clauses. For structural differences between the three languages involved, some Turkish non-finite motion verbs were also reconsidered on the [CONFPAT]-tier. Therefore, Turkish motion converbs, which were used as clause linking devices (e.g. *-Ip*, *-ken*, *-IncA*, *diye*, *-dIkten sonra*, see §3.2.6.3), were also tagged on the [CONFPAT]-tier. Note that this relates also to constructions where (non-finite) Path, Manner or Generic converbs are subordinated or coordinated to non-motion verbs (see (79)). However, converbs which were used as Manner or Path adverbials (e.g. *-ErEk*, *-E -E*) and subordinated to a (non) motion verb were not considered on the [CONFPAT]-tier.

Motion verbs, which were corrected by a speaker, were tagged only once. Either the corrected motion verb was tagged or the more expressive (on the basis of the DGD 2 classification). In (80), the Manner verb *kriechen* 'to creep' was tagged instead of *laufen* 'to walk'.

(79) ara-sın-dan   geç-er-ken • •   kedin-in   zil-i   çal-dı
      between-POSS-ABL   pass-AOR-CVB   cat-POSS   bell-ACC   ring-PST.3SG
      'When the cat passed through, it rang (the bell)' (Sevgi, TUR, 410–416)

(80) und   ist   dann   ganz   nach   oben • [[ee]] •   also • •
      and   AUX.PR   then   completely   to   above   well
      gelaufn . • •   gekrochn
      =walk.PTCP   =creep.PTCP
      'And then he walked to the top, he crept' (Eda, TURGER, 342–356)

7. Linguistic devices

Other linguistic devices which express Manner and Path were tagged on the [LINGDEV]-tier, further specifying the part of speech (among others prepositional phrases, separable and inseparable verb prefixes, Manner adverbs, Manner/Path *-ErEk/-E -E* converbs/gerunds, adverbial directionals, case marking, postpositions, see Appendix B.II for further details), in order to get individual and group preferences for expressing Manner and Path outside the motion verb.

8. Verb construction

The verb construction type was tagged on the [VERBCONST]-tier, specifying the combination of the [CONFPAT] and [LINGDEV]-tiers. The part of speech was not further specified, just in the case that Manner, Path or no device was encoded outside the motion verb (e.g. Manner verb was combined with Path and/or Manner device, Path verb was combined with Path and/or Manner device, etc.). Constructions, in which the speaker corrected a motion verb, were tagged only once (the motion construction in (80) was tagged once with [VM_P]).

Furthermore, the tag-set also includes information about main verb and subordinate constructions. Consequently in (81), the main verb construction (*evine giriyo*) was tagged with [VP_P] (Path verb+Path device) and the subordinate (non-finite) construction (*borulara tırmanıp*) with [VCONVM_P] (non-finite Manner(Path) verb+Path device) on the [VERBCONST]-tier. The subordinate (finite) construction in (82) was tagged with [VSC_VGEN_P] (subordinate clause with Generic verb+Path device).

(81) boru-lar-a   tırman-ıp •   o-nun   ev-in-e   gir-iyo
     pipe-PL-DAT   climb-CVB   its-GEN   house-POSS-DAT   =enter-PROG.3SG
     'It climbed to the pipes and entered the house' (Zuhal, TUR, 79–86)

(82) après   il   a   pris   un   baton   pour   [[ee]]   • pour qu'
     later   he   AUX.PR   take.PTCP   INDF   stick   for   four that
     il   puisse   s'   en   aller
     he   can.SBJV   REFL   there   go.INF
     'Then he took a stick, so that he could go there' (Adile, TURFRE, 759–774)

This procedure allows a more adequate comparison on the constructional level between the three languages involved. In turn, constructions, in which the non-finite verb and the main verb relate to the same [EVENTTYPE], were tagged together. In (83), the non-finite element was thus tagged as Manner device in a [Path verb+Path device+Manner device]-construction (VP_P_M).

(83) yuvarlan-arak   bol / bovling   şey-in-e   gir-di
     roll-CVB   bowling   thing-POSS-DAT   enter-PST.3SG
     'It entered into the bowling thing rolling' (Melis, TURGER, 275–281)

Thus, it is possible to obtain individual and group specific constructional preferences of motion event encoding.

9. Path elaboration

Whether a speaker expresses no, one, two (or more) Path elements in one main clause or a separately tagged non-finite clause, was tagged on the [ELAB]-tier in order to analyse individual and group specific Path elaboration.

Figure 18 illustrates the extended extract of the transcription of the speaker Beren. The expressed event type is tagged on the [EVENTTYPE]-tier (*und ist reingegang* 'and he went in' = IN), the motion verb category on the [CONFPAT]-tier (*gehen* 'to go' = VGEN), the linguistic device on the [LINGDEV]-tier (*rein* 'into' = PART), the verb construction on the [VERBCONST]-tier (Generic verb with Path device = VGEN_P), and the Path elaboration on the [ELAB]-tier (one Path element = GROUND_1).

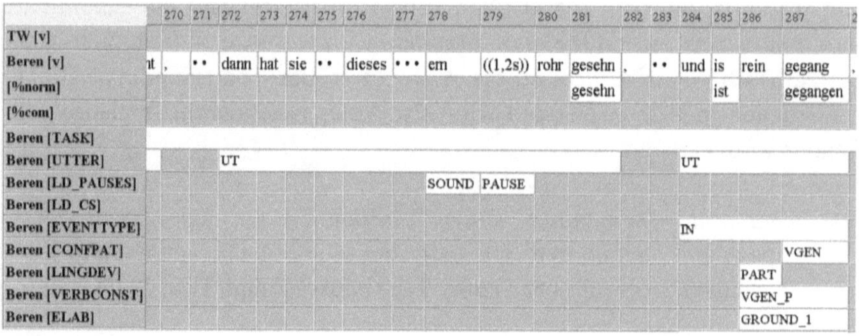

Figure 18: Annotation of specific motion event categories in EXMARaLDA.

In a second step, the transcriptions are merged with EXMARALDA Corpus-Manager (CoMa) in order to generate five subcorpora (bilingual: Turkish-German, Turkish-French; minimal bilingual: German, Turkish, French). The subcorpora are analysed in a third step with the EXMARALDA query tool EXAKT ("EXMARALDA Analysis and Concordancing Tool"), which is a tool for searching transcribed and annotated phenomena in an EXMARALDA corpus. It is then possible to analyse each single annotation tier for each group or individual speaker by using regular expressions and the defined annotation tags as parameters. Furthermore, the annotation tiers

#	S	Communication	Speaker	Left Context	Match	Right Context	CONFPAT	EVENTTYPE
19		tweety_shirin_tr	Shirin	şimdi , • ee	çıktığında	bowling topu karnın a ...	VP	GENERALIS
20		tweety_nezihe_tr	Nezi...	? • • ee elektrik ee • ipleri	bindi	, bi tane de tren keldi , ...	VP	GENERALIS
21		tweety_oezguer_tr	Oez...	sıl diyoduk ((1,2s)) em ((1s))	çıkarmamış	, • • • sonra şey gidyo •...	VP	GENERALIS
22		tweety_nihal_tr	Nihal	şey top onun ee karnının içine	girdi	? • ve bowling e gitti , ...	VP	IN
23		tweety_geza_tr	Geza	dikkatli • •	girmek	istiyo ,	VP	IN
24		tweety_shirin_tr	Shirin	inay a girmek istedi , ama sona	giremedi	. çünkü birisi attı onu v...	VP	IN
25		tweety_shirin_tr	Shirin	yo , • • sona da kedi o binay a	girmek	• istiyo ozaman tırman...	VP	IN
26		tweety_shirin_tr	Shirin	ıktığında bowling topu karnın a	girmiş	sona yuvarlanıyo yuva...	VP	IN
27		tweety_goezde_tr	Goe...	e düşme bi de ? ağzının içine	girdi	? sona da • kediyle top ...	VP	IN
28		tweety_dilsah_tr	Dilsah	• kedi bi tane yani apartman a	girmeye	çalışıyo ee şeyden tır...	VP	IN
29		tweety_dilsah_tr	Dilsah	attığı için . o da • midesin e	girmiş	,	VP	IN
30		tweety_adile_tr	Adile	((1,0)) ee kedinin ee ağzının a	girdi	bide ke / em şey kedi ...	VP	IN
31		tweety_nezihe_tr	Nezi...	k için , • • ama ee apartman ee	giremedi	ozaman ((loughs)) ee ...	VP	IN
32		tweety_bircan_tr	Bircan	burnunu kapatarak suyun altı...	girdi	,	VP	IN
33		tweety_devin_tr	Devin	e binyor , sonra ama • sonra ee	girmeye	çalışıyor , • ama gemi ...	VP	IN
34		tweety_devin_tr	Devin	üyo , ama ee gemi ee su altın a	giriyor	.	VP	IN
35		tweety_maide_tr	Maide	bi tane büyükanne var , • kedi	girmesin	diye içeriy e , • kovalı...	VP	IN
36		tweety_maide_tr	Maide	• ge / bi ta / tre / tren e	bindi	, • orda büyükanne de ...	VP	IN

Figure 19: Analysis of (multiple) annotation tiers with EXAKT

can be related with each other, by adding one or more annotation columns in EXAKT. Figure 19 illustrates an analysis of the motion verb choice [VP] (Path verbs) in the bilingual Turkish-French group and its use in different [EVENTTYPES].

In order to carry out dynamic data analysis according to the requirements for the current study (e.g. the individual proportion of used Path verbs in Turkish in EX-, IN-, PRO- and TRANS-events (telic Path phrases)) it is necessary to enter the results based on the analysis with EXAKT into a spreadsheet.[53] The resulting numbers per individual and group can be entered in the following into a statistics program in order to run descriptive and inferential statistics (for more details see subpoint "Statistical analysis" below).

6.5.2 Manner Verb Control Task

The MVC-Task was transcribed by using the same tool and conventions described above. The transcription exclusively includes speakers' descriptions of the elicited motion event situations; descriptions of fillers were not transcribed at all. Only one motion verb was tagged as a target event per task item. In cases of self-correction, the motion verb, which was semantically closer to the stimulus, was determined as target event (e.g. *atlıyor zı/ • zıplıyor* 'He jumps / hops'). With respect to Turkish, non-finite Manner converbs were tagged when they were semantically closer to the stimulus than the main motion verb to which the converb was subordinated (e.g. in *sallanarak atlıyor* 'She/he jumps swinging' the lemma *sallanmak* was

---

[53] For these kinds of dynamic data analysis the spreadsheet component LibreOffice Calc (Version 4.4.4.3) of the LibreOffice software package was used.

tagged as a target event instead of *atlamak*). However, disregarded lemmas were tagged separately, so that they can serve for individual analysis (for instance when a speaker does not express a disregarded motion verb in the vm-Task).

As shown in an extract of the transcription of the mvc-Task in Turkish, performed by the speaker Eda (see Figure 20), the transcript includes a transcription tier (Eda [v]), a normalisation tier [%norm], and three annotation tiers. The lemma of the expressed motion verb was tagged on the [LEMMA]-tier, the category on the [CONFPAT]-tier and the respective control task item (see Table 15), which was performed, was indicated on the [TASK]-tier.

	15	16	17	18	19	20	21	22	23	24	25	26	27	28	29
KBG [v]															
Eda [v]		adam	ağcının	üstünde	tır	/	tır	/	ee tırlandı	adam	koştu	adam	yur	/	yuvarlandı
[%norm]			ağacın	üstüne					tırmandı						
Eda [LEMMA]									tırmanmak		koşmak				yuvarlanmak
Eda [CONFPAT]									VMP		VM				VM
[%com]															
Eda [TASK]	9	2b								3b		4b			

Figure 20: Transcription and annotation of the lexical control task with EXMARaLDA.

In the following step, the search tool EXAKT, again, allows an analysis of the expressed motion verb lemmas of each individual speaker as well as the lemma frequency of each group tested. Furthermore, it is possible to relate the different annotation tiers in order to gain the number and variation of lemmas in a respective task item. The results of the relation of the annotation columns with EXAKT were entered in the following into a spreadsheet and analysed according to the required information (e.g. the individual amount of used Manner verbs in Turkish in the different target items).

6.5.3 Parental questionnaires

The questionnaire for parents of the bilingual participants comprises a total of 34 questions (see Appendix A.I). For the purpose of the current study, nine questions are not included in the analysis (QBILPAR4, QBILPAR5.1/2, QBILPAR6.2, QBILPAR13, QBILPAR19.1–4). The questionnaire for parents of the minimal bilingual participants comprises a total of 26 questions (see Appendix A.II). For the purpose of the current study, two questions are not included in the analysis (QMONOPAR4, QMONOPAR5.2).

The coding procedure of the questionnaires involves an assignment of numbers to the answers with respect to the different categories (see Appendix B.III.a and B.III.b for further details of the coding method).

1. The child's biographic information (QBILPAR2, QBILPAR3.2/3; QMONOPAR2, QMONOPAR3.1/2)
2. Parents' biographic information (QBILPAR14.1/2, QBILPAR15.1/2; QMONOPAR10.1/2, QMONOPAR11.1/2)
3. The child's acquisition context (QBILPAR7.1–3, QBILPAR8, QBILPAR9.2, QBILPAR10.2, QBILPAR11.2–5, QBILPAR12.2–5; QMONOPAR6.1–3, QMONOPAR7, QMONOPAR8, QMONOPAR9.1–4)
4. Parents' educational information (QBILPAR16.1/2, QBILPAR17.1/2, QBILPAR18.1/2, QBILPAR19.1/2; QMONOPAR12.1/2, QMONOPAR13.1/2, QMONOPAR14.1/2, QMONOPAR15.1/2)

The first two categories serve to determine or exclude the migration context of children and parents. Thus, it is possible to determine the exact generation of migration of each participant as well as the length of resistance of migrated children and parents. The third category involves an assessment of the child's acquisition context of L1, L2, L3 and the acquis0ition type (monolingual, minimal bilingual, simultaneous bilingual, child bilingual). Furthermore information about L1 and L3 instructions in/outside school can be assessed.

According to the highest educational qualification of one parent[54] an educational level has been determined for each family in the fourth category. Since the parents involved in this study having gone through different educational systems in Germany, Turkey and France, the levels are related to the International Standard Classification of Education (ISCED-2011), which facilitate standardised international comparisons of statistics across education systems (see Table 17, for more details concerning the classification of the parents' educational qualifications in this study see Appendix B.III.a and B.III.b).

The different levels of educations were divided into three categories "low" (levels 0–2), "medium" (levels 3–5), and "high" (levels 6–8).

6.5.4 Child questionnaire

The (bilingual) child questionnaire comprises a total of 73 questions (see Appendix B.III.c). For the purpose of the current study, only 30 questions are included in the analysis.

---

[54] When determining the educational background, generally the educational level of the child's reference person is used (usually the mother). Since the parental questionnaire does not provide any information with respect to the child's reference person, in this study the highest level of one parent is used to determine the educational background.

Table 17: Levels of education among the International Standard Classification of Education (ISCED-2011).

Level 0	Early childhood education
Level 1	Primary education
Level 2	Lower secondary education
Level 3	Upper secondary education
Level 4	Post secondary non-tertiary education
Level 5	Short cycle tertiary education
Level 6	Bachelor or equivalent education
Level 7	Master or equivalent education
Level 8	Doctoral or equivalent education

The coding procedure of the questionnaires involves, again, an assignment of numbers to the answers with respect to different categories which serve to determine the domain of language dominance (see Appendix B.III.c for further details of the coding method).

Domain language use with Parents (QBIL4.1.1–4, QBIL4.2.1–4)
Domain language use with siblings/peers (QBIL4.1.5–10, QBIL4.2.5–10)
Domain Media/Reading (QBIL9.1/2, QBIL11.1/2, QBIL15.2.1/2, QBIL16.2.1/2)

An interval mean score (pseudo-ratio-scaled) has been calculated for 1. and 2. Depending on the closeness to one pole (1=German/French, 3=Turkish) of the interval, a dominance for one language or "no dominance" in the respective domain has been determined (1.0–1.66 = "German/French dominant"; 1.67–2.33 = "no dominance"; 2.34–3.0 = "Turkish dominant").

3. Coding numbers of answers regarding the frequency of media consumed (three questions) or reading activities (two questions) in German/French and Turkish (0=never; 1=sometimes; 2=often) were subtracted from each other. Because the questions are listed in the order German/French>Turkish, positive results indicate a dominance towards German or French, negative results a dominance towards Turkish, and a zero result no dominance.

6.5.5 Statistical analysis

In Study 1 and 2 the results are generally presented as average group and/or individual values (based on ordinal (e.g. the language use with the mother at home), interval (e.g. the frequency of reading in one language) and ratio scales (e.g. numbers/proportion of used Manner verbs)). The statistical analyses comprised of descriptive and inferential statistics and are carried out in the program R, which is a free software environment for statistical computing and graphics (R Core Team 2013).[55] In the following we discuss the relevant statistical concepts that are the basis for the statistical tests in this study, and which, furthermore, allow a more adequate assessment of intra-group differences.

Any indicated group performance represents the mean (in the reported results indicated as *M*). Furthermore, the range (in the reported results indicated as *R*) and the standard deviation (in the reported results indicated as *SD*) are indicated for each (quantitative) analysis. The range indicates the dispersion for interval or ratio data that is the difference of the largest and the smallest value within a group (Gries 2013: 121) (e.g. the largest proportion of Manner verb usage by a Turkish-German bilingual speaker in Turkish). The standard deviation represents a computed distance of each data point (e.g. the individual proportion of a Turkish-German speakers' Manner verb usage in Turkish) to the mean (of Manner verb usage in Turkish of all Turkish-German bilinguals) (see Gries (2013: 124) for more details regarding the computational measurement).

In order to obtain a more detailed individual variation between a speaker's performance of a single group and to determine his or her individual usage preferences, "*z*-scores" are calculated. The calculation of a *z*-score is relative to the mean and the standard deviation of one group. For instance, in a data set with a mean of 44% Manner verb usage and an *SD* of 13.2, a positive *z*-score of +2.33 by speaker *N* means that speaker *N*'s performance is more than two standard deviations above the mean (74.76%). Thus, a negative (below the mean) or positive (above the mean) *z*-score is an indication that the performance of a speaker varies within the same group. Note that in statistical theory only values which indicate a distance of three (Sincich 1986) or four *SD* (Younger 1979) are classified as outliers. In addition, Shiffler (1988) notes that *z*-scores are constrained as regards small data sets. Since the sub-group size in this study is maximally 15, it is statistically not possible to exceed an *SD* of 4. Thus, according to a four *SD* definition, no speaker can be considered as an outlier. However, we include speakers in the qualitative analysis whose *z*-values are the highest in one group in order to examine intra-group differences as well as the interaction of usage preferences in L1 and L2 individually. In this context *z*-scores are a more appropriate indication of a speakers' variation in L1 and L2 than for instance individual proportions; therefore we consider general differences, which can occur between means of a group X in L1 (and L2).

---

[55] In this study, statistical analyses are carried out with R version 3.2.2 (2015-08-14) (for further details see https://www.r-project.org/ [accessed 2018-01-15]).

Inferential statistics are generally carried out in order to test the differences between i) the mean of an independent sample of a group A (e.g. Turkish-German bilinguals) and a group B (e.g. Turkish-French bilinguals), or ii) between the mean of a dependent sample (Manner verb usage in Turkish and German) of a group A (e.g. Turkish-German bilinguals). The choice of the statistical test is dependent on the distribution of the data points. Many statistical tests require a normal distribution of the data points within one sample. A normal distribution is related to the mean, the median (that is the middle value of distributed values according to their size) and the mode (that is the value which is most often observed within a sample) (Gries 2013 :115–116). In normally distributed data the mean, the median and the mode are equal. Provided that 68% of the data points are within one standard deviation of the mean and approximately 95% of the data points are within two standard deviations of the mean, a normal distribution can be assumed (Lane n.d.: 251–252). Thus, in normally distributed data, 2.5% are expected to be greater than 1.96 SD above the mean and 2.5% to be more than 1.96 SD below the mean (Crawley 2014: 76). The normality assumption can be tested by the verification or falsification of the so called null-hypothesis (e.g. H_0: "The Manner verb usage by Turkish-German and Turkish-French bilinguals does not differ from a normal distribution"). In this study we use the Lilliefors test, which is a test for rejecting or accepting the normality assumption (H_0) (Conover 1999). For all statistical tests we define a significance level "$p_{critical}$" and follow the usual significance value 0.05.[56] This value represents the threshold value for rejecting or accepting H_0 (Gries 2013: 27). When running, for instance, the Lilliefors Test, we obtain the probability of error which is generally called the 'p-value'. The p-value indicates the probability of error when accepting the alternative hypothesis (e.g. H_1 "The Manner verb usage by Turkish-German and Turkish-French bilinguals differs from a normal distribution"). When the computed p-value is lower than the defined $p_{critical}$ (<0.05), or in a technical sense "significant", it is more likely to reject H_0, since the error probability that H_1 is true is smaller than 5%. Vice versa, a p-value ≥0.5 suggests that H_0 can not be falsified, since the error probability that H_1 is true is larger than 5%. (Gries 2013: 28).

Given the fact that the (in)dependent samples are normally distributed, (parametrical) two sample t-tests (for independent samples, see context (i) above) or paired t-tests (for dependent samples, see context (ii) above) are carried out. In

---

[56] In this study p-values are rounded up or down; a p-value < 0.001 is referred to as highly significant and indicated with ***; 0.001 ≤ p < 0.01 is referred to as very significant and indicated with **; 0.01 ≤ p < 0.05 is referred to as significant and indicated with *; ≥ 0.05 is referred to as not significant.

order to specify further arguments for these tests, the (normally distributed) data is again tested for variance homogeneity by using the F-test (Gries 2013:218–221).

The two sample t-test for independent samples tests that the means of two independent samples (or populations) are equal (by testing H_0). When referring to our example above, H_0 may be "Turkish-German and Turkish-French bilinguals do not differ in their Manner-verb usage in Turkish". In this context, every speaker provides just one data point and the data points are not related to each other. Thus, the sample is independent. A two sample t-test would test that the mean of the (normally distributed) Manner verb usage (dependent ratio-scaled variable y) of Turkish-German bilinguals (independent nominal variable g_1) and Turkish-French bilinguals (independent nominal variable g_2) is equal. H_0 is rejected when the p-value is <0.05, which means that the error probability of the alternative hypothesis (H_1 "Turkish-German and Turkish-French bilinguals differ in their Manner-verb usage in Turkish") is smaller than 5%.

The paired t-test for dependent samples tests that the means of two dependent populations are equal (by testing H_0). When referring to our example above, H_0 may be "Turkish-German bilinguals do not differ in their Manner-verb usage in Turkish and German". The sample is dependent since each speaker provides two data points: Manner verb usage in German and Manner verb usage in Turkish. Thus, the values of Manner verb usage are connected to each other. A paired t-test would test that the mean difference of Turkish-German bilinguals' (normally distributed) Manner verb usage (dependent ratio-scaled variable y) in Turkish (independent nominal variable g_1) and German (independent nominal variable g_2) is equal. H_0 is rejected when the p-value is <0.05, which means that the error probability of the alternative H_1 ("Turkish-German bilinguals' Manner verb usage differs in Turkish and German") is smaller than 5%.

In cases of violations of the normality assumption (e.g. H_0 "The Manner verb usage by Turkish-German and Turkish-French bilinguals differs from a normal distribution"), parametric tests, such as the t-test, cannot be used, instead, alternative, non-parametric tests are carried out. Whenever a sample is not normally distributed we use the Wilcoxon Sign Rank Test with continuity correction for two independent or dependent samples. Similarly to the t-test it tests whether the mean differences of two (in)dependent samples are equal, but, in contrast, without assuming that they are normally distributed. In comparison with the parametric test the non-parametric Wilcoxon test is more appropriate when a sample is not normally distributed (for more details see Crawley (2014:96–97). The test provides again a p-value, which is used in relation to $p_{critical}$ (<0.05) in order to accept or reject the null hypotheses.

When examining a relationship (e.g. Turkish-German bilinguals' Manner verb usage in Turkish and in German) between a dependent ratio-scaled variable (e.g. var$_1$=Manner verb usage in German) and an independent ratio-scaled variable (e.g. var$_2$=Manner verb usage in Turkish) a Pearson product-moment correlation is carried out. When examining a relationship between variables of ordinal measurement levels (e.g. var$_1$= "1", which stands for language dominance in L2; var$_2$= "2" (no language dominance); var$_3$= "3" (language dominance in L1)), a Spearman's rank correlation is conducted. Whereas the Pearson's correlation measures a linear relationship, the Spearman's correlation measures monotonic relationships. On the basis of the variables tested, in both tests, a correlation coefficient (*rho*, commonly indicated as *r*) between -1 and +1 is calculated. A positive correlation indicates that the more/higher a value X, the more/higher a value y, a negative correlation indicates that the more/higher a value X, the less/lower a value Y, or vice versa, the less/lower a value X, the more/higher a value Y. In cases of $r \approx 0$, no correlation can be assumed (H$_0$).[57] The correlation is tested against the null hypothesis (e.g. H$_0$ "There is no correlation between Turkish-German bilinguals Manner-verb usage in German and Turkish"). Given the case that in our example above *r* is +0.9 and statistically significant ($p<0.05$), we can argue that Turkish-German bilinguals significantly used more Manner verbs in Turkish, the more they used Manner verbs in German.

In addition to *p*-values, further test statistics are indicated in this study when reporting the results of a statistical analysis. When using a two sample or paired *t*-test, the mean (*M*) and standard deviation (*SD*) of each sample, the sample size minus the degrees of freedom (*df*)[58] as well as the *t*-value[59] are indicated. When using a Wilcoxon Sign Rank Test, the median (in the reported results indicated as *med*) of each sample, as well as the sum of the signed ranks (abbreviated by *W*), are additionally indicated. In addition to the correlation coefficient, the sample size minus 2 *df*, as well as the *t*-value, are indicated. To simplify matters, we will not refer to the test statistics of testing normality. Whenever the use of parametric and non-parametric tests is indicated in the current study, this means that the normality assumption and variance homogeneity was tested in advance. Furthermore, we will only refer to the exact *p*-values and test statistics when the statistical tests revealed a significant difference of a <0.05 level.

---

[57] In this study we follow the usual interpretation and labelling of correlation coefficients: +0.7 < r ≤ +1/ -0.7 > r ≥ -1 *very high*; +0.5 < r ≤ +0.7/ -0.5 > r ≥ -0.7 *high* ; +0.2 < r ≤ +0.5/-0.2 > r ≥ -0.5 *intermediate*; 0 < r ≤ +0.2/ 0 > r ≥ -0.2 *low*; $r \approx 0$ *no statistical correlation* (Gries 2013:147).
[58] The degrees of freedom are the sample size (e.g. the data points of 15 Turkish-German and 15 Turkish-French speakers), minus the number of parameters amount of data points (here two, namely "Turkish-German" and "Turkish-French") (Crawley 2014:53).
[59] The *t*-value indicates the size of the difference in relation to the variation in a sample.

7 Study on language dominance patterns and motion encoding by Turkish-German and Turkish-French bilinguals

The current study is based on the recent research findings on bilingual language dominance patterns as well as monolingual and bilingual acquisition and the development of motion events in German, Turkish and French established in Chapters 1–3. The study is divided into two sub-studies which follow the methodology described in Chapter 5. First, the focus is on language dominance patterns of Turkish-German and Turkish-French bilinguals (§7.1). The results of the first study serve as reference values for the individual interpretation of the second (voluntary motion, §7.2).

7.1 Study 1: Language dominance

Study 1 aims to provide language dominance profiles for each Turkish-German and Turkish-French bilingual speaker in two dominance levels, namely language skills and language knowledge (dimensions) and language use (domain). Thus, besides the commonly employed assessment of linguistic repertoires in language dominance research, this study also takes into account the different social functions of the speaker's languages (to which Grosjean (1985: 469) refers to "what a language is used for, with whom and where"). In this holistic view of bilingualism, we therefore achieve the bilingual speaker's reality.

More concretely, the question is explored of whether there are intra- and inter-group differences among Turkish-German and Turkish-French bilinguals according to language dominance patterns (domain, dimension) (RQ1). On the basis of the literature on language maintenance and dominance among bilingual Turkish-German and Turkish-French speakers (see §2.3.2 and 2.3.4), it would be expected that a language dominance shift from Turkish towards the surrounding majority language is already in place for the participants under study. We hypothesise that this applies instead to dimension rather than to domain as a result of schooling in an L2 context on the one hand, and the high vitality of Turkish in the German and French diaspora on the other hand. In this context, what is of further interest is whether language dominance in the language use with parents, siblings and peers at and outside home, as well as media/reading activity, is interconnected with language dominance in language skills (verbal fluency, code-mixing) and language knowledge (lemma diversity) (RQ 2). We assume that a high L1-usage (L1-dominance in domain) can prevent L1>L2-dominance shift in dimension (L2-dominance) and that dominance patterns in dimension are related to the use of L1 and L2 (domain). In sum, the following hypotheses are tested in Study 1:

- H_0 There are no differences between L1 and L2 with respect to language dominance in domain and dimension by Turkish-German and Turkish-French bilinguals;
- H_1 Language dominance (domain) is related to the interlocutor;
- $H_{1.1}$ Turkish-German and Turkish-French bilinguals are dominant in their L1 as regards language use with parents;
- $H_{1.2}$ Turkish-German and Turkish-French bilinguals are dominant in their L2 as regards language use with siblings and peers;
- H_2 Turkish-German and Turkish-French bilinguals with an "L1-dominance" in domain are L1-dominant in dimension;
- H_3 Turkish-German and Turkish-French bilinguals with L2-dominance in domain are also L2 dominant as regards verbal fluency, lemma diversity and code-mixing.

7.1.1 Results domain

We referred to domains as situations and contexts of language use by assuming that bilinguals' language dominance is distributed differently (see §2.1.2.1). In order to determine the dominance patterns of each individual bilingual speaker and of both bilingual groups, three situations/contexts are distinguished: (i) language use with parents, (ii) language use with siblings and peers, and (iii) language use when watching television or video clips in the internet (media) as well as reading activities. The results are based on the parental and child questionnaires, described in §6.2 and §6.5. Let us first examine each situation/context per group, in order to find out whether there are inter- and intra-group differences in domain among Turkish-German and Turkish-French bilinguals.

7.1.1.1 Turkish-German bilinguals

The numbers in Table 18 indicate that Turkish dominance according to language use with parents is predominant. Only two participants are dominant in German in conversations with parents, and one participant does not indicate a dominance. With respect to the dominance according to language use with sibling and peers, bilinguals either have "no dominance" (eight participants) or are dominant in German (seven participants). According to media and reading, six participants

Table 18: Language dominance patterns (domain) of Turkish-German bilinguals (intra-group comparison).

	TURGER
Domain language use Parents	
German	2
no	1
Turkish	12
Domain language use siblings/peers	
German	7
no	8
Turkish	0
Domain Media/Reading	
German	6
no	5
Turkish	4

are dominant in German, four are dominant in Turkish and five do not have a dominance. When interpreting the group results with respect to the three situations/contexts, it turns out that mainly media and reading lead to the heterogeneous dominance patterns.

When comparing the results individually, a high heterogeneity can be observed. Only one participant (Beren) indicates a consistent dominance pattern in one language (here German). However, some overlap can be observed, when categorizing the results by assigning letters to the individual patterns (fine pattern, see Table 19). We briefly discuss these patterns in the following in order to highlight the inter-individual variation of language dominance patterns.

Table 19: Language dominance patterns (domain) of Turkish-German bilinguals (individual results).

Speaker	Language use with Parents	Language use with siblings & peers	Language use Media & Reading	Dominance pattern fine	global
Alisa	3	1	2	E	mixed
Beren	1	1	1	A	L2
Dana	3	2	2	G	no
Eda	3	1	1	D	L2
Ela	3	1	2	E	mixed
Esna	3	2	3	H	L1
Gamze	3	1	1	D	L2

(continued)

Table 19 (continued)

Speaker	Language use with Parents	Language use with siblings & peers	Language use Media & Reading	Dominance pattern fine	Dominance pattern global
Kurt	3	2	1	F	mixed
Melis	3	2	3	H	L1
Ozan	2	1	1	C	L2
Sefar	3	2	2	G	no
Serkan	3	2	3	H	L1
Taylan	3	2	3	H	L1
Tuba	3	1	1	D	L2
Yiğit	1	2	2	B	no

1=dominant in German; 2=no dominance; 3=dominant in Turkish

Pattern H (Esna, Melis, Serkan, Taylan): A dominance in Turkish with parents, "no dominance" with siblings and peers and a Turkish dominance in media and reading.
Pattern D (Eda, Gamze, Tuba): Turkish dominance according to language use with parents, and German dominance according to language use with siblings and peers as well as according to media and reading activities.
Pattern E (Alisa, Ela): Turkish dominance with parents, and with respect to media/reading; German dominance with siblings/peers;
Pattern G (Dana, Sefar): Turkish dominance with parents, "no dominance" with siblings/peers and "no dominance" according to media/reading.

The other patterns (A, B, C, F) occur only once each (Beren, Yiğit, Ozan, Kurt). These results highlight that bilinguals are predominantly not only dominant in one language, but use their languages in different domains in their life, in which one language may be more required than another. However, the sum of such domain-specific dominance can still provide a global language dominance in domain, which would simplify matters when including the individual dominance profiles in further analyses of the current study. Thus, the dominance patterns have been transformed into more global patterns, namely:

"**L1**": at least two of three situations/contexts indicate an "L1-dominance";
"**L2**": at least two of three situations/contexts indicate an "L2-dominance";
"**no**": at least two of three situations/contexts do not indicate an "L1-/L2-dominance";
"**mixed**": Each situation/context indicates a distinct dominance.

The results show that four speakers are L1-dominant, five speakers are L2 dominant, three speakers are neither L1 nor L2 dominant, and three speakers display distinct dominance patterns in each category.

7.1.1.2 Turkish-French bilinguals

When regarding each situation/context per group (see Table 20), Turkish dominance according to language use with parents applies to six bilinguals, whereas eight bilinguals indicate "no dominance" and one is French dominant. Nine bilinguals are French dominant according to language use with siblings and peers, six indicate no dominance, and no one is dominant in Turkish. With respect to media and reading, eleven bilinguals are dominant in French, three indicate no dominance, and only one is dominant in Turkish.

Table 20: Language dominance patterns (domain) by Turkish-French bilinguals (intra-group comparison).

	TURFRE
Domain language use Parents	
French	1
No	8
Turkish	6
Domain language use siblings/peers	
French	9
No	6
Turkish	0
Domain Media/Reading	
French	11
No	3
Turkish	1

When comparing the results individually, a high heterogeneity can be observed in the Turkish-French bilingual group as well (see Table 21). However, three participants indicate a consistent dominance pattern: Devin is dominant in French, Nihal and Shirin indicate "no dominance" among the three situations/contexts. Again, some overlap can be observed, when categorizing the results by assigning letters to the individual patterns (fine pattern), which we will also briefly discuss in the following.

Table 21: Language dominance pattern domain by Turkish-French bilinguals (individual results).

Speaker	Language use with Parents	Language use with siblings & peers	Language use Media/ Reading	Dominance pattern	
				fine	global
Adile	3	2	2	H	no
Arda	2	2	1	D	no
Bircan	2	1	3	C	mixed
Devin	1	1	1	A	L2
Dilşah	3	1	1	F	L2
Emre	2	1	1	B	L2
Geza	3	1	1	F	L2
Gözde	3	2	1	G	mixed
Maide	3	2	1	G	mixed
Mert	2	1	1	B	L2
Nezihe	2	1	1	B	L2
Nihal	2	2	2	E	no
Özgür	3	1	1	F	L2
Seçkin	2	1	1	B	L2
Shirin	2	2	2	E	no

1=dominant in French; 2=no dominance; 3=dominant in Turkish

> **Pattern B** (Emre, Mert, Nezihe, Seçkin): "no dominance" according to language use with parents, and a dominance in French according to language use with siblings and peers, as well as media and reading;
> **Pattern F** (Dilşah, Geza, and Özgür): dominance in Turkish according to language use with parents, and dominance in French according to language use with siblings and peers as well as media and reading;
> **Pattern E** (Nihal, Shirin): "no dominance" at all;
> **Pattern G** (Gözde, Maide): Turkish dominance with parents, "no dominance" with siblings/peers, French dominance according to media/reading.

The other patterns (A, C, D, H) occur only once each (Devin, Bircan, Arda, Adile). Again, the results highlight that bilinguals are predominantly not only dominant in one language, but use their languages in different domains in their life, in which one language may be more required than another. Due to the high heterogeneity and to simplify matters, the dominance pattern have been transformed as well ("L1", "L2", "no", "mixed", see Turkish-German context above). The results indicate that no speaker is L1-dominant, three speakers display distinct dominance patterns in each category ("mixed"), four speakers are neither L1 nor L2 dominant, and eight speakers are L2-dominant.

Let us now compare the results of both bilingual groups in order to obtain possible inter-group differences of bilingual speakers in Germany and France.

7.1.1.3 Inter-group comparison

Regarding each situation/context per group, the numbers in Table 22 show that Turkish-French bilinguals are more heterogeneous with respect to language use with parents as compared to Turkish-German bilinguals in terms of a weaker dominance in Turkish. Furthermore, the results indicate a similar picture in terms of language use with siblings and peers. With respect to media and reading the picture is different, inasmuch for Turkish-French bilinguals the most dominant language is their L2.

Table 22: Amount of language dominance patterns (domain) by Turkish-German and Turkish-French bilinguals (in numbers).

Dominance	TURGER	TURFRE
Domain language use Parents		
German/French	2	1
no	1	8
Turkish	12	6
Domain language use siblings/peers		
German/French	7	9
no	8	6
Turkish	0	0
Domain Media/Reading		
German/French	6	11
no	5	3
Turkish	4	1

When comparing the global dominance patterns, the numbers in Table 23 show that more Turkish-French bilinguals indicate an "L2-dominance" in domain as compared to Turkish-German bilinguals, who more frequently indicate an "L1-dominance".

Let us now examine the bilingual speakers' dominance in dimension. In order to further determine possible inter- and intra-group differences, we first have to measure each participants' individual dominance in the operationalised categories for dimension. §7.1.2.1 examines the proportion of disfluency signals per utterances (verbal fluency), §7.1.2.2 the diversity of expressed

Table 23: Amount of L1-, L2-dominance, no dominance and mixed patterns (domain) per group (in numbers).

Dominance domain	TURGER	TURFRE
L1	4	0
L2	5	8
no	3	4
mixed	3	3

lemmas in each language (lexical repertoire) and §7.1.2.3 the amount and direction of mixing elements from one language into the other language (code-mixing).

7.1.2 Results dimension

7.1.2.1 Verbal fluency

In this study, we include unfilled pauses ≥ 1.0 s and filled pauses (such as "em, ee, mh, bah") as well as repairs or word truncation as disfluency signals ("hesitation and monitoring phenomena" Hlavac 2011). In order to measure a speaker's verbal fluency in L1 and L2, the individual mean of disfluency signals per utterance in the VM-Task was, as a first step, calculated in each language by using the EXMARALDA query tool EXAKT (see §6.5). As a second step, the difference between L1 and L2 disfluency signals was calculated for each speaker by subtracting the L2-value from the L1-value. A resulting difference > 0 indicates that more disfluency signals were measured in Turkish than in German/French. A difference < 0 analogously indicates that disfluency signals were higher in German/French. In order to determine a bilingual speakers' dominance in L1 or L2, the *SD* of difference-values per group was calculated as a third step and each individual difference-value was divided by the *SD*. The resulting value, which we term dominance score (*ds*), follows a distribution *D* with a variance of 1 and an unknown mean. Thus, as a norm of dominance we can set $ds \geq 1$ for "L2-dominance" and $ds \leq -1$ for "L1-dominance". A ds $-1 < 0 < 1$ is determined as "no dominance". As an illustration, when assuming an individual difference-value of 1.0 and an *SD* of 0.5, the *ds* would be 2.00. An L2-dominance can be determined, since the speaker indicates a $ds \geq 1$. This procedure allows an evaluation of individual verbal fluency in L1 and L2 in relation to the group and an assignment of three categories ("L1-dominance", "L2-dominance", "no dominance") as applied in the measurement of domain in §7.1.1.

Turkish-German bilinguals

Figure 21 shows the difference-values of measured verbal fluency per utterance in Turkish and German as well as the individual ds[60] of each Turkish-German bilingual speaker. The results indicate that seven speakers display a $ds \geq 1$, which means that a dominance in verbal fluency in German can be assumed (Beren, Yiğit, Ela, Ozan, Gamze, Dana, Alisa). The ds of five speakers are very close to each other ($-1 < 0 < 1$), which is an indication for that the verbal fluency is relatively balanced in both languages (Serkan, Taylan, Kurt, Esna, Tuba). Moreover, the figures reveal that three speakers are dominant in the sense of verbal fluency in Turkish, since they indicate a $ds \geq -1$ (Eda, Melis, Sefar).

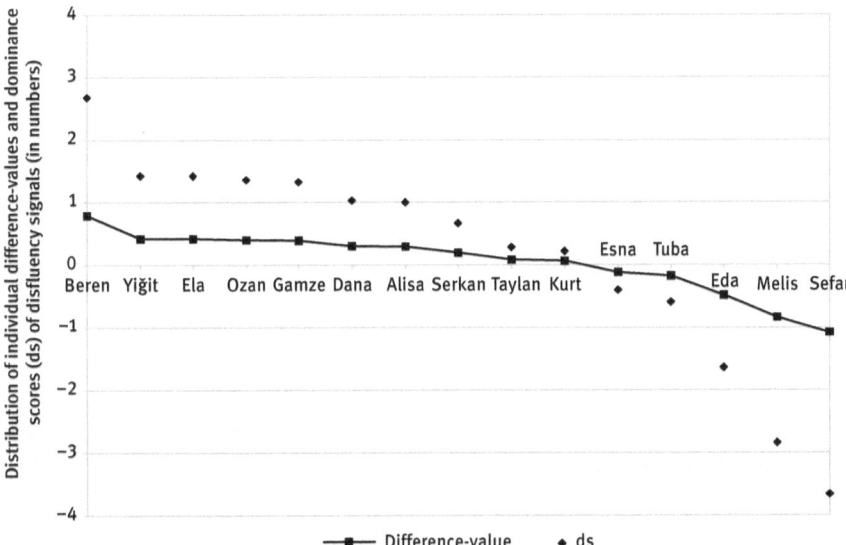

Figure 21: Individual difference-values of verbal fluency in L1 and L2 and individual dominance-score (ds) for Turkish-German bilinguals

Turkish-French bilinguals

Figure 22 summarises again the difference between measured verbal fluency per utterance in Turkish and French and the calculated ds[61] of each Turkish-French bilingual speaker. The results indicate that four speakers display a $ds \geq 1$ (Devin, Nezihe, Adile, Arda), which means that a dominance in the sense of verbal fluency

---

[60] The SD of difference-values in the Turkish-German group was 0.29.
[61] The SD of difference-values in the Turkish-French group was 0.27.

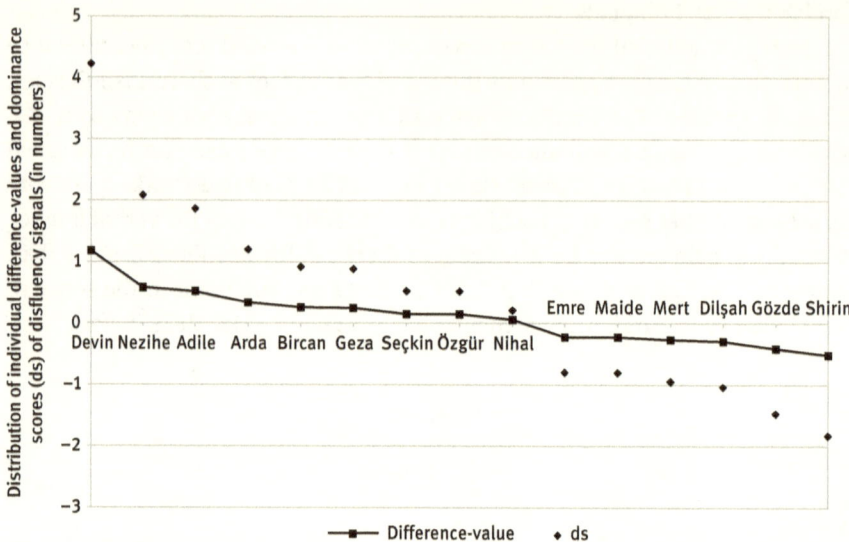

Figure 22: Individual difference-values of verbal fluency in L1 and L2 and individual dominance-score (ds) for Turkish-French bilinguals.

towards French can be assumed. The *ds* of eight speakers (Bircan, Geza, Seçkin, Özgür, Nihal, Emre, Maide, Mert) are very close to each other (-1 < 0 < 1), which is an indication that their verbal fluency is relatively balanced in both languages. Three speakers are dominant in the sense of verbal fluency in Turkish (Dilşah, Gözde, Shirin), since they display each a *ds* ≥ -1.

Inter-group comparison

When comparing the results between both bilingual groups, the numbers in Table 24 show that Turkish-German bilinguals indicate more often an "L2-dominance" in the sense of verbal fluency as compared to Turkish-French bilinguals who rather indicate no dominance. In each group, only three speakers are L1-dominant. Let us now turn to the lexical repertoire in each language and language group.

Table 24: Summary of L1-, L2-dominance, and no dominance (verbal fluency) per group.

Dominance verbal fluency	TURGER	TURFRE
L1	3	3
L2	7	4
no	5	8

7.1.2.2 Lexical repertoire

All tagged utterances in the vm-Task except for code-mixing serve as a data basis for the analysis of the speakers' lexical repertoire. For structural differences of the languages examined, the analysis excludes closed class elements (except for separable verb prefixes and (directional) adverbs encoding Path[62]) as well as auxiliary verbs.[63]

The lemma diversity is determined by tokens per lemma (TpL). A low TpL score in one language indicates a more diverse lexical repertoire in the task, and vice versa, a high TpL score in one language is an indication of a less diverse lexical repertoire. In order to determine language dominance, we follow the procedure described in §7.1.2.1 above. First, the difference between the TpL scores in L1 and L2 was calculated for each speaker by subtracting the L2 score from the L1 score. A resulting difference > 0 indicates that the lexical repertoire was lower in Turkish than in German/French. A difference < 0 analogously indicates that lexical repertoire was lower in German/French. In the following step, the individual difference-value was divided by the calculated *SD*. Again, the resulting value, the dominance score (*ds*) follows a distribution *D* with a variance of 1 and an unknown mean. A speakers' language dominance was determined by the *ds* ("L1-dominance": $ds \geq -1$; "L2-dominance": $ds \geq 1$; "no dominance": $-1 < 0 < 1$). As noted above, this procedure allows an evaluation of individual lexical repertoire in L1 and L2 in relation to the group and an assignment of three categories ("L1-dominance", "L2-dominance", "no dominance").

Turkish-German bilinguals

As regards Turkish-German bilinguals, the mean TpL-score for L1 ($M=2.34$, $SD=0.34$, $R=1.94–3.37$) and L2 ($M=2.27$; $SD=0.33$; $R=1.72–2.92$) is quite similar, which is proven by a paired *t*-test which did not reveal a significant difference. However, when looking into the individual results, some intra-group differences were found.

---

[62] As regards German, highly productive separable Path prefixes such as adverbial double particles (*rein, raus*) were counted as single lemma. Separable Path prefixes which belong to lexicalised verb-constructions were counted as one lemma (e.g. *Er schmeißt eine Bowlingkugel rein* 'He throws a bowling ball inside' (two lemmas; *rein, schmeißen* 'inside, throw') vs. *Er schmeißt die Kegel um* 'He knocks down the pin' (one lemma; *umschmeißen* 'down.knock').

[63] In French, the verb *aller* serves as auxiliary verb, e.g. for building the (near) future (*Elle va nager* 'She is going to swim) or past tense (*Hier elle a nagé* 'Yesterday she swam'). However, as noted in §3.2.6.1 *aller* can also be used as (Generic) verb in motion expressions (e.g. *Elle est allé au bowling* 'She went to the bowling (centre)'. Such motion contexts were manually extracted and included in the analysis.

The numbers in Figure 23 indicate that on the basis of the dominance norm an "L2-dominance" can be assumed for Eda, Yiğit, Beren, Taylan ($ds \geq 1$),[64] whereas Gamze, Alisa, and Melis are L1-dominant ($ds \geq -1$). For the other speakers "no dominance" can be determined ($ds\ -1 < 0 < 1$).

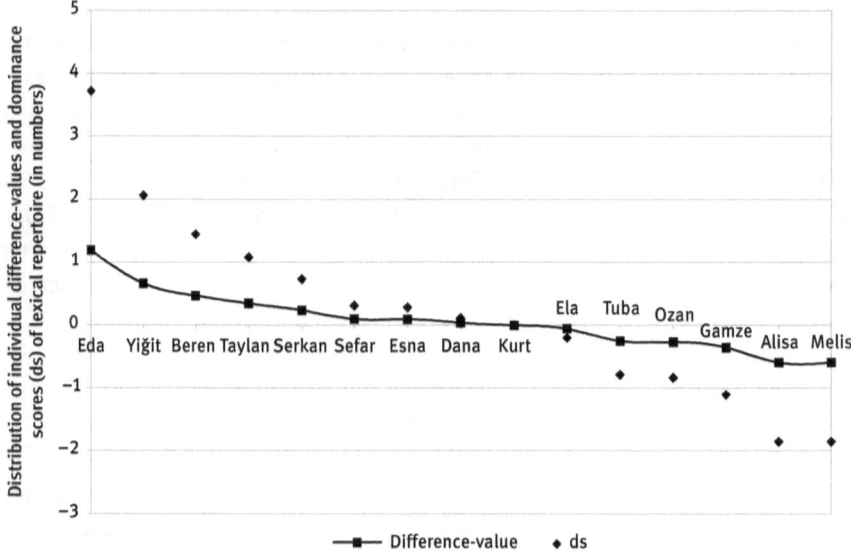

Figure 23: Individual difference-values of lexical repertoire in L1 and L2 and individual dominance-scores (ds) for Turkish-German bilinguals (in numbers).

Let us now also examine each language separately, in order to gain a more detailed picture of inter-individual variation in each group.

Because a comparison with minimal bilinguals would not be appropriate when analysing each language separately, we take as a reference point the lowest TpL score in the sense of a more diverse lexical repertoire among the bilingual participants (in Turkish Ela (1.94); in German Yiğit (1.72)). In relation to the reference value, the measured amount of lemmas of each speaker (given lemmas) was transformed into a value of expected lemmas, which indicates the individual variation within the group and language.

The results reveal differences between the speakers' L1 and L2. Figures 24 and 25 demonstrate that numbers of given lemmas and expected lemmas are greater in German compared with Turkish. As regards Turkish, only Eda displays a considerable difference between given and excepted lemmas. A subtle difference is

---

[64] The *SD* of difference-values in the Turkish-German group was 0.32.

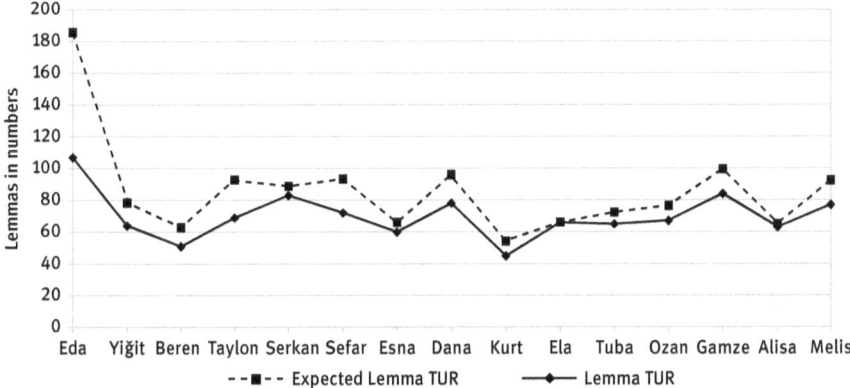

Figure 24: Given and expected lemmas in Turkish of Turkish-German bilinguals.

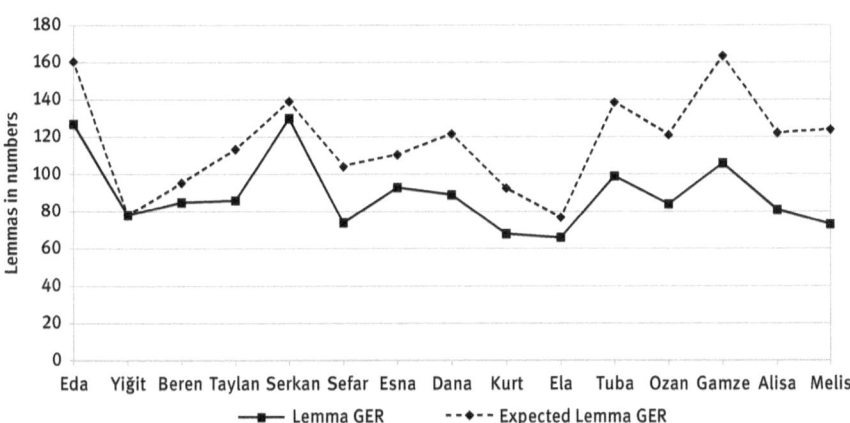

Figure 25: Given and expected lemmas in German of Turkish-German bilinguals.

found among Taylan, Sefar, Dana and Gamze. A non-parametric test was chosen to compare the TpL under expected (EXP) and given (GIVEN) conditions in Turkish, which did not indicate a significant difference.

As regards German, subtle differences between given and expected lemmas are only found for Ela and Beren, and Serkan almost reaches the excepted lemmas on the basis of Yiğit's reference point. All the other participants display considerable differences. A paired t-test was conducted to compare the TpL under expected (EXP) and given (GIVEN) lemma conditions in German. There was a highly significant difference in the scores under EXP ($M=117.47$, $SD=26.12$) and GIVEN ($M=89.27$, $SD=19.3$) conditions; $t(14)=6.7$, $p<0.001***$.

The findings suggest a greater inter-individual variation as regards the participants' lexical repertoire in German than in Turkish. However, the mean of used lemmas is greater in German (89.27) compared with Turkish (70.07). On average, the participants also used more tokens in German (201.8) than in Turkish (166.67).

Turkish-French bilinguals
In the case of Turkish-French bilinguals, the results of a paired *t*-test indicate that the mean TpL score in French is significantly lower (*M*=1.81; *SD*=0.29; *R*=1.16–2.18) in comparison with Turkish (*M*=2.23; *SD*=0.27), *t*(14)=−5.84, *p*<0.001***. The individual results confirm this tendency. Figure 26 shows that no participants indicates a higher lexical repertoire in L1. Eight participants display a *ds* ≥ 1,[65] which is an indication of an L2-dominance. The *ds* of the other seven speakers are quite similar in both languages (–1 < 0 < 1), consequently "no dominance" can be determined.

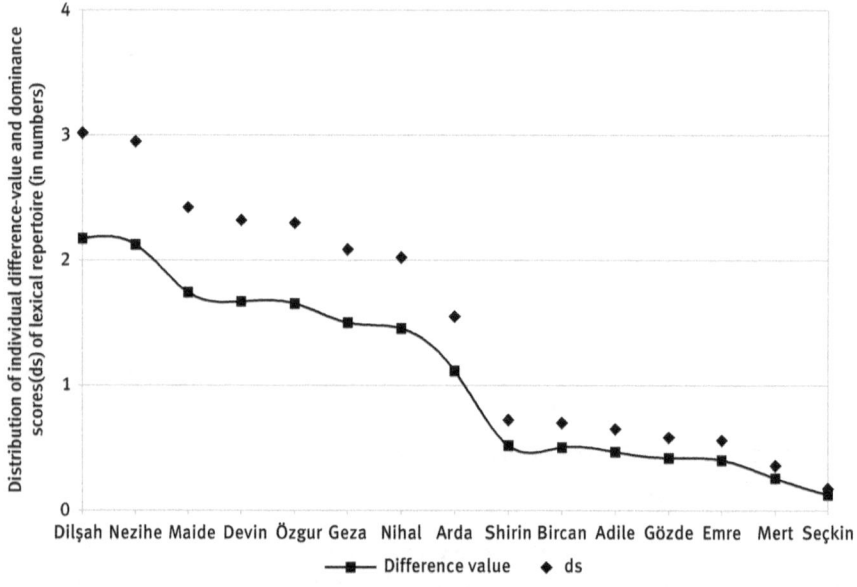

Figure 26: Individual difference-values of lexical repertoire in L1 and L2 and individual dominance-scores (ds) for Turkish-French bilinguals (in numbers).

In order to gain inter-individual variation in both languages, each language was again analysed separately by taking again as a reference point the lowest TpL-score in the sense of a more diverse lexical repertoire among the bilingual

---

[65] The *SD* of distance-values in the Turkish-French group was 0.28.

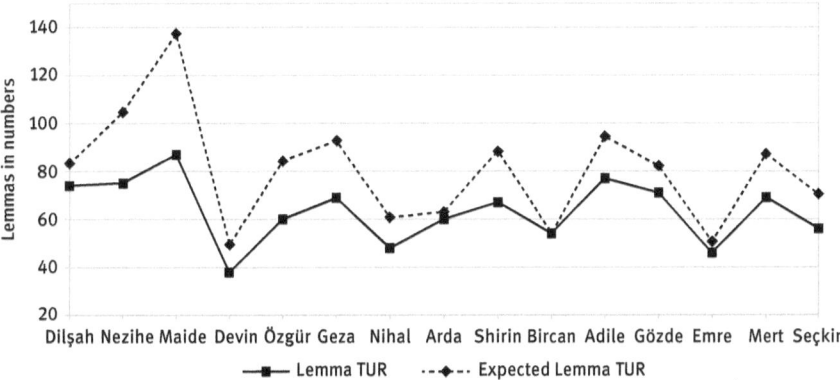

Figure 27: Given and expected lemmas in Turkish of Turkish-French bilinguals.

participants (Turkish Bircan (1.78); French Dilşah (1.16)). The results reveal differences in both speakers' L1 and L2 (see Figures 27 and 28). With regard to Turkish, only three participants display a subtle difference between given and expected lemmas (Arda, Bircan, Emre). A paired t-test was conducted to compare the TpL score under expected (EXP) and given (GIVEN) lemma conditions in Turkish. There was a highly significant difference in the scores under EXP (M=80.17, SD=23.35) and GIVEN (M=63.4, SD=13.29) conditions; $t(14)$=6.7, p<0.001***.

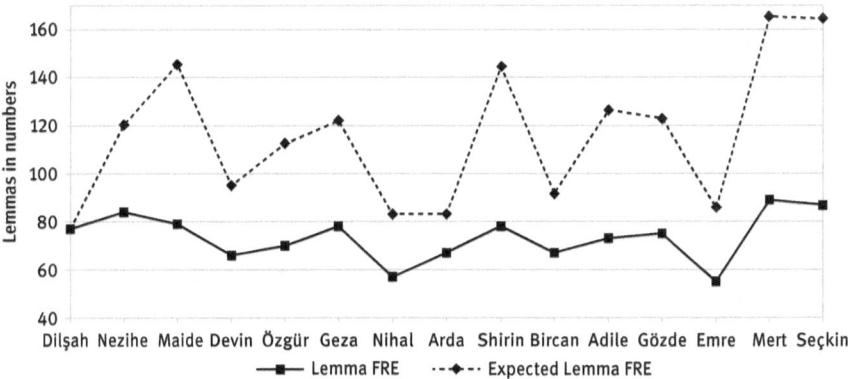

Figure 28: Given and expected lemmas in French of Turkish-French bilinguals.

As regards French only, Nihal, Arda, Bircan and Emre do not display considerable differences between given and expected lemmas in French on the basis of Dilşah's reference point. A non-parametric test was chosen in order to compare the TpL under expected (EXP) and given (GIVEN) lemma conditions. The Wilcoxon rank sum test revealed a highly significant difference under EXP (*med*=120.26) and GIVEN (*med*=75.0) conditions in French (*W*=210.5, *p*<0.001***).

The findings suggest that Turkish-French bilingual speakers vary inter-individually in both languages. The figures, however, demonstrate that the inter-individual variation is greater in French than in Turkish. Nevertheless, Turkish-French bilinguals are more dominant in French on the basis of their lexical repertoire (TpL). The mean of used lemmas is greater in French (73.47) compared with Turkish (63.4) and, on average, the participants used more tokens in French (134) than in Turkish (115.93).

Inter-group comparison

When comparing the dominance profiles of both bilingual groups, the numbers in Table 25 indicate a different picture by contrast to the findings of verbal fluency. Turkish-French bilinguals are more often L2-dominant in their lexical repertoire and do not indicate an "L1-dominance" at all in comparison with Turkish-German bilinguals.

Table 25: Amount of L1-, L2-dominance, and no dominance (lexical repertoire) per group (in numbers).

Dominance lexical repertoire	TURGER	TURFRE
L1	3	0
L2	4	8
No	8	7

When examining the results in greater detail, it turns out that this difference is mainly related to the bilingual speaker's lexical repertoire in the L2. Although inter-individual variation in Turkish is less pronounced in Turkish-German bilingual speakers than in Turkish-French bilinguals, the mean TpL scores in Turkish are quite similar among both groups (TURGER *M*=2.34; TURFRE *M*=2.23), which is also supported by the statistical analysis. A Wilcoxon Sign Rank Test did not reveal a significant difference between TpL scores under Turkish-German and Turkish-French conditions. In contrast, the mean TpL scores for the speakers' L2 reveal differences between the groups in terms of a higher lexical diversity in French than in German. Turkish-French bilinguals used significantly fewer tokens per lemma in French (*M*=1.81; *SD*=0.29) as compared to Turkish-German bilinguals in German (*M*=2.28; *SD*=0.33); *t*(28)=−4.11 *p*<0.001***. Thus, the fact that Turkish-French bilinguals are more often dominant in French than Turkish-German bilinguals are in German is related to a more diverse lexical repertoire in French by Turkish-French bilinguals.

A further indication of language dominance on the dimension level is the amount and direction of code-mixing utterances. Along with Muysken (2000:1), we are using the term code-mixing "to refer to all cases where lexical items and grammatical features from two languages appear in one sentence". All the lexical items considered were pronounced with the respective L1- or L2-phonology. Incidences which can be identified as direct answers to an investigators' request were not counted.

7.1.2.3 Code-mixing

Code-mixing utterances which were found in the corpus of the VM-Task occur, for instance ad hoc, when one word is borrowed from the other language and integrated into the sentence (insertion). This type of code-mixing has a referential function "because it often involves lack of knowledge of one language or lack of facility in that language on a certain subject" (Appel & Muysken 2005: 118).

Examples (84) to (87) illustrate the insertion of German and French lexical material into a Turkish matrix clause. In all examples the speakers integrate L2 words into the Turkish grammar. Yiğit adds the accusative suffix -*I* to the inserted French word *balle* 'ball' in example (84) which is required by the verb *atmak* 'to throw' in an equivalent transitive construction in Turkish (*topu atmak* 'to throw the ball'). Nihal, too, retains the L1 grammar in example (85) by marking the dative (-*(y)E*) to the inserted L2 words (*tuyauy-a* 'towards the pipe'). In contrast, the ablative suffix (-*dEn*) which is added to the integrated German word in example (86) does not corresponds to an equivalent Turkish construction (*dürbünle bakmak* 'watching with (a) binocular').

On the contrary, in example (87) Serkan uses a bare noun compound instead of a -*(s)I* noun compound.[66] The inserted German word *Kugel* 'bowl' is not marked with the possessive suffix -*(s)I* which would be required for this type of noun compound in Turkish (*bovling topu* 'bowling ball'). One can also argue that the speaker refers to his L2 grammar regarding compound nouns of the type substantive+substantive (*Bowlingkugel* 'bowling ball'), which is much less restrictive in German compared with the Turkish equivalent form of bare noun compounds (Eisenberg 2006; Göksel & Kerslake 2005: 95).

---

[66] In Turkish, there are basically two types of noun compounds:bare noun compounds with no suffixation to mark the relation between them and -*s(I)* noun compounds, where the head of minimally two juxtaposed nouns is marked with the third person possessive suffix (-*(s)I*). Where the first type is much more restricted in Turkish, the latter is the more common type of compounding (Göksel & Kerslake 2005:95–98).

(84) boling   **ball-ı**   at-tı
     =bowling ball-ACC throw-PST.3SG
     'It threw the bowling **ball**' (Yiğit, TURGER, 250–252)

(85) bi   top   [[em]] **tuyauy**-a at-tı
     one ball   pipe-DAT   throw-PST.3SG
     'It threw a **ball** to the pipe' (Nihal, TURFRE, 95–99)

(86) *onun için   ((1s)) **fernglas**-dan bak-tı
     the reason why   binocular-ABL   watch-PST.3SG
     'This is the reason why it watched from (with) her/his **binocular(s)**
     (Serkan, TURGER, 189–194)

(87) bi • • bovling **kugel** • • su   boru-nun   için-e   koy-du
     one   bowling ball   water   pipe-GEN   inside.DAT put-PST.3SG
     'It put a bowling **ball** inside the drain pipe' (Serkan, TURGER, 371–379)

A few speakers immediately replace the borrowed word by a word of the language of investigation. In example (88), Geza inserts the French word *balle* 'ball' and corrects himself subsequently by adding the appropriate Turkish lexical (*top* 'ball') and grammatical forms (accusative suffix *-I*). In example (89), Alisa makes use of the German word *S-Bahn* 'city train' when referring to the vehicle in the stimulus.[67] She replaces and corrects the German word immediately by the Turkish word *otobüs* 'bus'.

(88) kuş   da • bowling **balle** [[ee]] top-u   alı-yo ?
     bird FOC bowling ball   ball-ACC =take.PROG.3SG
     'The bird also takes a ball, um, a bowling **ball**' (Geza, TURFRE, 188–196)

(89) o zamda • **s-bahn**   gel-iyo ,   otobüs gel-iyo
     =that time city train =come-PROG.3SG   bus   =come-PROG.3SG
     'In that time the city train is coming, the bus is coming' (Alisa, TURGER, 415–422)

---

[67] It is possible that the conceptualisation of the vehicle as city train ("*S-Bahn*") is related to the speakers' interaction with her physical-social world. It is quite possible that in the individual speaker's environment (suburban district in Berlin, Germany) this sort of public transport plays a more significant role than e.g. tramway or bus. However, the concept of city train is closer to the concept of the vehicle actually shown in the stimulus (tramway) than bus ("*autobus*"). We can only hypothesise that the domain of vehicles of public transport is lexically more distinct in German than in Turkish, which leads to the lexical choice of *autobus* in Turkish.

Moreover, some code-mixing utterances have a metalinguistic function. In the following examples, the speakers directly comment on the languages involved, either in a language different from the rest of the utterance (see examples (90) and (91)) or in the same language (see examples (92) and (93)). The type of mixing in examples (90) and (91) is often referred to as alternation, since it takes place between utterances in a turn (Muysken 2000: 5).

(90) burda   kedi   şime/ •   **oh   wie   heisst   noch mal   fernrohr**
     there   cat   oh   how   mean.PR   again   binocular
     'There the cat **oh what was the name for binocular**' (Ozan, TURGER, 182–188)

(91) ((1,9s))   mit   dem   messa   ((1,2s))   **kes-di**   **ne**   **de-mek**
                with   DET.DAT   =knife   cut-PST.3SG   what   mean-INF
     kes-di
     cut-PST.3SG
     'With the knife she/he cut what does it mean she/he cut' (Melis, TURGER, 1544–1552)

(92) sie   hat • •   in   einem ((3,0s))   **isch**   **weiß**   **nisch**
     she   AUX.PR   in   DET.DAT   =I   know.PR   = NEG
     is   **des**   **heiß** • • kafes   ne ,   kafes   kafes
     =AUX.PR   =this   =mean.PR   cage   what   cage   cage
     hani   gış   kafes
     well   =bird   cage
     'She was in a ... I don't know what this means, cage what ... cage cage like bird cage' (Melis, TURGER, 330–351)

(93) ev-in   kenar-ın-da   böyle   şey-ler   var
     house-GEN   border-POSS-LOC   like   thing-PL   exist
     ((1s)) ((3,5s)) [[ee]] ((3s)) [[ee]] **schornstein**   **almanca-sı** ((3s))
                                          chimney   German-POSS
     'At the border of the house there were like things, **chimney in German**' (Eda, TURGER, 390–402)

Another type of ad hoc borrowing is a tag-switch, which involves discourse particles such as *nein* (94) 'no', *oui* 'yes' (95) or *also* 'well' (96) in a language different from the rest of the sentence. Such discourse particles can be interpreted as inner speech, which occasionally occur in the speech in a language different from that of the sentence. We suggest that the language from which these discourse particles are inserted is the more dominant. In some cases responses to the investigator's questions are in the other language (see (97)).

(94) twee - ty , • • **nein** kedi
    tweety   no   cat
    'Tweety, **no**, the cat' (Alisa, TURGER, 522–526)

(95) gid-iyo-sun   **oui**   gidi-yo-sun   böyle
    go-PROG-2SG   yes   go-PROG-2SG   like
    'You are going, **yes**, you are going' (Shirin, TURFRE, 494–497)

(96) bun-lar-ın   alt-ın-a   gel-ince   **also**   alt-ın-a
    this-PL-GEN   bottom-POSS-DAT   come-CVB   well   bottom-POSS-DAT
    derken ,   o / onlar-ın   kab – lo-sun-a   gel-ince
    saying   their-POSS   cable-POSS-DAT   come-CVB
    'When she/he comes to their bottom, **well**, saying to the bottom, when she/he comes to their cable' (Taylan TURGER, 526–538)

(97) Interviewer: köpekler kediye saldırdı ?
                  'Did the dogs attacked the cat?'
    Ozan: **ja**
                  '**Yes**' (Ozan, TURGER, 630–635)

Furthermore, there are some few utterances, which involve the English word "strike". Such expression are also considered as code-mixing, since it is common to say in German *einen Strike machen/werfen* 'to make/bowl a strike', and also used in French (*faire un strike* 'to make a strike') whereas it is commonly not used in Turkish. This is supported by the fact that "strike"-constructions were used by German and French minimal bilinguals, but they were not found at all in the corpus of Turkish minimal bilinguals. The latter rather used expressions such as *bovlinglere çarpıyor* 'it hits the bowlings' or *bovling topu oldu* 'it made the bowling balls'. Esna's (see (98)) and Seçkin's (see (99)) expressions can therefore be interpreted as loan translations from their L2 (German *Strike werfen* 'to throw a strike'; French *faire un strike* 'to make a strike').

(98) strike   at-tı
    strike   throw-PST.3SG
    'She/he threw a strike' (Esna, TURGER, 261–262)

(99) *strike yap-tı*
strike make-PST.3SG
'She/he made a strike' (Seçkin, TURFRE 176–177)

Let us now examine the total amount of code-mixing utterances and the direction of mixing for each individual speaker. As a norm for language dominance, we set the direction of influence. Thus, unidirectional code-mixing is determined as "L1-dominance" (L1>L2) or "L2-dominance" (L2>L1), no code-mixing is determined as "no dominance". In cases of bidirectional code-mixing, the amount of code-mixing utterances in one language is used to determine language dominance (in cases of same numbers in each language, "no dominance" is determined). It has to be noted that this procedure generally does not account for individual differences of the amount of code-mixing. Thus, a speaker who displays significantly more code-mixing utterances in one language than another speaker is not further distinguished within the respective dominance category.

The numbers in Table 26 indicate that code-mixing predominantly occurs in Turkish-German bilinguals' descriptions. The vast majority of Turkish-French bilinguals do not code-mix at all. Only three speakers mix French elements into their Turkish descriptions, whereas nine Turkish-German bilinguals mix German elements into their Turkish descriptions (see also Table 27 for a summary).

Table 26: Amount of code-mixing utterances and direction of mixing in Turkish-German and Turkish French bilinguals.

Code-mixing TURGER				Code-mixing TURFRE			
Speaker	L1>L2	L2>L1	Dominance	Speaker	L1>L2	L2>L1	Dominance
Alisa	0	4	L2	Adile	0	0	no
Beren	0	2	L2	Arda	0	0	no
Dana	0	0	no	Bircan	0	0	no
Eda	0	2	L2	Devin	0	0	no
Ela	0	0	no	Dilşah	0	1	L2
Esna	0	2	L2	Emre	0	0	no
Gamze	0	3	L2	Geza	0	3	L2
Kurt	0	0	no	Gözde	0	0	no
Melis	15	0	L1	Maide	0	0	no
Ozan	0	6	L2	Mert	0	0	no
Sefar	0	0	no	Nezihe	0	0	no

(continued)

Table 26 (continued)

	Code-mixing TURGER				Code-mixing TURFRE		
Speaker	L1>L2	L2>L1	Dominance	Speaker	L1>L2	L2>L1	Dominance
Serkan	0	5	L2	Nihal	0	0	no
Taylan	0	1	L2	Özgür	0	0	no
Tuba	1	0	L1	Seçkin	0	0	no
Yiğit	0	1	L2	Shirin	0	3	L2

In these cases an "L2-dominance" can be assumed. The only exceptions are Melis (15 occurrences) and Tuba (1 occurrence), who mix Turkish elements into their German descriptions, which is an indication of an "L1-dominance". No speaker indicates bidirectional code-mixing.

Table 27: Amount of L1-, L2-dominance, and no dominance (code-mixing) per group (in numbers).

Dominance code-mixing	TURGER	TURFRE
L1	2	0
L2	9	3
no	4	12

On the basis of measured language dominance in dimension in §7.1.2.1–7.1.2.3, we can now determine individual language dominance patterns for each bilingual speaker and find out whether the observed inter- and intra-group difference in domain can also be observed for dimension among Turkish-German and Turkish-French bilinguals.

7.1.2.4 Language dominance pattern dimension
Turkish-German bilinguals

Table 28 summarises the findings of the explored categories which served for determining language dominance in dimension. The figures indicate a high heterogeneity among Turkish-German bilinguals. When assigning letters to the different patterns (as applied in the context of language dominance in domain above), only a few speakers display a consistent pattern across all categories (Melis, pattern A; Beren, Yiğit, pattern B; Kurt, pattern C). However, in a few other patterns, some overlap can be observed as well. In the following, we briefly discuss these patterns in order to highlight the observed inter-individual variation.

Table 28: Summarised results (dimension) for Turkish-German bilinguals.

Speaker	Dominance TpL	Dominance Verbal Fluency	Dominance Code Switching	Dominance	
				fine	refined
Alisa	3	1	1	E	L2
Beren	1	1	1	B	L2
Dana	2	1	2	F	no
Eda	1	3	1	G	L2
Ela	2	1	2	F	no
Esna	2	2	1	D	no
Gamze	3	1	1	E	L2
Kurt	2	2	2	C	no
Melis	3	3	3	A	L1
Ozan	2	1	1	H	L2
Sefar	2	3	2	I	no
Serkan	2	2	1	D	no
Taylan	1	2	2	J	no
Tuba	2	2	3	K	no
Yiğit	1	1	1	B	L2

1 = German dominant; 2 = no dominance; 3 = Turkish dominant

Pattern A (Melis): "L1-dominance" in each category;
Pattern B (Beren, Yiğit): "L2-dominance" in any category;
Pattern C (Kurt): "no dominance" in each category;
Pattern D (Esna, Serkan): "no dominance" in verbal fluency and TpL and an "L2-dominance" in code-mixing;
Pattern E (Alisa and Gamze): "L1-dominance" in TpL and "L2-dominance" in verbal fluency and code-mixing;
Pattern F (Dana, Ela): "L2-dominance" in verbal fluency and "no dominance" in TpL and code-mixing.

All the other speakers display distinct patterns (pattern G, H, I, J, K). These results are consistent with our observation in the context of language use inasmuch as speakers' language dominance is dimension specific. However, the sum of such dimension-specific dominance can still provide a global language dominance in dimension, which would simplify matters, when including the individual dominance profiles in further analyses of the current study. Consequently, the dominance patterns have been transformed into global patterns by following the same procedure of §7.1.1:

"**L1**": at least two of three categories indicate an "L1-dominance";
"**L2**": at least two of three categories indicate an "L2-dominance";
"**no**": at least two of three categories do not indicate an "L1-/L2-dominance";
"**mixed**": Each category indicates a distinct dominance.

The results show that only one speaker is L1-dominant, whereas six speakers are L2-dominant. Most of the speakers indicate "no dominance".

Turkish-French bilinguals

As regards Turkish-French bilinguals, the individual results in Table 29 indicate again a high heterogeneity. Only four speakers display a consistent pattern (Bircan, Emre, Mert and Seçkin, pattern A). However, in a few other patterns some overlap can be observed as well. In the following, we briefly discuss these patterns in order to highlight the observed inter-individual variation.

Table 29: Summarised results (dimension) for Turkish French bilinguals.

Speaker	Dominance TpL	Dominance PAUSES	Dominance Code Switching	Dominance profile	
				fine	refined
Adile	2	1	2	D	no
Arda	1	1	2	C	L2
Bircan	2	2	2	A	no
Devin	1	1	2	C	L2
Dilşah	1	3	1	E	L2
Emre	2	2	2	A	no
Geza	1	2	1	F	L2
Gözde	2	3	2	G	no
Maide	1	2	2	B	no
Mert	2	2	2	A	no
Nezihe	1	1	2	C	L2
Nihal	1	2	2	B	no
Özgür	1	2	2	B	no
Seçkin	2	2	2	A	no
Shirin	2	3	1	H	mixed

1 = French dominant; 2 = no dominance; 3 = Turkish dominant

Pattern A (Bircan, Emre, Mert and Seçkin): "no dominance" in each category;

Pattern B (Maide, Nihal, Özgür): "L2-dominance" in TpL and code-mixing and "no dominance" in verbal fluency;
Pattern C (Arda, Devin, Nezihe): "L2-dominance" in TpL and in verbal fluency and "no dominance" in code-mixing.

All the other speakers display distinct patterns (pattern D, E, F, G, H). Among those Shirin indicates a mixed pattern, since she is L1 dominant in verbal fluency, L2-dominant in code-mixing and neither L1- nor L2-dominant in TpL.

While the dominance patterns in dimension are less heterogeneous as compared to those of Turkish-German bilinguals, a dimension-specific dominance can be observed for Turkish-French bilinguals as well. To simplify matters, when including the individual dominance profiles in further analysis of the current study, the dominance patterns have been transformed into global patterns ("L1", "L2", "no", "mixed", see above) as well. The results show that no Turkish-French bilingual speaker is L1-dominant, whereas five speakers are L2-dominant and nine speakers are neither L1- nor L2-dominant.

Inter-group comparison
When comparing the results based on the global dominance patterns in dimension of both bilingual groups, there were no major differences found between the two bilingual groups (see Table 30).

Table 30: Summary of L1-, L2-dominance, no dominance and mixed patterns (dimension) per group.

Dominance dimension	TURGER	TURFRE
L1	1	0
L2	6	5
no	8	9
mixed	0	1

We can now examine the relation between the dominance profiles of the individual speakers as regards domain and dimension in order to find out whether "L1/no/L2-dominance" in language use is interconnected with "L1/no/L2-dominance" in language skills and language knowledge and if a dominance in domain prevents an L1>L2-dominance shift in dimension. In order to do so, the determined fine patterns (based on categorical variables) as well as global dominance patterns (based on transformed categorical variables) in both domain and dimension are reconsidered.

7.1.3 The relation of domain and dimension

In order to answer the second research question whether L1/L2-dominance in domain is interrelated to L1/L2-dominance in dimension, let us first investigate the relation between the fine patterns of language dominance in domain ("L2-dominance", coded as "1"; "no dominance", coded as "2"; "L1-dominance", coded as "3") and the fine patterns of language dominance levels in dimension ("L2-dominance", coded as "1"; "no dominance", coded as "2"; "L1-dominance", coded as "3").

The overall results of a Spearman's correlation indicate no strong relationships among the six variables tested. As illustrated by the heat map in Figure 29, which indicates the correlation strength among the six variables tested, an intermediate correlation was only found with respect to language dominance in media/reading activities and language use with siblings/peers: the more dominant in one language in media/reading activities, the more dominant in language use with siblings and peers.

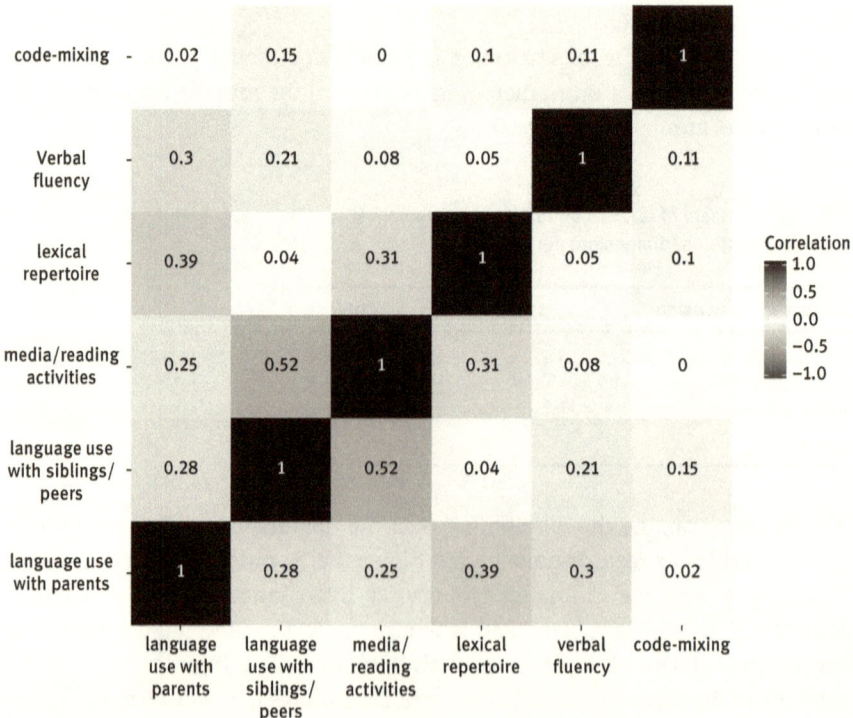

Figure 29: Correlation coefficients in both groups.

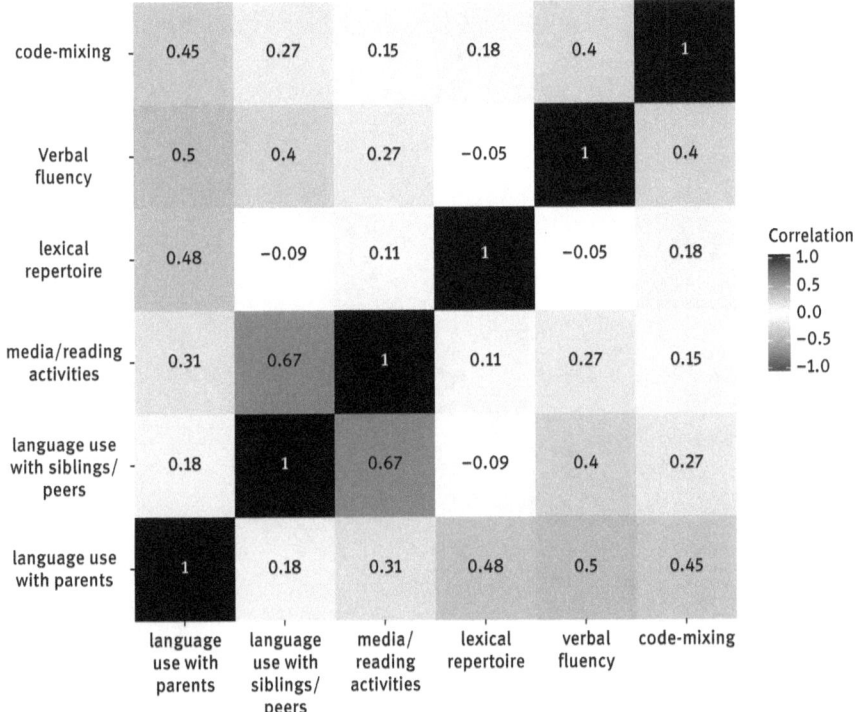

Figure 30: Correlation coefficients in the Turkish-German group.

Since the results of the language dominance patterns in §7.1.1 and §7.1.2 indicated some striking inter-group differences, let us also look into the correlation results within each group. The results of a Spearman's correlation (see Figure 30) indicate that in the Turkish-German group, next to media/reading activities and language use with siblings/peers, there is an intermediate positive correlation between verbal fluency and language use with parents: the more dominant in one language with regard to verbal fluency, the more dominant in the other language in language use with parents.

On the other hand, in the Turkish-French group, the results of a Spearman's correlation (see Figure 31) indicate an intermediate negative correlation between language dominance in code-mixing and verbal fluency: the more dominant in one language in code-mixing, the less dominant in the other language in verbal fluency or vice versa, the less dominant in code-mixing, the more dominant in verbal fluency.

Based on this statistical analysis, we can conclude that there is no striking relation among the variables which have been considered in this study with regard to domain-specific language dominance and language skills and knowledge.

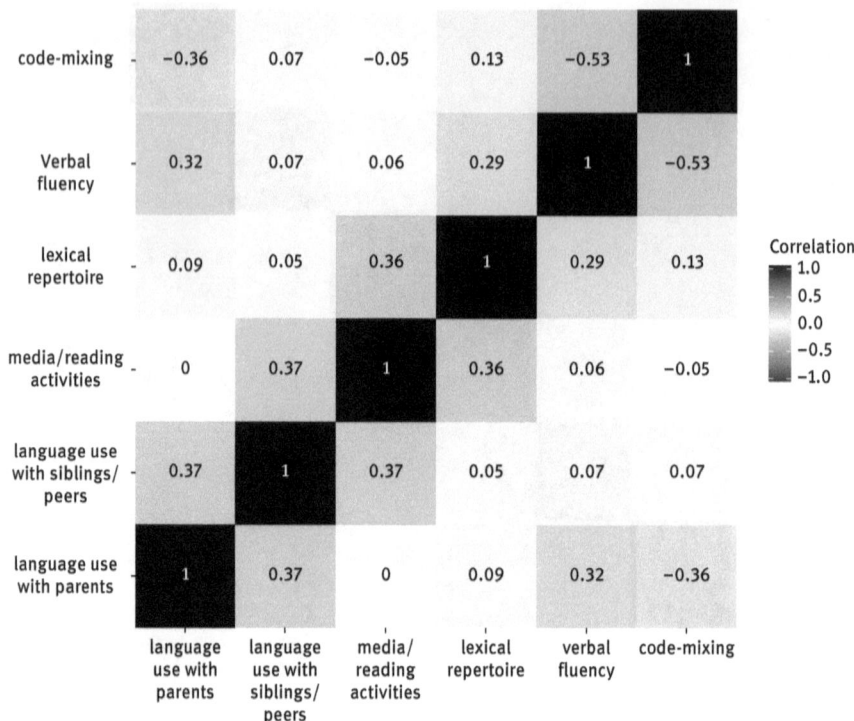

Figure 31: Correlation coefficients in the Turkish-French group.

Moreover, the argument can be put forward that interrelations between domain and dimension are rather individual, and differ at the group level.

In order to get a different perspective and to explore whether a dominance in domain prevents an L1>L2-dominance shift in dimension, let us now also take into account the global dominance patterns (based on transformed categorical variables) in domain and dimension.

The combinations of each individual bilingual speakers' global language dominance in domain and dimension are summarised in Figure 32. The numbers indicate that, in all, nine different pattern combinations can be observed. The figures support the suggested relation between dominance in domain and dimension. Speakers who are L1-dominant in domain are in any case L2-dominant in dimension. Furthermore, in cases where speakers are L2-dominant in domain they are most likely L2-dominant or do not display a dominance in dimension. However, since these patterns are generally limited, the results have to be interpreted with caution.

When comparing the bilingual speakers' individual patterns the figures show that the assumed relation between "L2-dominance" in domain and an "L2-/no

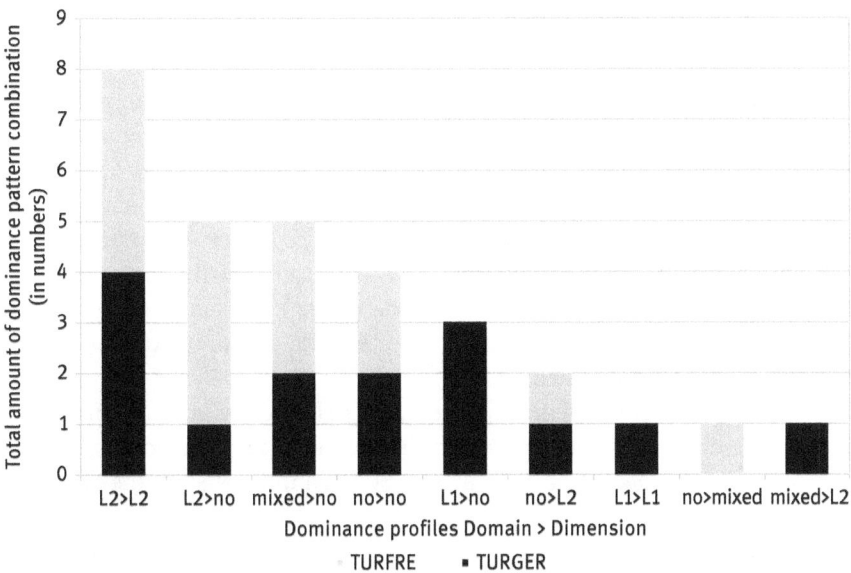

Figure 32: Amount of combinations of dominance profiles (domain and dimension).

dominance" in dimension was found more often among Turkish-French bilinguals. In contrast, "L1-/no dominance" (domain) and "L1-/no dominance" (dimension) combinations are limited to Turkish-German bilinguals (for a more detailed overview of each participant's individual combination see Table 109 in Appendix C.I). When considering the speakers' biographical information, it turns out that the only speaker who consistently displays an "L1-dominance" is Melis. Similarly, she is the only participant within the Turkish-German bilingual group who was born in Turkey (thus indicating the highest AoO in the group) and attended a Turkish kindergarten before she moved to Germany. Thus, we could assume that her language dominance in domain and dimension is further influenced by the (lower) length of resistance in Germany. However, in the Turkish-French bilingual group there is also one speaker who was born in Turkey (Dilşah). In contrast to Melis, Dilşah indicates in both dominance categories an "L2-dominance". In this context, the argument of length of resistance can not be put forward. We assume instead that the individual language use (and presumably the environment) has a more significant impact on the observed differences between these two speakers.

In sum, we can state that about two thirds of all speakers display "no dominance" or an "L1-dominance" in dimension. In contrast, only one third of all speakers display "no dominance" or an "L1-dominance" in domain (the other speakers display an "L2-dominance" or mixed pattern).

7.1.4 Summary and discussion

The purpose of the first study was to examine language dominance patterns in Turkish-German and Turkish-French bilinguals. We defined language dominance in two categories: domain and dimension. Domain was related to language use in different situations/contexts and was operationalised as language use with parents at and outside home, with siblings and peers at and outside home and in reading and media activities. Dimension captured the language skills (operationalised as verbal fluency and code-mixing) and language knowledge (operationalised as lexical repertoire). Two research questions were addressed and various hypotheses tested.

To answer the first research question (RQ_1) of whether there are intra- and inter-group differences among Turkish-German and Turkish-French bilinguals according to language dominance patterns (domain, dimension) the following hypotheses were tested:

H_0 There are no differences between L1 and L2 with respect to language dominance in domain and dimension by Turkish-German and Turkish-French bilinguals;
H_1 Language dominance (domain) is related to the interlocutor;
$H_{1.1}$ Turkish-German and Turkish-French bilinguals are dominant in their L1 as regards language use with parents;
$H_{1.2}$ Turkish-German and Turkish-French bilinguals are dominant in their L2 as regards language use with siblings and peers.

$H_{1.1}$ was only partially confirmed for the Turkish-German group, but not for the Turkish-French group. The results indicated that Turkish-German bilinguals are more frequently L1-dominant regarding language use with parents as compared to Turkish-French bilinguals. In addition, the findings show that Turkish-German bilinguals made more use of Turkish for media and reading activities in comparison with Turkish-French bilinguals. $H_{1.2}$ can be considered partially confirmed, since most speakers of both bilingual groups indicate an "L2-dominance" in their language use with siblings and peers.

The second research question (RQ_2) was concerned with the relation of language dominance in language use (with parents, siblings and peers as well as media/reading activities) and language dominance in language skills (verbal fluency, code-mixing) and language knowledge (lemma diversity) in L1/L2. The further aim was to answer whether a dominance in L1 in domain would prevent an L1>L2-dominance shift in dimension. The following hypotheses were tested:

H_2 Turkish-German and Turkish-French bilinguals with an "L1-dominance" in domain are L1-dominant in dimension;

H₃ Turkish-German and Turkish-French bilinguals with "L2-dominance" in domain are also L2-dominant as regards verbal fluency, lemma diversity and code-mixing.

The examination of the fine dominance patterns in domain and dimension has shown that there is no general prediction of language dominance in verbal fluency, lexical repertoire and code-mixing on the basis of language dominance in language use with parents, siblings/peers and media/reading activities. A correlation among the variables can rather be assumed at the individual level. Thus, the validity of H_2 was disproved. In addition, the analysis of the global language patterns indicated that global "L1-dominance" in dimension was related to global "L1-dominance" in domain. However, this finding is limited to only a few Turkish-German bilinguals, since the rest of the speakers (including Turkish-French bilinguals) did not indicate an "L1-dominance" in domain at all.

Moreover, the results of the combinations of fine and global dominance patterns in domain and dimension suggest that bilingual speakers are more likely to display an "L2-dominance" or "no dominance" in dimension when they are "L2 dominant" in domain, which tend to confirm H_3.

Let us now discuss some specific inter-group differences found with regard to RQ_1 which go beyond the hypotheses tested. The overall picture implies that Turkish-German bilinguals are generally more L1-dominant or do not indicate a dominance in domain as compared to Turkish-French bilinguals. This may be related to a slower decrease of Turkish input in the Turkish-German context as a result of differences in language policy in France and its smaller Turkish community. The quantitative results did not show major differences between the groups as regards dimension. However, inter-group differences were found for the different measurements of language skills and language knowledge.

First, with regard to verbal fluency, there were only subtle inter-group differences found: a few Turkish-French bilinguals more frequently displayed "no dominance" in comparison with Turkish-German bilinguals who were L2 dominant slightly more often.

Second, Turkish-French bilinguals are more often L2 dominant in their lexical repertoire as compared to Turkish-German bilinguals. Moreover, it was noted that the two groups do not differ with respect to their lexical repertoire in Turkish. Thus, the difference is related to a greater lexical repertoire in the L2 for Turkish-French bilinguals as compared to Turkish-German bilinguals. In §6.1, it was reported that the two groups differed as regards the quantity and quality of Turkish instructions in the school context. Whereas Turkish-German bilinguals attend a biliteracy program where instruction in Turkish and German is coordinated in regular classes (five hours a week and two hours of "only-Turkish"-instruction), only seven Turkish-French bilinguals attended L1-instruction (*ELCO*, see §2.3.2), or private classes offered by Turkish cultural associations (on average two hours per week). Surprisingly, this difference does not lead to differences between Turkish-German and Turkish-French bilinguals' language knowledge and skills in Turkish. In the context of the differences found for the lexical repertoire of the bilinguals' L2, the question of "time on tasks" arises. Advocates of the time on task argument would claim that a greater input and use of Turkish in the school context involves a lower input and use of the L2, which entails a slower lexical development in German. Due to the absence of Turkish instruction in regular classes, we can, indeed, assume that Turkish-French bilinguals had more L2 input in the school context as compared to Turkish-German bilinguals. From a "time on tasks" perspective, this fact would lead to a faster increase of the Turkish-French bilinguals L2 lexicon. However, the context of the current analysis neither allows us to confirm nor to negate the "time on tasks" argument. In order to prove its assumption, further global language assessment tests would be needed. The crucial question here is instead whether no effect of bilingual schooling on the lexical repertoire in Turkish of Turkish-German bilinguals could be detected. We can only assume that there are other factors which have a greater impact than the quantity and quality of L1-instruction, such as the quality and quantity of Turkish in the speaker's everyday interactions.

Third, Turkish-French bilinguals code-mix less frequently than Turkish-German bilinguals. This finding supports the research in this field which provides evidence of that code-mixing is much less prominent among second generation Turkish-French bilinguals in France as compared to other Turkish diaspora in Europe (see §2.3.6). In this study, the observed difference may also be related to the fact that code-mixing is generally more often reported for language use within the family (outside and at home) by the Turkish-German bilinguals' parents than by the Turkish-French bilinguals' parents. This could be a factor which leads to a greater routine of code-mixing in the Turkish-German bilinguals' speech.

The results not only indicate differences between the two bilingual populations. When taken together, the figures reveal that approximately two thirds of all speakers do not display an "L2-dominance" in dimension. Since the participants had all reached their ninth year of age, this finding generally challenges the consensus among researchers, outlined in §2.3.4, that for Turkish-German and Turkish French bilinguals an L2-dominance shift sets in by age eight. In contrast, the findings suggest that Turkish-German and Turkish-French bilinguals have a great chance of preventing a language-dominance shift.

The overall observed heterogeneous picture of language dominance reinforces the assertion that the dimensions along which language dominance were operationalised in this study ("situations of language use", "contexts of language use", "language skills", "language knowledge") are instead "inherently *gradual or continuous*, not categorical" (Birdsong 2016: 86 emphasis in the original). Although for methodological reasons, we attempt to determine a direction of dominance for each speaker in both domain and dimension, it has to be noted that there is no general categorical "L1-/L2-dominance". Furthermore, due to the fact that the operationalisation of language dominance was limited to each of the three categories, the results of Study 1 only provide a limited view of the multidimensional construct of language dominance.

We now turn to the second study, which investigates motion event descriptions in Turkish, German and French. Whenever it is required, the individual dominance patterns determined in Study 1 are taken into account to further specify the direction of cross-linguistic influence.

7.2 Study 2: Voluntary Motion

Study 2 focuses on cross-linguistic influences in oral motion event descriptions of video stimuli (Voluntary Motion (VM-) Task, see §6.2) given by Turkish-German and Turkish-French bilinguals, in order to evaluate the impact of language-specific properties as well as language dominance patterns. To account for the need for substantial extensions and refinements in motion research (as outlined in §3.2.6), the linguistic analysis also covers verb conflation, the verbal periphery (adverbal and adnominal encoding), motion event constructions (combinations of motion verbs and other linguistic devices), Path elaboration (Plus- vs. Minus-Ground) and specific motion event types (here Path focus vs. boundary focus) in greater detail. Furthermore, the bilingual speakers' Manner verb lexicon was separately tested (Manner Verb Control (MVC-) Task, see §6.2) and analysed in order to further identify lexical gaps and explain a possible avoidance of Manner verbs in the participants' performance. The methodical approach provides in addition to quantitative also qualitative statistical analysis, in order to consider inter-individual performances. The study addresses the following research questions:

Are there inter- and intra-group differences in the encoding of motion events in L1 and L2 between the groups tested with regard to

The proportion and diversity of Manner, Path, Manner-Path and Generic motion verbs?
The proportion of expressing Manner and Path in other linguistic devices?
The proportion of combining Manner, Path, Manner-Path and Generic verbs with other linguistic devices and the elaboration of Path?

The proportion of expressing Manner and Path in verb roots in locative and telic Path phrases?

The motion verb repertoire which can explain individual motion verb choices?

Based on the multicompetence framework in which it is assumed that ramifications of L1 and L2 apply to different areas of language, a bidirectional influence in bilinguals' motion description is predicted. Furthermore, this influence is expected to correlate with the similarity or distance of conceptualisation patterns in L1 and L2. Due to the successive acquisition of distinct L2-encoding patterns, it is hypothesised that the conceptualisation patterns of Turkish-German bilinguals vary from those of Turkish and French minimal bilinguals as well as from Turkish-French bilinguals. At the level of linguistic encoding, it is hypothesised that differences occur most likely in overlapping structures (that are patterns within a split system such as expressing Path outside the main verb in Turkish or using more frequently Path verbs or Manner devices in German), constructional preferences (e.g. combining more frequently Manner and Path verbs with disambiguating Path elements in Turkish due to an L2-influence), and conflicting linguistic constraints (e.g. the use of Path or Generic verbs in telic Path phrases in German due to an L1-influence or violations of the boundary crossing constraint in Turkish due to an L2 influence). In contrast, the typological proximity of Turkish-French bilinguals' L1 and L2 is assumed to lead to conceptualisation patterns similar to French and Turkish minimal bilinguals. Thus, a positive conceptual transfer (e.g. in the preference for Path over Manner verbs) is presumed. Bidirectional influence is only expected with respect to intra-typological differences in certain domains (e.g. lower Path elaboration in Turkish due to an L2 influence). Based on the theoretical and empirical background established in Chapters 2–4, the following hypotheses are tested in Study 2:

H_0 Turkish-German and Turkish-French bilinguals do not differ when comparing the groups with each other and with minimal bilingual speakers;

H_1 Turkish-German and Turkish-French bilinguals exhibit an "in-between performance" in L1 and L2 inasmuch as they differ in their performance in comparison with minimal bilingual speakers of the respective languages;

$H_{1.1}$ Turkish-German bilinguals differ in their performance in German when comparing them with German minimal bilinguals;

$H_{1.2}$ Turkish-French bilinguals differ in their performance in French when comparing them with French minimal bilinguals;

$H_{1.3}$ Turkish-German and Turkish-French bilinguals differ in their performance in Turkish descriptions when comparing the groups with each other and with Turkish minimal bilinguals.

Furthermore, the findings of Study 1 are taken into account when further specifying a possible direction of cross-linguistic influence and to answer the research question of whether L1/L2-dominance impact the direction of L1/L2 influence in motion event encoding. It is expected that the direction of influence is supported by language dominance patterns. The more L2 dominant a speaker in domain and dimension, the higher the impact of the L2 on the L1, and, vice versa, the more L1-dominant a speaker is in domain and dimension, the higher the impact of L1 on the L2. The following hypotheses are tested in Study 2 as well:

- H_0 Language dominance does not impact the direction of cross-linguistic influence in Turkish-German and Turkish-French bilinguals' motion expressions;
- H_1 Language dominance impacts the direction of cross-linguistic influence in Turkish-German and Turkish-French bilinguals' motion expressions;
- $H_{1.1}$ Turkish-German and Turkish-French bilinguals display a higher degree of L2 influence on Turkish when they are L2 dominant in domain and dimension;
- $H_{1.2}$ Turkish-German and Turkish-French bilinguals display a higher degree of L1 influence on their L2 when they are L1 dominant in domain and dimension.

In the following, the results of the MVC-Task (elicitation of different types of motion in which Manner is foregrounded in order to control the speaker's Manner verb lexicon in L1 and L2) and the VM-Task (elicitation of re-narrations of "Tweety and Sylvester" sequences in order to analyse the encoding of different types of voluntary motion events in L1 and L2) are presented. The results are based on the analytic procedure presented in §6.5. Because the interpretation of the particular analytical levels of the VM-Task requires further information on the bilingual speakers' Manner verb lexicon, the analysis of the MVC-Task is presented first (§7.2.1). The following sections (§7.2.2–7.2.6) present the results of the particular analytical levels of the VM-Task. In §7.2.2 motion verb choices, frequency and diversity are examined; §7.2.3 includes the encoding of Manner and Path in other linguistic devices and §7.2.4 the Path elaboration. In §7.2.5, the combination of motion verbs with other linguistic devices are examined. §7.2.6 focuses on motion verb choices in locative and telic Path phrases.

The results in §7.2.2–7.2.6 are presented by language in the following order: Turkish, German, French. Thus, at the first step, the results of the bilingual speakers' L1 in the particular analytical level are compared with each other as well as with the results of the Turkish minimal bilingual speakers. At the second and the third step, the results of the bilinguals' L2 in the particular analytical level are compared with those of the minimal bilingual speakers of the respective language.

The analysis for each language includes a quantitative as well as a qualitative analytical procedure. Quantitative analyses are carried out in order to determine inter-group differences and are generally presented in percentages, since the expressed motion events vary across participants, groups and languages. The indicated percentage per group represents the mean of summed proportions per participant. The following qualitative analysis focuses on individual performances which indicate a high variation within a respective group in order to highlight intra-group differences. The qualitative analyses are generally presented as z-scores, which are relative to the mean and the standard deviation of one group. This procedure aims to determine and discuss individual cross-linguistic influence on the basis of individual usage preferences. Furthermore, participants' individual results in the MVC-Task (§7.2.1), as well as bilingual speakers' language dominance profiles in Study 1 (§7.1), are included in the analysis. This allows a more detailed examination of the relation between the individual speakers' lexical repertoire and their individual motion verb choices as well as of the relation between cross-linguistic influence and language dominance in the bilingual speakers' motion descriptions.

As noted in §6.5, this analytical procedure allows a detailed analysis of inter- and intra-group differences between bilingual speakers, bilingual and minimal bilingual speakers as well as individual cross-linguistic influences in bilingual speakers' motion descriptions.

7.2.1 Results of Manner Verb Control Task

As announced above, we will begin with the analysis of the MVC-Task. As noted in §6.2 the task was designed to elicit the speakers' encoding of Manner of motion and controlling of their Manner verb lexicon. The following analysis comprises, at a first step, a general view of the frequency and the diversity of encoded motion verbs in each language and group on the basis of the MVC-Task.

Turkish

Table 31 shows percentages of all encoded motion verbs in the MVC-Task. In all, 165 target events were elicited. The average numbers indicate that Turkish minimal bilinguals encoded slightly more target events (93.94%) compared with the bilingual groups (both 89.09%). Turkish-German and Turkish French bilinguals encoded Manner more frequently (TURGER 69.39%; TURFRE 68.71%) and Manner and Path less frequently (TURGER 16.33%; TURFRE 15.65%) in the verbal slot compared with Turkish minimal bilinguals (Manner verbs 60.65%; Manner-Path verbs 18.71%).

7.2 Study 2: Voluntary Motion — 179

Table 31: Encoded motion verbs in MVC-Task Turkish (in %); diversity of motion verbs (in numbers).

Motion verb category	Encoded motion verbs Turkish			Diversity of motion verbs Turkish		
	TURGER	TURFRE	TUR	TURGER	TURFRE	TUR
VM	69.39	68.71	60.65	11	11	9
VMP	16.33	15.65	18.71	2	3	2
VP	8.16	11.56	14.19	4	4	4
VGEN	6.12	2.72	3.87	1	1	1
VLV	0.00	1.36	2.58	0	2	3
Total encoding	89.09	89.09	93.94			

Figure 33 (based on the numbers in Table 110, see Appendix C.II) indicates that differences in Manner verb choices between bilingual speakers and Turkish minimal bilinguals can be traced back to a few particular lemmas: *zıplamak* 'to bounce', *hoplamak* 'to hop', and *yürümek* 'to walk'. Furthermore, Turkish-French bilinguals use *dönmek* 'to turn(back)' more frequently. Moreover, Turkish minimal bilinguals more frequently use the Manner-Path verb *tırmanmak* 'to climb', which explains the subtle difference in this category. The figures also indicate that in all groups there are speakers who used Path verbs in their descriptions. Interestingly, Path is more frequently encoded in main verbs by Turkish-French and Turkish minimal bilinguals (TURFRE 11.56%; TUR 14.19%) in comparison with Turkish-German bilinguals (8.16%). Differences in Path verb choices can be traced back to the more frequent use of *geçmek* 'to pass' by Turkish-French and Turkish minimal bilinguals as well as the use of *çıkmak* 'ascend' by Turkish-French bilinguals and *inmek* 'descend' and *girmek* 'to enter' by Turkish minimal bilinguals (see Figure 33). In comparison, Turkish-German bilinguals used *binmek* 'to get on' more frequently than the other two groups did. Moreover, Turkish-German bilinguals used Generic verbs more frequently (6.12%) compared to the other two groups (TURFRE 2.72%; TUR 3.87%). Instead of a single Manner verb (e.g. *dengelemek* 'to balance'), a few other motion constructions, such as **denge durmak*[68] 'to stay in balance', *denge sağlamak* 'to redress balance', **denge tutmak*[69] 'to keep one's balance' were used by Turkish-French and Turkish minimal bilinguals.

When examining the diversity of expressed motion verbs, the figures indicate that Turkish minimal bilinguals used somewhat fewer Manner verb lemmas compared to bilingual speakers and did not use *dönmek* 'to spin', *hoplamak* 'to hop' and *sürünmek* 'to crawl' at all. Turkish-French bilinguals used one

---

[68] Target utterance: *dengede durmak*.
[69] Target utterance: *dengede tutmak*.

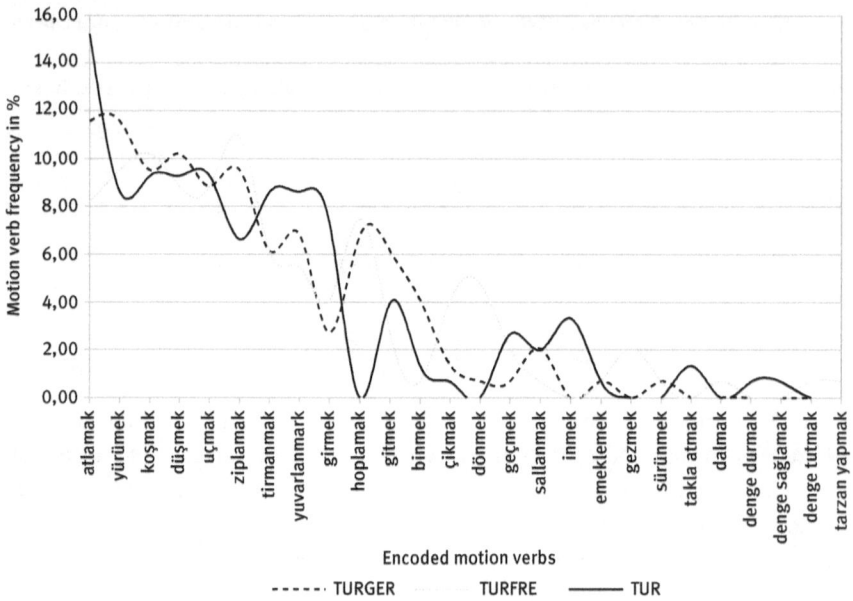

Figure 33: Inter-group differences in motion verb choices Turkish (in %).

Manner-Path lemma (*dalmak* 'to dive') more often in comparison with Turkish-German and Turkish minimal bilinguals. The Path diversity is equal among all groups.

Let us have a look into the Manner verb choices in greater detail. Figure 34 shows that in target items 2b, 7b, 11b, 12b and 14b, Manner verbs were generally less frequently used. Four tendencies could be observed which serve to explain the avoidance of Manner verbs in these items. First, in targets 2b (man climbing up a tree) and 14b (child falling from a pole), various speakers used a Manner-Path verb (*tırmanmak* 'to climb'). This is not surprising, since minimal bilingual speakers of Turkish, German and French also typically used Manner-Path verbs for these types of motion.

Second, some speakers in each group encoded the Figure's preceding Motion (which was not shown in the stimulus) in target item 7b (man balancing on a bench) by using the Path verb *binmek* 'to get on'. Third, various speakers did not use motion verbs at all; the number of motion events not encoded reaches the highest point in target event 11b (man sneaking across a corridor towards a door; TUR 9; TURGER 7; TURFRE 6), which explains the low frequency of Manner verbs used in this target. The high numbers in each group are not surprising, since Turkish does not provide a Manner verb which encodes "to sneak". Instead of using another Manner or Generic verb, some speakers inferred a traversal into

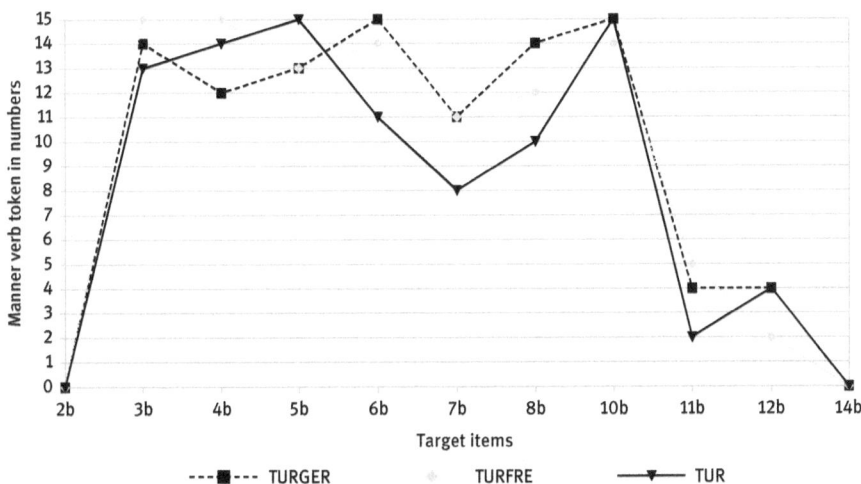

Figure 34: Numbers of Turkish Manner verb choices in target events.

the imagined ground behind the door (which was not shown in the stimulus) by using the verb *girmek* 'to enter'. Fourth, a Figure's traversal into a bounded space as shown in target item 12b (man creeping under a table) led in particular Turkish minimal bilinguals and Turkish-French bilinguals to make use of the Path verb *girmek* (TUR 8; TURFRE 7; TURGER 4, see also Figure 35 below).

At first sight, the numbers in Figure 34 reveal that there are no striking differences between the groups, except for certain target events. In target event 6b (man jumping from a tree), 7b (man balancing on a bench) and 8b (man swinging with a rope into a lake), Turkish-German and Turkish-French bilinguals more frequently encoded Manner by using for instance *atlamak* 'to jump', *hoplamak* 'to hop', or *sallanmak* 'to swing' in comparison with Turkish minimal bilinguals.

Based on the corpus analysis of written texts in the TNC in §3.2.6.1, we classified Manner verbs in the categories "expressive" (less frequent) and "everyday" (more frequent). When applying this classification to the Manner verbs (except for other motion constructions) used by the bilingual and minimal bilingual speakers in Turkish, the average numbers in Table 32 show that bilingual speakers made use of expressive Manner verbs twice as much as Turkish minimal bilinguals.[70]

---

[70] Manner verbs were classified on the basis of the TNC classification in §3.2.6.1.

Table 32: Manner verb usage according to the TNC classification (in %).

Manner verbs	TURGER	TURFRE	TUR
expressive	28.43	30.61	15.22
everyday	71.57	69.39	84.78
total verbs in numbers	102	98	92

Although the MVC-Task aimed to elicit Manner verbs, the numbers in Table 31 above indicated that several speakers in all groups tend to use Path verbs. When examining Path verb choices per group, the figures show that this tendency is consistent among all target events except one. Figure 35 indicates that bilingual speakers more frequently used Path verbs compared with Turkish minimal bilinguals in target event 2b (man climbing up a tree). Whereas Turkish minimal bilinguals preferred the Manner-Path verb *tırmanmak* 'to climb' (13), it was less frequently used by Turkish-German (8) and Turkish-French bilinguals (9). Alternatively, bilingual speakers used the Path verbs *binmek* 'to get on' (TURFRE (5); TURGER (1)) and *çıkmak* 'to ascend' (TURGER (6); TURFRE (1)).

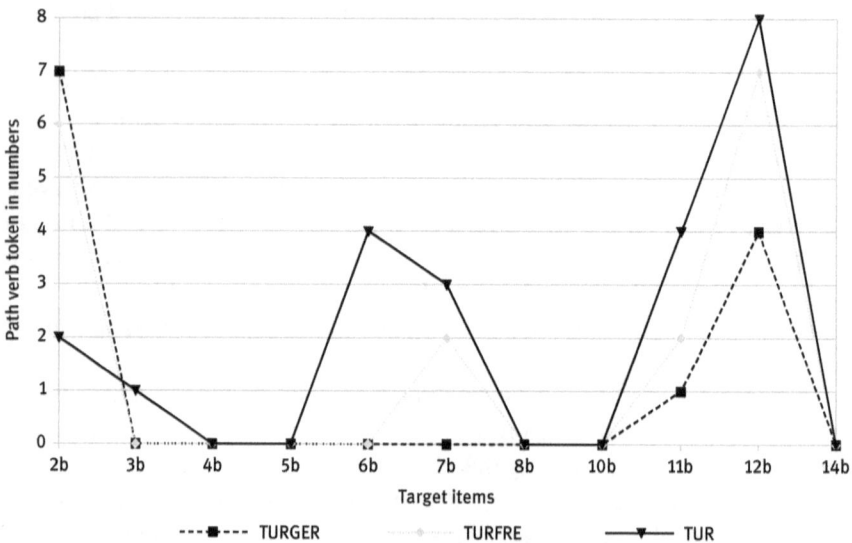

Figure 35: Numbers of Turkish Path verb choices in test items.

On the contrary, Turkish minimal bilinguals more frequently used Path verbs (*inmek* 'to descend' (4)) in target event 6b (man jumping from tree), whereas bilingual speakers only used Manner verbs (*atlamak* 'to jump' TURGER (7), TURFRE (3); *hoplamak* 'to hop' TURGER (2), TURFRE (4); *zıplamak* 'to bounce' TURGER (6)), TURFRE (7). In target event 7b (man balancing on a bench), some speakers used the verb *geçmek* (TUR (3)). As noted above, several speakers used Path verbs when inferring the Figure's motion (which was not shown in the stimulus) in target 7b and 11b (man balancing on a bench plus man sneaking across a corridor towards a door) as well as the Figure's traversal into a bounded space in 12b (man creeping under a table).

In sum, the analysis of the MVC-Task in Turkish revealed that several speakers in all groups used Path verbs instead of Manner or Manner-Path verbs. We assume that on the basis of their mental images, bilingual and minimal bilingual speakers tend to focus in their linguistic symbolisation on the Figure's Path or a traversal over a plane or into a bounded space. Interestingly, the figures reveal that Turkish-French and Turkish minimal bilinguals are more likely to do so. It is possible that this finding is an indication of varying conceptualisation patterns due to differing impact of the speakers' L2. Turkish-German bilinguals tended instead to focus on the Figure's Manner and therefore less frequently used Path verbs in the target items, since they are confronted with distinct conceptualisation patterns in the L1 and L2 in comparison with the other two groups.

However, as regards Manner verb choices, the results indicate that bilingual and minimal bilingual speakers of Turkish display quite a wide range of different Manner lemmas. The inter-group differences found are related to only a few specific Manner verb choices between bilingual speakers and Turkish minimal bilinguals. Turkish-German and Turkish-French bilinguals used slightly more Manner lemmas than Turkish minimal bilinguals. Furthermore, the difference is more obvious in a higher usage of expressive Manner verbs.

German

Table 33 shows percentages of all encoded motion verbs in the MVC-Task. In all, 165 target events were elicited. The average numbers show that both groups used a motion verb in 98% of the target events. German minimal bilinguals encode Manner slightly more often, whereas Turkish-German bilinguals use Manner-Path more.

Table 33: Encoded motion verbs in MVC-Task German (in %); diversity of motion verbs (in numbers).

Motion verb type	Encoded motion verbs German		Diversity of motion verbs German	
	TURGER	GER	TURGER	GER
VM	78.40	80.98	12	16
VMP	17.90	15.95	2	3

(continued)

Table 33 (continued)

Motion verb type	Encoded motion verbs German		Diversity of motion verbs German	
	TURGER	GER	TURGER	GER
VP	0.00	0.00	0	0
VGEN	3.70	0.61	1	1
VLV	0.00	2.45	0	2
Total encoding	98.18	98.79		

Figure 36 (based on the numbers in Table 111, see Appendix C.II) indicates that differences in Manner verb choices between the two groups are related to some specific verbs, which were less frequently used by German minimal bilinguals, but virtually not used at all by Turkish-German bilinguals (*rutschen* 'to slide', *hüpfen* 'to bounce', *fahren* 'to drive', *gleiten* 'to glide', *kullern* 'to wobble', *schaukeln* 'to swing/rock'). Furthermore, German minimal bilinguals used *schwingen* 'to swing' more frequently in comparison with Turkish-German bilinguals. In comparison, Turkish-German bilinguals more frequently used *springen* 'to jump' and *rennen*

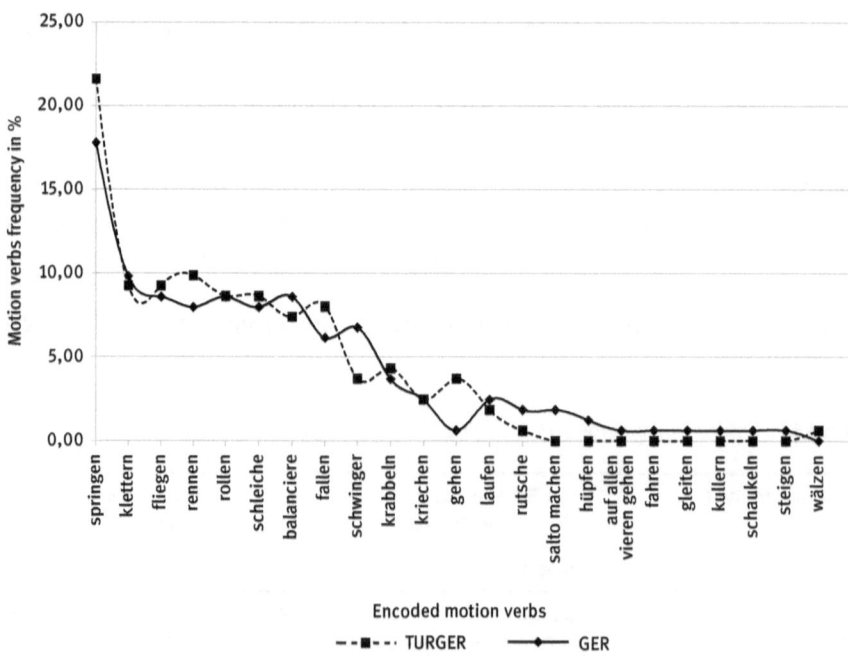

Figure 36: Inter-group differences in motion verb choices German (in %).

'to run'. As regards differences in Manner-Path verb choices, the figures reveal that they can be traced back to a more frequent usage of *fallen* 'to fall' among Turkish-German bilinguals. A few German minimal bilinguals used some other motion constructions which encode a specific Manner (e.g. *einen Salto machen* 'to do a somersault').

Although the Generic verb usage is limited among Turkish-German bilinguals (6 occurrences), German minimal bilinguals hardly used them at all (1 occurrence). Generic verbs were used most often in target event 12b (man creeping under a table). Several few other motion constructions were used by German minimal bilinguals, but never by Turkish-German bilinguals.

Path verbs were not used at all by speakers in the two groups, thus the following examination includes only the domain Manner of motion.

When examining the Manner verb choices in greater detail, the numbers in Figure 37 reveal that there are no striking differences between the groups regarding their Manner verb choices except for four targets. In target events 7b (man balancing on a bench), and 14b (child falling from a pole) German minimal bilinguals used more Manner verbs compared with Turkish-German bilinguals. The latter, however, encoded Manner more frequently in target event 8b (man swinging with a rope into a lake) as compared to German minimal bilinguals. Note that

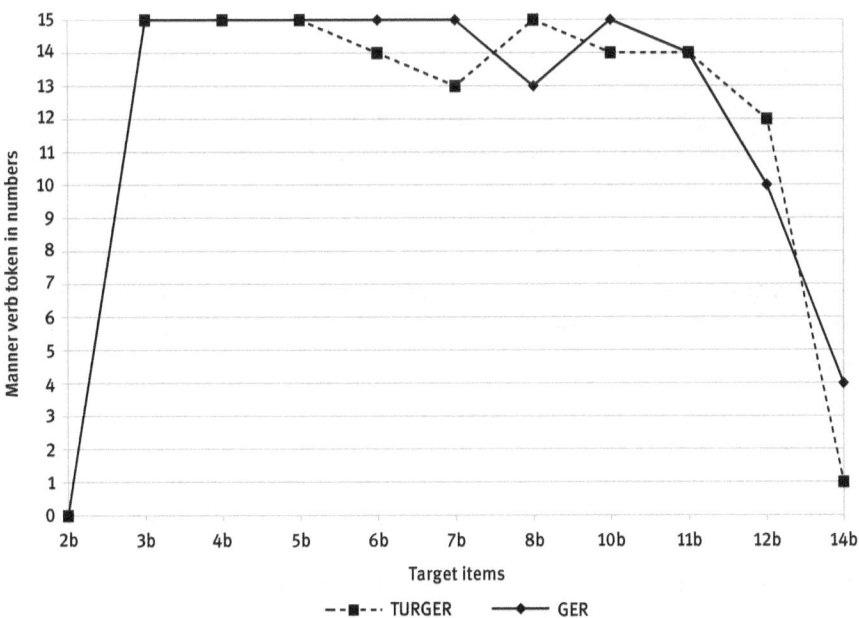

Figure 37: Numbers of German Manner verb choices in target items.

this is only due to the fact that other motion constructions were classified into a single category. The difference in target event 12b (man creeping under a table) is related to a more diverse encoding pattern among German minimal bilinguals, who dominantly used *krabbeln* 'to crawl' (6) and *kriechen* 'to creep' (4) but also the Manner-Path verb *klettern* 'to climb' (2) and the construction *auf allen Vieren gehen* 'to go on all fours'. In contrast, Turkish-German bilinguals used *krabbeln* (7), *kriechen* (4), *schleichen* 'to sneak' (1) but also three times *gehen* 'to go'.

When classifying the Manner verbs (except for other motion constructions which encode Manner) on the basis of the corpus analysis of oral texts in German (DGD 2) in §3.2.6.1 into the categories "expressive" (less frequent) and "everyday" (more frequent), the numbers in Table 34 show that Turkish-German bilinguals used slightly more everyday Manner verbs (65.63%) in comparison with German minimal bilinguals (60.31%).

Table 34: Manner verb usage in German according to DGD 2-classification (in %).

Manner verbs	TURGER	GER
everyday	65.63	60.31
expressive	34.37	39.69
Total verbs in numbers	128	131

In sum, the results of the MVC-Task revealed that there are no major differences between Turkish-German and German minimal bilinguals in the frequency of motion verbs used. Inter-group differences in Manner verb choices between the two groups are related to some specific verbs. The differences are obvious in a lower usage of different Manner lemmas and of expressive Manner verbs by Turkish-German bilinguals. The figures also indicated that Path verbs were not used at all. However, a few Turkish-German bilinguals made use of Generic verbs – most frequently when describing a motion situation which involved a traversal into a bounded space. In contrast, Generic verbs were virtually not used at all by German minimal bilinguals.

French

Table 35 again presents percentages of all the encoded motion verbs in the MVC-Task in French. The average numbers show that Turkish-French bilinguals encoded a few more target events (90.96%) in comparison with French minimal bilinguals (87.88%). Whereas Turkish-French bilinguals encoded Manner more frequently (TURFRE 65.56%; FRE 60.69%), French minimal bilinguals more frequently used Manner-Path verbs (TURFRE 15.89%; FRE 19.31%).

7.2 Study 2: Voluntary Motion — 187

Table 35: Encoded motion verbs in MVC-Task French (in %) and diversity of motion verbs (in numbers).

Motion verb categorys	Encoded motion verbs in French		Diversity of motion verbs in French	
	TURFRE	FRE	TURFRE	FRE
VM	65.56	60.69	6.00	7.00
VMP	15.89	19.31	2.00	2.00
VP	9.27	6.21	6.00	3.00
VGEN	1.32	2.76	1.00	1.00
VLV	7.95	11.03	9.00	8.00
Total encoding	90.96	87.88		

Figure 38 (based on the numbers in Table 112, see Appendix C.II) indicates that differences in Manner verb choices between the two groups are related to *sauter* 'to jump', which was more frequently used by Turkish-French bilinguals. Nevertheless, the figures indicate, that some French minimal bilinguals used one specific Manner verb (*se balancer* 'to swing') which was not used at all by

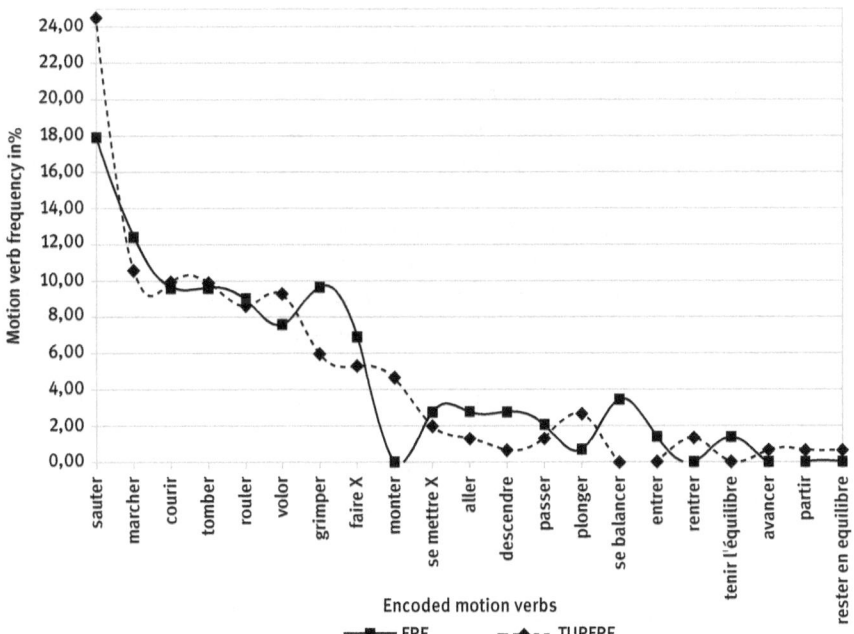

Figure 38: Inter-group differences in motion verb choices French (in %).

bilingual speakers. In contrast, French minimal bilinguals more frequently made use of the Manner-Path verb *grimper* 'to climb', which explains the differences in this category.

In French, speakers of both groups also used Path verbs in their descriptions. These were more diverse and more frequently used by Turkish-French bilinguals (TURFRE 9.27%; FRE 6.21%). The difference can be traced back to a more frequent usage of the Path verb *monter* 'to ascend' by Turkish-French bilinguals. Generic verbs were generally limited to a few speakers in both groups (TURFRE 1.32%; FRE 2.76%).

Moreover, French minimal bilinguals particularly made use of other motion constructions (TURFRE 7.95%; FRE 11.03%). Such constructions most frequently contain the verb *faire* 'to do' and a Manner adverb (e.g. *faire (tout) doucement* 'doing it (very) slowly/quite') or noun (*faire (comme) tarzan* 'doing (it like) tarzan'; *faire l'équilibre* 'doing the balance'; *faire un salto* 'doing a salto'; *faire des roulades* 'doing roll-overs') or the verb *se mettre* 'to get' and a Manner adverb (*se mettre à quatre pattes* 'to get(move) on all fours' or a preposition encoding Path (*se mettre sous la table* 'to get under the table'). A few other constructions were found, such as *rester en équilibre* 'staying in equilibrum' or *tenir l'équilibre* 'keeping the balance'.

Let us now have a look into Manner verb choices in the different target items. The numbers in Figure 39 reveal that both groups used Manner verbs less frequently in target events 2b (man climbing up a tree), 7b (man balancing on a bench), 11b (man sneaking across a corridor towards a door), 12b (man creeping under a table) and 14b (child falling from a rope). In 2b and 14b, most of the speakers used Manner-Path verbs (as in Turkish and German, see above) or Path verbs (for more details see examination of Path verb choices below), which explains the absence of Manner verbs in these targets. A lower frequency of Manner verbs in target items 7b, 11b and 12b was also observed in the Turkish context above (but not for German). Similarly to Turkish, some Turkish-French bilingual and French minimal bilingual speakers used Path verbs when linguistically encoding the Figure's traversal into a bounded space in 12b and/or inferred the Figure's preceding motion in 7b or a following traversal into a bounded space in 8b.

However, some subtle inter-group differences can be observed for certain target events. The difference in 5b (bird flying in the sky) is related to the fact that French minimal bilinguals more frequently did not encode a motion verb but described the perspective of an other agent (*il a vu un oiseau* 'he saw a bird'. In 7b and 8b, French minimal bilinguals more frequently used other motion constructions as compared to Turkish-French bilinguals, which explains the inter-group differences for these targets.

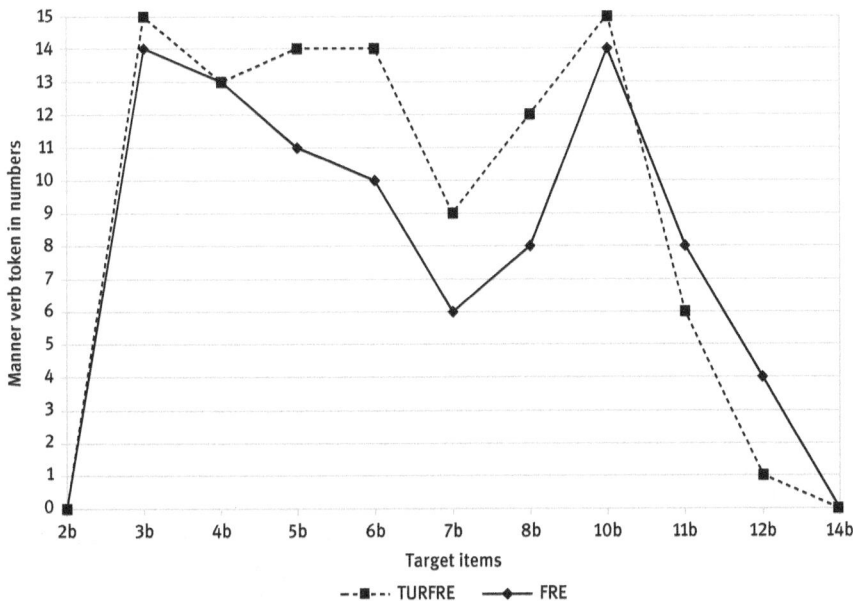

Figure 39: Numbers of French Manner verb choices in target items.

When classifying the Manner verbs (except for other motion constructions which encode Manner) on the basis of the corpus analysis of oral texts in French (CLAPI) in §3.2.6.1 into the categories "expressive" (less frequent) and "everyday" (more frequent) Manner verbs, the numbers in Table 36 show that Turkish-French bilinguals made use of more expressive Manner verbs slightly more often as compared to French minimal bilinguals (TURFRE 16.38%; FRE 13.82%).

When examining the Path verb choices, the numbers in Figure 40 show that, in targets where a traversal into a bounded space was inferred (11b, 12b), speakers tended to use Path verbs. Furthermore, the Path verb choices in 2b (man climbing up a tree) explain the differences found for the more frequent usage of *monter* 'to ascend' by Turkish-French bilinguals and *grimper* 'to climb' by French minimal bilinguals. Bilingual speakers tended to prefer encoding Path in SUPER-event

Table 36: Manner verb usage in French according to CLAPI-classification.

Manner verbs	TURFRE	FRE
everyday	83.62	86.18
expressive	16.38	13.82
Total verbs in numbers	116	123

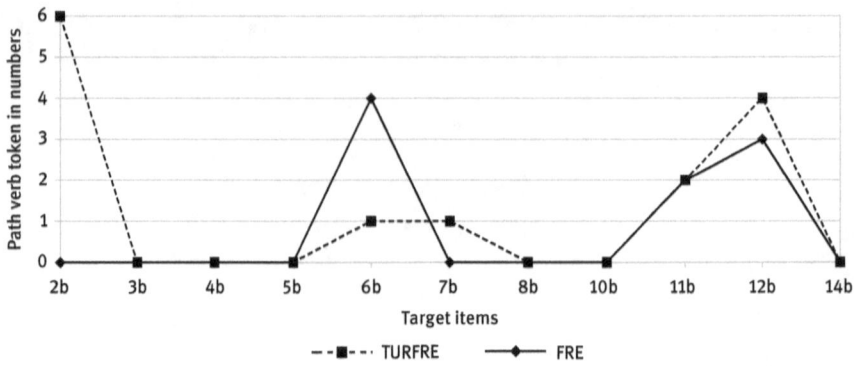

Figure 40: Numbers of French Path verb choices in target items.

types. Vice versa, some French minimal bilinguals tended to use the Path verbs *descendre* 'to descend' in DE-event types (6b, man jumping from a tree), in which bilingual speakers generally used the verb *sauter* 'to jump'.

In sum, the analysis of the MVC-Task in French revealed that several speakers in both groups used Path verbs instead of Manner or Manner-Path verbs. As in the Turkish context discussed, we assume that on the basis of their mental images, bilingual and minimal bilingual speakers tend to focus in their linguistic symbolisation on the Figure's Path or a traversal over a plane or into a bounded space. On the one hand, this is an indication that in V-languages Motion situations which would require more expressive Manner verbs (here to balance, to swing, to creep) lead to different encoding strategies. In contrast to Turkish, speakers of French more frequently expressed Manner of motion in different fashions by making use of other motion constructions. This might be the reason they made use of Path verbs less frequently and also used less diverse Path verbs in French as compared to Turkish-French bilinguals. Nevertheless, the results of the MVC-Task in French supports the assertion that speakers of V-languages tend to focus more on Path for typological reasons and therefore more frequently encoded the Figure's traversal into a bounded space or inferred the Figure's Motion.

As regards the frequency and diversity of Manner and Manner-Path verb choices, the results revealed only subtle inter-group differences. Generally, Turkish-French bilinguals and French minimal bilinguals both display small numbers of Manner lemmas but might compensate for their limited usage by using other motion constructions which serve to express Manner alternatively. Intra-group differences were found for a higher usage of Path verbs in SUPER-event types and a higher usage of Manner verbs in DE-event types by Turkish-French bilinguals. Since the same tendency was found for the Turkish-French bilinguals' as well as Turkish minimal bilinguals' Turkish descriptions, we can assume that these cases indicate an L1 motivated influence.

Summary
The findings of the motion descriptions based on the MVC-Task suggest that speakers of Turkish and French make use of the "Path-in-verb" pattern, even if Manner of motion was foregrounded in the stimulus set. This is particularly the case in motion situations where the Figure crosses a spatial boundary. With regard to the speakers Manner verb repertoire, which the MVC-Task aimed to assess, the findings suggest, that speakers of Turkish generally display a considerable number of Manner lemmas. Whereas there are only subtle differences found between speakers of Turkish and French as regards their Manner verb frequency, bilingual and minimal bilingual speakers used, on average, more diverse Manner verbs in Turkish as compared to the bilingual and minimal bilinguals' performance in French. This finding suggests that speakers made more use of the Manner verb repertoire in Turkish than in French. In French, speakers were more likely to use a limited number of Manner verbs, which are further specified by Manner adverbs (e.g. *marcher à quatre pattes/sur la pointe des pieds/doucement* 'walking on all fours/on tiptoe/slowly'). As regards the Manner verb usage in German, the results showed that Turkish-German bilinguals do not dramatically differ in their frequency of Manner verbs. However, they hardly reached the diversity of Manner lemmas used by German minimal bilinguals.

In the case that Path verb usage by bilingual and minimal bilingual speakers of Turkish and French suggests a typological motivation, it can be assumed that the use of Path verbs in telic Path phrases is an indication of the boundary crossing constraint in V-languages, which leads speakers to encode Path in the main verb and to omit Manner of motion (see §3.2.6.4). Furthermore, bilingual and minimal bilingual speakers tend to "upgrade" some motion situations in Turkish and French and thus might construct different motion images than those of bilingual and minimal bilingual speakers of German. As a consequence, the former focus in their linguistic symbolisation on the Figure's Path, a traversal over a plane or into a bounded space, while the latter focus rather on the Manner of motion. This observation could be typologically motivated. V-speakers might generally be more routinised to focus on the Figure's Path and add this information when it is missing. The fact that Turkish-German bilinguals do so less frequently in their Turkish descriptions is possibly related to their L2 conceptualisation, which influences the way they encode in their L1 the Motion situations shown in the stimuli. On the other hand, a few Turkish-German bilinguals made use of Generic verbs when linguistically encoding a Figure's traversal into a bounded space. In these cases the avoidance of Manner verbs seems to be related to their L1-conceptualisation and reflects an L1>L2 influence. Among Turkish-French bilinguals, a cross-linguistic influence could also be observed for some specific event types. When linguistically encoding SUPER- and DE-events in French, Turkish-French bilinguals reflect their preference for Manner-Path in SUPER- and Path verbs in DE-events. These cases are possibly due to an intra-typological difference of Turkish and French.

The differences found in the Manner verb diversity between bilingual and minimal bilingual speakers are not surprising when it is assumed that bilingual speakers' language development takes longer than that of minimal bilinguals (see §2.2).

Let us now turn to the results of the VM-Task. Note that the task was carried out for eliciting different types of voluntary motion events which are within the cross-linguistic focus of the current study.

7.2.2 Results of motion verb choices

7.2.2.1 Overall picture

In Chapters 3 and 4, we predicted that speakers of V- and S-languages differ as regards their preferences for conflation patterns: Turkish and French speakers are expected to prefer the "Path in verb" pattern and German speakers the "Manner in verb" pattern (for the concept of conflation see §3.2.4 and the coding §6.5). When examining, at a first step, the three languages cross-linguistically, the quantitative results confirm these predictions. The average numbers in Table 37 show that, first, the "Path-in-verb" pattern is more dominant in Turkish and French among Turkish-German and Turkish-French bilinguals as well as Turkish and French minimal bilinguals, and that, second, the "Manner-in-verb" is more dominant in German among Turkish-German and German minimal bilinguals.

Table 37: Motion verb choices in motion descriptions of all participants (in %).

Motion verb category	Turkish			German		French	
	TURGER	TURFRE	TUR	TURGER	GER	TURFRE	FRE
VM	30.59	23.56	30.00	43.06	57.08	25.21	34.74
VMP	7.22	12.78	15.35	11.89	16.54	9.24	6.19
VP	38.42	39.36	36.52	0.00	0.39	53.00	45.98
VGEN	23.77	22.77	17.71	43.05	18.00	10.61	11.09
VLV	/	1.53	0.42	/	0.39	1.93	2.00
VAUX/VMOD	/	/	/	2.00	7.60	/	/
Total verbs in numbers	282	252	293	338	330	241	205

In the context of distinct preferences of conflation patterns in L1 and L2, we further predicted that conceptual transfer would lead to differences in Turkish-German bilinguals' motion verb choices in their L1 and L2. In contrast, Turkish-French bilinguals' are expected to display a positive conceptual transfer in their motion verb choices in L1 and L2. In order to examine these predictions, let us now take a closer look at the motion verb choices of bilingual and minimal bilingual speakers in the respective languages.

Turkish (quantitative)
The figures in Table 38 display a few inter-group differences as regards the use of motion verbs in the speakers' motion descriptions in Turkish.

Whereas Turkish-German bilinguals more frequently used Manner verbs (TURGER 30.59%; TURFRE 23.56%, see example (100)), Turkish-French bilinguals used more frequently Manner-Path verbs (see example (101)) (TURFRE 12.78% vs. TURGER 7.22%). As regards Path (see example (102)) and Generic verbs (see example (103)) both groups are relatively close.

(100) kedi hemen • •   kuş-a • • • [[ee]] ((2s)) koş-tu
      cat   immediately bird-DAT   run-PST.3SG
      'Immediately the cat ran to the bird' (Kurt, TURGER, 54–62)

(101) suy-un   için-e   düş-tü
      water-GEN inside-DAT   fall-PST.3SG
      'It fell into the water' (Adile, TURFRE, 448–451)

(102) kedi öbü / öbür [[ee]] taraf-dan geç-mey-e   çalış-tı
      cat   other   side-ABL   pass-NMLZ-DAT try-PST.3SG
      'The cat tried to pass from the other side' (Devin, TURFRE, 145–153)

(103) tam   yukarı gel-iyodu
      almost up   come-PST.IPFV.3SG
      'It was almost coming up' (Gamze, TURGER, 296–298)

Generally, parametric and non-parametric tests did not reveal a significant difference under TURGER and TURFRE conditions in the usage of VM, VMP, VP and VGEN. In comparison with the Turkish minimal bilingual group, the figures indicate that Turkish-French bilinguals are closer to Turkish minimal bilinguals when encoding Manner and Path together (such as *tırmanmak* 'to climb', *düşmek* 'to fall'; TURFRE 12.78%, TUR 15.35%), whereas Turkish-German bilinguals less frequently

Table 38: Means (M), Standard deviations (SD) and ranges (R) of motion verb choices in Turkish motion descriptions of Turkish-German (TURGER) and Turkish-French bilinguals (TURFRE) as well as Turkish minimal bilinguals (TUR) (in %).

Motion verb category	Turkish								
	TURGER			TURFRE			TUR		
	M	SD	R	M	SD	R	M	SD	R
VM	30.59	13.12	0–50	23.56	13.24	6.66–50	30.00	10.08	10.71–43.75
VMP	7.22	8.52	0–12	12.78	9.7	0–30.77	15.35	7.22	4.76–33.33
VP	38.42	13.85	17.39–58.33	39.36	16.91	15.38–84.62	36.52	10.64	23.08–57.14
VGEN	23.77	19.77	0–72.22	22.77	13.32	0–46.67	17.71	8.39	4.76–29.41
VLV	/	/	/	1.53	3.36	0–11.11	0.42	1.61	0–6.25
VAUX/VMOD	/	/	/	/	/	/	/	/	/
Total verbs in numbers	282			252			293		

used such verbs (7.22%). This observation is supported by the results of the statistical analysis. Independent two sample *t*-tests were conducted to compare the Manner (VM) and Manner-Path verb (VMP) usage under Turkish-German bilingual (TURGER), Turkish-French bilingual (TURFRE) and Turkish minimal bilingual (TUR) conditions. Turkish-German bilinguals (M=7.22, SD=8.52) used Manner-Path verbs significantly less often than Turkish minimal bilinguals (M=15.35, SD=7.22), $t(28)$=–2.82, p=<.01**). Under TURFRE and TUR, as well as under TURGER and TURFRE conditions, no significant differences were found.

In turn, Turkish-German bilinguals' and Turkish minimal bilinguals' total Manner verb (such as *koşmak* 'to run'; TURGER 30.59%, TUR 30%) and Path verb (such as *girmek* 'to enter'; TURGER 38.42%, TUR 36.52%) encoding is more similar. Parametric tests did not reveal significant differences under TURGER and TUR conditions.

It is striking that both bilingual groups made use of Generic verbs more frequently compared to Turkish minimal bilinguals (17.71%). However, parametric and non-parametric tests did not reveal a significant difference under TURGER and TUR as well as TURFRE and FRE conditions in VGEN-usage.

Other motion constructions with semantically weak verbs such as *yapmak* 'to make' or *etmek* 'to do' were rarely used and only found among Turkish-French bilinguals (see example (104)) and Turkish minimal bilinguals (e.g. *takip etmek* 'to do a chase' see example (105)).

(104) kedi de   tarzan gibi yap-mak   ist-iyo
      cat FOC tarzan like make-INF =want-PROG.3SG
      'The cat also wants to do it like Tarzan' (Geza, TURFRE, 294–299)

(105) gel-ip   o-nu   takip et-ti
      come-CVB   she/he-ACC   chase do.PST.3SG
      'It came and chased him' (Sevgi, TUR, 87–91)

Generally, a considerable number of Manner and Manner-Path verbs across bilingual and minimal bilingual speakers were observed (see §7.2.2.2 below for an overview).

Let us now analyse the results qualitatively in order to obtain and discuss intra-group differences and individual speakers' usage preferences.

Turkish (qualitative analysis)
As regards motion verb choices in Turkish the figures reveal intra-group differences. For instance, as regards Turkish German-bilinguals, Melis did not use a

single Manner verb in Turkish, whereas Kurt used a Manner verb in about 50% of his motion utterances. In order to detect speakers with highest and lowest values in a respective motion verb category in one language, z-scores were calculated for each speaker as illustrated in §6.5.

The numbers in Table 39 show that Alisa, Kurt and Yiğit more frequently used Manner verbs, which is possibly an indication of an L2>L1 influence. Furthermore, Melis indicates a negative z-score as regards her Manner verb usage and a positive z-score in the use of Path verbs, which seems to be an indication of a more typical V-pattern. We will include these cases in the qualitative analysis of motion descriptions in German.

Table 39: Turkish-German bilinguals with a distance of one or more standard deviations (SD) in Manner verb (VM), Manner-Path verb (VMP), Path verb (VP) and Generic verb (VGEN) usage in Turkish, their educational background (SES) and standard deviation in types per lemma (TpL).

Speaker	VM	VMP	VP	VGEN	SES	TpL
Alisa	+1.02		−1.33			
Kurt	+1.48			−1.20	*	−0.03
Yiğit	+1.10					
Ela		+1.50		−1.20	low	−1.18
Tuba		+1.67				
Beren	−1.91		−1.17	+2.45	middle	+0.15
Gamze			−1.52	+1.22	low	−0.11
Esna			−1.07	+1.18	*	−0.62
Melis	−2.33	+2.09	+1.29			

*incomplete questionnaire

The figures further indicate that Beren's performance differs strongly in comparison with the other speakers; his lower usage of Manner and Path verbs in Turkish is possibly related to a higher usage of Generic verbs (+2.45 SD). Furthermore, there were a few other speakers who used Path verbs less frequently (Alisa, Gamze, Esna).

As regards Turkish-French bilinguals, the highest variation can be observed for the individual use of Manner verbs (see Table 40). Arda and Nihal used Manner verbs more frequently (and similarly Path verbs less frequently). In contrast, Bircan, Devin, Dilşah and Seçkin indicate a negative z-score in their Manner verb usage. Furthermore, the speakers vary in their Path verb usage. Arda, Nihal and Seçkin indicate a negative z-score, whereas Devin and Mert used Path verbs

Table 40: Turkish-French bilinguals with a distance of one or more standard deviations (*SD*) in Manner verb (VM), Manner-Path verb (VMP), Path verb (VP) and Generic verb (VGEN) usage in Turkish.

Speaker	VM	VMP	VP	VGEN	SES	TpL
Arda	+1.99		−1.15			
Nihal	+1.24		−1.15			
Bircan	−1.20	+1.85				
Devin	−1.20	−1.32	+2.68	−1.13	middle	+0.35
Dilşah	−1.26			+1.79	low	−0.85
Seçkin	−1.20	+1.85	−1.42	+1.76	middle	+0.01
Geza		−1.32				
Mert			+1.22	−1.71	middle	+0.08

more frequently. Moreover, Dilşah and Seçkin made more frequent and Devin and Mert less frequent use of Generic verbs.

In all, Devin and Seçkin display the highest variations, since their *z*-scores are, in all motion verb categories, more than 1 *SD* below or above the mean. We will include these speakers in our qualitative analysis as regards their motion descriptions in French in order to further specify the nature of variation.

Note that the phenomenon of intra-group difference does not exclusively account for bilingual speakers. A few Turkish minimal bilinguals also indicate in each category positive or negative *z*-scores (at least 1 *SD* above or below the mean).[71]

Generally, we have seen that speakers in each group more frequently used Generic verbs in their motion descriptions. In §2.1.3, it was argued that a speaker's lexical development can be influenced by her or his educational background. In this context, the question arises of whether a lower lexical repertoire, which might be reflected in a preference for semantically weak verbs, is related to a speaker's educational background. When considering the individual educational background profiles of speakers with the highest and lowest Generic verb usage, the figures indicate that there is no general interrelation between parental education and Generic verb usage among these speakers. Although Gamze (TURGER) and

---

[71] Manner verbs below mean: Seval, Sevgi; Manner verbs above mean: Başak, Musa, Zeren; Manner-Path verbs below mean: Helin, Musa; Manner-Path verbs above mean Akay, Onur; Path verbs below mean: Musa, Nilsu; Path verbs above mean Kerim, Seval; Generic verbs below mean: Zeren, Onur, Kerim; Generic verbs above mean: Helin, Musa, Nilsu, Zuhal.

Dilşah (TURFRE) indicate a higher Generic verb usage and a low educational background, their z-values of TpL are below the mean for both speakers, which is an indication that they display a more diverse lexical repertoire in comparison with other speakers of their group. Moreover, Devin and Mert (both TURFRE) indicate a middle educational background and used Generic verbs less frequently. Their lexical repertoire is, however, not strikingly different. In contrast to these cases, Beren (TURGER) and Seçkin (TURFRE) used Generic verbs more often but indicate a middle educational background. Both speakers are near the mean of their groups as regards their TpL-scores. Thus, we can conclude that a middle educational background does not necessarily lead to a lower usage of Generic verbs. Furthermore, there is no relation between the speaker's lexical repertoire and their educational background. Consequently, the use of Generic verbs in Turkish motion descriptions, then, is possibly a more common pattern and not due to lexical development.

Let us now turn to the bilingual speakers' performance in their respective L2. We first examine the motion verb usage in German among Turkish-German and German minimal bilinguals.

German (quantitative)

As already noted, Turkish-German and German minimal bilinguals used Manner verbs (see example (106)) more frequently compared to speakers of Turkish and French (see Table 41). Furthermore, they hardly used Path verbs at all (there was only one incidence found in the corpus of German minimal bilinguals, see example (107)).

(106) er   is   auf   diesn   • • [[em]] linien   balangsiert
      he   =AUX.PR   on   =these   line.PL   =balance.PTCP
      'He balanced on these lines' (Eda, TURGER, 849–856)

(107) tweety verschwand   ürgndwie •   mit granny smith   in • •
      tweety disappear.PST   =somehow   with =Granny Smith   in
      die   straßnbahn
      DET   =tramway
      'He disappeared with Granny Smith in the tramway' (Moritz, GER, 860–871)

Moreover, the figures summarised in Table 41 indicate multiple inter-group differences. Turkish-German bilinguals used Manner less frequently (43.06%) and Manner-Path verbs (11.89%) in comparison with German minimal bilinguals (VM 57.08%; VMP 16.54%).

Table 41: Means, Standard deviations (SD) and ranges (R) of motion verb choices in German (in %).

Motion verb category	German					
	TURGER			GER		
	M	SD	R	M	SD	R
VM	43.06	13.87	18.52–65.52	57.08	11.38	40–78.57
VMP	11.89	4.68	5.13–20	16.54	5.91	10–32
VP	/	/	/	0.39	1.52	0–5.88
VGEN	43.05	11.76	11.76–70.37	18.00	12.28	0–40
VLV	0.00	/	/	0.39	1.52	0–5.88
VAUX/VMOD	2.00	2.68	0–7.41	7.60	7.35	0–25
Total verbs in numbers	338			330		

The results of an independent two sample *t*-tests support these differences. Turkish-German bilinguals (*M*=43.06, *SD*=13.87) significantly less frequently used Manner verbs than German minimal bilinguals (*M*=57.08, *SD*=11.38); *t*(28)=3.02, *p*<0.01**. Furthermore, a significant difference for Manner-Path verb usage was found under Turkish-German bilingual (*M*=11.89, *SD*=4.68) and German minimal bilingual (*M*=16.54, *SD*=5.91) conditions; *t*(28)=2.35, *p*<0.05*.

Furthermore, Turkish-German bilinguals (*M*=43.06, *SD*=11.76) used significantly more Generic verbs (such as *kommen* 'to come' in example (108)) as compared to German minimal bilinguals (*M*=18.00, *SD*=12.28); *t*(28)=–4.66, *p*<0.001***. Note that Turkish-German bilinguals used Generic verbs as often as Manner verbs in their German motion descriptions.

(108) dann is   se•   ist   die katze rein   gekommen
      then =AUX.PR =she AUX.PR DET cat   inside come.PTCP
      'Then the cat came in' (Michel, GER, 548–556)

The statistics also show that German minimal bilinguals more frequently used modal or auxiliary verbs (in motion constructions without motion verb, see example (109)) in comparison with Turkish-German bilinguals. A Wilcoxon rank sum test revealed a significant difference under TURGER (*med*=0) and GER (*med*=5.0) conditions; *W*=172.5, *p*<0.01**. Note that only one third of the Turkish-German bilingual speakers used this type of construction at all.

(109) die katze wollte   hinterher
      DET cat   want-PST   afterwards
      'The cat wanted [to go] after [him]' (Nicole, GER, 252–255)

There are several possible reasons for the differences found. First, the lower frequency of Manner verbs among Turkish-German bilinguals is possibly due to a typologically motivated L1-influence, since Manner verbs were less frequently used in Turkish as compared to German. However, the results of a Pearson's correlation did not reveal a significant correlation of lower Manner verb usage in Turkish and German ($r=0.35$).

Second, the greater amount of Generic verbs among Turkish-German bilinguals may also reflect a compensation strategy as a result of a lack of German Path verbs. Due to their low semantic degree, German Generic verbs may be an appropriate strategy among Turkish-German bilinguals, who similarly used these verbs in the way in which they used Path verbs in Turkish (VGEN German: 43.05%; VP Turkish: 38.42%). The conceptualisation may then be L1 based, the lexical material in the L2 is "adjusted", insofar Generic verbs are extended to Path verbs (Schroeder 2009; Goschler et al. 2013). In this case, a conceptual transfer can be assumed which is reflected in a lower Manner and Manner-Path encoding in German motion descriptions. When correlating the bilingual speakers' proportion of Manner and Generic verbs in German, this assumption can be confirmed. A Pearson's correlation indicates that there is a significant negative correlation between Turkish-German bilinguals' Manner verb and Generic verb usage ($r=-0.95$; $t(13)=-10.705$, $p<0.01***$); the lower the use of Manner verbs, the higher the use of Generic verbs (and vice versa) in Turkish-German bilinguals' motion descriptions.

Third, the lower frequency of Manner and Manner-Path verbs is possibly also a result of a general higher usage of Generic verbs, a phenomenon which is well known in child language acquisition as well as second language acquisition research. Although Generic verbs were also found in the motion descriptions of German minimal bilinguals of the same age, they used these verbs much less frequently. This may be related to their minimal bilingual background; they have had more input in only one language (German) compared to the bilingual speakers (see §2.2.1). Consequently, it can be assumed that German minimal bilinguals are one step further in their lexical development, which may be reflected in a lower usage of Generic and a higher usage of Manner/Manner-Path verbs in German. In order to further specify this aspect and to exclude the possibility of lexical gaps or of a lower lexical repertoire, it is necessary to take into account the results of the MVC-Task (§7.2.1), TpL-scores (§7.1.2.2) and educational profiles.

By doing so, Generic verb and no motion-constructions of the VM-Task were checked in a first step with elicited Manner and Manner-Path verbs in the MVC-Task. Lexical gaps were excluded from the individual amount of Generic/no-motion constructions used.

The analysis indicates that there are only four incidences in which a lexical gap can not be excluded. This concerns the speakers Melis (*schleichen* 'to sneak' (2)), Taylan (*klettern* 'to climb' (1)), and Ozan (*fallen* 'to fall' (1)), who used the appropriate Manner verb in neither the VM- nor the MVC-Task. Those incidences were subtracted from the individual numbers of Generic verbs.

The numbers in Table 42 indicate the individual results of the VM-Task, which were subdivided into "no Manner/Manner-Path verbs" (z-scores of Generic verb and no motion verb constructions) as well as the total number of "Manner/Manner-Path lemmas". The individual results of the MVC-Task indicate the total number of Manner/Manner-Path lemmas as well as the proportion of used Manner/Manner-Path verb choice per target events. In addition, z-scores were calculated for the speaker's TpL-scores as well as their individual educational

Table 42: Z-scores of Generic/no motion verbs in German, Manner/Manner-Path repertoire in German, z-scores of tokens per lemma (TpL) in German and educational background profiles of Turkish-German bilinguals.

	Voluntary Motion Task		Manner Verb Control Task				
	no Manner/ Manner-Path verb	Manner/ Manner-Path lemmas	Manner/ Manner-Path lemmas	Manner/ Manner-Path verb choice per target events	Tokens per lemma (TpL)	SES
Speaker	SD	numbers	numbers	%	SD	level
Melis	1.52	6	8	90.91	+1.97	high
Alisa	1.26	9	7	81.82	+0.96	low
Kurt	1.14	5	9	100.00	+0.20	*
Dana	0.80	6	7	100.00	+0.23	low
Tuba	0.67	7	8	100.00	+0.38	middle
Taylan	0.67	7	8	81.82	−0.01	middle
Beren	0.21	8	10	100.00	−1.05	middle
Gamze	0.07	9	10	81.82	+1.15	low
Yiğit	−0.42	10	10	90.91	−1.69	middle
Ela	−0.53	8	9	100.00	−0.84	low
Esna	−0.73	9	10	100.00	−0.71	*
Ozan	−0.73	9	9	90.91	+0.63	low
Sefar	−0.86	7	8	100.00	+0.44	low
Eda	−1.25	13	10	100.00	−0.32	middle
Serkan	−1.83	8	9	100.00	−1.33	middle
mean	39.71% (SD 15.24)	8.06	8.8	94.55	2.27 (SD 0.33)	

*incomplete questionnaire

profiles indicated. The results must be interpreted with caution, since the differences between the participants are, in some cases, relatively small.

Let us first have a look into the individual results of the VM-Task. The figures indicate a tendency for a lower Manner/Manner-Path verb repertoire (lemmas) to cause a higher use of Generic verbs in all event types. The only exception is the speaker Alisa, who displays a high Manner/Path verb repertoire (nine different lemmas) and has one of the highest z-scores for Generic verb usage (+1.26 SD). The results of the MVC-Task confirm these findings; except for Kurt, the Manner/Manner-Path verb lexicon of speakers with a high usage of Generic verbs in the VM-Task, is below average. However, there are speakers who used Generic verbs more frequently in the VM-Task but indicate a 100% Manner verb choice in the MVC-Task. Thus the proportion of Manner/Manner-Path verb choices in the MVC-Task does not seem to be related to a higher usage of Generic verbs in the VM-Task.

Moreover, when considering the speaker's TpL-scores (see §7.1.2.2) a Pearson's correlation indicates a highly significant negative correlation ($r=-0.77$) between a lower TpL (in the sense of a higher lexical repertoire) and a lower usage of Generic verbs ($t(13)=-4.31$, $p<0.001***$).

When examining the speaker's educational background and their Generic verb usage, Alisa and Dana indicate a low educational background and used Generic verbs more frequently, however, there are th ree speakers who also have a low educational background but used Generic verbs less frequently (Ela, Ozan, Sefar). Thus, the speakers' educational background and a higher or lower usage of Generic verbs do not seem to have any relation.

We can conclude that the higher usage of Generic verbs is not due to gaps in the speakers' Manner/Manner-Path verb lexicon nor to their educational background. However, for a few speakers a lower Manner/Manner-Path verb repertoire and a general lower lexical repertoire seem to trigger the use of Generic verbs and possibly reinforce a conceptual L1-transfer.

The results will now be analysed qualitatively in order to obtain and discuss intra-group differences as well as to determine individual speakers' usage preferences and individual cross-linguistic influences in the bilingual speakers' performance in L1 and L2.

German (qualitative analysis)

In regard to German, there are considerable intra-group differences (see z-scores in Table 43). For instance some Turkish-German bilingual speakers used Manner verbs less frequently compared to other speakers (e.g. Dana, Melis, and Tuba vs. Eda and Serkan). Whereas Tuba preferred Manner-Path verbs (+1.29 SD) over Manner verbs (−1.14 SD), Dana (+1.18 SD) and Melis (+1.62) indicate a higher Generic

Table 43: Turkish-German bilinguals with a distance of one or more standard deviations (*SD*) in Manner verb (vm), Manner-Path verb (vmp), and Generic verb (vgen) usage in German.

Speaker	VM	VMP	VGEN
Dana	−1.24		+1.18
Eda	+1.62	−1.03	−1.12
Serkan	+1.56	+1.18	−1.86
Tuba	−1.14	+1.29	
Melis	−1.77		+1.62
Alisa		−1.39	
Taylan		−1.30	
Sefar		+1.67	

verb usage. In contrast, Serkan more frequently used Manner (+1.56 *SD*) and Manner-Path verbs (+1.18 *SD*) and less frequently Generic verbs (−1.86 *SD*). Among all Turkish-German bilinguals, Eda and Serkan display the highest variation within the Turkish-German bilingual group (both indicate more than one *SD* above or below the mean in Manner, Manner-Path and Generic verb usage). Again, the phenomenon of intra-group differences is not limited to bilingual speakers, since a few German minimal bilingual speakers also vary strongly within their group.[72]

When examining the bilingual speakers' L1 and L2 the focus is on possible cross-linguistic influences. We assumed that this is the case for speakers who indicate a higher usage of Manner verbs in Turkish. Vice versa, this should also account for speakers with a lower frequency of Manner verbs as well as with a higher frequency of Generic verbs in German. The numbers show that among speakers who indicate more than +1 *SD* in their Manner verb usage in Turkish (Alisa, Kurt and Yiğit), only Yiğit also more frequently used Manner verbs in German (+0.67 *SD*). In contrast, Alisa (−0.52 *SD*) and Kurt (−0.54 *SD*) display a lower proportion of Manner verbs in German as compared to their Turkish motion descriptions. For Ozan, the same tendency can be observed as for Yiğit; he more frequently used Manner verbs in his German motion descriptions (+0.67 *SD*) and also indicates a higher proportion in Turkish (+0.53 *SD*). In the cases of Yiğit and

---

[72] Manner verbs below mean: Alex, Katharina, Manner verbs above mean: Max, Nicole, Sophie (+1 *SD*); Manner-Path verbs below mean: Melanie; Manner-Path verbs above mean: Christian, Katharina; Generic verbs below mean: Christian, Philip, Sophie; Generic verbs above mean: Alex, Michel.

Ozan, an L2>L1 influence can be maintained, which is possibly related to conceptualisation restructuring. When taking the Turkish-German bilinguals' language dominance profiles (§7.1) into account, the direction of influence seems to be supported for Ozan and Yiğit. Ozan displays an "L2-dominance" in both domain and dimension, whereas Yiğit is L2 dominant in dimension but does not display a clear dominance pattern as regards domain.

For speakers who indicate a lower Manner verb usage in German (Dana, Tuba, Melis), the figures reveal a relation between a higher Path verb and lower Manner verb usage in Turkish only for Melis. In her case, an L1>L2 influence can be maintained. By contrast, the scores of Dana and Tuba show that they used even slightly more Manner verbs in Turkish as compared to their German motion descriptions. Because their values in Turkish do not strikingly differ from the mean, an influence can not be maintained. Instead, Tuba more frequently used Manner-Path verbs in both Turkish (+1.47 *SD*) and German (+1.29 *SD*); since Manner-Path verbs were generally more frequently used in German, the direction of influence is probably L2 based. Moreover, Dana and Melis indicate a high Generic verb usage in German, which is assumed to be influenced by an L1-conceptualisation pattern. Language dominance seems to support the direction of transfer for Melis, who is L1-dominant in both domain and dimension and partly for Tuba who does not indicate a dominance in dimension and is more L2-dominant as regards domain. Dana, in contrast, indicates a dominance in neither domain nor dimension.

In sum, a higher use of Manner verbs in German does not necessarily imply a higher usage in Turkish, and this would be an indication of an L2>L1 influence. Consequently, we can conclude that Turkish-German bilinguals are closer to Turkish minimal bilinguals than to German minimal bilinguals. The direction of influence is, except for some few speakers, L1 based instead, and reflected in a lower frequency of Manner verbs and a higher frequency of Generic verbs in the L2. The direction of transfer is, for some speakers, supported by language dominance, but not for all.

Nevertheless, as regards the Manner, Manner-Path and Generic verb usage, further details with respect to the respective verb construction (§7.2.5) and event types (§7.2.6) are required in order to specify possible L1 effects. Let us now turn to the motion verb usage in French.

French

As already noted, Turkish-French and French minimal bilinguals generally preferred Path verbs (see example (110)) but also display a considerable number of Manner (see example (111)) and Manner-Path verbs (see example (112)).

(110) puis [[ee]] elle sort   de   la   cage
      then   she exit.PR from DET cage
      'Then she exits from the cage' (Shirin, TURFRE, 218–224)

(111) après il a   roul-é • dans une descente
      later he AUX.PR roll-PTCP in DET descent
      'Later he rolled on a decent' (Ethan, FRE, 190–197)

(112) puis [[ee]] il il a   grimp-é   sur un poteau
      then   he he AUX.PR climb-PTCP on DET pole
      'Then he … he climbed on a pole' (Seçkin, TURFRE, 502–510)

The figures in Table 44 also indicate some inter-group differences. On the one hand, the results of an independent sample t-test show that Turkish-French bilinguals used Manner verbs significantly less frequently (M=25.21, SD=9.89) than French minimal bilinguals (M=34.74, SD=12.33); $t(27)$=2.3, p<0.05*).

Table 44: Means (M), Standard deviations (SD) and ranges (R) of motion verb choices in French (in %).

Motion verb category	French					
	TURFRE			FRE		
	M	SD	R	M	SD	R
VM	25.21	9.89	6.67–36.84	34.74	12.33	14.29–57.14
VMP	9.24	9.11	0–33.33	6.19	8.06	0–21.05
VP	53.00	9.49	36.84–71.43	45.98	14.42	21.43–71.43
VGEN	10.61	6.16	0–21.43	11.09	11.36	0–38.89
VLV	1.93	4.9	0–18.18	2.00	3.99	0–10.53
VAUX/VMOD	/	/	/	/	/	/
Total verbs in numbers	241			205		

On the other hand, Turkish-French bilinguals encoded Path (53%) as well as Manner and Path (9.24%) slightly more often in verbs, compared to French minimal bilinguals (VP 45.98%; VMP 6.19%). Non-parametric tests did not reveal significant differences.

As regards the use of Generic verbs (e.g. *aller* 'to go', *venir* 'to come' TURFRE 10.61%; FRE 11.09%, see example (113)) as well as other motion constructions (*faire comme tarzan* 'doing like Tarzan' TURFRE 1.93%; FRE 2.00%, see example (114) below), both groups are relatively equal. Parametric and non-parametric tests did not reveal a significant difference, which supports these findings.

(113) puis   il   va •   dans   la   maison   de   l'   oiseau
       then   he   go.PR in   DET   house   of   DET   bird
       'Then he went into the bird's house' (Zoé, FRE, 47-56)

The differences found are distributed among certain phenomena (see Table 45). In both languages, Turkish-French bilinguals exhibit a lower Manner-verb usage in comparison with minimal bilinguals of the respective language. Therefore, a general cross-linguistic influence has to be excluded. As regards Manner-Path and Path verb usage, Turkish-French bilinguals are closer to Turkish minimal bilinguals, whereas they are closer to French minimal bilinguals with respect to the use of Generic verbs and other motion constructions with semantically weak verbs.

Table 45: Proportion of motion verb choices in Turkish and French (in %).

Motion verb category	Turkish		French	
	TURFRE	TUR	TURFRE	FRE
VM	23.56	32.03	25.21	34.74
VMP	12.78	13.32	9.24	6.19
VP	39.36	36.52	53.00	45.98
VGEN	22.77	17.71	10.61	11.09
VLV	1.53	0.42	1.93	2.00
VAUX/VMOD	/	/	/	/
Total verbs in numbers	252	293	241	205

The higher usage of Manner-Path verbs in French by Turkish-French bilinguals is possibly due to a more frequent and routine use of Manner-Path verbs in Turkish. However, this assumption is not supported by the statistical analysis. A Pearson's correlation revealed a negative correlation ($r=-0.25$), which means that the higher the Manner-Path verb usage in Turkish, the lower it is in French. Furthermore, the correlation is not significant.

Similarly, there is no significant correlation between the higher use of Path verbs in Turkish and the general higher frequency of Path verbs in French. Although a Pearson's correlation indicates a positive correlation, which means that the use of Path verbs in Turkish is greater, when Path verbs are more frequently used in French, the correlation coefficient is very small ($r=0.15$).

One crucial question remains with respect to the Generic verb usage in Turkish and French. As regards the lower usage in the L2 among Turkish-French bilinguals in comparison with the higher usage in L2 by Turkish-German bilinguals, a possible explanation could be explained typologically. Since Turkish-French bilinguals are confronted with distinct conflation patterns and constraints in their L2 to a lesser degree, they do not have to adjust lexical material in their L2, as argued above. However, we have seen that the use of Generic verbs is generally much higher in Turkish compared to French among both bilingual and minimal bilingual groups. As argued above, a lower frequency in Manner or Path verb usage can be evoked by a general higher Generic verb usage. Since Turkish-French bilinguals and French minimal bilinguals both used Generic verbs in French much less frequently, the question arises of whether *aller* 'to go' and *venir* 'to come' are less prototypic in French motion constructions as compared to Turkish Generic verbs *gitmek* 'to go' and *gelmek* 'to come' in Turkish motion constructions. Furthermore, if there are developmental constraints in child bilingualism, as argued in the Turkish-German context above, we also have to question why this is not the case for Turkish-French bilinguals, and we will return to this aspect in the qualitative analysis.

The above-mentioned limited, but more frequent usage of constructions with the semantically weak verb *yapmak* 'to do' in Turkish can be explained by a loan transfer of the French expression *faire comme Tarzan* 'doing like Tarzan', which was also used by French minimal bilinguals. As an illustration, the speaker Özgür transfers the construction in example (114) into his Turkish description (see example (115)), which reflects an enrichment of his linguistic and conceptual repertoire due to his bilingual background. A construction such as in example (115) was not used at all by Turkish minimal bilinguals.

(114) le   chat   il   a   une   idée, • il   essaye de faire comme   tarzan
      the   cat   he   AUX.PR DET   idea   he   try.PR to do   like   tarzan
      'The cat has an idea, it tries to do it like Tarzan' (Özgür, TURFRE, 345–358)

(115) şey   kedi tarzan gibi yap-mak   isti-yo
      thing cat   tarzan like make-INF   =want-PROG.3SG
      'The cat wants to do it like Tarzan' (Özgür, TURFRE, 179–184)

In sum, Turkish-French bilinguals' motion descriptions display subtle bidirectional influences which are generally related to conflation preferences and loan transfers.

Let us analyse the results qualitatively, in order to obtain and discuss intra-group differences as well as to determine individual cross-linguistic influences in the bilingual speakers' performance in L1 and L2.

French (qualitative analysis)

Again, the figures in Table 46 reveal intra-group differences in both groups. For instance, four Turkish-French bilingual speakers did not use Manner-Path verbs at all, whereas a higher frequency was found among other speakers (for instance Seçkin +2.64 SD).

Table 46: Turkish-French bilinguals with a distance of one or more standard deviations (SD) in Manner verb (VM), Manner-Path verb (VMP), Path verb (VP) and Generic verb (VGEN) usage in French, their standard deviation of tokens per lemma (TpL) in French as well as educational background (SES) profiles

Speaker	VM	VMP	VP	VGEN	TpL	SES
Arda	−1.29		+1.00	+1.32	−1.30	middle
Gözde	−1.00					middle
Devin	−1.83	−1.01	+1.94	+1.76	−0.48	middle
Seçkin	−1.87	+2.64		−1.76	+1.27	middle
Bircan	+1.18		−1.7			low
Emre	+1.06		−1.07			low
Geza		−1.01				low
Nihal			−1.37			*
Nezihe		−1.01				middle
Özgür		−1.01				middle
Shirin				−1.76	+1.14	*

*incomplete questionnaire

Furthermore, two speakers did not use Generic verbs at all (Seçkin, Shirin), while others display a higher usage (Arda, Devin). Similarly, the range in Manner verb usage shows that some speakers rarely used Manner verbs (e.g. TURFRE Arda, Sevin, Seçkin), whereas other speakers made use of this pattern more frequently (Bircan, Emre). Generally Devin displays the most variation in French since his values are, in each category, more than one SD above or below the mean.

As regards the lower usage of Manner verbs in French, we assumed that there is no relation to Turkish, since bilingual speakers generally used Manner verbs less frequently in comparison with minimal bilingual speakers in both languages. The individual results show that there are individual relations in the preferred motion verbs. Devin and Seçkin both display lower z-scores in their French Manner verb usage; the lower frequency in Devin's case is possibly related to a general preference for Path and Generic verbs in French, whereas Seçkin prefers Manner-Path verbs instead.

Similarly, the higher use of Path verbs in French seems to reinforce Devin's higher usage in Turkish (+2.68 *SD*). Since Path verbs are generally more often used in French, the direction of influence is here L2 based instead. Furthermore, Seçkin's preference for Manner-Path verbs in French is possibly related to a higher frequency in Turkish (+1.84 *SD*). Here an L1>L2 influence can be assumed, since Manner-Path verbs are generally more often used in Turkish as compared to French. When considering their language dominance profiles, the direction of influence is confirmed for Devin, who is clearly L2 dominant in both domain and dimension, but not for Seçkin, who is L2-dominant in domain and does not indicate a clear dominance in dimension.

When considering the use of Generic verbs in Turkish and French, we pursued the question of whether the observed difference is due to general restrictions in French or whether other reasons, such as a lower lexical repertoire or educational background can be considered. Let us examine some individual cases. We have seen, that Dilşah and Seçkin indicate the highest proportions of Generic verbs in Turkish and similarly used Manner verbs less frequently. In French, Seçkin did not use a single Generic verb, and Dilşah's *z*-score is only +0.17 *SD* above the mean. Consequently, a relation between their Generic verb usage in L1 and L2 can be excluded. Furthermore, Seçkin indicates a lower lexical repertoire in French, which could have an influence on his Generic verb usage, as argued in the Turkish-German context above. However, this is obviously not the case. When taking into account their language dominance profiles, Dilşah indicates an "L2-dominance" in both domain and dimension. As illustrated above, Seçkin is L2-dominant in domain and does not indicate a clear dominance in dimension. This finding suggests, that the higher use of Generic verbs in Turkish is possibly related to a lower dominance in Turkish. However, this suggestion is disproved when relating the lowest proportions of Generic verbs of Turkish-French bilinguals in Turkish (Devin, Mert) and their language dominance profiles. Devin is clearly L2-dominant in both domain and dimension; Mert is L2-dominant in domain and does not indicate a dominance as regards dimension. Both, Devin's and Mert's dominance profiles resemble those of Dilşah and Seçkin, whereas their Generic verb usage in Turkish is inverted. Neither does further qualitative analysis including their educational profiles reveal any relation. For instance, among those speakers who used Generic verbs more frequently in French, Arda and Devin, both, indicate a middle educational background and similarly a greater lexical repertoire.

On the basis of these findings we can conclude, that neither "L1-dominance" indicates a lower Generic verb usage, nor "L2-dominance" a higher Generic verb usage in Turkish; just as small is the impact of the speakers' educational background and their lexical repertoire on the use of Generic verbs in French. We therefore can maintain that the use of Generic verbs is generally less restricted in Turkish, as compared to French.

In order to further specify the inter-group differences found for the analytical level of motion verb choices, let us now have a closer look into the motion verb lemmas which were used by each group in the VM-Task. The results are presented for each language and group. Lemmas are sorted by falling numbers of a total group's lemma tokens.

7.2.2.2 Lemma frequency

Turkish

The inter-group differences of the motion verb patterns illustrated above are also reflected in the lemma frequency of Turkish motion verbs in Figure 41 (based on the numbers in Table 113, see Appendix C.III). There is a more frequent usage of the Manner-Path verbs *düşmek* 'to fall' and *tırmanmak* 'to climb' by Turkish-French bilinguals and Turkish minimal bilinguals, a more frequent usage of the Generic verbs *gitmek* 'to go' and *gelmek* 'to come' by Turkish-German and Turkish-French bilinguals as well as a more frequent usage of the Path verb *binmek* 'to get in/on' by Turkish French bilinguals.

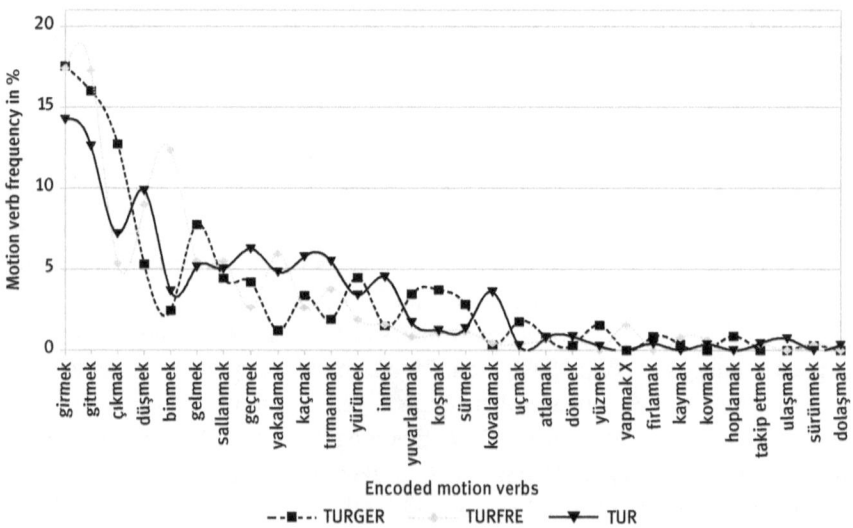

Figure 41: Inter-group differences in motion verb choices Turkish (in %).

However, the groups differ further with regard to choices of some specific motion verbs. Turkish-German bilinguals used the Path verb *çıkmak* 'move up'/'ascend' more frequently as well as the Generic verb *gelmek* 'to come'. Furthermore, a difference is also visible in a limited, but more frequent use of more expressive

Manner verbs (*yuvarlanmak* 'to roll', *sürmek* 'to drive', *hoplamak* 'to hop/bounce') by Turkish-German bilinguals. Other (less expressive) Manner verbs are also, although limited, more frequently used by Turkish-German bilinguals in comparison with the other two groups (*yürümek* 'to walk', *koşmak* 'to run', *uçmak* 'to fly', *yüzmek* 'to swim'). One exception is the Manner verb *yakalamak* 'to catch' which was much less frequently used by Turkish-German bilinguals compared with the other two groups.

In comparison with the bilingual groups, Turkish minimal bilinguals made more frequent use of the (less expressive) Manner verbs *kovalamak* 'to pursue/chase' and *kaçmak* 'to escape' and the Path verb *inmek* 'to descend/to get off'. With Turkish-French bilinguals, the most striking difference in the sense of a more frequent usage in comparison with the other two groups is limited to the Path verb *binmek* 'to get in/on' and the Generic verb *gitmek* 'to go'.

German

The inter-group differences of the motion verb patterns illustrated above are also reflected in the lemma frequency of German motion verbs in Figure 42 (based on the numbers in Table 114, see Appendix C.III). However, the numbers indicate that the difference in Generic motion verb usage is particularly related to the verb *gehen* 'to go', since the distance between the frequency of *gehen* and *kommen* 'to come' is far greater (as predicted by the corpus analysis in §3.2.6.1).

The figures reveal that there are some Manner verbs which were used more frequently by German minimal bilinguals (*rollen* 'to roll', *laufen* 'to walk'). Furthermore, the observed difference of Manner verb usage between the two groups is also related to a greater diversity of expressive Manner verbs which were infrequently used by German minimal bilinguals, but not at all by Turkish-German bilinguals (*schlüpfen* 'to slip', *schnappen* 'to grap', *hechten* 'to dive', *kugeln* 'to bowl/roll', *rasen* 'to dash'). Instead, Turkish-German bilinguals used *rennen* 'to run' more frequently as compared to German minimal bilinguals. However, there are also several expressive Manner verbs among Turkish-German bilinguals which were not used at all by German minimal bilinguals (*krabbeln* 'to crawl', *hüpfen* 'to bounce'). Furthermore, one utterance (see (116)) was found with the Turkish-German bilingual speaker Tuba, which reflects, on the one hand, the productivity of denominalisation in German (the noun *Murmel* 'marble' is denominalised by adding the suffix -n). In this context, the verb *murmeln* denotes 'playing with marbles'. On the other hand, the usage of *murmeln* in combination with the directional Path device (*weg* 'away') reflects instead a continuation of lexical innovation in the category Manner of motion verbs in German.

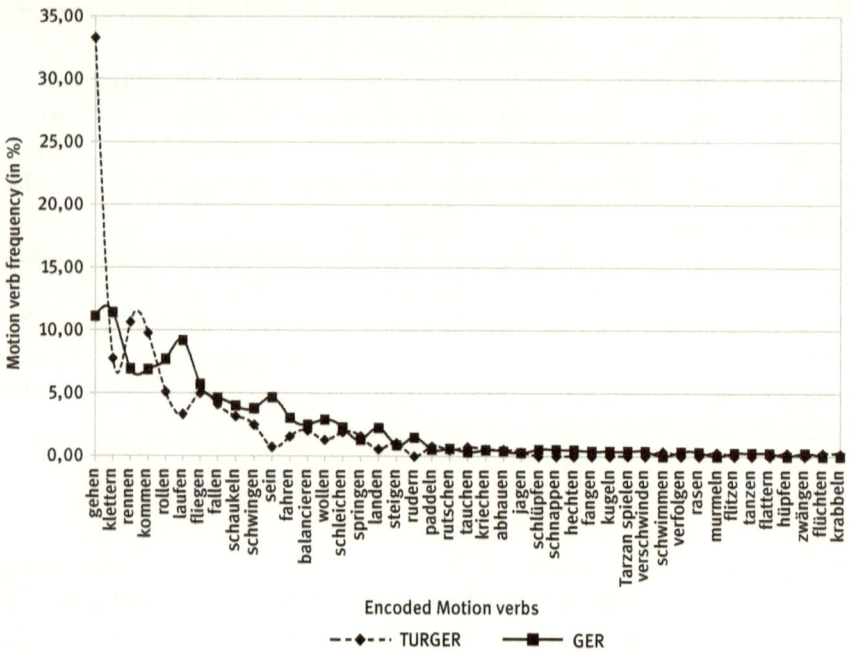

Figure 42: Inter-group differences in motion verb choices German (in %).

(116) und • dann ist die so weg-gemurmelt, zu-m bowlingcenter
and than AUX.PR DET like off-roll like.PTCP to-DET.DAT bowling centre
'Then she rolled off to the bowling centre like a marble' (Tuba, TURGER, 458–468)

Furthermore, the observed difference in the category Manner-Path verbs is related to a higher usage of *klettern* 'to climb' by German minimal bilinguals. As regards motion descriptions without motion verbs, the higher frequency among German minimal bilinguals can be traced back to a higher usage of *sein* 'to be' constructions.

French

The average numbers in Figure 43 (based on the numbers in Table 115, see Appendix C.III) illustrate that the observed differences of Manner verb usage between both groups is related to a higher frequency of *rouler* 'to roll', *se balancer* 'to swing', *conduire* 'to drive', *atterir* 'to land' and *marcher* 'to walk' by French minimal bilinguals. Furthermore, there are some infrequently used Manner verbs among French minimal bilinguals which were not used at all by Turkish French bilinguals (e.g. *avancer* 'to advance', *tourner* 'to turn', *chasser* 'to chase', *faufiler*

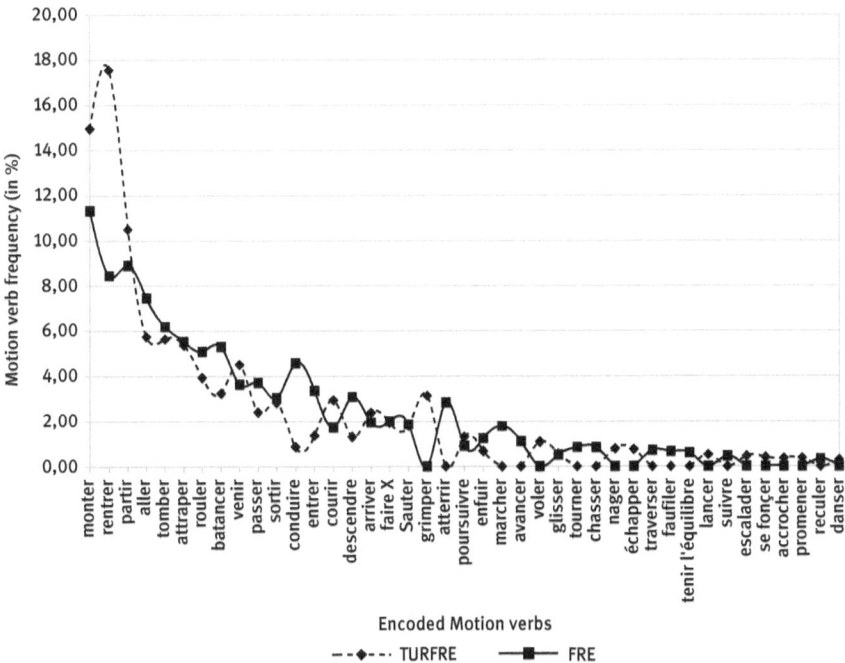

Figure 43: Inter-group differences in motion verb choices French (in %).

'to sneak'). Vice versa, there are some infrequently used Manner verbs among Turkish-French bilinguals which were not used at all by French minimal bilinguals (e.g. *voler* 'to fly', *nager* 'to swim', *échapper* 'to escape', *se fonçer* 'to rush oneself', *s'accrocher* 'to cling to sth.', *promener* 'to stroll').

The figures indicate that the higher usage of Manner-Path verbs among Turkish-French bilinguals is related to a more frequent usage of *grimper* 'to climb', which was not used at all by French minimal bilinguals. Note that the opposite was observed in the MVC-Task (see §7.2.1). In contrast, the difference between French minimal bilinguals and Turkish-French bilinguals as regards the usage of the verb *monter* 'to ascend' is also evident in the VM-Task. Here, it seems that Turkish-French bilinguals are more ready to encode SUPER-events in the VM-Task, which we will analyse in greater details in §7.2.6. Furthermore, it is striking that Turkish-French bilinguals made use more frequently of *rentrer* 'to enter (again)' and *partir* 'to leave', which explains the differences found for Path encoding between both groups.

The results in this section have indicated some inter-group differences which are possibly related to the motion lemma diversity. Let us now examine this aspect in greater details. For reasons of clarity, the category of "Manner diversity" includes Manner, Manner-Path verbs as well as other motion constructions with

Manner devices. Motion constructions without motion verb (with *sein* 'to be' or *wollen* 'to want') were not taken into account.

7.2.2.3 Lemma diversity

Turkish

The numbers in Table 47 show that in the case of Turkish, the means of different Motion as well as Manner/Manner-Path and Path verbs are lower among the bilingual groups compared to the Turkish minimal bilingual group.

Table 47: Means (*M*) and ranges (*R*) of Motion, Manner/Manner-Path and Path verb diversity Turkish (in numbers).

	Turkish					
	TURGER		TURFRE		TUR	
	M	R	M	R	M	R
Motion verbs	9.2	5–13	8.87	5–13	10.53	7–13
Manner verbs	4.73	1–7	4.53	1–9	5.73	4–8
Path verbs	3.07	2–4	2.87	2–5	3.47	1–5

Table 48: Means (*M*) and ranges (*R*) of everyday and expressive Manner verbs Turkish (in %).

Manner/ Manner- Path verbs	Turkish								
	TURGER		TOT (in numbers)	TURFRE		TOT (in numbers)	TUR		TOT (in numbers)
	M	R		M	R		M	R	
everyday	88.72	62.5–100		94	80–100	97	96.52	84.62–100	126
expressive	11.28	0–37.5		14	0–20	3	3.48	0–15.38	5

As regards the diversity of motion verbs (including Generic verbs), Turkish-German bilinguals used on average slightly more motion verbs (9.2) in comparison with Turkish-French bilinguals (8.87). When looking at the distribution of motion verbs, the figures reveal that there are, in each group, speakers who used only five different motion verbs (Beren, TURGER; Devin/Dilşah TURFRE), other speakers display a higher diversity (Sefar TURGER (13); Maide/Nezihe TURFRE (13)). The difference between the lowest and highest values in each group is exactly the same. In comparison with the bilingual groups, Turkish minimal bilinguals used more different motion verbs (10.53); the range of motion verbs is also smaller (7–13).

Furthermore, the numbers show that, on average, Turkish-German bilinguals display a slightly higher Manner diversity (TURGER 4.73) compared to Turkish-French bilinguals (4.53). However, neither group reached the diversity of Turkish minimal bilinguals (5.73). Moreover, the differences between Manner verbs used is much greater among the bilingual groups. In each bilingual group, there are speakers who only used one type of Manner verbs (TURGER Beren; TURFRE Seçkin); other speakers used seven (TURGER Ela) or even nine types (TURFRE Nezihe). The distribution of used Manner verbs is much more limited in the minimal bilingual group. Among Turkish minimal bilinguals, Helin and Seval display the lowest number of Manner verbs (4), whereas Başak and Rüya used each eight different Manner verbs.

As regards the diversity of Path verbs, Turkish-German bilinguals again used slightly more different Path verbs (3.07) in comparison with Turkish-French bilinguals (2.87). On average, Turkish minimal bilinguals used some more diverse Path verbs (3.47). The difference between lowest and highest values of Path verbs was relatively equal in all groups. A few speakers in each group only used two different Path verbs, others four (TURGER) or five (TURFRE, TUR).

On the basis of this analysis, the assumption that Turkish-German bilinguals used more diverse Manner verbs than the other two groups (see §7.2.2.2) cannot be maintained. Moreover, the figures show that bilingual speakers lag somewhat behind their Manner/Manner-Path and Path verb diversity when comparing them with minimal bilingual speakers. Again, considerable intra-group differences were observed in each group.

Furthermore, when classifying the Manner and Manner-Path verbs used by bilingual and minimal bilingual speakers of Turkish on the basis of the corpus analysis of written texts in Turkish (TNC) (see §3.2.6.1) in the categories "expressive" (less frequent) and "everyday" (more frequent), the numbers in Table 48 indicate that Turkish-German bilinguals, on average, made strikingly more often use of expressive Manner verbs[73] (11.28%) in comparison with Turkish-French bilinguals (3%)[74] and Turkish minimal bilinguals (3.48%)[75]. Whereas most of the Turkish-French (12) and Turkish minimal bilinguals (11) never used expressive Manner verbs, the numbers are much smaller among Turkish-German bilinguals. Note that these numbers have to be interpreted carefully when comparing them with those of speakers of German and French, since the classification of Turkish expressive and everyday Manner verbs is based on a written corpus analysis, whereas the classification in German and French is based on oral corpora analyses.

---

73 *hoplamak* 'to hop'; *sürünmek* 'to creep'; *yuvarlanmak* 'to roll'.
74 *sürünmek* 'to creep'; *yuvarlanmak* 'to roll'.
75 *yuvarlanmak* 'to roll'.

German

As regards German, again, differences of Motion and Manner verbs used between bilingual and minimal bilingual speakers were found. The figures in Table 49 indicate, that, on average, Turkish-German bilinguals used less diverse motion verbs (9.87) in comparison with German minimal bilinguals (12.0). Furthermore, German minimal bilinguals used at least ten different motion verbs, whereas the minimum value among Turkish-German bilinguals is seven. Again, there are some speakers in each group who used more diverse motion verbs (Eda TURGER (15); Mia GER (16)).

Table 49: Means (*M*) and ranges (*R*) of Motion, Manner and Path verb diversity German (in numbers).

	German			
	TURGER		GER	
	M	R	M	R
Motion verbs	9.87	7–15	12.0	10–16
Manner verbs	8.07	5–13	10.6	8–14
Path verbs	/	/	0.06	0–1

When regarding the different Manner verb types (see Table 50), the range of lowest and highest values is also greater among Turkish-German bilinguals. Kurt (TURGER), for instance, used only five different Manner verbs, whereas Eda made use of thirteen different Manner verbs. In the German minimal bilingual group, Katharina and Moritz used the lowest number of different Manner verbs (8), Mia, in contrast, used fourteen different Manner verbs. On average, German minimal bilinguals display a higher diversity of Manner verbs (10.6) compared to Turkish-German bilinguals (8.07).

Moreover, when applying the Manner and Manner-Path verbs used by Turkish-German bilinguals and German minimal bilinguals to the classification of expressive (less frequent) and everyday (more frequent) which we determined in §3.2.6.1 on the basis of the corpus analysis of oral texts in German (DGD 2), the numbers in Table 50 indicate that Turkish-German bilinguals made, on average, less frequent (12.63%) use of expressive Manner verbs[76] in comparison with German minimal bilinguals (15.92%).[77] The ranges of lowest and highest values

---

[76] *balancieren* 'to balance'; *hüpfen* 'to bounce'; *krabbeln* 'to crawl'; *kriechen* 'to creep'; *schleichen* 'to sneak'; *schwingen* 'to swing'.
[77] *balancieren* 'to balance'; *flattern* 'to flap'; *flitzen* 'to dash'; *hechten* 'to dive'; *kriechen* 'to crawl; *kugeln* 'to bowl/roll'; *rasen* 'to rush'; *schleichen* 'to sneak'; *schlüpfen* 'to slip'; *schnappen* 'to grab'; *schwingen* 'to swing'; *zwängen* 'to jam'.

Table 50: Means (*M*) and ranges (*R*) of everyday and expressive Manner verbs German (in %).

Manner verbs	German						
	TURGER		TOT (in numbers)	GER		TOT (in numbers)
	M	*R*		*M*	*R*	
everyday	87.37	71.43–100	155	84.08	72.43–92.31	207
expressive	12.63	0–28.57	25	15.92	7.69–28.57	39

differ very little between the two groups. However, among the bilingual group there are speakers who used no expressive Manner verbs at all (Melis, Taylan), which is not the case for German minimal bilinguals.

French

The numbers in Table 51 indicate no striking differences between the means and the distribution of different Motion (TURFRE M=9.4; FRE M=9.2), Manner (TURFRE M=4.4; FRE M=4.6) and Path (TURFRE M=3.93; FRE M=3.8) verbs by Turkish-French and French minimal bilinguals. However, there were striking intra-group differences found. Whereas Lola (FRE) used sixteen and Geza (TURFRE) fourteen different motion verbs, Devin (TURFRE) only used seven and Yanis (FRE) five different motion verbs. Furthermore, Mathis (FRE) used nine different Manner verbs; the highest value in the bilingual group is seven (Geza, Mert). In contrast there is one speaker in each group who only used one Manner verb (TURFRE: Devin; FRE: Lilou). As for Path verbs, Jeanne and Mathis (FRE) used seven, Arda, Devin, Geza, Shirin (TURFRE) five, Yanis (FRE) only two, Dilşah, Mert, Nezihe, Nihal, and Özgür (TURFRE) only three different lemmas.

Table 51: Means and ranges Motion, Manner and Path verb diversity French (in numbers).

	French			
	TURFRE		FRE	
	M	*R*	*M*	*R*
Motion verbs	9.4	7–12	9.2	5–16
Manner verbs	4.4	1–7	4.6	1–9
Path verbs	3.93	3–5	3.8	2–7

When applying the Manner and Manner-Path verbs used by Turkish-French bilinguals and French minimal bilinguals in French to the determined categories

Table 52: Means (*M*) and ranges (*R*) of everyday and expressive Manner verbs French (in %).

Manner verbs	French					
	TURFRE			FRE		
	M	R	TOT (in numbers)	M	R	TOT (in numbers)
everyday	79.25	50–100	26	71.72	50–100	66
expressive	20.75	0–50	17	28.28	0–50	24

expressive (less frequent) and everyday (more frequent) based on the corpus analysis of oral texts in French (CLAPI) (see §3.2.6.1), the numbers in Table 52 reveal that French minimal bilinguals made more frequent use of expressive Manner verbs (28.28%)[78] compared to Turkish-French bilinguals (20.75%).[79]

Summary

The findings of this section indicate that inter-group differences were primarily found in Turkish-German bilinguals' motion verb choices in German: they less frequently made use of Manner and Manner-Path verbs and displayed a strikingly higher usage of Generic verbs. In contrast, Turkish-German bilinguals only differ in their motion verb choices in Turkish in a lower Manner-Path verb usage in comparison with Turkish minimal bilinguals. Except for a lower frequency of Manner verbs by Turkish-French bilinguals, there were no striking differences found between the three groups. Similarly, the only difference between Turkish-French and French minimal bilinguals was limited to a lower Manner verb usage in French by Turkish-French bilinguals.

Moreover, as regards motion verb choices, some intra-typological differences between Turkish and French were found, which are mainly reflected in a more common usage of Generic verbs in Turkish. This usage is independent of the speakers' lexical repertoire and educational background.

On the basis of the analysis of motion verb frequency and diversity, we can state that bilingual speakers generally displayed a lower diversity of Manner, Manner-Path and Path verbs and less frequently used expressive Manner verbs in comparison with minimal bilingual speakers of the respective language. The only exception was found for Turkish-German bilinguals who more frequently

---

[78] French minimal bilinguals used *balancer* 'to balance'; *faufiler* 'to slip through'; *glisser* 'to slide'; *rouler* 'to roll'.
[79] Turkish-French bilingual used *balancer* 'to balance'; *escalader* 'climb.up'; *glisser* 'to slide'; *rouler* 'to roll'.

used expressive Manner verbs in Turkish in comparison with Turkish-French bilinguals and Turkish minimal bilinguals.

When taking the results of the MVC-Task into account, the figures indicate that the Manner diversity in the VM-Task was generally lower among all groups. This is due to the fact, that on the one hand, Manner was foregrounded in the MVC-Task and, on the other hand, the re-narration in the VM-Task was more complex and cognitively demanding, which might have had an influence on speakers' lexical choices.

The overall results of motion verb choices have shown that the distance of average numbers in each conflation category is generally smaller between Turkish-French bilinguals and French minimal bilinguals in French than between Turkish-French bilinguals and Turkish minimal bilinguals in Turkish. In contrast, the distance of average numbers in each conflation category is smaller between Turkish-German bilinguals and Turkish minimal bilinguals in Turkish and greater in comparison with Turkish-French bilinguals and with German minimal bilinguals in German. In the case of Turkish, this is surprising, since we predicted that due to the greater distance of conflation preferences in L1 and L2, Turkish-German bilinguals would display a higher L2 impact in their L1 than Turkish-French bilinguals.

Nevertheless, we can conclude that our predictions that distinct preferences of conflation patterns in L1 and L2 would lead to a greater impact on Turkish-German bilinguals' motion verb choices in their L1 and L2 could be confirmed. The influence is, however, particularly evident in the speakers' L2, while the L2 impact is only obvious in individual speakers' performances and detectable in the more detailed analysis of the speakers' Manner verb choices. As regards the more varying L2-performance of Turkish-German bilinguals, we suggest that this is related to the greater typological distance of their L1 and L2 as regards the language-specific conflation patterns. In contrast to the observed usage of Generic verbs in Turkish, it is assumed that the much higher frequency in German is related to a typologically motivated conceptual L1>L2 transfer, which in some cases is further reinforced by a lower Manner/Manner-Path verb lexicon and a general lower lexical repertoire. The impact of the L2 is evident only for individual Turkish-German bilingual speakers and reflected in a higher Manner verb usage in Turkish. Furthermore, we assume that the differences found for the usage of expressive Manner verbs in Turkish-German bilinguals' motion descriptions in Turkish is related to the influence of German, in which bilingual speakers are more routinised in making use of expressive Manner verbs than Turkish minimal bilingual speakers in Turkish and Turkish-French bilinguals in Turkish and French.

From a typological perspective, the findings in this section generally challenge Talmy's assertion of a striking preference for Path verbs by speakers of V-languages. Although the "Path-in-verb" pattern was the most frequently used conflation pattern in the Turkish and French motion descriptions by

Turkish-German and Turkish-French bilinguals as well as Turkish minimal bilinguals, a considerable number and diversity of Manner and Manner-Path verbs could be observed as well.

We now turn to the linguistic devices which were used to encode Path and Manner outside the motion verb. These are considered from a parts of speech perspective (see §3.2.6.2) as well as from Wälchli's "clines of Path salience" (see §3.2.5.3). The statistics in the following section only give a descriptive overview in order to expand the typological perspective on Path encoding (see §3.2.5.3). Inferential statistics, as well as qualitative analysis, were therefore not conducted (and in most of the cases not possible due to the relatively small set of values).

7.2.3 Results of other linguistic devices

In §3.2.6.2 we predicted that the locus of the highest differentiation of Path encoding is verbal and adverbal encoding for speakers of Turkish and French, while for speakers of German it is adverbal and adnominal encoding. Furthermore, due to a higher differentiation of Path in adnominal encoding in Turkish, we predicted that speakers of Turkish differ from speakers of French. Moreover, the latter are expected to be more similar to German with respect to the Path differentiation achieved by adverbal encoding.

In the encoding of Manner, we presumed, that due to typological differences between the three languages, speakers of Turkish and French more frequently make use of other linguistic devices in subordinate, adverbial or other Manner encoding strategies as compared to speakers of German.

Let us now examine the other linguistic devices which were used to encode Path and Manner in the motion descriptions in Turkish, German and French.

7.2.3.1 Overall picture
Turkish

Regarding the linguistic devices, which were used to encode Manner and Path outside the motion verb in Turkish, the average numbers in Table 53 show that directional case marking (see example (117)) and adverbial directionals (see example (118)) are most frequently used by the three groups.

(117) bi   gemiy-e   bin-mek   isti-yodu
       a   boat-DAT   get.in-INF   =want-PST.IPFV.3SG
       'It was wanting to get into a boat' (Nihal, TURFRE, 268–272)

Table 53: Manner and Path devices Turkish (in %).

Devices	Turkish		
	TURGER	TURFRE	TUR
POSTCASE	77.29	82.46	77.18
POSTPOS	0.80	2.34	2.07
ADVDIR	16.33	9.94	16.18
ADV_M	4.78	2.92	0.83
CONV_M	0.40	1.17	0.41
CONV_P	0.00	0.58	1.66
OTHER_M	0.00	0.58	1.24
OTHER_P	0.40	0.00	0.41
PATH (all)	94.82	95.32	97.51
MANNER (all)	5.18	4.68	2.49
total devices (in numbers)	251	171	241

(118) dışarı kaç-ıyor
 out escape-PROG.3SG
 'It is escaping out' (Seval, TUR, 183–184)

The figures show that Turkish-French bilinguals made slightly more use of case marking (TURFRE 82.46%) in comparison with Turkish-German and Turkish minimal bilinguals (TURGER 77.29%; TUR 77.18%). Turkish-German and Turkish minimal bilinguals used adverbial directionals more often (TURGER 16.33%; TUR 16.18%) in comparison with Turkish-French bilinguals (9.94%). Moreover, Turkish-French and Turkish minimal bilinguals used postpositions (see example (119)) more frequently (TURFRE 2.34%; TUR 2.07%), albeit limitedly, compared to Turkish-German bilinguals (0.80%).

(119) bovling salon-un-a doğru yürü-dü
 bowling saloon-POSS-DAT towards walk-PST.3SG
 'It walked towards the bowling saloon' (Bircan, TURFRE, 139–143)

From the figures it is apparent that the use of -ErEk and -E -E Manner and Path converbs (see (120) and (121)) is limited. However, Turkish-French and Turkish minimal bilinguals made use of these complex subordinate structures more often compared to German-Turkish bilinguals.

(120) yürüy-erek geç-ti
 walk-CVB pass-PST.3SG
 'It passed walking' (Helin, TUR, 400–401)

(121) sonra kedi koş-a koş-a [[ee]] • kuş-u   yakala-mak ist-iyodu
       later cat   run-CVB   bird-ACC   catch-INF   =want-PST.IPFV.3SG
       'Then the cat was willing to catch the bird by running' (Emre, TURFRE, 55–63)

When encoding Manner outside the main verb, Turkish-German bilinguals preferred adverbs (4.78%, see example (122)) over converbs or other Manner devices. Manner adverbs were less preferred by Turkish-French (2.92%) and Turkish minimal bilinguals (0.83%). Turkish-French bilinguals used instead some more -*erek* Manner converbs (1.24%) in comparison with the other two groups (TURGER 0.4%; TUR 0.41%). Turkish minimal bilinguals made limited use of other Manner encoding strategies such as *küreklen* 'with the oar', *bisiklet gibi* 'like a bicycle' (see example (123))[80] (TUR 1.24%; TURFRE 0.54%; TURGER 0.00%), in which the Manner of motion is not encoded directly but has to be inferred.

(122) hızlıca • • orda   yürü-dü
       fastly   there   walk-PST.3SG
       'It walked fastly' (Eda, TURGER, 906–909)

(123) bisiklet gibi • • geri   gel-di
       bicycle like   back   come-PST.3SG
       'It came back like a bicycle' (Helin, TUR, 338–342)

In all, the numbers show that Manner is generally much less frequently encoded outside the main verb. Turkish-German and Turkish-French bilinguals encoded Path slightly less frequently (TURGER 94.82%; TURFRE 95.32%) in other linguistic devices in comparison with Turkish minimal bilinguals (97.51%). Consequently, they encoded Manner more frequently outside the main verb (TURGER 5.18%; TURFRE 4.68%) compared to Turkish minimal bilinguals (2.49%).

German

The average numbers in Table 54 show that prepositional phrases (see example (124)) and adverbs (mostly adverbial double particles, see example (125)) were commonly used among Turkish-German and German minimal bilinguals when expressing Path outside the motion verb in German.

Furthermore, the numbers indicate that German minimal bilinguals used Path adverbs slightly more often (GER 39.5%; TURGER 36.29%) and less frequently

---

[80] Note, that *yapmak/etmek* constructions were not counted here, since they have been considered in the motion verb category in §7.2.2.

Table 54: Manner and Path devices German (in %).

Devices	German	
	TURGER	GER
ADV_P	36.29	39.50
ADV_M	2.87	5.25
PART	15.67	14.64
PP	45.17	38.40
PREF	0.00	0.00
OTHER_M	0.00	2.21
PATH (all)	97.13	92.54
MANNER (all)	2.87	7.46
total devices (in numbers)	383	362

made use of prepositional phrases (GER 38.4%; TURGER 45.17%) in comparison with Turkish-German bilinguals. Whereas the numbers of separable Path prefixes (see (126)) is quite similar (TURGER 15.67%; GER 14.64), inseparable Path prefixes (such as *-über(queren)* 'over(cross)' etc.) were not used at all.

(124) dann is • die katze zu-m hotel gerannt
 then AUX.PR DET cat to-DET.DAT hotel run.PTCP
 'Then the cat ran to the hotel' (Taylan, TURGER, 112–119)

(125) also ers dann runter gerannt
 well =he.AUX.PR then down run.PTCP
 'Well then he ran down' (Ron, GER, 331–335)

(126) [[em]] die katze geht vom rohr hoch
 DET cat go.PR from.DAT pipe up
 'From the pipe the cat goes up' (Tuba, TURGER, 372–378)

As regards Manner devices, German minimal bilinguals made more frequent, albeit limited, use of Manner adverbs (5.25%, see example (127)) in comparison with Turkish-German bilinguals (2.87%). Furthermore, German minimal bilinguals described, in some cases, Manner in other fashions, where Manner of motion has to be inferred (see example (128)). Because Turkish-German bilinguals never made use of such strategies, their average numbers of directional Path devices is slightly higher than those of German minimal bilinguals (TURGER 97.13%; GER 92.54%).

(127) dann   is   sie ganz schnell gerannt
      then   AUX.PR she very fast   run.PTCP
      'Then she ran very fast' (Nicole, GER, 598–603)

(128) die   katze • • läuft   auf zehnspitz-n an   den   hund-n   vorbei
      DET   cat   walk.PR   on   =tiptoe-PL   at   DET.ACC =dog.PL over
      'Then she ran over the dogs on tiptoes' (Max, GER, 1377–1386)

French

The average numbers in Table 55 indicate that, among Turkish-French and French minimal bilinguals, Path was largely encoded in prepositional phrases (TURFRE 82.76; FRE 84.00%, see example (129)).

Table 55: Manner and Path devices French (in %).

Devices	French	
	TURFRE	FRE
ADV_P	4.83	1.60
ADV_M	1.38	1.60
GERUND_M	0.69	0.00
GERUND_P	0.00	0.80
GERUND_VLV(M)	0.69	0.00
OTHER_M	4.83	4.00
PART	1.38	0.80
PP	82.76	84.00
PREF	3.45	7.20
PATH (all)	92.41	94.40
MANNER (all)	7.59	5.60
total devices (in numbers)	145	125

Differences were found in adverbial Path phrases (see example (130)), which were more frequently used by Turkish-French bilinguals (4.83%) compared to French minimal bilinguals (1.6%). The latter, in contrast, used (inseparable) Path prefixes more frequently (FRE 7.2%; TURFRE 3.45%, see also example).

(129) il   a   a-tterri   dans des   poubelle-s
      he   AUX.PR to-land.PTCP   in   INDF trash-PL
      'He landed in trashes' (Ethan, FRE, 30–36)

(130) le   chat il   a   couru   en bas
      DET   cat   he   AUX.PR   run.PTCP   down
      'The cat ran down' (Adile, TURFRE, 242–248)

In general, gerunds (see example (131)) and Path particles (see example (132)) were very limitedly used by speakers of both groups.

(131) il   est   parti   en courant
      he   AUX.PR   leave.PTCP   run.PTCP
      'He left running' (Adile, TURFRE, 97–101)

(132) après   i   rentre   dedans
      then   =he   back.enter.PR   inside
      'Then he comes back inside' (Geza, TURFRE, 494–497)

Both groups made use of other Manner encoding strategies, where Manner has to be inferred (e.g. *comme une liane* 'like a creeper', see example (133) or *sans faire de bruit* 'without making noise', see example (134)). In general, the figures reveal that Manner encoding in other linguistic devices is generally limited.

(133) elle   s   balance   comme   une   liane
      she   =REFL   swing.PR   like   DET   creeper
      'She swings like a creeper' (Zoe, FRE, 402–408)

(134) après le   chat le   soir   i   rent [[ee]] • • • sans   faire de   bruit
      then   DET   cat   DET   night   =he   =back.enter.PR   without   make   of   noise
      'Then, at night, the cat enters again without making any noise' (Dilşah, TURFRE, 394–406)

7.2.3.2 Adnominal and adverbal Path encoding

According to Wälchli's typology of Path encoding (see §3.2.5.3), there are similarities and differences between all groups and languages with regard to verbal, adnominal and adverbal Path encoding. The figures in Table 56 show the percentage of Path encoding, including the numbers of the verbal, adnominal and adverbal slot. The verbal slot includes the proportions of Path (con)verbs, the adnominal slot includes case marking, postpositions and prepositional phrases and the adverbal slot includes adverbial directionals, Path adverbs as well as (in)separable verb prefixes (particles).

Table 56: Verbal (V), adnominal (AN) and adverbal (AV) Path encoding of all participants (in %).

Path encoding	Turkish			German		French	
	TURGER	TURFRE	TUR	TURGER	GER	TURFRE	FRE
V	30.70	37.93	31.95	0.00	0.30	48.66	43.75
AN	57.31	55.56	56.51	46.51	41.37	45.98	50.48
AV	11.99	6.51	11.54	53.49	58.33	5.36	5.77
total Path devices (in numbers)	342	261	338	383	362	145	125

The results emphasise again that Path was largely encoded outside the main verb – not only in German but also in Turkish and French. Let us now have a more detailed look at the results per languages.

Turkish
The figures reveal that Turkish-French bilingual speakers display differences in verbal and adverbal Path encoding. Turkish-French bilinguals more frequently encoded Path in the verbal slot (37.93%) compared to the other two groups (TURGER 30.7%; TUR 31.95%). Furthermore, they encoded Path in the adverbal slot less frequently (6.51%) in comparison with Turkish-German and Turkish minimal bilinguals, whose values are again similar (TURGER 11.99%; TUR 11.54%).

German
Path was virtually not encoded in the verbal slot. Most frequently, speakers of both groups encoded Path in the adverbal slot. The average numbers indicate that Turkish-German bilinguals did so slightly less frequently (TURGER 53.49%, GER 58.33%), but slightly more often encoded Path in the adnominal slot (TURGER 46.51%, GER 41.37%). However, the differences found are very small.

French
Turkish-French bilinguals most frequently used the verbal slot when encoding Path in French (TURFRE 48.66%; FRE 43.75%), whereas French minimal bilinguals more frequently used the adnominal slot (FRE 50.48%; TURFRE 45.98%). However, the differences are very small. When considering the performance of all speakers in Turkish, the figures indicate that generally Path encoding in the V-slot is more common in French as compared to Turkish. As illustrated above, Turkish-French bilinguals indicate a higher use of the V-slot in Turkish in comparison with the

other two groups. This might be due to a more routine use of this encoding strategy in French. Both, Turkish-French and French minimal bilinguals made only limited use of the adverbal slot. Again, the differences found for Turkish-French bilinguals in Turkish are possibly related to the lower use in French, which is probably due to the fact that adverbial Path encoding in French is generally restricted.

Summary
The findings in this section suggest that bilingual speakers generally acquire and use other linguistic devices similarly to minimal bilinguals. This is mainly reflected in the frequent usage of prepositional phrases in German and French, the frequent usage of separable Path prefixes and adverbs in German and, as predicted, the avoidance of more complex subordinate Path or Manner devices in Turkish and French. Nevertheless, subtle differences were found mainly in a higher avoidance of complex subordinate structures in Turkish by bilingual speakers and a more frequent usage of adverbial directionals in Turkish by Turkish-German bilinguals.

As regards the avoidance of more complex Manner/Path converbs, we could observe that the speakers tend to express Manner in adverbs or other Manner encoding strategies instead, which might be due to less heavier processing demands. In addition, we can assume that the differences observed in the usage of Manner/Path converbs between bilingual and minimal bilingual speakers is related to developmental constraints, since the *-erek* converb is generally acquired later (Berman & Slobin 1994: 547–551). The same might apply for the lower usage of (Manner/Path) gerunds in French. Recent empirical studies (among others (Harr 2012) have shown that young speakers of French rarely use constructions involving one or more subordinate elements, which might also be due to a more economic strategy in motion event encoding. Both developmental and processing economy can lead to a higher encoding of Manner in main verbs (as the results in §7.2.2 have shown) and the less typical V-pattern observed in Turkish and French.

Moreover, the preference for adverbial directionals in Turkish-German bilinguals' motion descriptions in Turkish might be related to their similarity to German separable (adverbial) verb prefixes.

The analysis on the basis of Path slots provided evidence of some more details of Path encoding in the three languages. Speakers of French and Turkish less frequently encoded Path in the adverbal slot as compared to speakers of German. However, the results suggest that Path is often encoded in other linguistic devices in V-languages, whereas this is more frequently the case for Turkish than for French. This finding contributes to a stronger intra-typological perspective of Path encoding in V-languages and suggests that Turkish is more S-framed than French, in the sense of a higher productivity of adverbal Path encoding.

According to the statistics, we have seen that Path was considerably encoded in all languages in other linguistic devices. We now go one step further and examine how predicted linguistic constraints in Turkish and French have an impact on how many directional Path elements are expressed per motion verb construction (see §3.2.6.3).

7.2.4 Results of Path elaboration

In §3.2.6.3 we predicted that, due to limitations in combining motion verbs with directional Path devices in Turkish and French, speakers of Turkish and French use Minus-Ground constructions more frequently than Plus-Ground constructions. Whereas Minus-Ground constructions cover motion verb constructions which are combined with "no" (see (135)) or only "one" directional Path device (e.g. a single prepositional phrase, see example (136)), in Plus-Ground constructions the motion verb is combined with two (or more) directional Path devices (e.g. a prepositional phrase and a separable Path prefix in German, see example (137)). Since German speakers are more free to combine motion verbs with several directional Path devices, we predicted that they more frequently use Plus-Ground constructions and less frequently Minus-Ground constructions in comparison with speakers of Turkish and French.

(135) gemiy-len   git-mey-e   çalış-ıyo
      boat-INST   go-NMLZ-DAT   =try-PROG.3SG
      'It is trying to go with the boat' (Zuhal, TUR, 374–376)

(136) là   y a   le   chat   qui   grimpe   sur   un   poteau
      there   =there is DET   cat   who   climb.PR on   INDF   post
      'At that place, there is the cat who climbs on a post' (Shirin, TURFRE, 418–427)

(137) er   is   aus   dem   käfisch   raus   gekomm
      he   =AUX.PR   from   DET.DAT   =cage   out   =come.PST
      'He came out of (from) the cage' (Ozan, TURGER, 204–210)

Before comparing the performances in Turkish, German and French, let us first analyse the results in greater detail language by language.

Turkish (quantitative)

As regards Turkish, the figures in Table 57 show that, on average, Turkish-German bilinguals expressed two (or more) directional Path elements per motion construction (see example (138)) more frequently (10.4%) in comparison with Turkish-French bilinguals (5.92%). However, between the two groups, no significant difference was found. The same applies for one directional Path element per motion construction (TURGER 59.04%; TURFRE 52.96%, see example (139)).

Table 57: Means (*M*) and ranges (*R*) of Path elaboration Turkish (in %).

Directional Path elements per motion verb	Turkish					
	TURGER		TURFRE		TUR	
	M	R	M	R	M	R
no	30.56	8.33–58.82	41.13	15.38–61.11	34.16	6.25–52.94
one	59.04	38.39–87.5	52.96	37.5–76.92	56.03	29.41–87.5
two (or more)	10.40	0–25	5.92	0–20	9.81	0–23.81
total constructions	282		252		293	

As regards no directional Path element per motion construction (see example (140)), Turkish-French bilinguals (M=41.13; SD=14.99) used this pattern significantly more often (t(28)=2.09, p<0.05*) in comparison with Turkish-German bilinguals (M=30.56, SD=12.56).

(138) *boru-dan aşağ yuvarlan-dı*
 pipe-ABL =down roll-PST.3SG
 'It rolled down (from) the pipe' (Alisa, TURGER, 265–268)

(139) *boru-lar-dan in-di*
 pipe-PL-ABL descend-PST.3SG
 'It descended (from) the pipes' (Maide, TURFRE, 505–507)

(140) *yol-da sürün-dü*
 path-LOC creep-PST.3SG
 'It crept on the road' (Mert, TURFRE, 228–229)

In comparison with Turkish minimal bilinguals, Turkish-German and Turkish-French bilinguals do not significantly differ with respect to the expression of "no", "one" and "two (or more)" directional Path elements per motion construction. However, regarding the proportions in each category there is a greater differences between Turkish-French bilinguals and Turkish minimal bilinguals concerning the expression of "two (or more)" as well as "no" directional Path elements per motion construction compared to Turkish-German bilinguals.

Let us now analyse the results qualitatively in order to obtain and discuss intra-group differences and individual speakers' usage preferences.

Turkish (qualitative)

The individual numbers of Path elaboration indicate, again, considerable intra-group differences (see Table 58). Notably in the category "no directional Path element", the distribution of lowest and highest values in each group is very high. Some speakers in each group more frequently made use of this pattern (e.g. TURGER Esna; TURFRE Geza; TUR Musa), whereas it is less frequently used among others (e.g. TURGER Serkan, Melis; TURFRE Bircan, Dilşah). Furthermore, whereas Melis (TURGER), Bircan and Seçkin (both TURFRE) more frequently expressed one directional Path device (+2.23 SD), Kurt (TURGER) and Özgür (TURFRE) less frequently made use of it (–1.58 SD).

Table 58: Turkish-German and Turkish-French bilinguals with a distance of one or more standard deviations (SD) in expressing no, one or two (or more) directional Path elements in Turkish.

Group	Speaker	no	one	two (or more)
TURGER	Esna	+2.25	–1.44	–1.32
	Kurt	+1.11	–1.58	
	Melis	–1.44	+2.23	–1.32
	Serkan	–1.77		+1.85
	Ela		–1.1	+1.22
	Sefar		+1.17	–1.32
	Dana			+1.1
	Esna			
	Melis	–1.44		
TURFRE	Bircan	–1.72	+1.82	
	Devin	–1.20		+1.48
	Dilşah	–1.40	+1.04	+1.16
	Geza	+1.33	–1.07	
	Nihal	+1.26		
	Özgür	+1.01	–1.18	
	Seçkin	–1.20	+1.82	
	Arda			+2.20

In the category "two (or more) directional Path elements", there are speakers in each group who did not use this pattern at all (TURGER: Esna, Melis, Sefar; TURFRE: (Emre, Geza, Nezihe, Nihal, Seçkin, Shirin); TUR: two speakers (Rüya, Zeren)), others made use of it more frequently (e.g. TURGER Serkan; TURFRE Arda; TUR Helin 23.81%).

These cases of intra-group variation will be taken into account when comparing the bilinguals' performance in L1 and L2 in the following.

German (quantitative)
The figures in Table 59 reveal inter-group differences in German between German-Turkish and German minimal bilinguals.

Table 59: Means (*M*) and Ranges (*R*) of Path elaboration German (in %).

Directional Path elements per motion verb	German			
	TURGER		GER	
	M	R	M	R
no	21.08	9.52–38.46	18.26	5.88–35.29
one	49.24	21.43–82.76	62.04	35.29–85
two (or more)	29.68	6.9–52.38	19.69	0–85
total constructions	338		330	

Turkish-German bilinguals (med=11.12) used significantly more often two (or more) Path elements per motion verb in comparison with German minimal bilinguals (med=5.56) (W=630, p<0.01**). Moreover, Turkish-German bilinguals (*M*=49.24; SD=17.53) expressed one directional Path element (see example (141)) significantly less often in comparison with German minimal bilinguals (*M*=62.04; SD=15.04) (t(28)=2.15, p<0.05*). Constructions with no directional Path elements (see example (142)) were slightly more frequently used by Turkish minimal bilinguals (TURGER 21.08%; GER 18.26%). However, between the groups there was no significant difference found.

(141) dann is-sie • • •   runta   gerollt
      then =AUX.PR-she   =down   roll.PTCP
      'Then she rolled down' (Melanie, GER, 321–325)

(142) dann is   der balangsiert
      then =AUX.PR   he   =balance.PTCP
      'Then he balanced' (Yiğit, TURGER, 660–663)

When correlating the performance of Turkish-German bilinguals in Turkish and German motion descriptions, the results of a Pearson's correlation indicate for no directional Path elements an intermediate positive correlation ($r=0.43$), and for one directional Path element ($r=0.20$) as well as for two (or more) Path elements ($r=0.15$) a low positive correlation. None of the correlations were statistically significant. We can surmise that neither a lower nor a higher usage of two (or more) directional Path elements per motion verb in one language has an impact on its frequency in the other language. Nevertheless, we will look into the qualitative results, in order to detect possible intra-group variation and to further determine individual speakers' usage preferences and cross-linguistic influences in the bilingual speakers' motion descriptions in L1 and L2.

German (qualitative)

When looking at the individual results, the numbers in Table 60 indicate that there are some speakers whose preference in one language might be reflected in the other language, although the statistical analysis did not reveal a significant correlation. From a cross-linguistic perspective, "no" as well as "two (or more)" Path elements are of particular interest, since they reflect typical patterns in Turkish and German. Kurt (+1.1 *SD*) and Esna (+2.23 *SD*) display the highest values in Turkish as regards no directional Path elements. However, only Kurt also displays a high value in German (Kurt +1.46 *SD*; Esna 0.27 *SD*). In his case we can assume an L1>L2 influence, which is reflected in a lower usage of directional Path devices in German and is considered as less typical for German. Similarly, Alisa (+1.74 *SD*) and Yiğit (+1.70 *SD*) display high values in German. They generally express motion verbs with no directional Path elements more often in comparison with German, whereas their performance in Turkish does not strikingly differ with respect to the mean (Alisa +0.75 *SD*, Yiğit −0.04 *SD*). Nevertheless, we can hypothesise an L1-influence on their L2-performance.

Table 60: Turkish-German bilinguals with a distance of one or more standard deviations (*SD*) in expressing no, one or two (or more) directional Path elements in German.

Speaker	no	one	two (or more)
Alisa	+1.74		−1.20
Eda	−1.07	+1.91	−1.62
Ela	−1.05		

(continued)

Table 60 (continued)

Kurt	+1.46	−1.58	
Ozan	−1.15		+1.62
Yiğit	+1.70	−1.18	
Dana		+1.84	−1.59
Tuba		−1.25	+1.45

Moreover, Serkan reaches the highest value of two (or more) Path elements in Turkish (+1.85 *SD*); his value in German is also above the mean (+0.82 *SD*). His higher usage of two (or more) directional Path devices in Turkish probably indicates an L2>L1 influence.

Generally we can assume that L1>L2 and L2>L1 influences are caused by constructional preferences in one language. However, it has to be noted that this only accounts for a single category (Alisa, Kurt, Yiğit no directional Path element; Serkan two (or more) Path elements), but it is never consistent across all categories. Thus, a higher usage of one pattern rather seems to decrease the usage of another pattern (e.g. Kurt used more frequently no directional Path elements and less frequently one directional Path element).

Let us also include the language dominance profiles for the speakers, where a cross-linguistic influence was assumed. In all cases the dominance profiles do not support the direction of influence. Alisa is more L2-dominant in dimension and indicates a mixed pattern in domain. Kurt also displays a mixed pattern as regards domain and does not indicate a dominance in dimension. Serkan is neither L1- nor L2-dominant as regards dimension, and indicates a "L1-dominance" in domain.

In general, the values of most speakers are distributed along the mean in L1 and L2, which is an indication of no bidirectional influence. For instance Melis and Sefar did not use two (or more) Path elements in Turkish at all, whereas their values in German are along the mean or even higher (Melis −0.004 *SD*, Sefar +0.74 *SD*). When considering their language dominance profiles, only Sefar indicates a balanced dominance in both domain and dimension, whereas Melis, as shown above, is clearly L1 dominant in both, domain and dimension.

French (quantitative)

The average numbers in Table 61 reveal that Turkish-French and French minimal bilinguals rarely used "two (or more)" Path elements per motion verb in French.

Table 61: Means (*M*) and ranges (*R*) of Path elaboration French (in %).

Directional Path elements per motion verb	French			
	TURFRE		FRE	
	M	*R*	*M*	*R*
no	44.61	23.08–73.33	47.02	27.27–66.67
one	54.21	26.67–76.92	50.45	30.43–72.72
two (or more)	1.18	0–17.65	2.53	0–21.43
total constructions	241		205	

Note that the "two (or more)" pattern occurs only due to the fact that inseparable Latin prefixes were taken into account in the analysis (see example (143)), since no other multiple Path combinations were found in the corpus. Moreover, both groups rather used one (see example (136) above) or no directional Path element (see example (144)).

(143) après il s'   en-fuit   de sa cage
      later he REFL away-escape from his cage
      'Later he escapes from his cage' (Mert, TURFRE, 262–268)

(144) là •   grosminet, i - l s'   balance   avec • • une corde
      there =Sylvester he =REFL swing.PR with   DET rope
      'There, Sylvester swings with a rope' (Eva, FRE, 277–285)

Some subtle inter-group difference can be observed. Turkish-French bilinguals display a slightly higher usage of one directional Path element (TURFRE 54.21%; FRE 50.45%), on the contrary, they used slightly less frequently no Path element (44.61%) as well as two (or more) Path elements (1.18%) in comparison with French minimal bilinguals (no: 47.02%; two (or more): 2.53%). However, parametric tests did not reveal significant differences under TURFRE and FRE conditions.

When examining the bilingual speakers' performance in L1 and L2 we can surmise that the difference observed between Turkish-French bilinguals and the other two groups in Turkish is related to the speakers' L2. From a cross-linguistic perspective, we can assume that the higher usage of no directional Path element in French by Turkish-French bilinguals may be reflected in a higher usage of this pattern in Turkish. A Pearson's correlation revealed a positive correlation ($r=0.44$) between a higher usage of no directional Path element in French and Turkish; however, the impact is statistically not significant. Further qualitative analyses are required to prove these assumptions individually.

The lower frequency of two (or more) Path elements in Turkish, is possibly influenced by the absence of this pattern in French. Note that since Mert is the only Turkish-French bilingual speaker who made use of two (or more) directional Path elements in French, we will not further elaborate this pattern in the following.[81]

We again analyse the results qualitatively in order to obtain and discuss intra-group differences and to further determine individual speakers' usage preferences and cross-linguistic influence in the domain of Path elaboration in Turkish-French bilinguals' motion descriptions in L1 and L2.

French (qualitative)

The figures also reveal for both groups intra-group differences with respect to the smallest and highest values (see ranges in Table 61 and *SD* differences in Table 62). A few bilingual speakers less frequently used no directional Path elements (Gözde, Devin). Both speakers also display the highest values in the category one directional Path element. In contrast, Nihal used one directional Path element less frequently, but more frequently no directional Path elements.

Table 62: Turkish-French bilinguals with a distance of one or more standard deviations (*SD*) in expressing no or one directional Path elements in French.

Speaker	no	one
Devin	−1.18	+1.23
Dilşah	+1.05	
Geza	+1.02	
Gözde	−1.60	+1.63
Nihal	+2.13	−1.98
Bircan		+1.02

As regards the assumption that the usage of no directional Path element in French is reflected in the usage of this pattern in Turkish, the individual results indicate that speakers who display a high frequency of no directional Path element in French tend to use this pattern more frequently in Turkish. This is the case for Nihal (+1.26 *SD* in Turkish, +2.13 *SD* in French) and Geza (+1.02 *SD* in French, +1.33

---

[81] Two thirds of the minimal bilingual speakers did not use this pattern at all; one speaker (Ethan) used two (or more) directional Path elements in 21.43% of his motion descriptions.

SD in Turkish). Here an L2>L1 influence can be maintained. However, this does not account for Dilşah, who more frequently used no directional Path elements in French (+1.05 *SD*) but indicates a higher negative *z*-score in Turkish (−1.41 *SD*). The same can be observed for Seçkin (+0.15 *SD* in French, −1.20 *SD* in Turkish). Both speakers clearly display distinct values in their L1 and L2.

Let us now also include the participants' language dominance profiles, in order to examine whereas the direction of influence is supported by a dominance pattern. Geza indicates an "L2-dominance" and Nihal "no dominance" in both domain and dimension. Thus, we can hypothesise that solely the language dominance profile of Geza supports an L2>L1 influence. In the cases for Dilşah and Seçkin, the scores of their dominance profiles indicate an "L2-dominance" in both domain and dimension for Dilşah, whereas Seçkin is L2-dominant in domain and does not indicate a dominance as regards dimension.

Two speakers, whose values in Turkish are below/beneath the mean, display lower values in French (Gözde in Turkish −0.53 *SD*, in French −1.6 *SD*; Bircan in Turkish −0.08 *SD*. −0.97 *SD* in French. In these cases an L1>L2 influence can be assumed. Their language dominance profiles, however, do not indicate a support of the direction of influence. Both indicate "no dominance" in dimension and display a mixed pattern as regards domain.

When regarding two (or more) directional Path elements, six of the speakers who did not use this pattern in French at all also did not make use of it in Turkish (Emre, Geza, Nezihe, Nihal, Seçkin, Shirin). In this context an L2>L1 influence can be assumed, since this pattern is generally more restricted in French as compared to Turkish. The direction of influence is supported for Geza and Nezihe (L2-dominant in both domain and dimension) and partly for Emre and Seçkin who are L2-dominant in domain, but display "no dominance" as regards dimension. For the other speakers the direction of influence is not supported (Nihal displays "no dominance" in both domain and dimension and Shirin "no dominance" in domain and a mixed pattern in dimension).

Taking the results together, only Nihal and Geza display in two categories, no and two (or more) directional Path elements, consistently an L2>L1 influence, which is only supported by an "L2-dominance" for Geza.

Summary

The results in this section have shown that speakers of Turkish and French generally less frequently used more than one directional Path element per motion verb (Plus-Ground constructions) as compared to speakers of German. In German, Turkish-German bilinguals in particular made use of this pattern (see Table 63). Furthermore, some intra-typological differences were observed. Bilingual and

Table 63: Path elaboration in Turkish, German and French of all participants (in %).

Directional Path elements per motion verb	Turkish			German		French	
	TURGER	TURFRE	TUR	TURGER	GER	TURFRE	FRE
no	30.56	41.13	34.16	21.08	18.26	44.61	47.02
one	59.04	52.96	56.03	49.24	62.04	54.21	50.45
two (or more)	10.40	5.92	9.81	29.68	19.69	1.18	2.53
total constructions	282	252	293	338	330	241	205

minimal bilingual speakers of Turkish more frequently expressed two (or more) Path elements in Turkish in comparison with bilingual and minimal bilingual speakers of French.

The overall results of Path elaboration suggest that Turkish provides structures which are considered "more S-framed" as compared to French. On the one hand, this leads Turkish-French bilinguals to express Plus-Ground constructions less frequently in Turkish as compared to Turkish-German and Turkish minimal bilinguals. On the other hand, since Path elaboration in Turkish is less productive as compared to German, Turkish-German bilinguals express two (or more) Path elements less frequently in German in comparison with German minimal bilinguals. The lower Path elaboration in French is also obvious in a preference for bare motion constructions by expressing no directional Path device in French by Turkish-French bilinguals and French minimal bilinguals. This leads Turkish-French bilinguals to make use of this pattern more often in Turkish than Turkish-German bilinguals and Turkish minimal bilinguals.

The findings reinforce the prediction that speakers of S-languages tend to express more Path elements per motion verb (see §3.2.6.3). However, the results further indicate intra-typological differences between Turkish and French. These differences lead to cross-linguistic influences in Turkish-German as well as Turkish-French bilingual speakers' motion expression in L1 and L2.

The analysis in this section did not provide any details regarding the combination of motion verbs and other linguistic devices. This aspect is examined in the following, in order to gain constructional preferences per languages and groups and to examine possible cross-linguistic influences.

7.2.5 Results of motion verb constructions

In §3.2.5.1 we discussed that, according to Talmy's lexicalisation patterns, speakers of Turkish and French more frequently combine Path verbs with Manner devices and, vice versa, that speakers of German, more frequently combine Manner verbs with directional Path devices. However, we predicted that due to the Path encoding in adverbal and adnominal slots in Turkish and French "pseudo-satellite" and hybrid constructions are possible which generally challenges Talmy's assertion. In this context, we predicted intra-typological variation in the verb constructions by speakers of French and Turkish. Furthermore, as a result of constructional constraints in one language (here Turkish) or constructional "allowance" in the other language (here German), cross-linguistic influence in Turkish-German bilinguals was presumed. In addition, we assumed in §7.2.3 that the speakers' language development as well as their cognitive capacity inhibit the usage of more complex subordinate constructions which are required to express the typical V-pattern (Path verb with Manner device [VP_M], for the analytical procedure see §6.5). In order to make our observations above precise, the statistics also include information about whether a construction was used in a main clause (MC) or a subordinate clause (VSC, VCONV) or an infinitive construction with modal or other non motion verbs (VMOD) was used. Since the numbers of several constructions found in the corpus are relatively small, we only refer to the most frequent constructions or to single phenomena (for an overview of all constructions see Tables 116 (Turkish), 117 (German) and 118 (French) in Appendix C.III).

Turkish (quantitative)
The average numbers in Table 64 indicate that in Turkish the most frequent construction is the combination of Path verbs with Path devices [VP_P].

Table 64: Means (*M*) and ranges (*R*) of motion verb constructions Turkish (in %).

Motion verb construction	Turkish					
	TURGER		TURFRE		TUR	
	M	R	M	R	M	R
VP_P	35.37	17.39–58.33	32.05	15.38–61.54	31.91	19.05–50.00
VM_0	19.34	0–44.44	17.96	0–40.00	22.65	3.57–41.18
VGEN_P	15.26	0–38.46	13.75	0–50.00	10.25	0–20.00
VM_P	10.51	0–25.00	5.59	0–23.08	9.67	0–18.75
VMP_P	5.84	0–17.39	7.00	0–21.43	10.14	0–18.75

The use of the [VP_P] construction (see example (145)) is almost identical in the Turkish-French and the Turkish minimal bilingual group (TURFRE 32.05%, TUR 31.91%). Turkish-German bilinguals made use of this construction slightly more often (TURGER 35.37%) in comparison with the other two groups. However, the differences between all groups were not statistically significant. Note that this type of motion verb construction is often considered redundant or pleonastic (which Croft et al. (2010:208) call "double framing construction", see §3.2.6.3).

(145) *ev-in   için-e   gir-di*
      house-GEN inside-DAT   enter-PST.3SG
      'It entered inside the house' (Geza, TURFRE, 124–127)

The constructions [VM_0] (bare Manner verb with no device, see example (146)) and [VGEN_P] (Generic verb with Path device, see example (147)) were also frequently found in the corpus. Parametric and non-parametric tests did not indicate any significant differences between the groups. Turkish-French and Turkish-German bilinguals used [VM_0] quite similarly (TURGER 19.34%; TURFRE 17.96%) and slightly less frequently in comparison with Turkish minimal bilinguals (22.65%). Both bilingual groups used [VGEN_P] more frequently (TURGER 15.26%, TURFRE 13.75%) in comparison with Turkish minimal bilinguals (10.25%).

(146) *sallan-dı*
      swing-PST.3SG
      'It swang' (Reyhan, TUR, 239)

(147) *aşağ-a   git-ti*
      =down-DAT   go.PST.3SG
      'It went down' (Beren, TURGER, 69–70)

Furthermore, the figures indicate several [VM_P] and [VMP_P] (Manner/Manner-Path verb with Path device, see examples (148) and (149)) constructions among the speakers. As illustrated in §3.2.5.1, this construction type is typically considered satellite-framed. Although there were no significant differences between the groups, the mean values indicate that Turkish-French bilinguals used [VM_P] constructions less frequently (5.59%) in comparison with the other two groups (TURGER 10.51%; TUR 9.67%). It is striking that Turkish minimal bilinguals made more frequent use of [VMP_P] (10.14%) as compared to Turkish-French (7.00%) and Turkish-German bilinguals (5.84%). Once again, the differences between the groups were not statistically significant.

(148) *yerin-e   yuvarlan-dı*
      place-DAT   roll.PST.3SG
      'It rolled to the place' (Dana, TURGER, 281–283)

(149) aşağı düş-üyor
down fall.PROG.3SG
'It is falling down' (Onur, TUR, 275–276)

Interestingly, constructions which are considered typically verb-framed in the motion literature were found less frequently. Table 65 summarises specific intergroup differences on the basis of the total constructions per group.

Table 65: V- and S-constructions Turkish (in %).

V/S	Turkish		
	TURGER	TURFRE	TUR
V-const	3.34	7.31	3.90
S-const	16.35	12.60	19.81
Total constructions	282	252	293

The figures reveal that typical V-constructions such as Path (con)verb with Manner device [VP_M, see example (150)], or Path (con)verb only [VP_O, see example (151)], where Manner is omitted, are rarely, but more frequently found in the Turkish-French bilingual group (TURFRE 7.31%; TURGER 3.34%; TUR 3.90%).

(150) seszizce gir-mey-e çalış-tı
quietly enter-NMLZ-DAT try-PST.3SG
'It tried to enter quietly' (Mert, TURFRE, 417–419)

(151) kedi bin-di
cat get on/in-PST.3SG
'The cat got on/in' (Nezihe, TURFRE, 125–126)

Typical S-constructions such as Manner/Manner-Path (con)verb with Path device ([VM_P]; [VMP_P], see examples (148) and (149) above) were more often used by Turkish minimal bilinguals (19.81%). Turkish-German bilinguals used these constructions slightly less frequently (16.35%), whereas the proportion of Turkish-French bilinguals is far lower (12.6%) as compared to the other two groups. Some few reverse framing constructions were also found (see (152)).

(152) tel-ler-in üzerin-den geç-erek, • • • yürü-mey-e çalış-ıyo
wire-PL-GEN above-ABL pass-CVB walk-NMLZ-DAT =try-PROG.3SG
'Passing from above the wires, it is trying to walk' (Seval, TUR, 448–455)

Table 66: Syntactic constructions in Turkish (in %).

Syntactic construction	Turkish		
	TURGER	TURFRE	TUR
VSC	1.14	1.39	1.97
VCONV	1.17	2.38	8.80
VMOD	11.59	17.11	12.42
Total constructions	282	252	293

As regards the syntactic construction, the average numbers in Table 66 show that subordinate constructions are generally limited.

In comparison with Turkish minimal bilinguals, Turkish-German bilinguals made minimally use of noun clauses (1.14%) and converbial clauses (1.17%) in their Turkish motion descriptions. Only a few converb (-*Ip*, -*IncA*) and -*dIk* clauses were found in the corpus. Also Turkish-French bilinguals used these constructions less frequently, albeit slightly more often (1.39% noun clauses; 2.38% converbial clauses) and were more diverse (-*Ip*, -*IncA*, -*ken*, *diye*, -*dIk*) in comparison with the Turkish-German group. Turkish minimal bilinguals used subordinate constructions more than twice as often in comparison with the other two groups (noun clauses 1.97%; converbial clauses 8.80%). As regards the diversity of subordinating suffixes, they do not differ from Turkish-French bilinguals (-*Ip*, -*IncA*, -*ken*, -*dIk*, -*dIktEn sonra*).

Modal verbs or other types of verbs which entail Manner, Manner-Path, Path or Generic nominalisations (see example (152) above) or infinitives (see example (153)) were used more frequently by Turkish-French bilinguals (17.11%) in comparison with the other two groups (TURGER 11.59%, TUR 12.42%).

(153)   *apartman-a   gir-mek   ist-iyo*
        building-DAT enter-INF   =want-PROG.3SG
        'It wants to enter in the building' (Nezihe, TURFRE, 62–65)

Let us now analyse the data qualitatively in order to obtain and discuss intra-group differences and individual speakers' usage preferences.

Turkish (qualitative)

When taking the speakers' individual results into account, intra-group differences can be observed for the usage of certain constructions (see Table 67).

Among bilingual speakers [VP_P] was used most diversely. Whereas Gamze (TURGER, –1.32 SD) and Seçkin (TURFRE, –1.41 SD) used this construction less

Table 67: Turkish-German and Turkish-French bilinguals with a distance of one or more standard deviations (SD) in VP_P, VM_0, VGEN_P, VM_P and VMP_P constructions in Turkish.

Group	Speaker	VP_P	VM_0	VGEN_P	VM_P	VMP_P
TURGER	Alisa	−1.13				
	Esna	−1.31			−1.40	
	Gamze	−1.32		+1.11		
	Kurt	+1.08	+2.20	−1.12		
	Melis	+1.08	−1.70			+1.76
	Serkan	+1.69			+1.92	
	Taylan	+1.08				
	Beren		−1.70	+2.54		
	Tuba				−1.40	+2.12
	Yiğit				+1.92	
	Ela			−1.12		+1.25
	Ozan			+1.17		
TURFRE	Dilşah			+1.94		−1.15
	Mert	+1.10		−1.36		
	Seçkin	−1.41	−1.45	+2.45		+1.38
	Bircan	+1.19	−1.45		+2.37	
	Devin	+2.50	−1.45			−1.15
	Nihal	−1.02	+1.77			
	Arda	+1.02			+1.95	
	Gözde					+1.59
	Geza					−1.15
	Nezihe					+1.71
	Shirin					−1.15

frequently, Serkan (TURGER, +1.69 SD) and Devin (+2.50 SD) made use of it more often.

In both bilingual groups, there are speakers who did not use [VM_0], [VGEN_P], [VM_P] and [VMP_P]-constructions at all. Other speakers in each group made use of these pattern more often and display a clear usage above the respective group mean. As regards [VM_0] Kurt (TURGER, +2.20 SD) and Nihal (TURFRE, +1.77 SD) made use of it more frequently, whereas Melis and Beren (TURGER, −1,70), as well as Seçkin, Bircan and Devin (TURFRE, −1.71 SD), did not use this construction at all. The same can be observed for [VGEN_P], which was not used at all by Ela and Kurt (TURGER, −1.12 SD) as well as by Mert (TURFRE, −1.36 SD).

Other speakers used this construction more frequently (TURGER: Beren +2.54 SD; TURFRE: Seçkin +2.45 SD, Dilşah +1.94 SD). The typical S-construction [VM_P] was more often not used at all by Turkish-French bilinguals (Dilşah, Emre, Geza, Mert, Nihal, Özgür, Shirin, each –1.15 SD) as compared to Turkish-German bilinguals (Esna, Tuba (TURGER, each –1.40 SD). Among Turkish-French bilinguals, Bircan (+2.37 SD) and Arda (+1.95 SD), among Turkish-German bilinguals Serkan (+1.92 SD) and Yiğit (+1.92 SD) more frequently made use of this construction.

Let us now examine the speaker's respective L2 in order to discuss possible L1-L2 interactions.

German (quantitative)

The average numbers in Table 68 indicate that there are several differences between Turkish-German and German minimal bilinguals' motion verb constructions.

Table 68: Means (M) and ranges (R) of motion verb constructions German (in %).

Motion verb construction	German			
	GERTUR		GER	
	M	R	M	R
VM_P	27.24	7.69–51.74	39.10	15.00–71.43
VGEN_P	38.17	11.76–62.96	13.70	0–30.00
VM_O	14.48	3.70–33.33	12.30	5.88–19.33
VMP_P	10.45	0–20.00	15.96	7.41–32.00
VAUX_P	0.71	4.76–5.88	4.35	3.85–20.00

The statistics indicate that Turkish-German bilinguals ($M=27.24$, $SD=13.48$) combined Manner verbs with Path devices [VM_P, see example (154))] significantly less frequently as compared to German minimal bilinguals ($M=39.10$, $SD=14.03$) ($t(28)=2.36$, $p=0.03*$). The same was observed for [VMP_P]-constructions (see example (155)) which were significantly more often used by German minimal bilinguals ($M=15.96$, $SD=6.43$) as compared to Turkish-German bilinguals ($M=10.45$, $SD=6.13$) ($t(28)=2.4$, $p<0.05*$).

(154) dann   is   er   dieser katze auch   hinterher   gerannt
       then   =AUX.PR   he   this   cat   also   afterwards   run.PTCP
       'Then he ran also after this cat' (Gamze, TURGER, 669–676)

(155) un   dann   klettert   die   katze   an   einer   regenrinne   hinauf
       =and   then   climb.PR   DET   cat   at   INDF   gutter   upwards
       'And then the cat climbs up a gutter' (Mia, GER, 149–157)

Furthermore, the difference between Turkish-German bilinguals (*M*=38.17, *SD*=14.77) and German minimal bilinguals (*M*=13.70, *SD*=9.93) is highly significant with respect to [VGEN_P] constructions (see (156)) ($t(28)=-5.33$, $p<0.001$***).

(156) un   danach is   die   katze darein   gegang
     =and   after   =AUX.PR   DET   cat   there.in   =go.PTCP
     'And later the cat went in' (Sefar, TURGER, 859–865)

The figures also show a slightly more frequent usage of bare Manner verbs without Path device [VM_0] (see example (157)) by Turkish-German bilinguals (TURGER 14.48%; GER 12.30%), however, no significant difference between the two groups was found.

(157) un   danach is   er •   gerollt
     =and   after   =AUX.PR   he   roll.PTCP
     'And later he rolled' (Beren, TURGER, 113–118)

Additionally, another type of construction, to which we referred in §3.2.4 and 7.2.2.1 as a motion construction without a motion verb, must be acknowledged. The figures show that only two Turkish-German bilinguals (Ozan and Serkan) used this construction with an auxiliary verb ([VAUX_P], see example (158)). The construction is limited, but more frequently used by German minimal bilinguals (4.35%, see example (159)). Furthermore, modal verb constructions without a motion verb ([VMOD_P], see example (160)) were also less frequently used by Turkish-German bilinguals (1.14%) in comparison with German minimal bilinguals (2.52%).

(158) un   danach is   er   von   diesn   kabel-n •   rüber
     =and   after   =AUX.PR   he   from   =these cable.PL   across
     '?And later he was across these cables' (Ozan, TURGER, 538–546)

(159) die   katze   ist   sofort   die   treppe-n runter
     the   cat   AUX.PR   immediately   DET   stair.PL downwards
     'Immediately the cat is down the stairs' (Philip, GER, 102–108)

(160) in •   diesem   video ,   wollte   der • •   kater , •   durch
     in   this   video   want.PST   DET   male cat   across
     den   garten   zu-m   vogel   in-s   haus   hoch   ,
     INDF   garden   =to-DET.DAT bird   =in-DET house   up
     '?In this video the tomcat wanted across the garden to the bird in up to the house' (Sören, GER, 793–811)

As regards the syntactic construction, both groups rarely used subordinate clauses (see example (161))(TURGER 4.14%; GER 5.45%, see Table 69).

Table 69: Syntactic constructions in German (in %).

Syntactic construction	GERTUR	GER
VSC	4.14	5.45
VMOD	7.69	11.82
Total constructions	338	330

Whereas Turkish-German bilinguals made use of modal verbs (see (162)) or other types of verbs (see (163)) which entail Manner, Manner-Path, Path or Generic infinitives in only 7.69% of their motion descriptions, German minimal bilinguals more frequently used this type of construction (11.82%).

(161) als   sie   in-s   haus   ge - [[ee]] laufen   is
      when she =in-DET.ACC house   walk.PTCP =AUX.PR
      'When she walked into the house' (Sören, GER, 134–142)

(162) er   wollte   zu   tweety gehn
      he want.PST to   tweety =go.INF
      'He wanted to go to Tweety' (Alisa, TURGER, 652–656)

(163) denn • • •   hat   sie   versucht   da • •   wieda   hoch   zu   komm
      =then   AUX.PR she   try.PTCP   there   =again   up   to   =come.INF
      'Then she tried again to get up there' (Ron, GER, 1066–1076)

When examining the bilingual speakers' performance in L1 and L2, the [VM_P] and [VGEN_P]-constructions are of particular interest. The results indicated no differences between Turkish-German bilinguals and Turkish minimal bilinguals of the [VM_P] usage in Turkish. As regards German, we have seen that Turkish-German bilinguals less frequently used this construction in comparison with German minimal bilinguals. In this context a typologically motivated L1>L2 influence can be assumed. The lower frequency of [VM_P] in Turkish seems to inhibit the usage in German. This is supported by the fact that Turkish-German bilinguals do not differ significantly from German minimal bilinguals in bare motion verb use [VM_0, VGEN_0] in German. Therefore, a preference for simpler constructions without any Path device can be excluded. Instead, [VGEN_P] constructions are strikingly preferred; an explanation might be the same as for the higher usage of Generic verbs and the lower usage of Manner verbs discussed in §7.2.2.1. The fact that [VP_P]-constructions were highly frequent among some Turkish-German bilinguals may trigger a higher usage of [VGEN_P] in German. Turkish-German bilinguals possibly extend the [VP_P]-construction to [VGEN_P] in German.

However, a Pearson's correlation indicated a low positive correlation of [VM_P] in German and Turkish ($r=0.12$) and did not reveal a significant effect.

In the following, further qualitative analysis will provide intra-group differences and individual speakers' usage preferences and cross-linguistic influences in the Turkish-German bilinguals' motion descriptions.

German (qualitative)

The individual analysis shows intra-group differences, mainly in the use of [VM_P] and [VMP_P] (see Table 70). Eda, for instance, combined Manner verbs with Path devices more frequently (+1.82 *SD*), whereas Alisa indicated a negative *z*-score (–1.45 *SD*). Kurt never combined Manner-Path verbs with Path devices. In contrast, Sefar used this construction more frequently (+1.56 *SD*). Bare Manner verb constructions, which were more frequently used in Turkish, as compared to German motion description, were also used by a few speakers more often (Yiğit +2.29, Alisa +1.67 *SD*), whereas Melis made use of it less frequently (–1.31 *SD*). As regards the combination of Generic verbs with directional Path devices, there are a few speakers who used this construction more frequently (Melis +1.68 *SD*, Kurt +1.28 *SD*) in comparison with other speakers (Serkan –1.79 *SD*, Sefar –1.23 *SD*).

Table 70: Turkish-German bilinguals with a distance of one or more standard deviations (*SD*) in VM_P, VGEN_P, VM_0, and VMP_P constructions in German.

Speaker	VM_P	VGEN_P	VM_0	VMP_P
Alisa	–1.45		+1.67	–1.29
Dana	–1.19			
Eda	+1.82			–1.14
Ozan	+1.16			
Sefar	+1.44	–1.23		+1.56
Serkan	+1.03	–1.79		+1.17
Kurt		+1.28		–1.71
Melis		+1.68	–1.31	
Yiğit			+2.29	
Tuba				+1.26

The assumption that speakers transfer the [VP_P] from their L1 into [VGEN_P] in their L2 is partly supported when examining bilingual speakers with the highest and lowest proportion of [VP_P] in Turkish. It turns out that except for Serkan, all the other speakers with higher [VP_P] proportions in Turkish (Melis, Kurt, Taylan) display a higher proportion of [VGEN_P] in German (Melis +1.68 *SD*, Kurt +1.28 *SD*, Taylan +0.80 *SD*). Vice versa, the proportions of [VGEN_P] in German of speakers with the lowest values of [VP_P] in Turkish (Esna, Gamze) are below the group mean (Esna −0.65 *SD*, Gamze −0.58 *SD*). Nevertheless, the direction of influence is only supported by language dominance in the case of Melis (L1-dominant in both domain and dimension), Gamze (L2-dominant both domain and dimension) and partly for Taylan (L1-dominant in domain, "no dominance" in dimension). As seen above, Kurt displays a mixed pattern in his language dominance profile for domain and "no dominance" as regards dimension, Esna is L1 dominant in domain and does not indicate a dominance in dimension.

In the case of Melis, it seems that there is a relation between her lower usage of [VM_0] in German (−1.31 *SD*) and Turkish (−1.70 *SD*). However, it is not clear whether the influence is L1 or L2 based. Due to her more limited use in Turkish, an L1>L2 influence can be assumed. On the contrary, since [VM_0] is less typical for German, the influence might also be L2>L1. Her language dominance profile, however, indicates a support for L1>L2 influence.

Among those speakers who indicate a high positive *z*-score in the use of [VM_P] in German Eda (+0.33 *SD*), Serkan (+1.92 *SD*) and Ozan (+0.26 *SD*) indicate a positive *z*-score in Turkish. In these cases an L2>L1 influence can be assumed; it is reflected in a higher usage of [VM_P] in Turkish. In contrast, Sefar less frequently made use of this construction in Turkish (−0.24 *SD*). He displays distinct patterns in his L1 and L2. Taking their dominance profiles into account, an L2-dominance supports the direction of influence for Eda and Ozan (L2-dominant in both domain and dimension). In contrast, Serkan is L1-dominant in domain and displays "no dominance" in dimension. Sefar indicates "no dominance" in either domain or dimension, which would also support his distinct motion verb construction patterns in both languages.

As regards the lower usage of motion constructions without motion verbs by Turkish-German bilinguals (which was not indicated in Table 70 due to its relative infrequency), it can be assumed that the absence of such constructions in Turkish influence bilingual speakers to make use of it. Among the two speakers who used this pattern in German only Ozan indicates an "L2-dominance" in both domain and dimension, whereas Serkan indicates an "L1-dominance" in domain and "no dominance" in dimension. Thus, dominance in German does not clearly support the use of these constructions, which are generally not typical in Turkish-German bilinguals' motion descriptions.

French (quantitative analysis)

The average numbers in Table 71 indicate a few inter-group differences, notably in the use of bare Manner verbs without other linguistic devices ([VM_0], see example (164)), which were more frequently used by French minimal bilinguals as compared to Turkish-French bilinguals. In contrast, the use of bare Path verbs without other linguistic devices ([VP_0], see example (165)) is quite similar (TURFRE 13.70%; FRE 14.40%).

Table 71: Means (*M*) and ranges (*R*) of motion verb constructions French (in %).

Motion verb construction	French			
	FRE		TURFRE	
	M	*R*	*M*	*R*
VP_P	31.68	7.14–58.33	36.46	17.65–61.54
VM_0	26.79	9.09–50.00	18.57	0–30.77
VP_0	13.70	5.88–42.86	14.40	7.14–33.33
VGEN_P	8.37	0–27.78	6.80	0–14.29
VM_P	7.56	5.26–21.43	6.20	4.16–17.65

The results of parametrical and non-parametrical tests indicate that Turkish-French bilingual and French minimal bilingual speakers do not significantly differ as regards the motion verb construction in French.

(164) après il   a   marché
      then   he   AUX.PR   walk.PTCP
      'Then he walked' (Ethan, FRE, 320–332)

(165) et   après elle est   sortie
      and   then   she   AUX.PR   exit.PTCP
      'And then she exited' (Arda, TURFRE, 157–161)

Moreover, Turkish-French bilinguals more frequently used Path verbs with Path devices ([VP_P], see example (166)) (TURFRE 36.46%; FRE 31.68%) and slightly less frequently Generic verbs with Path devices ([VGEN_P], see example (167)) (TURFRE 6.80%; FRE 8.37%). Manner verbs with Path devices ([VM_P], see example (168)) were limited, but slightly more often used by French minimal bilinguals (FRE 7.56%; TURFRE 6.20%).

(166) et   ensuite   il   est   rentré   dans le   tuyau
      and   thereafter   he   AUX.PR   enter.PTCP   in   DET   pipe
      'Thereafter he entered into the pipe' (Adile, TURFRE, 337–344)

(167) *du coup   il   va   dans   une   barque*
as a result he   go.PR in   INDF   small boat
'As a result he goes in a small boat' (Enzo, FRE, 482–488)

(168) *il   a   sauté   de   l'   autre   côté*
he   AUX.PR jump.PTCP from   DET   other   side
'He jumped from the other side' (Devin, TURFRE, 340–342)

Constructions which are considered typically verb-framed ([VP_M]; [VP_O]) in the motion literature were found less frequently. However, they were more often used by both groups than typical S-constructions (see Table 72).

Table 72: V- and S-constructions French (in %).

V/S	French	
	TURFRE	FRE
V-const	16.54	14.29
S-const	11.58	10.41
Total constructions	241	205

Furthermore, this finding suggests that bilingual and minimal bilingual speakers of French used more typical V-constructions in comparison with the Turkish-French bilinguals' as well as Turkish-German and Turkish minimal bilinguals' motion descriptions in Turkish; they more frequently used typical S-constructions ([VM_P]; [VMP_P]) as seen above.

The analysis of syntactic constructions in French indicate that subordinate clauses were slightly more often used by Turkish-French bilinguals (TURFRE 7.47%; FRE 6.34%, see Table 73). Turkish-French bilinguals also made more frequently use of modal verbs or other non motion verbs which entail Manner, Manner-Path, Path or Generic infinitives (TURFRE 14.52%; FRE 12.68%).

Table 73: Syntactic constructions in French (in %).

VCONST	TURFRE	FRE
VSC	7.47	6.34
VMOD	14.52	12.68
Total constructions	241	205

When considering the bilingual speakers' L1 and L2, three constructions, in which Turkish-French speakers display differences between both, Turkish-German and

Turkish minimal bilinguals, are of particular interest. As with a lower usage of [VM_P] by Turkish-French bilinguals in Turkish, a lower usage of this construction was found in French. In this context, the influence seems to be L2 based. Since it is more uncommon in French to combine multiple directional Path elements, speakers probably transfer this restriction into their L1.

Furthermore, Turkish-French bilinguals display a higher usage of [VP_O]-constructions in Turkish (see Table 118 in Appendix C.III), as compared to Turkish-German and Turkish minimal bilinguals. As seen above, this construction is more frequently used in French by both Turkish-French and French minimal bilinguals. These findings suggest an influence of the bilinguals' L2 on their performance in L1. However, the correlation coefficient is very low ($r=-0.14$) and statistically not significant. Therefore, further qualitative analyses are required in order to identify individual variation.

As regards the usage of [VM_O]-constructions, Turkish-French bilinguals made use of them less frequently in French as compared to French minimal bilinguals. In Turkish, they used this pattern slightly less frequently than Turkish minimal bilinguals; the dispersion, however, is lower as compared to the difference between French minimal bilinguals. In these cases an L1>L2 influence can be assumed.

Further differences were found with respect to the use of modal verbs or other non motion verbs with Motion infinitives; they were most frequently used in Turkish by Turkish-French bilinguals. The fact that this pattern is present in Turkish and French and similarly used by minimal bilinguals of each language, can not explain the higher usage by Turkish-French bilinguals in both languages. Since both languages are considered V-framed L2>L1 and L1>L2 influences can be seen as an intra-typological impact on how bilingual speakers encode motion events in two languages of the same type.

Let us now look into the qualitative results in order to determine and discuss intra-group differences and individual speakers' usage preferences and cross-linguistic influences in Turkish-French bilinguals' motion descriptions.

French (qualitative analysis)
Again, the figures in Table 74 reveal considerable intra-group differences as regards the lowest and highest values of motion constructions. For instance, Gözde (+1.95 SD) more frequently used [VP_P], whereas Mert indicates a negative z-score (–1.45 SD). Seçkin more often used bare Manner verb constructions (+1.85 SD) in comparison with Devin (–1.85 SD). In contrast, Devin combined Manner verbs with Path devices ([VM_P] more frequently (+2.18 SD), whereas Dilşah, Gözde, and Nezihe did not use this construction at all (–1.18 SD). As regards

7.2 Study 2: Voluntary Motion — 251

Table 74: Turkish-French bilinguals with a distance of one or more standard deviations (*SD*) in VP_P, VM_O, VP_O, VGEN_P and VM_P constructions in French.

Speaker	VP_P	VM_O	VP_O	VGEN_P	VM_P
Devin	+1.05	−1.85		+1.45	
Gözde	+1.95		−1.51		−1.18
Mert	−1.46				+2.18
Nezihe	+1.35	+1.22	−1.51		−1.18
Nihal	−1.28			−1.19	
Arda		−1.23		+1.12	
Dilşah		+1.08			−1.18
Seçkin		−1.85	+1.99	−1.19	
Bircan			−1.51		
Adile				−1.19	
Maide				−1.19	
Shirin				−1.19	−1.18
Emre					+1.54

[VGEN_P] there were even more speakers who did not use this construction (Adile, Maide, Nihal, Seçkin and Shirin, each −1.19 SD). In contrast, other speakers made use of it more frequently (Arda, +1.45 SD).

Regarding our assumption that a higher usage of [VP_O] in French is related to a higher usage of this construction in Turkish, the individual results indicate that only Devin (+0.74 in French) also displays a higher positive z-score in Turkish (+2.39 SD). In contrast, Seçkin, who has the highest z-score in French (+1.99), did not use [VP_O] in Turkish at all. The inverse case can be observed for Nezihe, who used this construction more frequently in Turkish (+1.74 SD) but never in French. Finally, the individual analysis shows that the higher use of [VP_O] in the Turkish-French bilingual group is related to a few speakers (Devin, Nezihe) and suggests that there is no general interaction between L1 and L2.

Among speakers who less frequently used bare Manner verb constructions [VM_O] in French, Devin (−1.45 *SD*) and Seçkin (−1.45 *SD*) did not use this construction in Turkish at all. In these cases, an L1>L2-dominance can be assumed. The direction of influence is, however, not supported by language dominance, since Devin displays an "L2-dominance" in both domain and dimension and Seçkin an "L2-dominance" in domain and "no dominance" in dimension.

Among speakers who never used [VM_P] in French, Dilşah also never used this construction in Turkish, and also Nezihe indicates a negative z-score (−0.17). These cases clearly suggest an L2>L1 influence, which is reflected in a lower usage of the [VM_P] construction in Turkish. When considering the language dominance profiles, the direction of influence is supported for all speakers since they are L2-dominant in both domain and dimension.

Summary
The finding in this section suggests that on a constructional level, speakers of Turkish and French usage of typical V-patterns is limited. Moreover, a higher usage of "double-framing" structures was found. Furthermore, on the syntactical level, bilingual speakers tend to avoid more complex structures in Turkish.

We assume that the observed transfer of certain constructions is generally due to constructional constraints or allowance in one of the bilinguals' languages. However, in the case of Turkish-German bilinguals who tend to avoid typical S-constructions, but routinely extend Path to Generic verbs in German, a convergence of the typical Turkish pattern ("Path-in-verb") and the typical German construction (Path outside the main verb) was observed ([VGEN_P]). This is in line with previous findings in Turkish-German bilingual settings (Goschler et al. 2013). and can be explained by the convergence approach introduced in §2.2.2.

The findings, again, contribute to an intra-typological perspective in motion research, and prove our findings in §7.2.3.2 that speakers of Turkish and French resort considerably to the adnominal and adverbal slot when encoding Path. The fact that the typical V-pattern [VP_M] was generally limited in Turkish and French is possibly due to the participants' language acquisition stage. Furthermore, it is possible that the cognitive requirements of the re-narration task generally inhibited the use of more complex structures and has led to an avoidance of encoding of Manner in subordinate clauses. Moreover, as noted above, it seems that bilingual speakers are behind the respective minimal bilingual age group as regards their usage of complex structures in Turkish (such as converbs in Turkish and gerunds in French).

Let us now turn to the motion verb choices in specific motion event types. In the context of linguistic constraints in Turkish and French, motion verb preferences in motion event types with Path and boundary focus (see §3.2.6.4) are of special interest in the following analysis. The distribution of cardinal kinds of displacements (see §3.2.5.3) allows a more detailed picture of conflation preferences as presented in §7.2.2.1 and can help to explain further inter- and intra-group differences.

7.2.6 Results of locative and telic Path phrases

7.2.6.1 Overall picture of locative Path phrases
Let us begin with the speakers' motion verb preferences in locative Path phrases, which are motion descriptions to which we referred as they do not predicate a specific locative endstate except for proximity to a ground (see §3.2.6.4). These include the AD, AB, SUPER and DE event types; furthermore GENERALIS was included in this category. In §3.2.6.4, we predicted that when using the "Manner-in-verb" pattern, speakers of Turkish and French only do so in locative Path phrases, while speakers of German are not restricted. Furthermore, the results of the MVC-Task (see §7.2.1) suggest that Turkish and French speakers differ in their preference for Manner and Path verbs in SUPER and DE-events. We predict a similar tendency in the motion verb choices in the VM-Task.

Turkish (quantitative)
Table 75 summarises the means and ranges of expressed motion verbs with Path focus in Turkish. The results show, that in each group approximately two thirds of the speakers' motion event descriptions display a Path focus (TURGER 69.27%; TURFRE 69.68%; TUR 70.93%).

The figures reveal that Manner verbs and Generic verbs were frequently used over Manner-Path and Path verbs, however, there are a few inter-group differences. Turkish-German bilinguals and Turkish minimal bilinguals made use of Manner verbs more frequently in locative Path phrases (TURGER 27.83%; TUR 29.08%) as compared to Turkish-French bilinguals (22.97%). The differences are, however, statistically not significant. In turn, Turkish-French bilinguals and Turkish minimal bilinguals more frequently used Manner-Path verbs in locative Path phrases (TURFRE 11.05%; TUR 14.30%) in comparison with Turkish-German bilinguals (6.47%). Whereas the difference between Turkish minimal ($M=14.30$, $SD=7.42$) and Turkish-German bilinguals ($M=6.47$, $SD=7.86$) is very significant ($t(28)=-2.81$, $p<0.01**$), it is not so under Turkish-German and Turkish-French conditions. Path verbs were more frequently used by Turkish-French bilinguals (13.15%) and slightly more frequently used by Turkish-German bilinguals (11.56%) as compared to Turkish minimal bilinguals (9.74%). The differences are statistically not significant. Generic verbs were more frequently used by both bilingual groups (TURGER 23.40%; TURFRE 20.99%) in comparison with Turkish minimal bilinguals (17.39%), however, the statistical tests also did not reveal a significant difference.

When we look more closely at the motion verb choice of corresponding event types in Table 76, the figures indicate that Turkish minimal bilinguals more often

Table 75: Means (M) and ranges (R) of motion verb choices in locative Path phrases Turkish (in %).

Group	VM		VMP		VP		VGEN		VLV		TOTAL	
	M	R	M	R	M	R	M	R	M	R	%	in nmb.
TURGER	27.83	0–50	6.47	0–25	11.56	0–25	23.40	0–66.7	0.00	0.00	69.27	198
TURFRE	22.97	6.67–50	11.05	0–30.77	13.15	0–33.33	20.99	0–46.15	1.53	0–11.11	69.68	173
TUR	29.08	7.14–43.75	14.30	4.76–33.33	9.74	0–28.57	17.39	4.76–29.41	0.42	0–6.25	70.93	206

Table 76: Motion verb choices per motion event type with Path focus Turkish (in %).

Motion verb category	Group	Locative Path phrases Turkish				
		AB	AD	DE	GENERALIS	SUPER
VM	TURGER	0.62	**6.79**	0.58	**19.83**	0.00
	TURFRE	1.84	2.14	0.00	**18.99**	0.00
	TUR	**5.00**	1.58	0.26	**22.24**	0.00
VMP	TURGER	0.00	0.42	3.49	0.67	1.90
	TURFRE	0.00	1.62	3.07	**4.24**	2.12
	TUR	0.42	3.00	4.32	**3.53**	3.04
VP	TURGER	0.00	0.81	1.51	0.00	**9.24**
	TURFRE	0.00	0.29	1.36	3.31	**8.18**
	TUR	0.00	1.02	**4.51**	0.32	3.89
VGEN	TURGER	1.63	**11.88**	1.40	6.47	2.03
	TURFRE	1.26	**11.98**	0.00	7.75	0.00
	TUR	1.10	**9.04**	0.00	7.00	0.26
VLV	TURGER	0.00	0.00	0.00	0.00	0.00
	TURFRE	0.00	0.00	0.00	1.53	0.00
	TUR	0.00	0.00	0.00	0.42	0.00
TOT	TURGER	2.25	19.90	6.98	26.97	13.17
	TURFRE	3.1	16.03	4.43	35.82	10.3
	TUR	6.52	14.64	9.09	33.51	7.19

encoded AB- and DE-events than bilingual speakers. In contrast, Turkish-German bilinguals more frequently encoded AD- and SUPER-events in comparison with Turkish-French and Turkish minimal bilinguals, whereas the latter used bare motion verbs (GENERALIS) more frequently as compared to Turkish-German bilinguals. However, GENERALIS-events were generally preferred in all groups.

With regard to the motion verb choices, Manner verbs were used most frequently in GENERALIS-events (TURGER 19.83%; TURFRE 18.99%; TUR 22.24%, see example (146) above). In AD-events Turkish-German bilinguals more frequently used Manner verbs (6.79%, see example (169)) as compared to the other two groups (TURFRE 2.14%; TUR 1.58%). On the contrary, Turkish minimal bilinguals more frequently used Manner verbs in AB-events (5.00%, see example (170)) in comparison with both bilingual groups (TURGER 0.62%; TURFRE 1.84%).

(169)   binay-e •   koş-uyo
        building-DAT   =run-PROG.3SG
        'It is running to the building' (Alisa, TURGER, 48–51)

(170) kedi boru-dan   yuvarlan-dı
      cat   pipe-ABL   roll-PST.3SG
      'The cat rolled from the pipe' (Başak, TUR, 291–294)

Turkish-French (4.24%) and Turkish minimal bilinguals (3.53%) used bare Manner-Path verbs (see example (171)) more frequently compared to Turkish-German bilinguals (0.67%). Path verbs were used more frequently in SUPER-events by Turkish-German (9.24%, see example (172)) and French bilinguals (8.18%) in comparison with Turkish minimal bilinguals (3.89%). The latter used Path verbs more frequently in DE-events (TUR 4.51%; TURGER 1.51%; TURFRE 1.36%, see example (173)). Generic verbs were generally used in AD- (see example (174)) and GENERALIS (see example (175)) event types.

(171) o zaman   tırman-ıyo
      that time   =climb-PROG.3SG
      'In that time it is climbing' (Shirin, TURFRE, 98–99)

(172) yukarıy-a   çık-tı
      up-DAT   ascend.PST.3SG
      'It ascended up' (Kurt, TURGER, 149–151)

(173) silvestir   aşağ-a   in-iyor
      =Sylvester   =down-DAT   descend.PROG.3SG
      'Sylvester is descending downwards' (Akay, TUR, 9–11)

(174) şey-in-e   git-ti
      thing-POSS-DAT   go-PST.3SG
      'It went to the thing' (Esna, TURGER, 248–250)

(175) kadın   da   gel-di
      woman   FOC   come-PST.3SG
      'Also the woman came' (Geza, TURFRE, 136–138)

Let us now analyse the data qualitatively in order to obtain and discuss intragroup differences and individual speakers' usage preferences in the Turkish-German and Turkish-French bilinguals' motion descriptions.

Turkish (qualitative)
The numbers in Table 77 indicate some intra-group differences. In each group, a few speakers used Manner verbs in locative Path phrases less frequently in

Table 77: Turkish-German and Turkish-French bilinguals with a distance of one or more standard deviations (*SD*) in Manner verb (VM), Manner-Path verb (VMP), Path verb (VP), and Generic verb (VGEN) usage in Turkish locative Path phrases.

Group	Speaker	VM	VMP	VP	VGEN
TURGER	Alisa	+1.31			
	Beren	−1.81			+2.30
	Kurt	+1.80			−1.24
	Melis	−2.26	+2.36	−1.27	
	Ela		+1.72		
	Tuba		+1.00		
	Esna			−1.27	+1.26
	Serkan			+1.48	
	Taylan			+1.48	
	Yiğit			+1.48	
	Ela				−1.24
	Gamze				+1.30
TURFRE	Arda	+2.09			
	Bircan	−1.18			
	Devin	−1.18	−1.26	+1.02	−1.17
	Dilşah	−1.26			
	Nihal	+1.32		−1.36	+1.09
	Seçkin	−1.18	+2.25	−1.36	+2.23
	Adile		−1.26		
	Geza		−1.26		
	Emre			+2.08	
	Mert			+1.22	−1.86

comparison with other speakers. For instance, among Turkish-German bilinguals, Melis did not use a single Manner verb in locative Path phrases (as illustrated above, she generally did not use Manner verbs at all) and Beren's usage is also limited (−1.81 *SD*), whereas Alisa (+1.31 *SD*) and Kurt (+1.80 *SD*) more frequently made use of them. The same can be observed for Turkish-French bilinguals (Dilşah −1.26 *SD*); +2.09 *SD*) and Turkish minimal bilinguals (Seval 7.14% vs. Musa 41.18; Zeren, 43.75%).

Manner-Path verbs were not used at all in locative Path phrases among Beren, Esna, Gamze, Kurt, Serkan and Taylan, but more frequently by Melis (+2.36 *SD*).

In each group there are speakers who did not use a single Path verb at all (TURGER Melis, Esna TURFRE Nihal), whereas other speakers more frequently made use of Path verbs (TURGER Serkan, Taylan, Yiğit, each +1.48 *SD*; TURFRE Emre, +2.08 *SD*). The highest dispersion between lowest and highest values can be observed for the use of Generic verbs in locative Path phrases among the bilingual speakers. In the Turkish-German group Ela and Kurt did not make use of Generic verbs at all, whereas Esna (+1.26 *SD*) and Gamze (+1.30 *SD*) used Generic verbs in nearly half of their locative Path phrases, Moreover, Beren even made use of it in almost two thirds of encoded locative Path phrases (+2.30 *SD*). Among Turkish-French bilingual speakers almost half of Seçkin's locative Path phrases contain a Generic verb (+2.23 *SD*), whereas Mert did not make use of them at all.

Let us now examine the speaker's respective L2 in order to discuss possible L1-L2 interactions.

German (quantitative)
Table 78 summarises the means and ranges of expressed motion verbs in locative Path phrases in German.

The results show, that Turkish-German bilinguals more frequently encoded locative Path phrases (64.06%) as compared to German minimal bilinguals (57.55%). Manner verbs were used equally among speakers of both groups (TURGER 32.05%; GER 31.47%), the difference is statistically not significant. Manner-Path verbs were more often used by German minimal bilinguals (13.9%) as compared to Turkish-German bilinguals 10.38%). This difference is again statistically not significant. The most striking inter-group difference relates to the use of Generic verbs in motion event descriptions with Path focus, which is significantly higher among Turkish-German bilinguals ($M=21.15$, $SD=13.52$) compared to German minimal bilinguals ($M=8.94$, $SD=8.26$) ($t(28)=2.98$, $p<0.01$**). This is not surprising, since Turkish-German bilinguals generally more often made use of Generic verbs as illustrated in §7.2.2.1. As regards motion constructions without motion verbs in locative Path phrases, German minimal bilinguals made more frequent, albeit limited, use of it in comparison with Turkish-German bilinguals. Because the use of these constructions is distributed among a few speakers, no statistical tests were conducted. The same situation accounts for other motion constructions with semantically weak verbs.

When examining the corresponding event types, the figures in Table 79 show further subtle inter-group differences which are reflected in a slightly higher use of AB-, AD- and GENERALIS-events by Turkish-German bilinguals.

Table 78: Means (M) and ranges (R) of motion verb choices in locative Path phrases German (in %).

Group	VM		VMP		VP		VGEN		VAUX/VMOD		VLV		TOTAL	
	M	R	M	R	M	R	M	R	M	R	M	R	%	in nmb.
TURGER	32.05	11.11–47.62	10.38	3.70–20.00	0.00	0.00	21.15	0–48.15	0.48	0–3.7	0	0	64.06	221
GER	31.47	17.65–48.39	13.91	5.88–21.43	0.00	0–5.88	8.94	0–23.81	2.84	0–10	0.39	0–5.88	57.55	190

Note:
[1] Note that in constructions where two events were segmented together by using the same verb (*wollte sisch • • dursch • den gartn ins haus schleisch* 'he wanted to sneak through the garden into the house' (Ozan, TURGER) only the Endpoint event (here IN) was considered.

Table 79: Motion verb choices per motion event type with Path focus German (in %).

Motion verb category	Group	Locative Path phrases German				
		AB	AD	DE	GENERALIS	SUPER
VM	TURGER	6.16	8.31	1.97	14.81	0.79
	GER	2.92	11.97	1.77	13.89	0.91
VMP	TURGER	0.00	0.56	3.23	0.74	5.85
	GER	0.00	0.00	3.92	0.67	9.32
VP	TURGER	0.00	0.00	0.00	0.00	0.00
	GER	0.00	0.00	0.00	0.00	0.00
VGEN	TURGER	0.92	8.27	1.95	4.77	5.24
	GER	0.33	2.06	1.59	2.98	1.98
VAUX/VMOD	TURGER	0.00	0.48	0.00	0.00	0.00
	GER	0.00	1.31	0.94	0.00	0.59
VLV	TURGER	0.00	0.00	0.00	0.00	0.00
	GER	0.00	0.00	0.00	0.39	0.00
TOT	TURGER	7.08	17.62	7.15	20.32	11.88
	GER	3.25	15.34	8.22	17.93	12.80

As regards the motion verb choices, German minimal bilinguals used Manner verbs in AB-events (TURGER 6.16%; GER 2.92%, see example (176)) less frequently, but more frequently in AD-events (TURGER 8.31%; GER 11.97%, see example (124) above). Furthermore, German minimal bilinguals more often made use of Manner-Path verbs in SUPER-events (TURGER 5.85%; GER 9.32%), which is generally due to a higher frequency of the verb *klettern* 'to climb' (see example (177)). As with a lower frequency use of Manner verbs in AD-events and Manner-Path-verbs in SUPER events by Turkish-German bilinguals, a higher usage of Generic verbs in the respective event types can be observed (AD: TURGER 8.27%, see example (178); GER 2.06%; SUPER: TURGER 5.24%; GER 1.98%, see example (126) above).

(176) und   dann   is   der • weg-gerannt
      and   then   =AUX.PR   he   off-run.PTCP
      'And then he ran off' (Yiğit, TURGER, 511–517)

(177) nh   dann   is-sie   da   rauf   geklettat
      =and   then   =AUX.PR-she   there   up   =climb.PTCP
      'And then she climbed up there' (Max, GER, 1066–1071)

(178) und dann is   er   zu-m   bowling center gegang
       and then AUX.PR   he   =to-DET.DAT   bowling centre =go.PTCP
       'And then he went to the bowling centre' (Eda, TURGER, 504–510)

When considering the bilingual speakers' L1 and L2, the differences found for Manner verb usage in AD-events in Turkish and Manner-Path verb usage in SUPER-events in German are probably due to cross-linguistic influences. A Pearson's correlation revealed a very significant negative correlation ($r=-0.71$) between a lower usage of Manner-Path verbs and a higher use of Generic verbs in SUPER-events in German ($t(13)=-3.67$, $p<0.01*$). We argued above that a lower usage of Manner verbs and the preference for Generic verbs are probably related to the general preference for Path over Manner verbs in Turkish. This possibly also account for the limited use of Manner-Path verbs in SUPER-events in German; as we have seen above, Path verbs are generally preferred in SUPER-events in Turkish. However, a Pearson's correlation revealed a low negative correlation ($r=-0.16$) which was statistically not significant. This finding suggests that the lower frequency of Manner-Path verbs in SUPER-events in German is more related to the use of Generic verbs in German than to a higher Path verb usage in Turkish. However, qualitative analyses are required in order to prove individual L1>L2 influences.

A higher usage of Generic verbs and a lower usage of Manner verbs in AD-events can be observed as well. However, since Turkish-German bilinguals rarely used Path verbs in Turkish, the higher usage of Generic verbs does not seem to be related to the L1. Moreover, the influence is rather L2 based and reflected in a higher usage of Manner verbs in Turkish in AD-events. A Pearson's correlation indicates an intermediate positive correlation, which was, however, statistically not significant ($r=0.41$). Again, further individual analysis will specify L2>L1 influences.

Similarly, the higher usage of Manner verbs in AB-events in German is not influenced by L1-usage patterns, since Turkish-German bilinguals predominantly avoid Manner verbs in AB-events in Turkish. In this context the question arises of whether bilingual speakers generally avoid the encoding of EX-events in German and more frequently encode an AB-event instead. In this case, the strategy is possibly typologically motivated. We will return to this issue in §7.2.6.2 when examining telic Path phrases.

In addition, the figures indicate that Turkish-German bilinguals more frequently encoded locative Path phrases than telic Path phrases in German (see Table 78 above), which is possibly a result of L1 strategies. As illustrated in §3.2.6.4, Özçalışkan (2013) observed an alternative encoding strategy in Turkish of parsing an event into multiple sub-events and leaving the traversal of the spatial boundary implicit. Consequently, the proportion of locative Path phrases increases when making use of this strategy. In this context it is possible that Turkish-German bilinguals' higher proportion of locative Path phrases in German is related to such (L1)-strategies. A Pearson's correlation indicated a positive, but statistically not significant correlation ($r=0.41$) between a higher proportion of locative Path phrases in Turkish and German.

In the following, qualitative analysis will provide further details as regards intra-group differences as well as individual speakers' usage preferences and cross-linguistic influences in Turkish-German bilinguals motion event descriptions in L1 and L2.

German (qualitative)

The figures in Table 80 reveal considerable intra-group differences among Turkish-German bilinguals. Such differences can also be observed for the use of Manner verbs in locative Path phrases. Whereas Melis' use of Manner verbs is limited (–1.84 *SD*), almost half of Ela's (+1.35 *SD*) and Yiğit's (+1.37 *SD*) encoded locative Path phrases contain a Manner verb.[82] Furthermore, Serkan did not use Generic verbs at all, Sefar's use is also limited (–1.07 *SD*), whereas Alisa (+1.47) and Dana (+1.99 *SD*) indicate much higher values.

Table 80: Turkish-German bilinguals with a distance of one or more standard deviations (*SD*) in Manner verb (VM), Manner-Path verb (VMP) and Generic verb (VGEN) usage in German locative Path phrases.

Speaker	VM	VMP	VGEN
Eda	+1.13		
Ela	+1.35	+1.18	
Melis	–1.84		
Ozan	–1.14		
Serkan	+1.13		–1.56
Yiğit	+1.37		
Alisa		–1.15	+1.47
Gamze		–1.46	
Sefar		+2.10	–1.07
Taylan		–1.05	
Dana			+1.99

---

[82] The same applies for German minimal bilinguals (Katharina 17.65% vs. Max 48.39%).

Table 81: Turkish-German bilinguals with highest standard deviations (*SD*) in Manner-Path verb (VMP) and Generic verb (VGEN) usage in SUPER events in German, Path verb (VP) usage in SUPER events in Turkish, Generic verb (VGEN) usage in AD-events in German and Turkish as well as in overall German and Turkish locative Path phrases.

Speaker	SUPER-events German		SUPER-events Turkish	VGEN in AD-events		VM in AD-events		Locative Path phrases	
	VMP	VGEN	VP	Turkish	German	German	Turkish	Turkish	German
Sefar	+1.72	−1.06						−0.85	−0.90
Serkan	+1.36	−1.06				+2.34	+1.78	−1.10	−0.44
Ela	+1.08	0.00							
Alisa								+1.08	+1.51
Beren								0,86	+0.22
Dana				1,51	2,5			0,7	+1.15
Gamze				+1.25	−0.1			+1.35	−0.40
Melis	−1.35	+1.93	−1.22					−2.58	−1.03
Esna	−1.35		−1.22	+1.47	−0.41				
Eda						+1.37	+1.13		
Taylan	−1.34	+1.18	+2.09			+1.54	−0.09		
Yiğit	−0.25	−1.06	+1.43						

In addition to our assumption that a lower usage of Manner-Path verbs is related to higher values in Generic verb usage in SUPER-events in German, the individual results show that, vice versa, there is also a relation between a higher usage of Manner-Path verbs and a lower usage of Generic verbs in SUPER-events in German among two speakers. Sefar (+1.72 *SD*) and Serkan (+1.36 *SD*) both displayed a positive z-score in their Manner-Path verb usage in SUPER-events in German and did not use Generic verbs at all (see Table 81). However, both speakers also did not use Manner-Path verbs in SUPER-events in Turkish at all. Therefore, a cross-linguistic influence can not be assumed. Among the four speakers[83] who used Manner-Path verbs in SUPER-events in Turkish, only Ela (+1.08 *SD*) and Ozan (+0.84 *SD*) also display higher values in both German and Turkish. In both cases an L2>L1 influence can be assumed. In contrast, for Taylan an L1>L2 influence can be assumed,

---

[83] Due to the limited use of Manner-Path verbs in Turkish SUPER-events, individual z-scores were not calculated.

since he more frequently used Path verbs in Turkish SUPER-events and similarly indicated a negative z-score for Manner-Path verbs and a positive z-score for Generic verbs in German SUPER-events. The language dominance profiles support the direction of influence for Ozan (L2-dominant in both domain and dimension) and partly for Taylan (L1-dominant in domain and "no dominance" in dimension), whereas Ela displays "no dominance" in dimension and a mixed pattern in domain.

As regards Generic verbs in AD-events, the numbers above indicated also a general higher degree of Generic verbs in Turkish locative Path phrases in all three groups. However, among speakers, who more frequently used Generic verbs in AD-events in Turkish, only Dana displays strikingly higher values in German (+2.50 *SD*). In her case an L1>L2 influence can be maintained. When examining speakers who more frequently used Manner verbs in AD-events in German, Serkan (+1.78 *SD*) and Eda (+1.13 *SD*) also display higher z-scores in Turkish. In contrast to Taylan, whose z-score in Turkish is negative (−0.09), for both an L2>L1 influence can be maintained. Only Eda's language dominance profile supports the direction of influence (L2-dominant in both domain and dimension). Serkan is L1-dominant in domain and displays "no dominance" in dimension, Dana is neither L1- nor L2-dominant in both domain and dimension).

When looking at the individual proportions of locative Path phrases in Turkish and German, the figures indicate that a few speakers with positive z-scores in Turkish more often encoded locative Path phrases in German (Alisa, Dana, Beren). On the basis of a general higher proportion of locative Path phrases observed in Turkish, an L1>L2 influence can be surmised. Let us illustrate this issue by examining some examples, which provide further event encoding strategies in German as a result for the speakers' L1.

Example (179) illustrates a strategy by encoding first the Figure's Manner with a bare Manner verb (*gekrabbelt* 'crawled') and subsequently the change of location into a bounded space by a Generic verb + directional Path device (*rein gegang* 'went into'). Such event segmentations were not found in Alisa's Turkish motion descriptions, but among several other speakers (see example (180)).

(179) un   dann   iss-er • •   so   ge- krabbelt • •   [diese ball hat
                                                                    ihn immer so
                                                                    gerollt ,
      and   then   =AUX.PR-he   like crawl.PTCP
      n • dann is er • • also oo - obn / obn steht so bowling ,]
      dann   iss-er   darein   gegang
      then   =AUX.PR-he   there.in   =go.PTCP
      'And then he like crawled…[this ball made him roll and then he… on the top there is written bowling]…then he went in' (Alisa, TURGER, 522–560)

(180) böyle   yuvarlan-dı , ((2,5s))   bovling [[ee]] ((1s))   halıs / • halı-sın-a
      like   roll-PST.3SG   bowling   rug-POSS-DAT
      gir-di
      enter-PST.3SG
      'It like rolled, it entered into the bowling alley' (Kurt, TURGER, 185–199)

Another strategy by implicitly encoding the change of location is illustrated in example (181). Again, Alisa used bare motion constructions (*kommt* 'comes'; *schleicht sich* 'sneaks'), but does not encode the Figure's entry into the bounded space, which has to be inferred by the listener. The same can be observed in her Turkish motion descriptions. In example (182) she first encoded a DE-event (*aşağ yuvarlandı* 'rolled downwards'), and subsequently describes the action (*topları attı* 'threw the balls') inside of another location (in the stimulus a bowling centre). When looking into Alisa's individual use of verb constructions in German, it is striking that she more often used [VM_0] (+1.67 *SD*).

(181) dann • • • kommt   die   katze , • • z-diesn   haus ? • •
      then   come.PR   DET   cat   =to-this   house
      er   macht   die   tür   auf • • er   schleicht   sich
      he   make.PR   DET   door   open   he   sneak.PR   REFL
      'In that time the cat is coming to this house. It opens the door (and then) it sneaks' (Alisa, TURGER, 846–866)

(182) ozanda ((1,5s))   boru-dan   aşağ   yuvarlan-dı , ozanda
      =that time   pipe-ABL   =down   roll-PST.3SG   =that time
      bovling   ((incomprehensible))   top-lar-ı   at-tı
      bowling   ball-PL-ACC   throw.PST.3SG
      'It rolled down from the pipe, in that time it threw the bowling balls' (Alisa, TURGER, 263–274)

In addition, Dana also omitted the Figure's entry into the bounded space in example (183) and subdivided the event into an AB- (*weggegang* 'away.went') and an AD-event (*zum bowling gegang* 'went to the bowling'. Similarly, in her Turkish motion descriptions the avoidance of encoding the Figure's change of location can be found as well (see (184)).

(183) un   danach   is   die • • katze   da   ganz   schnell
      and   later   AUX.PR   DET   cat   there   very   fast
      weg   gegang , und   un   danach   is   er   zu-m •
      away =go.PTCP and   =and   later   =AUX.PR   he   =to-DET.DAT

((incomprehensible))
bowling   gegang
bowling   =go.PTCP
'And later, the cat went very fast away and later it went to the bowling centre' (Dana, TURGER, 429–451)

(184)   bovling • •   yer-in-e   yuvarlan-dı
        bowling   place-POSS-DAT   roll-PST.3SG
        'It rolled to the bowling (centre) (Dana, TURGER, 279–283)

However, when looking at the other speakers' performance, Gamze indicates a positive z-score in Turkish and a negative z-score in German; in her case an influence can be excluded. The opposite was observed for Sefar, Serkan and Melis who less frequently encoded locative Path phrases in Turkish and also indicate a negative z-score in German. In these cases an L2>L1 influence can be surmised. The speakers' language dominance profiles indicate no support for those speakers for whom an L1>L2 influence was assumed. Alisa, Dana and Beren neither indicate an L1-dominance in domain nor in dimension. The same accounts for Sefar, Serkan and Melis, who neither indicate an "L2-dominance" in domain nor dimension; only Serkan indicates an "L2-dominance" in dimension.

French (quantitative)

Table 82 summarises means and ranges of expressed motion verbs in locative Path phrases in French.

Table 82: Means (*M*) and ranges (*R*) of motion verb choices in locative Path phrases French (in %).

Group	Locative Path phrases French										
	VM		VMP		VP		VGEN		VLV		TOTAL
	M	R	M	R	M	R	M	R	M	R	%
TURFRE	22.52	6.67–36.84	8.54	0–33.33	23.95	5.88–40	8.11	0–21.43	1.93	0–18.18	65.05
FRE	30.11	14.29–50	5.02	0–17.65	20.62	0–42.86	4.15	0–22.22	2.00	0–10.53	61.89

The average numbers show that Turkish-French bilinguals slightly more frequently encoded locative Path phrases (65.05%) in comparison with French minimal bilinguals (61.89%). Further inter-group differences are related to the Manner verb usage in locative Path phrases, which is higher among French minimal bilinguals (TURFRE 22.52%; FRE 30.11%), whereas bilingual speakers more frequently used Manner-Path verbs (TURFRE 8.54%; FRE 5.02%), Path verbs

(TURFRE 23.95%; FRE 20.62%) and Generic verbs (TURFRE 8.11%; FRE 4.15%). However, for all observed differences the results of (non) parametric tests were not significant.[84]

When looking at the corresponding motion event types in Table 83, the figures show that Turkish-French bilinguals generally more often encoded SUPER-events (17.48%) in comparison with French minimal bilinguals (7.87%), whereas French minimal bilingual slightly more often used bare motion verbs (GENERALIS-events: FRE 40.08% TURFRE 34.35%).

Table 83: Motion verb choices per motion event type with Path focus French (in %).

Motion verb category	Group	Locative Path phrases French				
		AB	AD	DE	GENERALIS	SUPER
VM	TURFRE	0.48	3.19	0.35	**18.50**	0.00
	FRE	0.51	2.46	0.38	**26.76**	0.00
VMP	TURFRE	0.00	0.00	1.64	3.38	3.52
	FRE	0.00	0.00	2.65	2.37	0.00
VP	TURFRE	0.00	1.52	1.27	7.59	**13.57**
	FRE	0.00	3.04	2.44	7.27	**7.87**
VGEN	TURFRE	0.00	**4.38**	0.39	2.95	0.39
	FRE	0.00	**2.47**	0.00	1.68	0.00
VLV	TURFRE	0.00	0.00	0.00	1.93	0.00
	FRE	0.00	0.00	0.00	2.00	0.00
TOT	TURFRE	0.48	9.09	3.65	34.35	17.48
	FRE	0.51	7.97	5.47	40.08	7.87

The inter-group difference in Manner verb usage is related to a higher frequency of bare Manner verbs by French minimal bilinguals (see example (185)). Based on the results of the MVC-Task, as well as the analysis of motion verb frequency in §7.2.2.2, we assumed that the observed more frequent use of Path verbs by Turkish-French bilinguals is related to SUPER-events. The numbers of Path verbs used in SUPER-events support this assumption. Turkish-French bilinguals more frequently encoded SUPER-events than French minimal bilinguals (predominantly by the verb *monter* 'to ascend', see example (186)). Furthermore, Generic

---

84 Due to the fact that only a few speakers used other motion constructions with semantically weak verbs, a statistical test has not been carried out for this variable.

verbs were more frequently used by Turkish-French bilinguals in AD- (see example (187)) and GENERALIS-events (see example (188)).

(185) il   devait   courir
       he   must.PST   run.INF
       'He had to run' (Eva, FRE, 406–408)

(186) il   était   monté   sur un   autre immeuble
       he   AUX.PST   ascend.PTCP   on   INDF   other building
       'He was ascending on another building' (Maide, TURFRE, 489–495)

(187) il   est   venu   à   côté de   titi
       he   AUX.PR come.PTCP   to   side of   =Tweety
       'He came to Tweety's side' (Bircan, TURFRE, 243–249)

(188) et   l'   oiseau i [[ee]] il   est   venu
       and   DET   bird   he   AUX.PR   come.PTCP
       'And the bird he came' (Adile, TURFRE, 288–295)

When considering the bilingual speakers' L1 and L2, the lower bare Manner verb usage in French locative Path phrases is possibly related to the lower usage of this pattern in Turkish; the mean of bare Manner verbs is quite the same in Turkish and French, as we have seen for the corresponding construction type ([VM_0]) in §7.2.5. A Pearson's correlation indicates an intermediate positive but statistically not significant correlation ($r=0.31$), which only partly supports this assumption. Thus, further individual analyses are required in order to detect possible intragroup variation.

Similarly, the assumption that the slightly higher use of Generic verbs in AD-events is possibly due to the relatively common usage of Generic verbs in Turkish AD-events is only partly supported by the statistical analysis. A Pearson's correlation revealed a not significant negative intermediate correlation ($r=-0.25$). Thus, a possible L1-influence might be related to a few speakers.

Furthermore, since Path verbs were generally used more frequently in Turkish SUPER-events, the direction of influence is possibly L1 based and reflected in a higher Path verb usage in French SUPER-events. The correlation analysis does not, however, confirm this assumption, since the correlation coefficient was low ($r=0.17$) and statistically not significant. Nevertheless, qualitative analysis will further specify whether there is a correlation among individual speakers.

As regards the subtle difference in the speakers' total encoding of locative Path phrases, it can be hypothesised that the higher usage among Turkish-French bilinguals is related to the higher usage in their Turkish descriptions and different encoding strategies in Turkish, as illustrated in the Turkish-German context. However, a Pearson's correlation did not reveal any relation between the higher usage of locative Path phrases in Turkish and French ($r=0.04$).

Let us analyse the data qualitatively in order to obtain and discuss intra-group differences as well as speakers' individual usage preferences and cross-linguistic influences in Turkish-French bilinguals' motion event descriptions in L1 and L2.

French (qualitative)
Again, the figures reveal considerable intra-group differences as regards the use of Manner, Manner-Path, Path and Generic verbs in French locative Path phrases (see Table 84). For instance, some speakers in each group used Manner verbs less frequently (Seçkin, Devin), other speakers displayed a higher usage (Bircan, Nihal). There are speakers who did not use Manner-Path (Devin, Özgür, Geza, Nezihe) and Generic verbs (Seçkin, Emre, Özgür, Shirin) at all, whereas other speakers displayed a high positive z-score (Manner Path verbs: Seçkin; Generic verbs: Devin, Arda).

Table 84: Turkish-French bilinguals with a distance of one or more standard deviations (*SD*) in Manner verb (vm), Manner-Path verb (vmp), Path verb (vp) and Generic verb (vgen) usage in French locative Path phrases.

Speaker	VM	VMP	VP	VGEN
Arda	−1.05			+1.58
Bircan	+1.51			
Devin	−1.62		+1.24	+1.98
Nihal	+1.14			
Seçkin	−1.67	+2.76	+1.69	−1.20
Mert		+1.01		
Adile			+1.36	
Mert			−1.91	
Emre				−1.20
Özgür				−1.20
Shirin				−1.20
Nezihe				+1.08

When considering the assumption that a lower Manner verb usage in GENERALIS-events is related to a speaker's L1, the figures indicate that among three speakers who did not use Manner verbs in GENERALIS-events in Turkish at all, two speakers also did not use Manner verbs in French GENERALIS-events at all (Devin, Seçkin). In both cases, an L1>L2 influence can be assumed, since the use of bare Manner verbs was less frequent in Turkish as compared to French. In contrast, Dilşah displays the highest z-score of Manner verb usage in GENERALIS-events in French, however, she used this pattern less frequently in Turkish. The direction of influence is for both, Devin and Seçkin not supported by language dominance. Devin is L2-dominant in both domain and dimension and Seçkin is L2-dominant in domain and does not indicate a dominance as regards dimension.

Table 85: Turkish-French bilinguals with highest standard deviations (SD) in Manner verb (VM) usage in GENERALIS-events, in Generic verb (VGEN) usage in AD-events and Path verb (VP) usage in SUPER events in Turkish and French.

Speaker	VM in GENERALIS-events VMP		VGEN in AD-events		VP in SUPER-events		Locative Path phrases	
	Turkish	French	Turkish	French	Turkish	French	Turkish	French
Arda			−0.22	+1.35	+1.68	−0.99	+1.78	−1.83
Bircan	−1.52	+0.80					−1.39	+0.32
Devin	−1.52	−1.89	−0.49	+1.65	+1.02	+1.07	−1.84	−0.07
Nihal	+1.69	+0.83			−1.16	−0.96	+0.61	+1.41
Seçkin	−1.52	−1.89	+3.01	−0.73	−1.16	+0.03	+0.88	+1.41
Dilşah	−1.00	+1.11			−0.21	+2.15	−1.35	+0.52
Emre					+2.00	+1.07	+1.13	−0.75
Mert			−1.36	−0.73	+0.26	−1,84	−0.57	−1.70
Shirin					−1.16	−0.94		
Nezihe			−0.37	+1.83	−1.16	+0.24		
Adile							+0.15	+1.81
Gözde							+0.15	−1.06

When looking at the individual results of Generic verbs in AD-events in French, it turns out that the values are distributed among only seven speakers. Furthermore, in Turkish Seçkin's z-score is +3.01 SD, which means that the higher mean of Generic verbs in Turkish AD-events is due to a single speaker. On the basis of the strongly varying values, it is generally difficult to make a clear assumption. We can, however, observe for Seçkin that the higher Generic verb usage in Turkish AD-events does not influence his verb choice in French AD-events.

As regards the use of Path verbs in SUPER-events, only two speakers of those who display higher values in French also more frequently used Path verbs in SUPER-events in Turkish (Devin, Emre, see Table 85). In both cases, an L1>L2 influence can be assumed, which is reflected in a higher use of Path verbs in French SUPER-events. Among speakers who did not use Path verbs in Turkish SUPER-events at all, Shirin and Nihal also display negative z-values in French. Here the influence is probably L2 based, since the use of Path verbs in SUPER-events is less common in French. L1>L2 influence is again not supported by the speakers language dominance profiles. As indicated above, Devin is L2-dominant in both domain and dimension, whereas Emre is L2-dominant in domain and indicates "no dominance" in dimension. Shirin and Nihal generally do not indicate a dominance as regards domain and dimension.

When examining Turkish-French bilinguals who display higher values of their total encoding of locative Path phrases in Turkish, the figures indicate that only Nihal, Seçkin and Adile also indicate a higher z-score in French. In these cases it is possible that individual L1-strategies influence the way these speakers encode motion descriptions in French. These strategies comprise i) subdividing the event into a GENERALIS-event (*roulé* 'rolled'), and subsequently an IN-event (*parti dans* 'left into') (see example (189)), ii) the avoidance of encoding the Figure's change of location into a bounded space (*jusqu'au bowling* 'as far as the bowling') (see example (190)) as well as iii) by implicitly encoding the traversal into a bounded space (see example (191)). All strategies were found in the Turkish-German context as well.

(189) et   puis   du coup   i   s'   est   roulé
       and   then   as a result   =he   REFL   AUX.PR   roll.PTCP
       et   ensuite   il   est   parti   dans   la
       and   after   he   AUX.PR   leave.PTCP   in   DET
       salle   de   bowling
       room   of   bowling
       'And then, as a result, he rolled himself and later he left into the bowling room' (Adile, TURFRE, 449–466)

(190) et   après   il   est • • •   he   s'   est   roulé   jusqu'au   bowling
       and   later   he   AUX.PR   il   REFL   AUX.PR   roll.PTCP   as far as.the bowling
       'And later he rolled himself as far as the bowling (centre)' (Nihal, TURFRE, 259–270)

(191) et   du coup   avec   ses   pieds il   a
      and   as a result   with   his   feet   he   AUX.PR
      commencé   à   rouler   rouler •jusqu'à le   bowling de la
      begin.PTCP to   roll   roll   as far as.to DET bowling of DET
      ville à   là bas , • • • et [[ee]] il   a   fait   un   strike
      town to   there   and   he AUX.PR make.PTCP INDF strike
'And as a result he began to roll, roll, with his feet as far as the bowling (centre) of the town there and he made a strike' (Seçkin, TURFRE, 408–443

In Devin's and Mert's case the figures show that their encoding of locative Path phrases is lower in French, which possibly influence their performance in Turkish, in which they indicate negative z-values. Here an L2>L1 influence can be hypothesised.

The language dominance profiles of Nihal, Seçkin and Adile indicate that none of the three speakers is L1-dominant in domain or dimension. In contrast, language dominance possibly supports the direction of influence for Devin, who is L2-dominant in both domain and dimension and partly for Mert, who is L2-dominant in domain and does not indicate a dominance in dimension.

Let us now examine the speakers' preferences for Manner and Path encoding in telic Path phrases.

7.2.6.2 Overall picture of telic Path phrases

We referred to telic Path phrases as a Figure's entry into a bounded space (IN), an exit out of a bounded space (EX) and a traversal over a plane to the other side of a threshold (TRANS, PRO)(see §3.2.6.4). We predicted that in contrast to speakers of S-languages, speakers of V-languages are constrained as regards the usage of Manner verbs in motion events with boundary focus and conceptualise such events differently. Therefore, we assumed that speakers of Turkish and French predominantly use Path verbs in telic Path phrases in Turkish and French, while speakers of German prefer Manner verbs. Furthermore, we assumed that as a result of the greater difference of L1- and L2-conceptualisations, Turkish-German bilinguals are more challenged than Turkish-French bilinguals when linguistically encoding motion events with boundary focus and display conceptual transfer in their L1 and L2.

Turkish (quantitative)
The results for motion verb choices in telic Path phrases in Turkish are summarised in Table 86. The average numbers show that, across all groups, Path verbs were dominantly used in telic Path phrases (TURGER 26.86%; TURFRE 26.22%;

TUR 26.79%). This is consistent with the predictions that the use of Manner verbs in motion events with boundary focus is generally restricted in V-languages.

Table 86: Means (*M*) and ranges (*R*) of motion verb choices in telic Path phrases Turkish (in %).

Group	Telic Path phrases Turkish										
	VM		VMP		VP		VGEN		VLV	TOTAL	
	M	*R*	*M*	*R*	*M*	*R*	*M*	*R*	*M R*	%	in numbers
TURGER	2.76	0–12.5	0.74	0–7.14	26.86	13.04–56.35	0.37	0–5.56	0 0	30.73	84
TURFRE	0.59	0–5.56	1.73	0–15.38	26.22	11.11–61.54	1.78	0–20	0 0	30.32	79
TUR	0.92	0–5.88	1.04	0.6.25	26.79	11.76–46.43	0.32	0–4.76	0 0	29.07	87

No significant differences were found between the groups. Nevertheless in all groups, a few violations of the boundary crossing constraint were found. Although the values are very low, the figures indicate that Turkish-German bilinguals more frequently used Manner verbs in telic Path phrases (2.76%) compared with Turkish-French (0.59%) and Turkish minimal bilinguals (0.92%). In contrast, Turkish-French more frequently used Manner-Path verbs in telic Path phrases (1.73%) in comparison with Turkish minimal (1.04%) and Turkish-German bilinguals (0.74%). Generic verbs were marginally used in telic Path phrases by Turkish-German bilinguals and Turkish minimal bilinguals (TURGER 0.37%; TUR 0.32%), whereas Turkish-French bilinguals made use of them more frequently (1.78%). Since the numbers of Manner, Manner-Path and Generic verbs were relatively low, (non)-parametric tests were not conducted.

When we look more closely at the corresponding event types of motion verb choices in Table 87, the figures indicate that both bilingual groups slightly more often encoded IN-events as compared to Turkish minimal bilinguals.

However, IN-events were generally more frequently encoded than EX-, PRO- and TRANS-events. Moreover, the latter were less frequently encoded by bilingual speakers as compared to Turkish minimal bilinguals (TURGER 3.10%, TURFRE 2.41%, TUR 6.24%). TRANS events were generally encoded with Path verbs (see example (192)). The inter-group differences as regards the use of Manner verbs are related to EX- and IN-events.

(192)   *karşı-dan   karşıy-a   geç-iyo   kedi*
        opposite-ABL opposite-DAT =cross-PROG.3SG cat
        'The cat is crossing over' (Seval, TUR, 56–61)

Table 87: Motion verb choices per motion event type with boundary focus Turkish (in %).

Motion verb category	Group	Telic Path phrases Turkish			
		EX	IN	PRO	TRANS
VM	TURGER	1.17	1.60	0.00	0.00
	TURFRE	0.00	0.59	0.00	0.00
	TUR	0.24	0.68	0.00	0.00
VMP	TURGER	0.00	0.74	0.00	0.00
	TURFRE	0.51	1.22	0.00	0.00
	TUR	0.00	1.04	0.00	0.00
VP	TURGER	2.67	19.99	1.10	3.10
	TURFRE	2.45	21.13	0.22	2.41
	TUR	2.97	17.57	0.00	6.24
VGEN	TURGER	0.00	0.37	0.00	0.00
	TURFRE	0.00	1.78	0.00	0.00
	TUR	0.00	0.32	0.00	0.00
VLV	TURGER	0.00	0.00	0.00	0.00
	TURFRE	0.00	0.00	0.00	0.00
	TUR	0.00	0.00	0.00	0.00
TOT	TURGER	3.84	22.70	1.10	3.10
	TURFRE	2.97	24.72	0.22	2.41
	TUR	3.21	19.62	0.00	6.24

The violation of the boundary crossing constraint in all groups requires a more detailed exploration. Whilst the use of Manner-Path verbs in telic Path phrases has been documented in the motion literature of V-languages, the use of Manner verbs is still problematic (see §3.2.6.4). We discuss this problem in the following by examining some examples, which were found in the corpus.

Examples (193) to (198) are all considered telic Path phrases, since the change of location of the Figure can be interpreted as traversal of a spatial boundary. In (193) and (194) an IN-event is encoded by using a Manner verb and Path device. In the corresponding motion situation of example (193), the Figure moves from a board-walk (Source Ground) into a boat (Goal/Endstate Ground), while in the motion situation to which example (194) is related, the Source Ground is located outside a house (windowsill) and the Goal Ground is inside the house (Grandmother's apartment).

(193) kedi o-nun için-e [[ee]] • yani • • için-e hopla-dı
cat his-GEN inside.DAT I mean inside.DAT hop-PST.3SG
'The cat hopped inside' (Gamze, TURGER, 717–726)

(194) kafes-in-den   çık-tı,   ((1s))   içeri   kaç-tı
      cage-POSS-ABL exit-PST   inside   escape-PST.3SG
      'It exited from the cage, it escaped inside' (Rüya, TUR, 63–69)

In both examples the speakers used a Manner verb in order to encode the way in which the Figure moves. As noted earlier, it is argued that Manner verbs cannot encode the change of location, therefore speakers of V-languages use Path verbs instead as predicates of the main clause. However, in the examples the speakers used the directional Path devices *içine* and *içeri*, which are supposed to encode a Figure's traversal into a bounded space.

The same type of construction was found for EX-events. In contrast to Rüya (see example (194) above), who used a Path verb (*çık-* 'exit') when encoding the Figure's change of location from the interior space (the bird's cage) to the exterior space (outside the cage), Yiğit made use of a Manner verb and an adverbial directional (see example (195)).

(195) dışarıy-a   f/uç-tu
      out-DAT   fly-PST.3SG
      'It flew out(wards)' (Yiğit, TURGER, 157–161)

In the corresponding motion situation of example (196), the Figure moves from the interior space of a drain pipe (Source Ground) to an exterior space (outside the drain pipe, Goal Ground). Again, in both examples, the Manner verb cannot encode the change of location, only the Path devices are supposed to encode the Figure's traversal out of a bounded space.

(196) bodu-dan   yani   dışarı   fırla-dı
      =pipe-ABL   I mean   outwards   pop-PST.3SG
      'It popped out of the pipe' (Ozan, TURGER, 403–406)

Examples (197) and (198) show how IN-events are encoded by Manner-Path verbs and Path devices. The Source Ground in the corresponding motion situation of example (197) is the Grandmother's house from which the Figure moves (vertically) into the Goal/Endstate Ground (the trash). In the corresponding motion situation of example (198), the Figure moves from a boat (Source Ground) into a river (Goal/Endstate Ground). The change of location is in both examples, again, encoded by the adverbial directional *içine*.

(197) kedi   çöp-ler-in   için-e   düş-üyor
      cat   trash-PL-GEN   inside.DAT   fall-PROG.3SG
      'The cat falls inside the trashes' (Fatih, TUR, 56–60)

(198) suy-un   için-e   düş-tü
       water-GEN   inside.DAT   fall-PST.3SG
       'It fell inside the water' (Adile, TURFRE, 448–451)

When taking into account our empirical observations established in §3.2.6.3, two central questions arise from the given examples. First, is there a "licence" for using certain Manner verbs in telic Path phrases in Turkish? Second, do Path devices such as directional adverbs and spatial nouns + case encode a Figure's traversal into or out of a bounded space?

In order to answer the first question, let us take a look at the Manner verbs, which were used in the examples. The use of the Manner-Path verb *düşmek* 'to fall' in (197) and (198) seems to be quite normal, since it is argued that motion verbs which encode uncontrolled motion can be conceptualised as change of location in V-languages (Slobin 2004b; Slobin 2006).

For the other Manner verbs which were used by the Turkish speakers, no exception is reported in the motion literature. However, note that Rüya (194) and Yiğit (195) used Manner verbs (*kaçmak* 'to escape'; *uçmak* 'to fly') which are frequently found in the corpus analysis of the TNC in §3.2.6.1. As noted earlier, we can assume that the Manner salience of such verbs is somewhat bleached compared to more expressive (and less frequently used) Manner verbs. Their Manner degree, therefore, might be so low that speakers are more free to use them, because they can conceptualise a change of location.

However, with *hoplamak* 'to hop' and *fırlamak* 'to pop (out)' Gamze (see example (193) above) and Ozan (see example (196) above) used more expressive Manner verbs in telic Path phrases. On the basis of our theoretical considerations, it should be truly problematic when conceptualising a change of location. Nevertheless, for both speakers it seems an appropriate strategy to linguistically encode their motion images.

Let us now look at the Path devices which were used in the examples and which were interpreted in the analysis as devices encoding the Figures' traversal into or out of a bounded space. At first sight, they resemble German adverbial verb prefixes and can be interpreted as Path satellites. On the one hand, Deny (1921: 242) states that adverbial directionals are combined with the dative when referring to the endstate (*aboutissement* 'culmination') of a Figure's motion. In this case, combinations of the directional adverbs *dışarı/içeri* and dative imply a Figure's traversal into a bounded space (endstate). On the other hand, the dative indicates directionality towards a Ground. When looking at example (195) the speaker might conceptualise the Figure's motion towards the Goal Ground (exterior). The Figure's traversal into the bounded space then stays implicit ("It flies towards outside").

We introduced *içine* in §3.2.6.2 as controversial when attributing the feature of encoding a Figures' motion into a bounded space ("(in)to its interior"). The incidences found in the corpus, however, give rise to doubts. In addition, *için* in combination with the dative marker, may vaguely encode "towards the inner". Consequently, the speakers might conceptualise and encode the Figure's motion towards a Goal Ground, and the traversal of the spatial boundary remains implicit in (195), (197) and (198).

A further aspect of the matter arises on the constructional level. In §3.2.6.3, the argument has been put forward that the combination of Manner verbs, which are used as predicates of a main sentence, with Path devices, is restricted. The Manner-Path verb *düşmek* 'to fall' canonically encodes a vertical (unintentional) direction and can therefore be classified into the category of Turkish motion verbs, which require a directional specification. Moreover, neither *uçmak*, nor *fırlamak* and *hoplamak* do necessarily require directional specifications. It is the speaker's intention when further specifying the Path outside the main verb. When examining the types of violations of the boundary crossing constraint, the argument can be put forward that Turkish-German bilinguals more frequently violate the boundary crossing constraint. The numbers of violations summarised in Table 88 indicate that Turkish-German bilinguals used a few more Manner verbs which encode other types of motion (*sürmek, hoplamak, uçmak*) in comparison with Turkish-French bilinguals and Turkish minimal bilinguals who slightly more often used the Manner-Path verb *düşmek* in telic Path phrases which encode uncontrolled motion. A closer look at the Manner/Manner-Path verb constructions indicates that Turkish-German bilinguals usually combined these verbs with *içine* '(in)to its interior'. As argued above, the Figure's traversal of a spatial boundary then remains implicit and is generally not habitual among speakers of Turkish.

Table 88: Summary of boundary crossing constraint violations (in numbers).

Group	violations	violations with Manner(-Path) verbs encoding uncontrolled motion
TURGER	7	2
TURFRE	6	4
TUR	3	3

Example (199) illustrates that in some cases speakers tend to correct themselves and prefer more habitual combinations of Path devices with Manner verbs.

(199) o   [[ee]] dışarı yani • • • [[ee]] pencere-den   hopla-dı.
       she/he/it   out   I mean   window-ABL   hop-PST.3SG
       'It hopped out, I mean from the window' (Gamze, TURGER, 254–263)

Let us now turn to the qualitative analysis which provides intra-group differences and individual speakers' usage preferences in Turkish-German and Turkish-French bilinguals' motion descriptions.

Turkish (qualitative)
The qualitative analysis indicates intra-group differences in the use of motion verbs in telic Path phrases. For instance, the use of Manner and Manner-Path verbs in telic Path phrases is distributed among only a few speakers[85] (Manner verbs: TURGER Gamze, Ozan, Serkan, Taylan, Yiğit; TURFRE Gözde, Maide; TUR Başak, Rüya, Seval; Manner-Path verbs: TURGER Alisa, Tuba; TURFRE Adile, Bircan, Mert; TUR Fatih, Nilsu, Sevgi). This means that most speakers did not use Manner and Manner-Path verbs in Turkish telic Path phrases at all. Furthermore, most speakers in each group did not use Generic verbs in telic Path phrases at all; the use is distributed among a few speakers in each group (TURGER, Beren; TURFRE Dilşah, Maide; TUR Helin).

Table 89: Turkish-German and Turkish-French bilinguals with a distance of one or more standard deviations (*SD*) in Path verb (VP) usage in Turkish telic Path phrases.

Group	Speaker	VP
TURGER	Melis	+2.62
	Sefar	+1.09
	Yiğit	−1.06
	Gamze	−1.23
TURFRE	Arda	−1.86
	Devin	+2.50
	Emre	−1.07

As regards the use of Path verbs in telic Path phrases, there are speakers in each group who made use of it less frequently in comparison with other speakers (TURGER Gamze; TURFRE Arda, see Table 89). In Arda's case, it turns out that he did not

---

[85] Because only a few speakers used Manner, Manner-Path and Generic verbs in Turkish telic Path phrases, *z*-scores were not calculated.

encode a single event with boundary focus in Turkish. In contrast, Melis (TURGER) and Devin (TURFRE) used Path verbs in Turkish telic Path phrases more frequently.

Attention must be drawn to the fact that "true" violations of the boundary crossing constraint (that are problematic cases as discussed above), in the Turkish-German bilingual group are distributed among three speakers (Gamze, Serkan, Yiğit). We will return to this aspect in the following, but we first examine the speakers' performance in their respective L2.

German (quantitative)
The statistical analysis based on the average numbers in Table 90 indicate that Turkish-German bilinguals used significantly fewer Manner verbs (M=11.02, SD=10.41) than German minimal bilinguals (M=25.61, SD=7.99) (t(28)=−4.31, p<0.001***). Furthermore, Turkish-German bilinguals used Generic verbs more frequently in telic Path phrases (M=21.90, SD=8.98) than German minimal bilinguals (M=8.72, SD=6.99); the difference is again highly significant (t(28)=4.48, p<0.001***). Manner-Path verbs were also used more frequently among German minimal bilinguals (GER 2.97%, TURGER 1.51%), however, the difference is statistically not significant.

When considering the group mean of telic Path phrases (TURGER 35.94%; GER 42.45%) as a reference point, the difference in Manner and Generic verb usage between both groups is even clearer. The numbers in Table 91 indicate that Turkish-German bilinguals used half as many Manner verbs and three times as many Generic verbs as compared to German minimal bilinguals. In comparison with the numbers of Generic verbs in locative Path phrases (see §7.2.6.1) the figures indicate a higher usage of Generic verbs in telic Path phrases in German among Turkish-German bilinguals.

When we look at the corresponding event types of motion verb choices, the average numbers in Table 92 indicate that German minimal bilinguals generally encoded more EX-, PRO-, and TRANS-events.

Most strikingly, German minimal bilinguals used Manner verbs in IN-events more frequently (TURGER 5.49%; GER 12.41%, see example (200), whereas Turkish-German bilinguals prefer Generic verbs (TURGER 17.82%; GER 4.79%, see example (201)).

(200) *und die katze is jetzt in eine bowlinghalle rein-gekugelt*
and DET cat AUX.PR now in INDF bowling.hall inside-bowl.PTCP
'And now the cat rolled into a bowling hall inside' (Katharina, GER, 218–227)

(201) *dann iss-er da rein-gegang*
then =AUX.PR-he there =inside-go.PTCP
'Then, he went in there' (Alisa, TURGER, 556–560)

Table 90: Means (M) and ranges (R) of motion verb choices in telic Path phrases German (in %).

Group	Telic Path phrases German												TOTAL	
	VM		VMP		VP		VGEN		VAUX/VMOD		VLV			
	M	R	M	R	M	R	M	R	M	R	M	R	%	numbers
TURGER	11.02	0–33.33	1.51	0–7.41	0	0	21.9	6.90–40.74	1.52	0–5.88	0	0	35.94	117
GER	25.61	15–42.86	2.97	0–12	0.39	0–5.88	8.72	0–17.65	4.76	0–15	0	0	42.45	140

Table 91: Motion verb choices with total telic Path phrases as a reference point (in %).

Group	Telic Path phrases German					
	VM	VMP	VP	VGEN	VAUX/VMOD	VLV
TURGER	30.65	4.19	0.00	60.93	4.23	0.00
GER	60.34	6.99	0.92	20.54	11.21	0.00

Table 92: Motion verb choices per motion event type with boundary focus German (in %).

Motion verb category	Group	Telic Path phrases German				
		EX	IN	PRAETER	PRO	TRANS
VM	TURGER	2.30	5.49	0.00	0.79	2.44
	GER	4.93	12.41	0.48	2.05	5.74
VMP	TURGER	0.00	0.80	0.00	0.00	0.71
	GER	0.00	2.43	0.00	0.53	0.00
VP	TURGER	0.00	0.00	0.00	0.00	0.00
	GER	0.00	0.39	0.00	0.00	0.00
VGEN	TURGER	2.12	17.82	0.44	0.56	0.95
	GER	1.78	4.79	0.26	0.93	0.97
VAUX/VMOD	TURGER	0.00	0.25	0.39	0.25	0.63
	GER	0.93	2.09	0.00	0.00	1.73
VLV	TURGER	0.00	0.00	0.00	0.00	0.00
	GER	0.00	0.00	0.00	0.00	0.00
TOT	TURGER	4.42	24.35	0.84	1.60	4.73
	GER	7.65	22.11	0.74	3.51	8.44

The results clearly show that Turkish-German bilinguals do not simply use more Generic verbs in general, but they particularly made use of them when encoding boundary crossing events. As suggested above, a semantic extension from Generic to Path can be assumed, which is expected to be a typologically motivated conceptual transfer from Turkish into German. Since the use of Manner verbs in telic Path phrases in Turkish is restricted, we can assume that Turkish-German bilinguals avoid Manner and Manner-Path verbs particularly in IN- and EX-events in their German motion descriptions. Instead, they resort to Generic verbs, which are semantically neutral and come closer to (Turkish) Path verbs or encode an AB-event instead (as illustrated above, in comparison with German minimal bilinguals, Turkish-German bilinguals more frequently used Manner verbs in AB-events).

Furthermore, we have seen above that Path verbs were predominantly used in Turkish telic Path phrases. The conceptualisation of the Figure's change of location may then be L1-based (Manner verbs cannot encode the change of location), whereas the motion construction is L2 based (use of Path satellites which encode the change of location). The results of a Pearson's correlation revealed an intermediate negative correlation ($r=-0.40$), which partly supports this assumption (the more Generic verbs are used, the lower is the Manner verb usage). However, the correlation was statistically not significant; further individual analyses are required in order to prove the assumption.

Let us now look at the results of the qualitative analysis in order to obtain and discuss intra-group differences as well as to determine individual speakers' usage preferences and cross-linguistic influences in Turkish-German bilinguals' motion descriptions.

German (qualitative)

The qualitative analysis reveals some intra-group differences. As regards the use of Manner verbs in telic Path phrases there are, for instance, three Turkish-German bilingual speakers who did not use a single Manner verb (Alisa, Taylan, Tuba), whereas other speakers indicate a higher usage (Ozan, Sefar) (see Table 93). Note that the latter surpass the use of Manner verbs of some German minimal bilingual speakers who indicate the lowest proportions (Alex, Melanie, Philip). Furthermore, there are bilingual speakers who more frequently used Generic verbs (Melis, Kurt) as compared to others (Eda, Serkan).[86] Only four speakers used Manner-Path verbs in telic Path phrases (Gamze, Ozan, Serkan, Tuba); therefore, z-scores were not calculated for this category.

An individual comparison of speakers' performance in L1 and L2 partly confirm the assumption, that there is a relation between the avoidance of Manner verbs in telic Path phrases in Turkish and a higher frequency of Generic verbs in telic Path phrases in German. Kurt and Melis (as well as Beren and Tuba) display the highest proportion of Generic verbs in telic Path phrases in German and did not use Manner verbs in telic Path phrases in Turkish at all. The only exception is Yiğit, who indicates a higher proportion of Generic verbs in German and similarly used a Manner verb in 10% of encoded telic Path phrases in Turkish. In the cases of Beren, Kurt, Melis and Tuba an L1>L2 influence can be maintained.

In order to verify this assumption and to exclude the possibility of lexical gaps, which may also influence the speaker's avoidance of Manner verbs in telic

---

[86] Among German minimal bilinguals, Philip, Sören, and Sophie did not use Generic verbs at all, whereas Michel and Moritz indicate a higher usage (17.65%).

Table 93: Turkish-German bilinguals with highest standard deviations (SD) in Manner verb (VM) and Generic verb (VGEN) usage in German telic Path phrases.

Speaker	VM	VGEN
Alisa	−1.06	
Ozan	+2.14	
Sefar	+1.50	
Taylan	−1.06	
Tuba	−1.06	+0.60
Eda		−1.67
Kurt		+1.54
Melis		+2.10
Serkan		−1.13
Beren		+0.74
Yiğit		+0.74

Path phrases, the results of the MVC-Task are reconsidered again. As outlined in §7.2.2.1, lexical gaps were excluded from the individual amount of Generic/no-motion constructions used.

The results in Table 94 indicate three tendencies. First, except for Gamze, the Generic verb usage in telic Path phrases in the VM-Task is generally higher than the usage in all events. Second, the use of Generic verbs in telic Path phrases is highest not only among those speakers whose Generic verb usage is above-average in all events, but also among speakers who indicate a lower use of Generic verbs (near or below mean) in all events (Beren, Yiğit, Ela). Third, in most of the cases, speakers provide an appropriate Manner/Manner-Path verb. These findings suggest that Generic/no motion verb choices are not due to lexical gaps, but are likely typologically motivated. This finally provides an answer to the question which we raised in §7.2.2.1.

Let us now also take the individual results of language dominance patterns into account, in order to acquire further details of the nature of the observed variation. We take as a reference point the highest and lowest proportions of Generic verb usage, in order to examine whether there is a relation between language dominance patterns and Generic verb usage. Alisa, Tuba and Beren display the highest Generic verb usage in telic Path phrases in German. The individual results of their language dominance patterns, however, do not indicate a clear direction.

Table 94: Generic/no motion verbs and Manner/Manner-Path repertoire among Turkish-German bilinguals.

	Voluntary Motion Task		Manner Verb Control Task	
	no Manner/ Manner-Path verbs (telic Path Phrases)	Manner/ Manner-Path lemmas (all events)	Manner/ Manner-Path lemmas	Manner/ Manner-Path verb choice per target events
Speaker	SD	numbers	numbers	%
Alisa	1.51	9.00	7.00	81.82
Tuba	0.92	7.00	8.00	100.00
Beren	0.92	8.00	10.00	100.00
Yiğit	0.92	10.00	10.00	90.91
Kurt	0.82	5.00	9.00	100.00
Ela	0.68	8.00	9.00	100.00
Taylan	0.47	7.00	8.00	81.82
Melis	0.23	6.00	8.00	90.91
Dana	0.13	6.00	7.00	100.00
Esna	−0.79	9.00	10.00	100.00
Sefar	−0.86	7.00	8.00	100.00
Serkan	−0.86	8.00	9.00	100.00
Gamze	−1.13	9.00	10.00	81.82
Ozan	−1.36	9.00	9.00	90.91
Eda	−1.60	13.00	10.00	100.00
mean	63.58	8.06	8.8	94.55

Alisa is more dominant in German as regards dimension and displays a mixed pattern in domain. Tuba does not indicate a dominance as regards dimension and is more L2-dominant in domain whereas Beren is L2-dominant in both domain and dimension. In all the cases, a support of typologically motivated transfer by language dominance can not be maintained. In contrast, we can hypothesise an impact of language dominance patterns when looking at the speakers with the lowest Generic verb proportions in telic Path phrases in German. Gamze, Ozan, and Eda are all L2-dominant in both domain and dimension.

These findings bring us to the question of whether L2 conceptualisations then also lead speakers to other encoding strategies in their L1. One possible influence of the L2 can be reflected in the use of Turkish Manner/Manner-Path verbs in boundary crossing events. The results have shown that Turkish-German bilinguals more frequently do so as compared to Turkish-French and Turkish minimal bilinguals. However, we argued that "true" violations in the Turkish-German bilingual group are extremely infrequent and are distributed among Gamze, Ozan and Yiğit. The L1 and L2 values of Gamze, Ozan, as well as of Serkan, reveal a relation between the use of Manner verbs in telic Path phrases in Turkish and a higher usage of Manner verbs in German (see Table 95).[87] The z-values of their Manner verb usage in German are above the mean, similarly they made use of Manner verbs in Turkish telic Path phrases. These cases suggest an L2>L1 influence of Manner verb usage in Turkish. However, this is not the case for Yiğit, nor for Taylan, who also used Manner verbs in Turkish telic Path phrases but did not use Manner verbs at all (Taylan) or less frequently (Yiğit) in German. Furthermore, in Gamze's and Serkan's case, this is supported by a lower Generic verb usage in telic Path phrases in German, whereas Yiğit's numbers of Generic verbs in telic Path phrases is one of the highest among the group.

Table 95: Individual Manner verb usage in telic Path phrases in German and Turkish (in %).

Speaker	Turkish	German
Gamze	4.34	14.81 (+0.37 SD)
Ozan	12.5	33.33 (+2.14 SD)
Serkan	8.33	17.65 (+0.64 SD)
Taylan	6.25	0 (−1.06 SD)
Yiğit	10	4.76 (−0.60 SD)

When taking the language dominance scores of these speakers into account, the picture is again quite diverse. An L2>L1 influence is possibly supported by language dominance patterns among Gamze and Ozan who are L2-dominant in domain and dimension. By contrast, Serkan displays an "L1-dominance" in domain, but "no dominance" in dimension. The same applies for Taylan (L1-dominance in domain and "no dominance" in dimension). Since the two speakers display inverse results as regards the Manner/Manner-Path verb usage in L1 and L2, but similarities as regards their language dominance patterns, a relation has to be rejected. The same is true for Yiğit, who displays "no dominance" in domain, but an "L2-dominance" in dimension.

French (quantitative)
The numbers of telic Path phrases in French indicate, again, that there are some incidences of violations of the boundary crossing constraint in each group

---

[87] Due to the limited use of Manner verbs in Turkish telic Path phrases, Table 95 only includes percentages for Turkish, since z-values were not calculated.

Table 96: Means (*M*) and ranges (*R*) of motion verb choices in telic Path phrases French (in %).

Group	Telic Path phrases French										TOTAL
	VM		VMP		VP		VGEN		VLV		
	M	*R*	*M*	*R*	*M*	*R*	*M*	*R*	*M*	*R*	%
TURFRE	2.69	0–14.29	0.70	0–10.53	29.05	14.29–46.15	2.51	0–14.29	0.00	0.00	34.95
FRE	4.64	0–21.43	1.17	0–11.11	25.36	7.14–50	6.94	0–16.67	0.00	0.00	38.11

(see Table 96). Moreover, French minimal bilinguals showed more frequent, albeit limited, usage of Manner (TURFRE 2.69%; FRE 4.64%) and Manner-Path verbs (TURFRE 0.70%; FRE 1.17%) as compared to Turkish-French bilinguals. Generally, Path verbs were dominantly used by both groups; Turkish-French bilinguals made use of them more frequently in comparison with French minimal bilinguals (TURFRE 29.05%; FRE 25.36%). Moreover, the latter used Generic verbs more frequently than Turkish-French bilinguals (TURFRE 2.51%; FRE 6.94%). The results of (non)parametric tests were not significant for all tested variables.[88]

The numbers of the corresponding event types in Table 97 illustrate that IN-events were most frequently encoded by speakers of both groups. The only difference between both groups is in the encoding of TRANS-events, which were more frequently encoded by French minimal bilinguals (FRE 4.42%; TURFRE 1.72%).

The observed differences of Manner verbs in telic Path phrases are related to EX- and IN-events. Turkish-French bilinguals used Path verbs in IN-events (see example (202)) more frequently, which explains the inter-group difference of Path verb usage in telic Path phrases, albeit French minimal bilinguals more frequently used Path verbs in TRANS-events (see example (203)). Instead French minimal bilinguals more frequently used Generic verbs in IN-events (see example (204)).

(202) il   rentre   dans   les   tuyaux
       he   enter.PR   in   DET.PL   pipe.PL
       'He enters into the pipes' (Devin, TURFRE, 223–237)

(203) et [[ee]] il   essaye   de • •   de passer   entre   les   chien-s
       and   he   try.PR   to   to pass   between   DET.PL   dog-PL
       'And he tries to pass between the dogs' (Lola, FRE, 726–736)

---

[88] For VMP and VLV variables no statistical tests have been carried out, since only a few speakers in each group made use of them.

Table 97: Motion verb choices per motion event type with boundary focus French (in %).

Motion verb category	Group	Telic Path phrases French			
		EX	IN	PRO	TRANS
VM	TURFRE	0.87	1.47	0.00	0.35
	FRE	1.24	2.75	0.65	0.00
VMP	TURFRE	0.00	0.70	0.00	0.00
	FRE	0.00	1.17	0.00	0.00
VP	TURFRE	2.84	24.15	0.69	1.37
	FRE	3.05	17.89	0.00	4.42
VGEN	TURFRE	0.00	2.51	0.00	0.00
	FRE	0.00	6.94	0.00	0.00
VLV	TURFRE	0.00	0.00	0.00	0.00
	FRE	0.00	0.00	0.00	0.00
Total	TURFRE	3.71	28.83	0.69	1.72
	FRE	4.29	28.75	0.65	4.42

(204) le   chat   il   est   allé   dans   le   bâteau
     DET   cat   he   AUX.PR   go.PTCP   in   DET   boat
     'The cat went into the boat' (Ethan, FRE, 374–381)

Let us discuss again the use of Manner and Manner-Path verbs in telic Path phrases in greater detail. As noted in §3.2.6.4, violations of the boundary crossing constraint are no exception in French. Examples (205) to (212) were all considered telic Path phrases and include a Manner or a Manner-Path verb. In example (205), the speaker Mathis used the Manner verb *atterir* 'to land' in order to describe the Figure's Manner of motion and a prepositional phrase (*dans les ordures* 'in(to) the trashes') to encode the change of location.

(205) il   a   a-tterri   dans   les   ordures
     he   AUX.PR   to-land.PTCP   in   DET.PL   trash.PL
     'He landed in the trashes' (Mathis, FRE, 57–63)

The figures indicate that *atterir* seems to be more acceptable in telic Path phrases than other Manner verbs, since French minimal bilinguals used this verb in five of six incidences of their total Manner verb usage in IN-events. However, the verb does not necessarily encode uncontrolled motion, which, as argued in the Turkish context above, might license the use in telic Path phrases in V-languages.

Furthermore, the verb is not highly frequent in spoken corpora of French (on the basis of the CLAPI-classification, see §3.2.6.1). The Latin prefix *a-* does not encode a traversal either, but an AD-event ("towards a goal"). A possible explanation may then be that the preposition *dans* 'in(to)' does not encode directions but location. Consequently, the speakers may focus on the Figure's Endstate Ground ("inside the trashes"), but not on the traversal from a Source Ground into an Endstate Ground ("into"). The same may apply for example (206). The preposition *dans* 'in(to)' can also encode a general location. However, the Motion situation to which the speaker refers shows the Figure (Sylvester) running across the street into a house. From a telic perspective the utterance is ungrammatical, since it is argued that the construction *courir dans* 'run in(to)' can not encode the Figure's traversal into a bounded space, but encodes Motion in a general location ("in the interior of the other house").

(206) après [[bah]] il   a   une   idée ((1,37s)) i   court
      later   he   AUX.PR   INDF idea   =he run.PR
      dans   l'   autre   maison
      in   DET   other   house
'Later he has an idea, he runs in(to) the other house' (Özgür, TURFRE, 49–62)

Example (207) illustrates an interesting strategy. When linguistically encoding the motion situation showing the Figure moving down a street into an Endstate Ground (a bowling centre), the speaker used a Manner verb (*rouler* 'to roll') and a prepositional phrase (*jusque* 'until/as far as') + *dans* 'in(to)' + nominal phrase. Whereas *jusque* unambiguously encodes the Endpoint of the Figure's change of location, *dans* + nominal phrase can also encode a general location ("in the interior of the bowling centre"). On this reading, the Figure's change of location proceeds with proximity to another Ground. As noted in §3.2.6.4 the use of Manner verbs in V-languages is common in such locative Path phrases. Since *dans* + nominal phrase can also be interpreted as general location, the Figure's traversal over or into the bounded space stays implicit and the utterance seems to be acceptable.

(207) il   a   roulé   jusque   dans un   centre de bowling
      he   AUX.PR   roll.PTCP   as far as   in   INDF   centre of bowling
'He rolled as far as inside a bowling centre' (Emma, FRE, 285–293)

In example (208), the speaker Camille described a PRO-event where the Motion situation shows the Figure sneaking through dogs lying in a garden. She used a

Manner verb (*se faufiler* 'to sneak') and a prepositional phrase *entre les chiens* 'through the dogs'. Since *se faufiler* is an expressive motion verb, the utterance does not seem acceptable in French. Maide used the Manner verb *se balancer* 'to swing' in example (209) and the preposition *à travers* 'across' when linguistically encoding the motion situation showing the Figure moving from a Source Ground (window sill) to the Goal Ground (window sill on the other side of a threshold). Both examples illustrate typical S-constructions and both are seen as problematic in the motion literature for V-languages.

(208) il   s'   est   faufilé entre   les   chien-s
       he   REF   AUX.PR sneak   between DET.PL dog-PL
       'He sneaked through the dogs' (Camille, FRE, 53–58 [transcript 2])

(209) il   s'   est   balancé   à travers l'   autre immeuble
       he   REF   AUX.PR swing.PTCP   across   DET   other building
       'He swang across to the other building' (Maide, TURFRE, 528–536)

Furthermore, there were also a few incidences of Manner verb usage in IN-events found. The speaker Mert in example (210) used the verb *se foncer* 'to rush oneself' and the preposition *dans* 'in(to)' which encodes the Figure's traversal into a bounded space when linguistically encoding the motion situation showing the Figure who moves (vertically) from the Source Ground (a house) into the Goal/Endstate Ground (a garbage can).

(210) il   s'   en   fonçait   dans   la   poubelle
       he   REFL   there   rush.PST   in   DET   trash
       'He rushed (himself) into the trash' (Mert, TURFRE, 94–100)

As regards the use of Manner-Path verbs in telic Path phrases, all incidences found in the corpus include the verb *tomber* 'to fall', such as in examples (211) and (212); the Figure's traversal into a bounded space is linguistically encoded by the preposition *dans* 'in(to)'. As argued in the Turkish context by the verb *düşmek* 'to fall', *tomber* can also be classified as a motion verb which encodes uncontrolled Motion and therefore seems to be common in French telic Path phrases.

(211) et   l'   est   tombé   dans   les   poubelle-s
       and   =he   AUX.PR fall.PTCP   in   DET.PL trash-PL
       'And he fell in the trashes' (Bircan, TURFRE, 131–137)

(212) et   l'   est   tom - bé • • dans • • dans un   bowling
      and =he AUX.PR fall.PTCP   in   in   INDF bowling
      'And he fell into a bowling (centre)' (Lou, FRE, 496–507)

Besides the usage of the verb *tomber*, the other Manner verbs which were used in telic Path phrases in French are generally seen as problematic in the motion literature. As noted above, we can assume that verbs such as *atterir*, *courir* or *rouler* (see examples (205), (206) and (207)), which were frequently found in the corpus analysis of the CLAPI in §3.2.6.1, might be somewhat bleached compared to more expressive (and less frequently used) Manner verbs (such as *faufiler* in example (208) or *se balancer* in example (209)). Thus, we could argue that speakers are more free to use them, because they can conceptualise a change of location. However, as pointed out by Berthele (2006:234) and Arias Oliveira (2012), it seems that in French such violations of the boundary crossing constraint are far more numerous than is discussed in the motion literature. When examining the numbers of violations of the boundary crossing constraint and the use of Manner-Path verbs which encode uncontrolled Motion, the figures in Table 98 show that, unlike Turkish-French bilinguals, French minimal bilinguals are more ready to use Manner verbs in telic Path phrases in French.

Table 98: Summary of boundary crossing constraint violations in French (number of occurrences).

Group	violations	violations including motion verbs which encode uncontrolled Motion
TURFRE	6	2
FRE	10	3

In comparison with the numbers of violations of the boundary crossing constraint in Turkish above, it seems that the use of Manner verbs in French is less restricted. This may cause some Turkish-French bilinguals to more often avoid the use of Manner verbs in motion events with a boundary focus in French as a result of an L1>L2 influence. We will take a closer look at the qualitative results in the following in order to verify this assumption by determining individual speakers' usage preferences as well as to obtain and discuss intra-group differences.

French (qualitative)
When considering the Turkish-French bilingual speakers' L1 and L2, the figures indeed prove that, except for Bircan and Maide, who used Manner verbs or Manner-Path verbs in telic Path phrases in both of their languages (see Table 99),

most of the speakers do not violate the boundary crossing constraint in either L1 or L2. When considering the language dominance patterns of both speakers, there is again, no clear relation. Both speakers display a mixed pattern in domain and "no dominance" in dimension.

Table 99: Turkish-French bilinguals' individual use of Manner and Manner-Path verbs in telic Path phrases in Turkish and French (in %).

Speaker	French		Turkish	
	VM	VMP	VM	VMP
Adile	/	/	/	5.56
Bircan	/	10.53	/	15.38
Emre	14.29	/	/	/
Maide	5.26	/	3.33	/
Mert	11.76	/	/	/
Özgür	9.09	/	/	/

As regards the observed difference in Path verb choices in French IN-events, the figures indicate that among speakers with higher values in Turkish only Devin also used Path verbs more frequently in French, which is an indication of an L1>L2 influence (see Table 100). Vice versa, speakers with lower values in French (Emre, Geza) also used Path verbs less frequently in IN-events in Turkish. Here an L2>L1 influence can be assumed.

In the case of L1>L2 influence, this influence is, again, not supported by language dominance patterns, since Devin is L2-dominant in both domain and dimension. As regards L2>L1 influences, only Geza is dominant in French in both

Table 100: Turkish-French bilinguals with highest standard deviations (SD) in Path verb (VP) usage in Turkish and French telic Path phrases.

Speaker	IN-events	
	Turkish	French
Arda	−1.89	0.09
Bircan	+1.55	−0.34
Devin	+2.23	+0.48
Emre	−0.89	−1.84
Geza	−0.40	−1.26

domain and dimension, which possibly supports an impact of French on Turkish. Emre is L2-dominant in domain and displays a mixed pattern in dimension. A relation of dominance patterns and Path verb usage in IN-events in French can not clearly assumed.

Summary
The results of motion verb choices in locative and telic Path phrases indicate that speakers of Turkish and French generally more frequently encoded locative Path phrases as compared to speakers of German. Furthermore, the results have shown that the considerable usage of Manner and Manner-Path verbs by bilingual and minimal bilingual speakers (see §7.2.2.1) is predominantly related to locative Path phrases. However, the use of Manner and Manner-Path verbs in telic Path phrases was observed in a few cases. The results have shown that such violations of the boundary crossing constraint are not only limited to L2>L1 transfer phenomena in a Turkish-German bilingual context. Besides a "licence" of motion verbs which encode uncontrolled Motion, less expressive Manner verbs can be used in combination with directional Path devices in telic Path phrases as well. Nevertheless, due to the relative frequency of Path verbs in motion events with boundary focus, there is a clear tendency towards a boundary crossing constraint in Turkish and French. However, it seems that the use of Manner and Manner-Path verbs in boundary crossing events is less restricted in French compared to Turkish. Instead, Turkish speakers tend to use alternative strategies to convey boundary crossing events implicitly, which leads to more segmentation of their descriptions and a less frequent encoding of telic Path phrases. Such strategies were also found in a few bilingual speakers' L2 motion descriptions.

When comparing the speakers' performances in Turkish, French and German, it is striking that inter-group differences are most evident in locative and telic Path phrases among Turkish-German and German minimal bilinguals. The results reinforce the assertion that Turkish-German bilinguals are more influenced in their L2 performance as compared to Turkish-French bilinguals as a result of distinct conceptualisations in L1 or L2. In Matras' view (Matras 2007), Turkish-German bilinguals are more inclined to maintain "demarcation boundaries" in their L2 as compared to Turkish-French bilinguals due to the greater differences of their L1 and L2. However, the reasons for the greater impact observed on Turkish-German-bilinguals are multifaceted.

First, on the basis of the corpus analysis (see §3.2.6.1), we can assume that the use of Generic verbs is generally highly frequent in spoken discourse. Furthermore, the higher usage of Generic verbs has been observed in monolingual first language acquisition (Goldberg, Casenhiser & Sethuraman 2004) and in second language acquisition as well (Ellis & Ferreira–Junior 2009). The results indicate that the usage of Generic verbs is higher among younger children as well as L2 learners as a result of developmental constraints as well as a lower processing cost. For both German minimal and Turkish-German bilingual speakers, the use of verbs such as *gehen* 'to go' or *kommen* 'to come' is much more economical than using a more expressive verb. The more frequent usage of Generic verbs by Turkish-German bilinguals can be explained by their acquisition stage. We have seen, that their lexical repertoire in German is somewhat behind German minimal bilinguals. This is not surprising and a well-known fact in bilingualism research. When looking at the Generic verb usage among older Turkish-German bilinguals, the usage seems to decrease with time. However, the results of a case study[89] indicates that only at around age 14 do the numbers of Generic verbs used by Turkish-German bilinguals approach the numbers of Generic verbs of ten-year-old German minimal bilinguals (Koch & Woerfel 2018). We can conclude that the higher Generic verb usage persists over time and is not only due to frequency, developmental constraints and acquisition stage. This leads us to another aspect of the matter.

Second, Turkish-German bilinguals' higher usage of Generic verbs, in particular in telic Path phrases, is a typologically motivated L1 influence. As illustrated in §3.2.6.4, bilinguals acquiring Turkish and German are confronted with different motion events conceptualisations. In the case of motion events, where the Figure crosses a spatial boundary, the change of location is generally encoded by Path verbs in Turkish. This might lead to a different conceptualisation of such events. The argument can be put forward that Turkish-German bilinguals' conceptualisation of boundary crossing events is L1 based (focus on Path which is typically encoded in the main verb) and the encoding in German therefore "adjusted". Since German generally lacks Path verbs, the use of semantically neutral verbs such as *gehen* 'to go' seems to be a strategy which fits into the L1 conceptualisation, since it does not encode Manner. However, *gehen* neither encodes Path, nor is the change of location encoded by a Path device outside the verb (which then explains the high usage of [VGEN_P] in German, as illustrated in §7.2.5). Consequently, the conceptual transfer appears to be convergent when Generic verbs replace Path verbs in German by similarly using a typical S-pattern (Path is encoded outside the main verb).

We now have completed the quantitative and qualitative analysis of Study 2. Due to the examination of different analytical levels (motion verb choices, Path elaboration, motion verb construction, locative and telic Path phrases), the qualitative analysis and the inclusion of the results of Study 1, as well as

---

89 The case study includes also eight older Turkish-German bilinguals (range 13–16 years).

extra-linguistic information, the bilingual speakers' individual L1-L2 interactions are "spread" over the entire analysis. As a last point, the assumed L1-L2 interactions are summarised in the following in order to give a conclusive overview of cross-linguistic influences and the relation of extra-linguistic factors.

7.2.7 Quantification of cross-linguistic influence and the (in)significance of language dominance

As noted in Chapter 1.2, the main idea of the multicompetence framework is an understanding of a bidirectional interaction of a bilingual speaker's languages as a natural and ongoing process. Empirical studies in this field are generally limited to their object of investigation. In the current study the "detection" of L1>L2 and/or L2>L1 influences is generally limited to the specific analysis of motion event encoding. Thus, the summary of cross-linguistic influence in the following does not claim to be exhaustive. Note that due to the analytical limitations of this study, there were multiple other interactions found which have been, up to this point, not further specified. For instance, the structure in (213) was found in the corpus of Turkish-German bilinguals and is assumed to be a convergence of German and Turkish patterns. In this context, Dirim & Auer (2004: 15) argue that the structure *devam gitti* 'he continued going', which was used by Turkish-German bilinguals, can be seen as a convergence of the frequent structure *weiter gehen* 'continue going' in German and the structure *geri gitti* 'she/he/it went back'. Whereas the latter is already present in Turkish, the structure *devam gitti* is generally infrequent. In line with this, the structure *devam yürüdü* ' she/he/it continued walking' can be seen as a convergence of the frequent structure *weiter x-en* 'continue x-ing' in German and the extended use of directional Path devices in the Turkish contact variety of Turkish-German bilinguals, which are less restricted combined with motion verbs. Note that the construction *devamlı* 'continuously'+Manner verb seems to be less restricted in (standard) written Turkish. In the TNC there were combinations found, albeit extremely limitedly, with *düş-* 'to fall', *dön-* 'to turn(back)' *kaç-* 'to escape' and *yürü-* 'to walk', but never with *devam*. Thus, the combination of *devam* with Manner verbs in the Turkish-German variety is possibly supported by *devamlı*-constructions in standard (written) Turkish. However, both assumptions need further support by analysing representative Turkish corpora in spoken discourse.

(213) devam   yürü-dü
       continue walk-PST.3SG
       'It continued walking' (Sefar, TURGER, 438–439)

Tables 101 to 103 summarise speakers' cross-linguistic influences which were identified on the basis of the specific analysis in Study 2 by indicating the analytical levels "motion verb choices" (VCONF), "Path elaboration" (ELAB), "motion verb construction" (VCONST), "locative Path phrases" (LOC) and "telic Path phrases" (TEL) and the corresponding direction of influence (L1>L2, L2>L1). Furthermore, language dominance profiles (domain and dimensions) are summarised into "L1-dominant" and "L2-dominant" (at least two of three domains indicate an L1- or L2-dominance), "no dominance" (at least two of three domains indicate no dominance) and "mixed" (each domain indicates a distinct dominance, e.g. L1-dominant in verbal fluency, L2-dominant in TpL, no dominance in code-mixing).

The figures in Table 101 show that some speakers indicate a unidirectional L1>L2 influence, but no L2>L1 influence in the domain of motion encoding. The results further show that incidences of L1>L2 influence were more often observed for Turkish-German bilinguals (five speakers) as compared to Turkish-French bilinguals (two speakers). Furthermore, Turkish-German bilinguals' L2 was affected in different analysed levels, whereas Turkish-French bilinguals' influence was only found in each on a single level. Most frequently, Turkish-German bilinguals display an L1>L2 influence in the domain of locative Path phrases.

Table 101: Unidirectional L1>L2 influence on analytical levels motion verb choices (VCONF), Path elaboration (ELAB), motion verb construction (VCONST), locative (LOC) and telic (TEL) Path phrases of Turkish-German and Turkish-French bilinguals and their language dominance profiles.

Speaker	Group	L1>L2	L2>L1	Dimension	Domain
Alisa	TURGER	ELAB, LOC	/	L2	mixed
Beren	TURGER	LOC; TEL	/	L2	L2
Dana	TURGER	VCONV; LOC (2)	/	no	no
Kurt	TURGER	ELAB; VCONST; TEL	/	no	mixed
Taylan	TURGER	VCONST, LOC	/	no	L1
Gözde	TURFRE	ELAB	/	no	mixed
Adile	TURFRE	LOC	/	no	no

Moreover, it is striking that the individual language dominance profiles do not clearly support the direction of influence. Except for the speaker Taylan, most speakers indicate no clear dominance towards their L1.

Table 102 indicates that there are many more speakers in the study who display a unidirectional L2>L1 influence (six Turkish-German bilinguals, seven Turkish-French bilinguals). The quantity of influence is quite similar between

Table 102: Unidirectional L2>L1 influence on analytical levels motion verb choices (VCONF), Path elaboration (ELAB), motion verb construction (VCONST), locative (LOC) and telic (TEL) Path phrases of Turkish German and Turkish-French bilinguals and their language dominance profiles.

Speaker	Group	L1>L2	L2>L1	Dimension	Domain
Eda	TURGER	/	VCONST, LOC	L2	L2
Esna	TURGER	/	VCONST	no	L1
Gamze	TURGER	/	VCONST; TEL	L2	L2
Ozan	TURGER	/	VCONV; VCONST, LOC, TEL	L2	L2
Sefar	TURGER	/	LOC	no	no
Serkan	TURGER	/	ELAB; VCONST, LOC (2), TEL	no	L1
Dilşah	TURFRE	/	VCONST	L2	L2
Geza	TURFRE	/	ELAB (2); TEL	L2	L2
Maide	TURFRE	/	TEL	no	mixed
Nezihe	TURFRE	/	VCONST, ELAB	L2	L2
Shirin	TURFRE	/	LOC, ELAB	mixed	no
Mert	TURFRE	/	LOC	no	L2

both groups, however, among Turkish-German bilinguals there are two speakers who display an L2>L1 influence in almost all domains (Ozan, Serkan). Most frequently, Turkish-German bilinguals display an L2>L1 influence in the domain of Verb construction and locative Path phrases.

The direction of influence is partly supported by language dominance. There are six speakers who display an "L2-dominance" in both domain and dimension (TURGER: Eda, Gamze, Ozan; TURFRE: Dilşah, Geza, Nezihe) and one speaker who displays at least an L2-dominance in domain and similarly "no dominance" in dimension (TURFRE: Mert). However, two speakers indicate an L1-dominance in at least one dominance level (Esna, Serkan).

The results further show that four Turkish-German bilingual speakers and five Turkish-French bilingual speakers display a bidirectional influence in the domain of motion encoding (see Table 103). As regards the language dominance profiles, most speakers, again, indicate an "L2-dominance" in at least one category and "no dominance" in the other (TURGER: Tuba, Yiğit; TURFRE: Emre, Seçkin). Only one speaker is either L1-dominant (Melis) or L2-dominant (Devin) in both domain and dimension. Thus, the dominance patterns do not dramatically differ from speakers who indicate a unidirectional L2>L1 influence.

Interestingly, speakers for whom no influence has been identified, all belong to the Turkish-French bilingual group (Arda, Özgür) and display an "L2-dominance" in one dominance level and "no dominance" in the other (see Table 104).

Table 103: Bidirectional influence on analytical levels motion verb choices (VCONF), Path elaboration (ELAB), motion verb construction (VCONST), locative (LOC) and telic (TEL) Path phrases of Turkish-German and Turkish-French bilinguals and their language dominance profiles.

Speaker	Group	L1>L2	L2>L1	Dimension	Domain
Ela	TURGER	TEL	LOC	no	mixed
Melis	TURGER	VCONV (2); VCONST; TEL	LOC	L1	L1
Tuba	TURGER	TEL	VCONV	no	L2
Yiğit	TURGER	ELAB, TEL	VCONV	L2	no
Bircan	TURFRE	ELAB	TEL	no	mixed
Devin	TURFRE	VCONST, LOC(2), TEL	VCONF, VCONST, LOC	L2	L2
Emre	TURFRE	LOC	TEL, ELAB	no	L2
Nihal	TURFRE	LOC	ELAB (2); LOC	no	no
Seçkin	TURFRE	VCONV, VCONST, LOC (2)	ELAB	no	L2

Table 104: Turkish-German and Turkish-French bilinguals with no influence and their language dominance profiles.

Speaker	Group	L1>L2 / L2>L1	Dimension	Domain
Arda	TURFRE	/	L2	no
Özgür	TURFRE	/	no	L2

When examining the quantity of cross-linguistic influences observed with respect to the different analytical levels, the numbers in Table 105 indicate that among Turkish-German bilinguals, L1>L2 influence mainly occurs in the domains of locative and telic Path phrases. L2>L1 influences are mainly evident in the domain of verb construction and locative Path phrases. Turkish-French bilinguals most frequently display L1>L2 influences in locative Path phrases. L2>L1 influences occur most frequently in the domain of Path elaboration.

7.2.8 Summary and discussion

The aim of Study 2 was to investigate cross-linguistic influences in motion event expressions in Turkish and German of Turkish-German bilinguals and in Turkish and French of Turkish-French bilinguals. We analysed the speakers' motion descriptions in L1 and L2 based on oral re-narrations of two video stimuli on various analytical levels: manner verb lexicon, motion verb choices, other

Table 105: Summary of observed influence on the analytical levels motion verb choices (VCONF), Path elaboration (ELAB), verb construction (VCONST), locative Path phrases (LOC) and telic Path phrases (TEL) of Turkish-German and Turkish-French bilinguals (in numbers).

Analytical levels	L1>L2		L2>L1	
	TURGER	TURFRE	TURGER	TURFRE
VCONV	3	1	3	1
ELAB	3	2	1	8
VCONST	3	2	5	3
LOC	5	7	7	4
TEL	6	1	3	4

linguistic devices, Path elaboration, motion verb constructions as well as locative and telic Path phrases. There were several research questions to be answered and various hypotheses to be tested. In order to answer the research questions (RQ_{1-4}) of whether there are inter- and intra-group differences in

- the proportion and diversity of Manner, Path, Manner-Path and Generic motion verbs;
- the proportion of expressing Manner and Path in other linguistic devices;
- the proportion of combining Manner, Path, Manner-Path and Generic verbs with other linguistic devices and the elaboration of Path; and
- the proportion of expressing Manner and Path in verb roots in locative and telic Path phrases

we compared the bilingual speakers' group performances in L1 with each other as well as the performances in L1 and L2 within the groups by using quantitative and qualitative methods. To further maintain an (intra-) typological motivated influence, the bilingual speakers' motion expressions in L1 and L2 were compared quantitatively with minimal bilingual speakers' motion expressions in German, Turkish and French. In addition, the bilingual speakers' performance in the MVC-Task, which tested the speakers' Manner verb repertoire, was considered to answer the RQ_5 of whether individual motion verb choices were related to the speakers' individual Manner verb lexicon.

We assumed that the degree of similarity or difference of language-specific patterns in speaker's L1 and L2 would lead to a similar or different motion conceptualisation. Thus, it was expected that Turkish-German bilinguals who are confronted with distinct language-specific patterns in their L1 and L2 are more likely display conceptual transfer than Turkish-French bilinguals. We predicted that this leads to differences in Turkish-German bilinguals' L2 motion descriptions in comparison with German minimal bilinguals. Furthermore, due to conceptualisation restructuring, we hypothesised that in comparison with Turkish-French bilinguals and Turkish minimal bilinguals, Turkish-German bilinguals also display greater differences in their L1 motion descriptions. By contrast, the similarity of language-specific patterns in L1 and L2 in Turkish-French bilinguals was expected to lead to a positive conceptual transfer, which is evident in weaker differences in their L1-motion descriptions in comparison with Turkish-German bilinguals and Turkish minimal bilinguals and in their L2 motion descriptions in comparison with French minimal bilinguals. Nevertheless, we expected that cross-linguistic transfer in L1 and L2 would still occur as a consequence of intra-typological differences between Turkish and French. Based on these assumptions, the following hypotheses were tested:

H_0 Turkish-German and Turkish-French bilinguals do not differ when comparing the groups with each other and with minimal bilingual speakers;

H_1 Turkish-German and Turkish-French bilinguals exhibit an "in-between performance" in L1 and L2 inasmuch as they differ in their performance in comparison with minimal bilingual speakers of the respective languages;

$H_{1.1}$ Turkish-German bilinguals differ in their performance in German when comparing them with German minimal bilinguals;

$H_{1.2}$ Turkish-French bilinguals differ in their performance in French when comparing them with French minimal bilinguals;

$H_{1.3}$ Turkish-German and Turkish-French bilinguals differ in their performance in Turkish descriptions when comparing the groups with each other and with Turkish minimal bilinguals.

The findings of the quantitative analysis, which aimed to answer RQ_{1-4}, indicated that inter-group differences were related to specific phenomena, but not for all particular analytical levels. The validity of $H_{1.1}$, that Turkish-German bilinguals differ in their performance in German when comparing them with German minimal bilinguals, tends to be confirmed. The statistics indicated significant differences in the German motion descriptions of Turkish-German bilinguals in comparison with German minimal bilinguals with respect to:

Motion verb choices: Turkish-German bilinguals used Manner, Manner-Path and Modal/auxiliary verbs less frequently in motion event descriptions without motion verbs and made use of Generic verbs more frequently in comparison with German minimal bilinguals;

Path elaboration: Turkish-German bilinguals indicated a higher usage of two (or more) directional Path elements per motion verb than German minimal bilinguals;

Motion verb construction: Turkish-German bilinguals combined Manner verbs with directional Path devices [VM_P] less frequently than German minimal bilinguals;

Locative and telic Path phrases: Unlike German minimal bilinguals, Turkish-German bilinguals encoded Generic verbs more frequently in locative Path phrases and made use of Manner verbs less frequently in telic Path phrases with a clear tendency to use Generic verbs instead.

Significant differences in the French motion descriptions between Turkish-French and French minimal bilinguals were only found in a lower Manner verb usage by Turkish-French bilinguals. Thus, $H_{1.2}$, that Turkish-French bilinguals differ in their performance in French when comparing them with French minimal bilinguals, tends not to be confirmed.

$H_{1.3}$, that Turkish-German and Turkish-French bilinguals differ in their performance in Turkish descriptions when comparing the groups with each other and with Turkish minimal bilinguals, also tends not to be confirmed. The significant differences found were limited to:

Motion verb choices: Turkish-German bilinguals indicated a lower Manner-Path verb usage in comparison with Turkish minimal bilinguals;

Path elaboration: Turkish-French bilinguals indicated a higher usage of "no" directional Path elements in comparison with Turkish-German bilinguals;

Locative Path phrases: Turkish-German bilinguals less frequently used Manner-Path verbs in locative Path phrases in comparison with Turkish minimal bilinguals.

The summarised findings of the quantitative analysis suggest that the degree of similarity and difference of language-specific patterns in bilingual speakers' L1 and L2 seem to impact particularly the L2 in Turkish-German bilinguals. The figures emphasise that differences in the L2 are mainly evident in the analytical levels of motion verb choices, motion verb construction and telic Path phrases between Turkish-German bilingual and German minimal bilingual speakers. Differences in L1 are more obvious between Turkish-French bilinguals and Turkish minimal bilinguals than between Turkish-German bilinguals and Turkish minimal bilinguals on the analytical level of Path elaboration.

With respect to motion verb choices we assumed that the lower frequency of Manner verbs and the parallel higher frequency of Generic verbs in German is related to a typologically motivated conceptual transfer which was only in a few individual cases further reinforced by a lower Manner/Manner-Path verb lexicon and a general lower lexical repertoire. Thus, as regards RQ_5 we can conclude that individual motion verb choices were generally not related to the speakers' individual Manner verb lexicon. As regards the analytical level of motion verb constructions, we assumed that the avoidance of typical S-constructions ([VM_P]) and an extension from Path to Generic verbs in German lead to a convergence of the typical Path encoding patterns in Turkish ("Path-in-verb") and German ("Path outside the motion verb"). This convergence is evident in the high frequency of the [VGEN_P]-construction in German. The results further indicated that the extension from Path to Generic verbs is mainly exhibited in telic Path phrases in German. This fact has led us to the assertion that Turkish-German bilinguals' conceptualisation of boundary crossing events is L1 based (by focusing on Path which is typically encoded in the main verb) and the linguistic symbolisation in German is therefore "adjusted".

In contrast to Turkish-German bilinguals, for Turkish-French bilinguals a positive conceptual transfer could be observed in the analytical level of motion verb choices. We assumed that the routine usage of Path verbs in L1 and L2 leads to an overuse of this category and a decrease of Manner verbs in motion descriptions in both Turkish and French. The quantitative findings suggest no major difference, neither between Turkish-French and Turkish-German bilinguals, nor between Turkish-French and Turkish minimal bilinguals. From this quantitative perspective, the findings support the assertion that, due to the typological closeness in motion event encoding of Turkish and French, Turkish-French bilinguals' motion descriptions in L1 and L2 display little influence. Vice versa, as a result of the typological difference in motion event encoding in Turkish and German, Turkish-German bilinguals' motion expressions, particularly in the L2, display a greater influence. When illustrating the mean differences on the particular analytical levels of motion verb choices, Path elaboration, motion verb construction, locative and telic Path phrases between bilingual speakers' performances and minimal bilingual speakers' performances, Figure 44 emphasises that Turkish-German and Turkish-French bilinguals are very close to each other with regard to their differences in L1. However, as shown above, they strikingly differ in their respective L2. Thus, we can conclude that on the basis of the quantitative measurements, bilingual speakers exhibit "in-between performances" in both of their languages, which are much more pronounced in the L2 of the Turkish-German bilingual group.

The reported quantitative comparisons only allowed relatively broad generalisations of similarities and differences between the groups under study. When taking the qualitative analysis into account, further evidence for the speakers' usage preferences and cross-linguistic influence could be maintained, which go beyond the results provided by the quantitative analysis. Furthermore, the individual results indicated considerable intra-group differences mainly in the bilinguals' motion descriptions in French and Turkish. As regards $H_{1,2}$ that

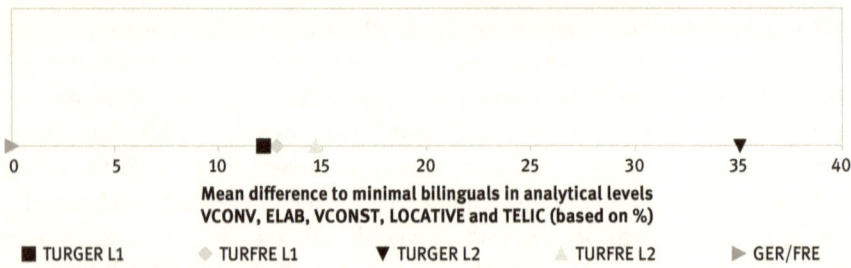

Figure 44: Mean difference of the particular analytical levels motion verb choices (VCONF), Path elaboration (ELAB), motion verb construction (VCONST), locative (LOC) and telic Path phrases (TEL) between bilingual (TURGER, TURFRE) and minimal bilingual speakers (GER, FRE) in the respective L1 and L2 (based on %).

Turkish-French bilinguals differ in their performance in French when comparing them with French minimal bilinguals, the individual analysis indicated that for some Turkish-French bilinguals intra-group differences are evident with regard to

1. **Motion verb choices**: some Turkish-French bilinguals more frequently used Path verbs in SUPER-events in comparison with French minimal bilinguals;
2. **Motion verb construction**: some Turkish-French bilinguals displayed a lower frequency of bare Manner verb constructions [VM_0] in comparison with French minimal bilinguals;
3. **Locative and telic Path phrases**: some Turkish-French bilinguals more frequently encoded locative Path phrases and less frequently violated the boundary crossing constraint in French in comparison with French minimal bilinguals.

Although the language-specific patterns of Turkish-French bilinguals' L1 and L2 are similar, the findings suggest L1>L2 influence in the individual speakers' motion descriptions. Such influence was observed most frequently in locative Path phrases, in which some Turkish-French bilinguals more frequently used Path verbs in SUPER-events in French. We assumed that this difference is related to intra-typological differences. The same intra-typological differences account for the avoidance of bare Manner verb constructions ([VM_0]) in French by a few Turkish-French bilinguals, since these constructions are more frequently employed in French than in Turkish. Furthermore, we observed a preference of paratactic organisation in French by some Turkish-French bilinguals who more frequently sub-divided their motion descriptions by expressing a GENERALIS-event and subsequently an IN-event in French (e.g. *Il s'est roulé et ensuite il est parti dans la salle de bowling* 'He rolled himself and afterwards he left into the bowling room'). In addition, some also tended to avoid the encoding of the Figure's change of location into a bounded space (*et après il s'est roulé jusqu' au bowling*) and/or implicitly encoded the traversal into a bounded space. Since these alternative strategies are commonly employed in Turkish (also by Turkish minimal bilinguals, e.g. *yuvarlandı bovling halısına girdi* 'It rolled, it entered into the bowling alley'), we assumed that the conceptualisation here is L1 based instead and reflected in the speakers' L2 descriptions. Note that these strategies could be observed for some Turkish-German bilinguals' motion descriptions in German (*Er ist gekrabbelt dann ist er darein gegangen* 'He crawled then he went in') which further contributes to $H_{1.1}$. The fact that these strategies were found in all the three groups of Turkish speakers supports the findings of Özçalışkan (2013) that speakers of Turkish tend to parse an event into a series of sub-events. However, it is possible that these strategies are a particular phenomenon related to the modality of the re-narration task, since this type of paratactic organisation is seen as typical for spoken Turkish (Schroeder 2009).

In addition to $H_{1.3}$ that Turkish-German and Turkish-French bilinguals differ in their performance in Turkish descriptions, when comparing the groups with each other and with Turkish minimal bilinguals, the qualitative results further indicated that the greater difference of language-specific patterns in German and Turkish as well as intra-typological differences in Turkish and French are also evident in the reverse way (L2>L1 influence). The individual differences found in Turkish-German and Turkish-French bilinguals' Turkish are related to:

Motion verb choices: some Turkish-German bilinguals indicated a higher usage of Manner verbs in comparison with Turkish-French bilinguals and Turkish minimal bilinguals;

Path elaboration: some Turkish-French bilinguals less frequently encoded "two (or more)" directional Path elements in comparison with Turkish minimal bilinguals;

Motion verb construction: some Turkish-German bilinguals displayed a higher usage of combinations of Manner verbs with directional Path devices [VM_P] in comparison with Turkish-French bilinguals and Turkish minimal bilinguals;

Locative and telic Path phrases: some Turkish-French bilinguals less frequently encoded locative Path phrases in comparison with Turkish-German bilinguals and Turkish minimal bilinguals; some Turkish-German bilinguals more often violated the boundary-crossing constraint in comparison with Turkish-French bilinguals and Turkish minimal bilinguals.

Thus, individual L2>L1 influence in Turkish-German motion descriptions was mainly found in the domains of motion verb choices, motion verb construction and telic Path phrases. In the observed cases, a conceptualisation restructuring was assumed, which was evident in a general higher usage of Manner verbs in Turkish as well as in particular when using Manner verbs in telic Path phrases. Furthermore, we assumed that the higher usage of combinations of Manner verbs with directional Path devices [VM_P] in Turkish, which is typical for S-languages, reflects an influence on the speakers' L1 due to constructional usage preferences in their L2. In the Turkish-French bilingual context individual L2>L1 influence was most frequently observed in the domains of Path elaboration, locative and telic Path phrases. The lower Path elaboration in some Turkish-French bilingual speakers' motion descriptions in Turkish was assumed to reflect an intra-typologically motivated L2>L1 transfer of usage preferences. This assumption is supported by recent research on intra-typological variation in romance languages (Hijazo-Gascón 2018). It is argued that native speakers of French generally display a lower Path elaboration in terms of using no or only one directional Path element as compared to e.g. native speakers of Italian and Basque. In §3.4 we discussed that Turkish has more complex morphological resources for spatial expression as compared to French and is therefore more similar to "Path salient" V-languages such as Basque. The results of Turkish and French minimal bilingual speakers' motion descriptions support this assertion. Furthermore, we assumed that the lower encoding of locative Path phrases in Turkish, as well as the lower usage of Path verbs in IN-events in Turkish, found among some speakers, reflect L2-usage preferences in the L1. Similarly to the difference found in the Path elaboration in Turkish and French, this effect is seen as an intra-typological impact. As illustrated, when linguistically encoding the motion images, French minimal bilinguals less frequently sub-divided the expressed motion events and rather expressed motion events with boundary focus explicitly. This motion encoding strategy differs from the paratactic organisation found for speakers of Turkish and leads to a lower frequency of locative Path phrases and similarly to a higher frequency of telic Path phrases in French. This was also observed in individual motion expressions in Turkish of some Turkish-French bilinguals; in these cases an L2>L1 influence could be maintained.

The overall results of the qualitative analysis which aimed to provide intra-group variation and cross-linguistic influence on the basis of individual speakers' usage preferences suggest that "direct transfer" from the L1 to the L2 (such as the use of Path verbs in German) or from the L2 to the L1 (such as the use of Manner verbs in telic Path phrases in Turkish), never or only very rarely occurred. Furthermore, although the numbers of a few bilinguals were on some particular analytical levels very close to minimal bilinguals in both L1 and L2, the general picture shows that they usually do not behave like minimal bilingual speakers. In fact, many of the differences found can be explained by usage preferences in the L1 and the L2. Several incidences which were determined as L1>L2 or L2>L1 influence can be related to the use of patterns which are provided by both of the bilinguals' languages. Thus, the speakers used L1-patterns in their L1 and L2-patterns in their L2 but preferred those which also exist in the other language, which similarly leads to an avoidance or less frequent usage of other patterns in L1 and L2. Within the convergence approach, introduced in §2.2, we can assume that, when encoding motion events, the bilingual speakers do not separate their languages, since they make use of their linguistic resources, which are at their disposal in L1 and L2 and lift their "demarcation boundaries" (Matras 2007) when displaying preferences for overlapping motion constructions. This type of influence which Goschler (2013: 127) refers to as a "'blend' of typological backgrounds" leads to differences between bilingual and minimal bilingual speakers. At first sight, the preferred structures that cause the differences between bilingual and minimal bilingual speakers are hardly obvious because they also exist in the L1 or L2. This kind of "hidden variation" (Bryant 2012) was detected by the quantitative and qualitative analysis and further contributes to an understanding of bilingual speakers' characteristics in L1 and L2.

In addition to the examination of the impact of language-specific patterns, the speakers' individual global language dominance patterns were included in the analysis. In order to answer RQ_6, of whether global language dominance patterns impact the direction of L1/L2 influence in motion event encoding, four groups were distinguished based on the direction of influence found in the qualitative analysis of Study 2: speakers who indicate "unidirectional L1>L2 influences", "unidirectional L2>L1 influences", "bidirectional influences" and "no influence". Furthermore, the direction of influence was analysed in relation to the individual global language dominance patterns in domain and dimension found in Study 1. We assumed that global dominance patterns in domain and dimension would support the direction of influence in the bilingual speakers' motion descriptions in L1 and L2 by testing the following hypotheses:

H_0 Language dominance does not impact the direction of cross-linguistic influence in Turkish-German and Turkish-French bilinguals' motion expressions;

H_1 Language dominance impacts the direction of cross-linguistic influence in Turkish-German and Turkish-French bilinguals' motion expressions;

$H_{1.1}$ Turkish-German and Turkish-French bilinguals display a higher degree of L2 influence on Turkish when they are L2 dominant in domain and dimension;

$H_{1.2}$ Turkish-German and Turkish-French bilinguals display a higher degree of L1 influence on their L2 when they are L1 dominant in domain and dimension.

The results revealed no clear picture, which is probably due to the quite heterogeneous results of language dominance patterns found in Study 1. Thus, the findings tend not to confirm $H_{1.1}$, that Turkish-German and Turkish-French bilinguals display a higher degree of L2 influence on Turkish when they are L2-dominant in domain and dimension. This is in line with the results of the study by Berthele & Stocker (2017), who did not find a statistically significant impact of bilingual dominance configurations for the choice of motion verbs and other related patterns in German-French bilinguals' motion descriptions. However, the qualitative analysis in the current study indicates that five of nine speakers, who indicated a unidirectional L2>L1-dominance, were also L2 dominant in both domain and dimension. These speakers also indicated quantitatively more incidences of L2>L1 influence than speakers who displayed an "L2-dominance", "no dominance" and/or "mixed patterns" in either domain or dimension. Thus, we assumed a tendency for speakers who are consistently L2-dominant in domain and dimension to more likely and more frequently transfer L2 elements into their L1. Among the speakers who display unidirectional L1>L2 influence, there was only one single speaker who displayed an L1-dominance in one category. Thus, $H_{1.2}$, that Turkish-German and Turkish-French bilinguals display a higher degree of L1 influence on their L2 when they are L1-dominant in domain and dimension, tend to also not be confirmed. Alternatively, the results suggest that L1>L2 influence is supported instead in cases where speakers indicate no clear dominance towards their L2. Most of the speakers who displayed a unidirectional L1>L2 influence indicated "no dominance" in dimension and "no dominance", "L1-dominance" or "mixed patterns" in domain. Speakers who displayed a bidirectional influence, mainly indicated an "L2-dominance" in at least one category and "no dominance" in the other. As regards their dominance patterns, they are situated between the group of speakers indicating "unidirectional L2>L1 influences" and the group of speakers indicating "unidirectional L1>L2 influences". There were also two speakers who did not indicate any individual cross-linguistic influence at all. Their dominance patterns are similar to those of speakers with "bidirectional influence" ("L2-dominance"/"no dominance" in domain or dimension).

8 General discussion and future directions

This empirical study aimed to provide insights into bilingual language usage and language dominance and the characteristics of bilingual speakers' performances. The goal of the investigation was to discover the nature of variation in L1- and L2-motion descriptions by evaluating the impact of language-specific properties (satellite- and verb-framed pattern) and language-dominance patterns. We focused on second, intermediate "2.5" and third generation Turkish-German and Turkish-French bilinguals. On the one hand, due to the vital linguistic communities of Turkish minority speakers in Germany and France, these two bilingual populations were seen as perfectly suitable for investigating language maintenance, language dominance and variation of the Turkish varieties spoken in Germany and France. On the other hand, we argued that the two populations are fruitful for investigating the nature of variation in the speakers' L1 and L2 since they indicate differences with regard to their language-specific patterns (S- and V-pattern by Turkish-German bilinguals and V- and V- pattern by Turkish-French bilinguals).

This research provides relevant findings which serve to answer the research questions as well as contribute to various aspects to the respective research area in which it is located: first, the study contributes to the domain of early second language acquisition by providing insights into the relation of language dominance patterns in domain and dimension as well as into sources of cross-linguistic differences in the bilingual speakers' L1 and L2. Second, the study serves to extend typological approaches towards motion event encoding by providing new perspectives of individual and intra-typological variation. And third, the study contributes to methodological aspects in language dominance, second language acquisition as well as in motion event research by considering not just quantitative, but also qualitative methods. In the following, we first discuss the main findings of this study and their relevance in the respective research area (§8.1 second language acquisition, §8.2 motion events, §8.3 methodology) and then emphasise the limitations of this study and suggest future directions (§8.4).

8.1 Contribution to second language acquisition research

8.1.1 Language use and language dominance

In this study, we argued that a bilingual person is not simply dominant in one language and that bilinguals' language dominance patterns are distributed between languages (see §2.1.2). In order to quantify speakers' language dominance to a measurable degree, we differentiated between dimensions (which included language skills and language knowledge) and domains (which cover the communicative function of language). The findings of Turkish-German and Turkish-French bilinguals' language dominance patterns mainly support our assumptions that bilinguals are generally not just only dominant in one language, but use their languages for different purposes or in different domains. This fact emphasises the importance of a conceptual and methodological distinction between the two levels – domain and dimension – in language dominance research. Furthermore, the distinction allowed us to examine the relation between the two dominance levels. Our results have shown that bilinguals' language dominance in domain does not necessarily predict their language dominance in dimension. However, we suggested that "L2-dominance" in domain predominantly co-occurs with "no dominance" or "L2-dominance" in dimension. However, our data provide evidence that Turkish-German and Turkish-French bilinguals have a great chance of preventing a language dominance shift, which generally challenges the consensus among researchers that for Turkish-German and Turkish French bilinguals an L2-dominance shift sets in by age eight.

Thus, our research provides new insights into the domain of language dominance in general and in the language use, the language skills and the language knowledge of second, intermediate "2.5" and third generation bilingual speakers in the Turkish diaspora in Europe in particular – until now, research on language maintenance and shift involving the language use and practices in the Turkish communities was predominantly carried out among adolescent or adult populations (but see the binational research project MULTILIT[90]).

8.1.2 The nature of variation in bilinguals

A further contribution to the domain of second language acquisition involves the understanding of the nature of variation in bilingual speakers' performances in L1 and L2. We argued that within a multicompetence perspective, ramifications of L1 and L2 apply to different areas of language (see §2.2). We further claimed that such ramifications are evident in cross-linguistic influences in both bilingual speakers' L1 and L2 but sometimes difficult to recognise, in particular in the domain of lexical-semantic variation (e.g. the use of semantically neutral over more expressive motion verbs, see §2.3.6). We assumed that the domain of motion

---

90 MULTILIT investigated the language abilities of multilingual children and adolescents with Turkish (and Kurdish) as home language(s) in France and Germany. For further details see http://www.uni-potsdam.de/daf/projekte/multilit.html [2018-01-15]

encoding (see §3.2) is a fruitful field for explaining sources of cross-linguistic differences in bilingual speakers' performances (see §3.3 and §4.2). In addition to language dominance, differences of language-specific motion encoding patterns (V/S-typology), which result in differences in motion event conceptualisation, were seen as the important factors of variation.

The findings support the assumption that different conceptualisation patterns in L1 and L2 lead to a greater bidirectional transfer in bilingual speakers' motion expressions than similar conceptualisation patterns in L1 and L2. In the motion expressions of Turkish-German bilinguals who acquired successively a V- (Turkish) and an S-language (German) within their first five years of life we found incidences of conceptual transfer (from L1 to L2), conceptual restructuring (from L2 to L1), semantic extension (in L2), convergence (of L1 and L2 patterns), and the use of alternative structures (in L2). Thus, these findings contribute to the assumption that interactions between bilinguals' two language knowledge systems include bidirectionality. In the context of conceptual restructuring, the acquisition of a second language can lead to a "new way of thinking" which can have an impact on the L2. In contrast, such an impact was much less when conceptualisation patterns in L1 and L2 were more similar. Quantitative analyses of the motion expressions in L1 and L2 of Turkish-French bilinguals who acquired successively two different V-languages within their first five years of life, did not show major differences to those of minimal bilingual speakers of French and Turkish. However, the perspective of this relatively broad generalisation is different when taking into account the findings of the qualitative analysis. It turned out that particularly speakers with similar conceptualisation patterns (Turkish-French bilinguals) showed considerable intra-group variation, which can be traced back to intra-typological differences between Turkish and French.

Furthermore, our results show that the direction of influence is not necessarily a result of language dominance. Only in those cases where speakers are L2 dominant in both domain and dimension are they more likely to and more frequently do transfer L2 elements into their L1. L1>L2 influence occurs instead in cases where bilingual speakers indicate no clear dominance towards their L2.

All in all, the resulting picture of language dominance and motion encoding suggests that there are more Turkish-French bilinguals who are L2-dominant in domain and/or dimension in comparison with Turkish-German bilinguals. In their L1 motion descriptions, the bilingual groups differed from Turkish minimal bilinguals on particular analytical levels, but the overall results indicated that the mean group difference between the bilingual groups was very small. In contrast, the difference was striking in their L2 performances. From the typological perspective of motion encoding, the greater L1>L2 influence supports our hypotheses. The subtle differences in the L1 are, however, surprising. It was expected instead that the greater typological difference of motion encoding patterns in the Turkish-German bilinguals' L2 would lead to a higher impact on the L1. Only in some cases were the differences found in the motion descriptions in Turkish assumed to be related to conceptualisation restructuring (Turkish-German) or to intra-typological differences (Turkish-French) and the direction of influence was supported by L2-dominance (both groups). However, the overall results did not provide evidence for the fact that these factors are general predictors for the differences found. Instead, the qualitative analysis revealed that "direct transfer" from the L1 to the L2, and vice versa, rarely occurs – and if so, it is mostly evident on only one particular analytical level in which conceptualisation patterns lead speakers' to a different linguistic symbolisation (e.g. the use of Manner verbs in telic Path phrases in Turkish-German bilinguals' motion descriptions). Furthermore, as predicted in §2.2.1, the general picture usually shows that bilingual speakers do not behave like "the mean minimal bilingual". In fact, the individual results suggest that most of the differences can be explained by usage preferences in L1 and L2: bilinguals most frequently make use of patterns which exist in both languages, but which are unequally preferred by minimal bilingual speakers. Since minimal bilingual speakers are not confronted with this sort of "'blend' of [intra-] typological backgrounds" (Goschler 2013: 127), their usage preferences are different.

The detection of the nature of variation in the form of different conceptualisation patterns, different usage preferences and the consequence of language dominance on bilingual speakers' motion description contributes to a better understanding of multilingual characteristics. The knowledge gained can also have didactic implications. The recognition that characteristics in the L2 performance of Turkish-German bilinguals – for instance a lower usage of expressive motion verbs and a higher usage of Generic verbs – are influenced by specific patterns of the L1, and not by incomplete L1/L2 acquisition, can shed a different light on the ongoing debate with respect to the language skills of Turkish-German bilinguals in Germany. As is argued by studies analysing the reasons for the educational failure of Turkish-German bilinguals in secondary schools, it is the lexical domain in which Turkish-German bilinguals display the largest difference from German monolingual students (DESI-Konsortium 2008: 217–218).

In sum, with the systematic detection of particular cross-linguistic differences and similarities as well as usage preferences in Turkish-German and Turkish-French bilingual children' L1 and L2, this study achieved new insights into second language acquisition research. This further provides a better understanding of the nature of variation in bilingual speakers' performances in L1 and L2.

As noted above, in addition to second language acquisition research, this study also contributes to perspectives on motion event research, which are discussed in the following.

8.2 Contribution to perspectives on motion event research

8.2 1 Motion encoding in multilingual settings

A vast empirical literature on motion event encoding has focused on monolingual first and then on foreign language learning. The domain of bilingual first language acquisition and particularly the domain of early second language acquisition has received much less attention. Furthermore, except for the study by Daller, Treffers-Daller & Furman (2011), the studies carried out in the Turkish-German bilingual setting solely investigated one of the bilinguals' languages, namely the L2 (Goschler 2009; Goschler et al. 2013; Schroeder 2009). Thus, on the one hand, this study contributes to the domain of motion event encoding in child bilinguals in general, and, by having considered both of the bilingual speakers' languages, to the desideratum in Turkish-German bilinguals' settings in particular. On the other hand, this is the first study which has investigated bilingual speakers' motion descriptions in Turkish-French bilingual settings; this makes an important contribution to the acquisition of two V-languages which has been investigated by a limited number of studies in foreign language acquisition, but, until now, not in the context of early second language acquisition.

Thus, we presented new insights into the motion event encoding in the L1 and the L2 of bilinguals who acquired (with Turkish and German) a V- and an S-language as well as (with Turkish and French) two V-languages in their early childhood.

8.2.2 Multilingual variation

More importantly, we argued that research on early second language acquisition contributes to necessary "extensions and refinements" (Goschler & Stefanowitsch 2013b: 10) in the domain of motion encoding (see §3.4). In this study, we discovered structures in Turkish, French and German motion descriptions which strikingly display variation as a result of interactions between the bilingual speakers' L1 and L2:
- the stable preference for Generic verbs (particularly in motion events with boundary focus) and the lower encoding of Manner in the German of Turkish-German bilinguals;
- the avoidance of typical S-constructions such as combinations of Manner verbs with directional Path devices in the German of Turkish-German bilinguals;

- the use of typical S-constructions such as combinations of Manner verbs with directional Path devices in the Turkish of Turkish-German bilinguals;
- the use of alternative strategies by sub-dividing the motion event into a GENERALIS-event and an IN-event or by implicitly encoding a traversal into a bounded space in the German of Turkish-German and in the French of Turkish-French bilinguals which leads to a higher encoding of locative Path phrases in French and German;
- the use of Manner verbs in boundary-crossing events in Turkish by Turkish-German bilinguals; and
- the avoidance of Manner verbs in boundary-crossing events in French by Turkish-French bilinguals.

Since these characteristics are considered as a result of cross-linguistic influences in L1 and L2, we suggest that they contribute a further reason of variation in motion encoding.

In addition to variation in multilingual settings, this study further supports recent intra-typological approaches which go beyond the S/V-typology proposed by Talmy.

8.2.3 Intra-typological variation

Our analytical procedure covered, in addition to verb conflation, the verbal periphery (adverbal and adnominal encoding), and resulting motion event constructions (combinations of motion verbs and other linguistic devices). The advocation of a broader definition of Talmy's satellites stricto sensu (see §3.2.5.2) by including prepositional phrases, directional adverbs and case-marking (as a morphological resource in Turkish) for directional Path encoding, revealed consequences for the results – particularly for the V-languages analysed.

The results provide evidence for the use of "(pseudo)-satellite constructions" in Turkish and French, which are both considered as V-languages in the motion literature. Our findings have shown that speakers of Turkish and French make, differently, but both to a considerable degree, use of adverbal and adnominal encoding. Consequently, they produce a great number of "double framing" constructions (combinations of Path verbs with directional Path devices), which are, according to Talmy's framework, generally not seen as prototypical for V-languages. In the case of French, it is claimed that there are, along with "double framing" constructions, various other patterns beyond the V-pattern and, therefore, French can not be considered as a typical V-language (Pourcel & Kopecka 2005). However, our data did not provide clear evidence for this assumption.

With respect to Path salience, the cross-linguistic comparisons of Turkish and French speakers' motion descriptions indicated that speakers of Turkish produced more elaborate Path descriptions than speakers of French. We assumed that the differences found are due to the more complex morphological resources for spatial expressions in Turkish, which leads speakers to more detailed Path descriptions. This finding led us to the assertion that Turkish is more Path salient than French. On the basis of recent intra-typological research on Romance languages, we suggest that Turkish can be classified on a continuum of Path salience in proximity to Italian and Basque which are both considered high Path salient languages (Ibarretxe-Antuñano 2009). This finding emphasises the importance of taking a usage-based approach into account, by focusing on the speakers' actual usage of linguistic resources for motion encoding instead or in addition to the analysis of the "possible range of linguistic resources a language might offer" (Hijazo-Gascón & Ibarretxe-Antuñano 2013: 49). Nevertheless, we have to emphasise that there are striking differences between Turkish, French and German. The analysis of combinations of motion verbs with directional Path devices indicated that, compared with German, they are much less frequent and more restricted with respect to their productivity and combination in Turkish and even more in French.

With regard to the level of conflation patterns, the results of motion verb choices revealed that Path verbs were most frequently used in Turkish and French, whereas Manner verbs were the most frequent choice in German. At first glance, this finding seems to support the premise of Talmy's framework which accounts for speakers' "first/habitual/most frequent/preferred choices" (Filipović & Ibarretxe-Antuñano 2015: 528). However, our results suggest some intra-typological variation: on the other hand, we observed that Manner verbs were used considerably in Turkish and French (predominantly in locative Path phrases). On the other hand, the analysis of the corpus-based distinction of a two-tiered lexicon of more frequently (everyday Manner/Manner-Path verbs) and less frequently (expressive Manner verbs) used Manner/Manner-Path verbs reveals that speakers predominantly make use of everyday Manner/Manner-Path verbs. However, differences were found between speakers of German/French and speakers of Turkish. Turkish speakers used expressive Manner verbs strikingly less frequently in comparison with speakers of German and French. This finding seems to fit Slobin's suggestion of a "cline/continuum of Manner salience" (Slobin 2004b). Contrary to our observation that Turkish is closer to German on a "cline of Path salience" than French, French is closer to German on a "cline of Manner salience" than Turkish.

Furthermore, we concluded that Generic verbs play an important role in Turkish motion descriptions by bilingual and minimal bilingual speakers and in German motion descriptions of Turkish-German bilinguals. In contrast, in French, the use of Generic verbs seems to be limited, and also plays a minor role in German minimal bilinguals' motion descriptions. We assumed that the use of Generic verbs in motion descriptions is more typical in Turkish than in French and more typical for Turkish-German bilinguals than for minimal bilingual speakers in German motion descriptions.

In sum, the study further contributes to variational approaches in motion research by providing new perspectives of intra-typological variation in Turkish and French and individual variation in (bilingual) speakers of German, Turkish, and French.

In addition to contributions to second language acquisition and perspectives on motion event research, this study also provides several methodical implications.

8.3 Contribution to methodological implications

8.3.1 Language dominance

In order to achieve the goals of this study, the methodology included the measurement of language dominance on two levels, namely language use (domain) and language skills and language knowledge (dimensions). The assessment of language dominance combined common methods in language dominance research: information on language use (in different contexts/situations) was gained in child questionnaires; information on language skills (verbal fluency, code-switching), and language knowledge (lexical repertoire) were gained by specific analysis of oral re-narrations in L1 and L2. More specifically, the measurement of verbal fluency and lexical repertoire provided an analytical procedure which considered, on the one hand, differences of protosyntactic fillers and true hesitation signals, and, on the other hand, structural differences between languages such as Turkish and German/French. To determine language dominance, we established a statistical method which took the group performances into account and provided a three-tiered language dominance level ("L1-dominance", "no dominance", "L2-dominance").

These methodological aspects contribute to further language dominance research by providing an analytical procedure which generally allows a more detailed comparison between different bilingual groups and of examine the relation between language dominance in domain and dimension.

8.3.2 Motion encoding

By considering not only group averages in the analysis of motion descriptions but also the distribution of the individual performances and the ranges within each bilingual group, the focus of this study was not only on inter-group differences, but also on intra-group differences. The additional qualitative analysis as well as the adoption of individual language dominance patterns allowed a detailed discussion of individual variation which has been mainly neglected in previous motion research. Most of the time, research in the domain of motion was carried out in quantitative comparisons which allow relatively broad generalisations of similarities and differences between groups. Our results indicate that the calculation of z-scores further specified intra-group variation and speakers' individual usage preferences which purely quantitative analyses could not provide. In addition, it was possible to highlight a speakers' variation with respect to the group mean and standard deviation – even though in cases in which a quantitative group comparison indicated no significant differences (and vice versa).

The study could demonstrate the importance of taking quantitative and qualitative measures into account, which not exclusively contributes to methodological aspects in motion research but is suitable for other research fields as well. Notably, when multilingual speakers are under investigation, qualitative measures achieve the characteristics of bilingual speakers' performances which are particularly characterised by inter-individual variation.

While the present study has supplied useful information about bilingual speakers' language dominance patterns, the nature of variation in their motion descriptions as well as methodological refinements, it has several limitations which have to be pointed out. Furthermore, we discuss in the following some directions which future research might go on the basis of our research.

8.4 Limitations and future directions

8.4.1 Limitations in language dominance and early second language acquisition and future directions

First, due to the fact that the operationalisation of language dominance was limited to three categories in domain and dimension in this study, our results only addresses a part of the multidimensional construct of language dominance. Furthermore, the use of questionnaires as a method to assess the bilingual speakers' language use only provides a rough picture of their actual language use. This is due to methodological limitations of this study, which only allowed the gathering of data by self-reports. Our data then may be determined by how the respective speaker wishes to view herself or himself, or limited to her or his temporary impression of language use. In order to present a more accurate assessment of a speakers' language use, as well as of their specific input patterns, future research should include methods which provide more detailed observation. Studies examining the language input and/or the language dominance commonly assess the relative amount of language exposure and language use in more detailed questionnaires (than those used in the present study) and/or with parental diary records or oral interviews. We believe that future investigations on language use and input patterns should go beyond these methods and focus instead on, or in addition to, the direct observation of a child's interactions. However, it is worth noting that the establishment of a high density corpus, which would be required to assess the actual amount of language exposure and language use, is a challenging and difficult undertaking. Particularly with increasing age, it is even more difficult, since a child's interaction is not primarily related to its parents but also to other interlocutors in societal interactions (such as on a playground, in a daycare centre, in a kindergarten, in school, etc.).

Second, since the focus of the Study 2 was on bilingual speakers, differences between minimal bilingual speakers of German, Turkish and French were not studied in detail, and no statistical analyses were provided to determine their extent. We suggested on the basis of a pilot study, which included older Turkish-German bilinguals, that patterns, such as the use of Generic verbs, tend to persist with age (see §7.2.6.2). However, the present study was limited only to one age group; thus it could not provide any further suggestions with regard to the dynamics of bilingualism such as the change of usage preferences and the shift or resistance of language dominance patterns and the interrelation to language development and language attrition. A (pseudo-) longitudinal study could provide insights into these aspects in relation to a possible change of communicative needs and a resulting language dominance change.

8.4.2 Limitations in motion encoding and future directions

First, since the experimental design of the present study is (semi-) controlled, our findings cannot make assumptions about the participants' behaviour in natural situations. A comparison of the speakers' elicited motion verb choices (see §7.2.2.2) and the corpus-based analysis of motion verb usage in corpora providing spontaneous data (in German and French, see §3.2.6.1), revealed that the numbers of Generic verbs such as "to go" or "to come" were different. The fact that they do not represent the most frequent motion verb choice in the speakers' re-narrations indicates that differences between elicited and spontaneous data can not be excluded. However, as regards the frequency of Manner/Manner-Path verbs (see §7.2.2.3), the results do not indicate major differences between spontaneous and experimental data. Future research should examine whether possible differences also account for the other analytical levels: investigations would be promising, particularly in the analytical level of motion verb constructions, by examining systematically the combinations of specific motion verbs (more frequent, less frequent) with particular directional Path devices (telic, atelic) in different languages (S and V) and different modalities (oral, written). Such a collocation based analysis could provide more detailed insights into possible restrictions of Path encoding in the verbal periphery (e.g. the combination of more frequent or less frequent Manner and Path verbs with telic or atelic Path devices) as well as the use of Manner verbs in telic Path phrases. Furthermore, the assumed greater flexibility in Turkish-German bilinguals' usage of Manner verbs (such as in telic Path phrases) due to the influence of the typical pattern of German should be further tested by taking acceptability tests into account. Such tests could provide evidence as regards the assumption that bilingual speakers acquiring a V- and an S- language display a greater tolerance towards constructions which include a Manner verb and a telic Path device (which we found in Turkish written texts such as *içeri koştu* 'it ran inside', see example (54) in §3.2.6.4 and Turkish oral descriptions, such as *içine hopladı* 'it hopped inside/(in)to its interior', see example (193) in §7.2.6.2) than minimal bilingual speakers of the respective V-language.

Second, since non-verbal tests have not been considered in the present study, the effects of the conceptual representation on the linguistic symbolisation of motion images are speculative. Furthermore, no answer to the question of what level of conceptualisation language may be involved and influence the way speakers conceptualise motion events could be provided either. In order to answer these questions, non-verbal tasks examining, for instance, the speakers' recognition or memory for motion and/or eye-movements would be required. However, research in the domain of motion has begun using such methods only recently and evidence for or against the relativistic hypothesis that conceptual processes are language-based in nature (Whorfian hypothesis) or are inter-dependent between conceptualisation and language knowledge (neo-Whorfian view) cannot be provided yet: several studies investigated whether speakers of S-languages pay more attention to Manner compared to speakers of V-languages, when language is not involved, by using recognition or forced-choice similarity judgements (Bohnemeyer, Eisenbeiss & Narasimhan 2006; Cardini 2010; Filipović 2011;

Gennari et al. 2002; Finkbeiner et al. 2002; Papafragou, Massey & Gleitman 2002; Zlatev, Blomberg & David 2010). The results, however, are extremely heterogeneous when speakers committed a motion event to memory and/or compared it to other motion events. While the results of some studies confirm that language-specific patterns have an impact on non-verbal recognition (Filipović 2011), others found a bias in all languages tested (Gennari et al. 2002 found a Path bias; Finkbeiner et al. 2002 found a Manner bias), or no bias (Papafragou, Massey & Gleitman 2002), independently of whether the participants spoke an S- or V-language. Moreover, Bohnemeyer, Eisenbeiss & Narasimhan (2006) did not find a simple categorical V/S-distinction and suggest a continuum in which various V-languages are distributed across the entire scale. The review of these studies indicates that the speakers' performances are less affected by their first language in general but instead by the procedure (whether the stimuli were pre-verbally described or not) and the used stimuli (natural vs. unnatural representation, lower vs. higher cognitive demands, objectivity vs. nonobjectivity). Furthermore, eye-tracking in non-verbal tasks has been considered very recently by a few studies to make assumptions about whether speakers of different languages pay attention to motion differently (Flecken et al. 2015; Flecken, von Stutterheim & Carroll 2014; Papafragou, Hulbert & Trueswell 2008; Soroli & Hickmann 2010; von Stutterheim et al. 2012). The results indicate that the speakers' pre-articulatory attention seems to reflect language-specific properties of the speakers' first languages. However, the validity of these results is limited. Since it is a great challenge to separate Manner and Path when designing a stimulus, eye-tracking can not exactly determine whether a speaker's attention was on the Figure's Manner or Path (Pavlenko 2014: 136).

The overall findings of studies involving non-verbal tasks imply that contradictory or ambiguous assumptions are due to possible methodological problems or differences in the research design. However, according to Pavlenko (2014: 136), the core problem is related instead to the limitations of Talmy's dichotomous typology. Thus, future research on language effects in motion perception and recognition should reconsider Talmy's framework in terms of a discursive continuum (Slobin 2004b), which includes "a range of typological options, where the members of the typological category vary in the degree to which they follow the same typological pattern or somehow deviate from it" (Jovanovic & Martinovic-Zic 2004: 224). When considering lexicalisation patterns as a theoretical framework, the findings of this study clearly give evidence for the need of extensions and refinements within the S- and V-typology by taking intra-typological as well as inter-individual variation in minimal as well as bilingual speakers' encoding of motion events into account.

Appendix

A. Questionnaires

I. *Parental questionnaire (child bilinguals)*

Translation

A General information about the child

1. Name of your child
2. Where was your child born?

   Date............................   in...................................... (city and country)
3. Did your child ever live in a foreign country?

   yes ☐   no ☐

   3.2 If your child lived in a foreign country please indicate the place of residence as well as the year of departure.

   - city/cities:
   - year(s) of departure:

4. Where do you currently live (city/district)?
5. Do other family members live in your neighbourhood?

   If yes, who are they? (multiple answers possible)

   ☐ uncle/aunt ☐ grandparents ☐ others (who?)

   5.2 If yes, how often do you see them ?

   - per week...........................
   - per month..........................
   - per year............................

6. Does your child have other siblings?

   yes ☐   no ☐

   6.2 If yes, how many and in what age?
   - numbers:
   - age?

B Information about the child's languages

7. Did your child attend a kindergarten?

    yes ☐   no ☐

    If yes,

    7.2 what was the language the most spoken to your child in kindergarten?

    ☐ German/French   ☐ Turkish   ☐ other

    7.3 what was the language your child itself most frequently used in kindergarten? (e.g. with friends)

    ☐ German/French   ☐ Turkish   ☐ other

8. Which language did your child acquire first?

    ☐ German/French   ☐ Turkish   ☐ other

9. Was your child exposed to German/French before entering kindergarten?

    yes ☐   no ☐

    9.2 If yes (multiple answers possible)

    ☐ within the family   ☐ with relatives
    ☐ with other children in the neighbourhood or on the playground
    ☐ by television   ☐ other

10. Did your child had problems when learning his or her language(s) (for instance did she/he only speak a few words by age two)?

    yes ☐   no ☐

    10.2 If yes, did your child visit a speech therapist?

    yes ☐   no ☐

11. Does or did your child attend/ed a class where his or her first language is/was instructed?

    yes ☐   no ☐

    If no,

    ☐ no instruction but learned with:

11.2 If yes,

☐ in Germany/France

☐ somewhere else (where?)

11.3 How long does/did she attend the class?

11.4 In which institution is/was the class offered?

☐ In school ☐ other (which?)

11.5 What was the main subject in class? (multiple answers possible)

☐ reading/writing ☐ Turkish culture/history of Turkey, ☐ religion

☐ other? (what subject?)_____

12. Is your child already learning a foreign language?

    If yes,

    12.2 which one?

    12.3 since when?

    12.4 which institution offers the foreign language class?

    ☐ school   ☐ private language class

    12.5 How many hours per week does your child attend the foreign language class?

13. Which language(s) does your child generally speak at home in Germany/France?

    ☐ German/French   ☐ Turkish   ☐ both   ☐ other (which?)

C Information about the parents

	Father	Mother
14. Where were you born (place of birth and country)	14.1	14.2
15. If you were born abroad, at what age did you move to Germany/France	15.1	15.2
16. What is your highest school-leaving (primary/secondary) qualification?	16.1 ☐ none ☐ primary education ☐ lower secondary education ☐ upper secondary education ☐ other	16.2 ☐ none ☐ primary education ☐ lower secondary education ☐ upper secondary education ☐ other
17. In what country did you obtain your highest school-leaving (primary/secondary) qualification?	17.1	17.2
18. What is your highest post-secondary qualification?	18.1 ☐ none ☐ post-secondary non-tertiary education ☐ short-cycle tertiary education ☐ Bachelor or equivalent education ☐ Master or equivalent education ☐ Doctoral or equivalent education ☐ other	18.2 ☐ none ☐ post-secondary non-tertiary education ☐ short-cycle tertiary education ☐ Bachelor or equivalent education ☐ Master or equivalent education ☐ Doctoral or equivalent education ☐ other
19. In what country did you obtain your highest school leaving (primary/secondary) qualification	19.1	19.2

20. When speaking to your child, which language(s) do you use most often?

	At home (20.1)				Outside home (20.2)			
	German	Turkish	both	other (which?)	German	Turkish	both	other (which?)
	☐	☐	☐	☐	☐	☐	☐	☐

21. Does it happen that you mix your languages (e.g. within one sentence)

    yes ☐ no ☐   yes ☐ no ☐

II. Parental questionnaire (minimal bilinguals)

Translation

A   General information about the child

1. Name of your child
2. Where was your child born?

   Date............................   in.................................... (city and country)

3. Did your child ever live in a foreign country?

   yes ☐   no ☐

   3.2 If your child lived in a foreign country please indicate the place of residence as well as the year of departure.

   - city/cities:
   - year(s) of departure:

4. Where do you currently live (city/district)?
5. Does your child have other siblings?

   yes ☐   no ☐

   5.2 If yes, how many and in what age?

   - numbers:
   - age?

B   Information about the child's languages

6. Did your child attend a kindergarten?

   yes ☐   no ☐
   If yes,

   6.2 what was the language the most spoken to your child in kindergarten?

   - ☐ German/French   ☐ other (which?)

   6.3 what was the language your child itself most frequently used in kindergarten? (e.g. with friends)

   - ☐ German/French   ☐ other (which?)

7. Which language did your child acquire first?

   ☐ German/French   ☐ other (which?)

8. Did your child had problems when learning his or her language(s) (for instance did she/he only speak a few words by age two)?

   yes ☐   no ☐

   8.2 If yes, did your child visit a speech therapist?

   yes ☐   no ☐

9. Is your child already learning a foreign language?

   If yes,

   9.2 which one?

   9.3 since when?

   9.4 which institution offers the foreign language class?

   ☐ school   ☐ private language class

   9.5 How many hours per week does your child attend the foreign language class?

C Information about the parents

	Father	Mother
10. Where were you born (place of birth and country)	10.1	10.2
11. If you were born abroad, at what age did you move to Germany/France	11.1	11.2
12. What is your highest school-leaving (primary/secondary) qualification?	12.1 ☐ none ☐ primary education ☐ lower secondary education ☐ upper secondary education ☐ other	12.2 ☐ none ☐ primary education ☐ lower secondary education ☐ upper secondary education ☐ other

		13.1	13.2
13	In what country did you obtain your highest school-leaving (primary/secondary) qualification?		
14.	What is your highest post-secondary qualification?	14.1 ☐ none ☐ post-secondary non-tertiary education ☐ short-cycle tertiary education ☐ Bachelor or equivalent education ☐ Master or equivalent education ☐ Doctoral or equivalent education ☐ other	14.2 ☐ none ☐ post-secondary non-tertiary education ☐ short-cycle tertiary education ☐ Bachelor or equivalent education ☐ Master or equivalent education ☐ Doctoral or equivalent education ☐ other
15.	In what country did you obtain your highest school leaving (primary/secondary) qualification	15.1	15.2

III. Child bilingual questionnaire

Translation

1. What is/are your mother tongue(s)?
2. Do you go on holidays to Turkey with your parents/grandparents/relatives?

   yes ☐   no ☐

   2.2 if yes

   ☐ every year   ☐ once in 2-3 years   ☐ once in 4-5 years

   2.3 Which language(s) do you speak when you are in Turkey?

   ☐ German/French ☐ Turkish ☐ both ☐ other (which?)

3. Which language(s) do you speak generally at home in Germany?

   ☐ German/French ☐ Turkish ☐ both ☐ other (which?)

4. Which language do you most frequently speak with the following persons? Which language does the following person speak most frequently with you?

		at home			
		German/French	Turkish	both	other
4.1.1	you to your mother	☐	☐	☐	☐
4.1.2	your mother with you	☐	☐	☐	☐
4.1.3	you to your father	☐	☐	☐	☐
4.1.4	your father with you	☐	☐	☐	☐
4.1.5	You with your younger siblings	☐	☐	☐	☐
4.1.6	your younger siblings to you	☐	☐	☐	☐
4.1.7	you with your older siblings	☐	☐	☐	☐
4.1.8	your older siblings to you	☐	☐	☐	☐
4.1.9	You to your Turkish speaking friends?	☐	☐	☐	☐
4.1.10	your Turkish speaking friends with you	☐	☐	☐	☐

		outside home			
		German/French	Turkish	both	other
4.2.1	you to your mother	☐	☐	☐	☐
4.2.2	your mother with you	☐	☐	☐	☐

4.2.3 you to your father	☐	☐	☐	☐
4.2.4 your father with you	☐	☐	☐	☐
4.2.5 You with your younger siblings	☐	☐	☐	☐
4.2.6 your younger siblings to you	☐	☐	☐	☐
4.2.7 you with your older siblings	☐	☐	☐	☐
4.2.8 your older siblings to you	☐	☐	☐	☐
4.2.9 You to your Turkish speaking friends?	☐	☐	☐	☐
4.2.10 your Turkish speaking friends with you	☐	☐	☐	☐

5. Would you say that you speak the following languages…:

5.1 German/ French	☐ very well	☐ well	☐ I get along	☐ poorly	☐ not at all
5.2 Turkish	☐ very well	☐ well	☐ I get along	☐ poorly	☐ not at all
5.3 other: _____	☐ very well	☐ well	☐ I get along	☐ poorly	☐ not at all

6. Would you say that you write the following languages…:

6.1 German/ French	☐ very well	☐ well	☐ I get along	☐ poorly	☐ not at all
6.2 Turkish	☐ very well	☐ well	☐ I get along	☐ poorly	☐ not at all
6.3 other: _____	☐ very well	☐ well	☐ I get along	☐ poorly	☐ not at all

7. Would you say that you read the following languages…:

7.1 German/ French	☐ very well	☐ well	☐ I get along	☐ poorly	☐ not at all
7.2 Turkish	☐ very well	☐ well	☐ I get along	☐ poorly	☐ not at all
7.3 other: _____	☐ very well	☐ well	☐ I get along	☐ poorly	☐ not at all

8. Would you say that you understand the following languages...:

8.1 German/ French	☐ very well	☐ well	☐ I get along	☐ poorly	☐ not at all
8.2 Turkish	☐ very well	☐ well	☐ I get along	☐ poorly	☐ not at all
8.3 other: _____	☐ very well	☐ well	☐ I get along	☐ poorly	☐ not at all

9. Do you watch TV and/or videos on the internet?

If yes, do you do this in	9.1 German/French	☐ often	☐ sometimes	☐ never
	9.2 Turkish	☐ often	☐ sometimes	☐ never
	9.3 English: _____	☐ often	☐ sometimes	☐ never
	9.4 other: _____	☐ often	☐ sometimes	☐ never

10. Do you listen to the radio (music, news...)?

yes ☐   no ☐

If yes, do you do this in	10.1 German/French	☐ often	☐ sometimes	☐ never
	10.2 Turkish	☐ often	☐ sometimes	☐ never
	10.3 English: _____	☐ often	☐ sometimes	☐ never
	10.4 other: _____	☐ often	☐ sometimes	☐ never

11. Do you have a PC or Laptop at home?

yes ☐   no ☐

If yes, do you do this in	11.1 German/French	☐ often	☐ sometimes	☐ never
	11.2 Turkish	☐ often	☐ sometimes	☐ never
	11.3 English: _____	☐ often	☐ sometimes	☐ never
	11.4 other: _____	☐ often	☐ sometimes	☐ never

12. Do you listen to music, do you do this in German/French?

    yes ☐   no ☐

    12.2 If yes, do you use it for

    ☐ playing games   ☐ doing homework   ☐ surfing in the internet (facebook, twitter...) ☐ chatting with friends (skype, facebook...) ☐ writing emails   ☐ other

    12.3 When writing on a PC/Laptop in which language(s) do you write?

German	☐ often	☐ sometimes	☐ never
Turkish	☐ often	☐ sometimes	☐ never
English	☐ often	☐ sometimes	☐ never
Other:	☐ often	☐ sometimes	☐ never

13. Do you have a mobile phone ?

    yes ☐   no ☐

    13.2 If yes in which language(s) do you write messages with your Turkish speaking friends?

German	☐ often	☐ sometimes	☐ never
Turkish	☐ often	☐ sometimes	☐ never
English	☐ often	☐ sometimes	☐ never
Other	☐ often	☐ sometimes	☐ never

14. Does it happen that you mix your languages when writing messages?

    yes ☐   no ☐

    14.2 If yes, does it happen

    ☐ rarely   ☐ often

15. Do you read newspapers, magazines, or journals?

    yes ☐   no ☐

If yes, do you do this in	15.2.1 German/ French	☐ often	☐ sometimes	☐ never
	15.2.2 Turkish	☐ often	☐ sometimes	☐ never
	15.2.3 English: _____	☐ often	☐ sometimes	☐ never
	15.2.4 other: _____	☐ often	☐ sometimes	☐ never

16. Do you read books?

    yes ☐   no ☐

If yes, do you do this in	16.2.1 German/ French	☐ often	☐ sometimes	☐ never
	16.2.2 Turkish	☐ often	☐ sometimes	☐ never
	16.2.3 English: _____	☐ often	☐ sometimes	☐ never
	16.2.4 other: _____	☐ often	☐ sometimes	☐ never

If you read, what do you prefer?

☐ novels (e.g.?)   ☐ science-fiction (e.g.?)   ☐ fantasy (e.g.?)
☐ stories   ☐ tales   ☐ comics   ☐ other:

17. Did your parents, grandparents or relatives read to you?

    yes ☐   no ☐

18. In which language(s) do you feel most secure...

	German	Turkish	both	other
18.1 when reading	☐	☐	☐	☐
18.2 when using the PC/laptop	☐	☐	☐	☐
18.3 when using a mobile phone	☐	☐	☐	☐
18.4 when working in a group at school	☐	☐	☐	☐

B. Methodology

I. Data collection: Instruction

Translation

The data collection will be made as follows:
1. Eight short sequences of the cartoon "Sylvester and Tweety" will be shown successively to the child. The child will be asked to retell precisely what it saw in each video sequence. Everything will be recorded with the voice recorder.
Introduction: "You will now watch some videos, which I don't know. When the video is finished, I'd like you to tell me exactly what happened. Please watch carefully, since I don't know the videos and I am not going to watch them with you. I will record everything. Please tell me now your first and last name" (begin the recording).
Note: If the child asks you for vocabulary (e.g. drain pipe), you are allowed to help with nouns, but never with verbs.
2. Short videos (totally 20 of 5–10 seconds), which show different motion scenes, are shown to the child. The child is instructed to watch the videos carefully and say after every video what the figure was doing.
Introduction: "You will watch some more videos and I'd like you to tell me what the person is doing. I will record everything again. Please tell me now your first and last name" (begin the recording).
Note: if the child asks for help, tell him or her: "If you don't know, try to describe it in other words". In cases when the child does not say anything, ask again: "What is the person doing?"
3. Start with the questionnaire by reading the questions to the child. Note down his or her answers. Again this task will be recorded, since the child answers verbally.
After having finished all the three tasks, thank the child for his or her participation.

[Translation, TW]

a. German

Die Erhebung erfolgt folgendermaßen:
    Acht kurze Videos aus dem Cartoon „Sylvester & Tweety" werden dem Kind nacheinander gezeigt. Das Kind wird aufgefordert nach jedem Video möglichst

genau zu erzählen, was passiert ist. Alles wird mit dem Aufnahmegerät aufgezeichnet.

Einführung: „Du wirst nun einige Videos, die ich nicht kenne, sehen. Ich bitte Dich, mir möglichst genau zu erzählen, was in den Videos passiert. Ich werde alles aufnehmen und bitte Dich jetzt Deinen Vor- und Nachnamen zu sagen." (Mit der Aufnahme beginnen)

Bemerkung: Falls das Kind nach Vokabeln fragt (z.B. Regenrohr) darfst Du ihm nur bei Nomen helfen, nicht aber bei Verben.

Kurze Videos (insg. 20, je 5 bis 10 Sekunden), die verschiedene Bewegungssituationen darstellen, werden dem Kind gezeigt. Das Kind soll diese kurz mündlich kommentieren.

Einführung: „Du wirst nun weitere Videos sehen und du sollst mir jedes mal sagen, was die Person macht. Ich werde alles aufnehmen und bitte Dich jetzt Deinen Vor- und Nachnamen zu sagen." (Mit der Aufnahme beginnen)

Bemerkung: Falls das Kind nach Hilfe fragt, antworte ihm: „Wenn Du es nicht weißt, versuche es zu umschreiben." Falls das Kind während der Präsentation schweigt, halte die Videos an und frage erneut: „Was macht die Person?"

Beginne nun mit dem Fragebogen, indem Du dem Kind die Fragen laut vorliest und die Antworten im Fragebogen entsprechend ankreuzt oder notierst. Auch dieser Task wird mit dem Aufnahmegerät aufgenommen, da das Kind mündlich antwortet.

Wenn die Tasks beendet sind, bedanke Dich bei dem Kind!

b. Turkish

Bu veri toplama çalışması aşağıda açıklandığı, gibi olacaktır:
1. Sylvester & Tweety çizgi filminden alıntı 8 kısa video birbiri ardına gösterilecektir. Her bir video gösterildikten sonra, öğrencilerden videoda geçenleri tam olarak anlatmaları istenecektir.
    Giriş: "Şimdi sana benim hiç bilmediğim bazı videolar göstereceğim. Bu videoları izledikten sonra, senden bana bu videolarda tam olarak neler olduğunu anlatmanı istiyorum. Şimdi her şeyi kaydedeceğim. Senden ismini ve soy ismini söylemeni rica ediyorum." (Kayıta başlama)
    Not: Eğer öğrenciler sana bilmedikleri kelimeleri sorarlarsa (ör. Su borusu), sadece isimleri söyleyebilirsin, fiilleri (ör. sallanmak) kesinlikle söyleme!
2. Öğrencilere farklı hareket durumlarını gösteren kısa videolar gösterilecektir. Öğrencilerden bu videoların içeriğini tanımlamaları istenecektir.

Giriş: "Şimdi daha farklı videolar izleyeceksin. Bana her seferinde videodaki figürün ne yaptığını söylemelisin. Şimdi her şeyi kaydedeceğim. Senden ismini ve soy ismini söylemeni rica ediyorum." (Kayıta başlama)
Not: Eğer öğrencinin yardıma ihtiyacı varsa: "Eğer bilmiyorsan, anlatmaya çalış" deyin. Eğer öğrenci birden susup konuşmazsa, videoyu durdurup tekrardan "O ne yapıyor" diye sorun.
Her iki görev de bittikten sonra katılımcılara teşekkür edin.

c. French

La collecte se déroulera de la manière suivante:

Huit courtes séquences vidéo extraites du dessin animé « Titi et Grosminet » seront montrées aux élèves et ils seront tenus de les raconter oralement en français. Tout/La production sera enregistrée.

Instructions: « Tu vas regarder quelques vidéos que je n'ai jamais vues, et tu devras ensuite me raconter précisément ce qui s'est passé dans le film. Je vais t'enregistrer et tu diras au début ton prénom et ton nom s'il te plait ». (Commencer l'enregistrement)

NB. Lorsque l'enfant demande du vocabulaire (par exemple, la gouttière), tu peux le lui dire mais seulement lorsqu'il s'agit de noms, en aucun cas des verbes.

Des courtes séquences vidéo (20 de 5 à 10 secondes) montrant différentes situations de mouvement) seront montrées aux sujets et ils seront tenus de les commenter oralement en français.

Instructions: « Tu vas regarder d'autres séquences de vidéos, et tu devras me dire à chaque fois ce que fait le personnage. Je vais t'enregistrer et tu diras au début ton prénom et ton nom s'il te plait ». (Commencer l'enregistrement)

NB. Lorsque l'enfant demande de l'aide, on lui répond, « si tu ne le sais pas, essaie de le dire autrement ». Si pendant la passation le silence se poursuit, on arrête/interrompt les séquences vidéo et on demande à l'enfant « Qu'est-ce qu'il fait? ».

Remplir le questionnaire en lisant les questions à l'enfant et en cochant ou écrivant les réponses. Cette séquence doit aussi être enregistrée puisque l'enfant répond aux questions oralement.

Une fois les trois phases effectuées, on remercie l'enfant.

II. Annotation tag-set for EXMARaLDA transcripts

Table 106: Annotation specifics for coding the Voluntary Motion Task.

Category	Specific annotation	Example
Type of event [EVENT]	AB	Locative Path phrases where the Figure's displacement is away from a Ground, such as *Sie ist ganz schnell weggegangen*; *Elle a quitté la maison*; *Yerden gidiyor*
	AD	Locative Path phrases where the Figure's displacement is to a Ground, such as *Sie ist da hingegangen*; *Elle roule jusqu' à la salle de bowling*; *Onun yanına gitti*
	DE	Locative Path phrases where the Figure's displacement is downward, such as *Sie ist runtergefallen*; *Elle descends une colline*; *Üzerine düştü*
	EX	Telic Path phrases where the Figure's displacement is out of a Ground, such as *Sie ist rausgeflogen*; *Elle sort de sa cage*; *Kafesten çıkıyor*
	GENERALIS	Locative Path phrases where the Figure's displacement is not further specified, such as *Sie balanciert*; *Elle glisse*; *Kaydı*
	IN	Telic Path phrases where the Figure's displacement is into a Ground, such as *Sie ist reingeflogen*; *Elle est rentré là-dedans*; *Yere girdi*;
	PRAETER	Telic Path phrases where the Figure 's displacement is a passing by a Ground, such as *Sie ist an den Kegeln vorbeigerollt*;
	PRO	Telic Path phrases were the Figure's displacement is through a Ground, such as *Sie ist durch die Hunde gelaufen*; *Elle s'est faufilé entre les chiens*; *Borunun içinden geçmeye çalıştı*
	SUPER	Locative Path phrases where the Figure's displacement is upward, such as *Sie ist hoch geklettert*; *Elle monte à la gouttière*; *Üstüne bindi*
	TRANS	Telic Path phrases where the Figure's displacement is over a Ground such as *Sie ist rüber balanciert*; *Elle essaye de traverser*; *Karşıya geçmeği çalıştı*
Motion verb choice [VCONF]	VM	A Manner verb, such as *rennen, courir, koşmak* etc.
	VP	A Path verb, such as *sich begeben; entrer; girmek* etc.
	VMP	A Manner-Path verb, such as *fallen; grimper; tırmanmak* etc.

(continued)

Table 106 (continued)

Category	Specific annotation	Example
	VGEN	A Generic motion verb, such as *gehen*; *aller*; *gitmek* etc.
	VMOD	A modal verb, non-motion verb (which is used in motion description), such as *wollen*, *beginnen*; *vouloir*, *commencer*; *istemek*, *başlamak* etc.
	VAUX	An auxiliary verb (which is used in motion description), such as *sein*
	VLV	A semantically weak verb used in other motion constructions, such as *machen*; *faire*; *yapmak*
Linguistic device [LINGDEV]	PART	(separable) Path particles, such as *hoch*; *dehors*; *dedans* 'inside';
	PREF	(inseparable) Path prefixes, such as *um-*; *em-/en-*; *dé(s)-* etc.
	PP	Prepositional phrases (associated with a motion verb), such as *in das Haus*; *à la maison* etc.;
	POSTCASE	Postpositional case marking (dative/ablative) associated with a motion verb, such as *ev-e/ev-den*;
	POSTPOS	Postpositions associated with a motion verb, such as *doğru* etc.;
	ADV_DIR	Directional adverbials specifying the source and/or goal of Motion, such as *dışarı* 'outwards'; *içeri* 'inside'; *yukarı* 'upwards'; *aşağı* 'downwards';
	ADV_P	Adverbs/double particles specifying Path, such as *rein*, *raus*, *runter*; *en bas*;
	ADV_M	Adverbs specifying Manner, such as *schnell*; *rapidement*; *çabuk* etc.;
	OTHER_P	Other Path devices such as *weiter*
	OTHER_M	Other Manner devices, which do not encode Manner directly, such as *auf Zehnenspitzen*; *comme une liane*; *bisiklet gibi*;
	CONV_M	Manner/Manner-Path converbs, such as *koşarak*, *koşa koşa* etc.;
	CONV_P	Path converbs, such as *çıkarak* etc.
	GERUND_M	Manner/Manner-Path participles/gerunds, such as *rennend*; *en courant* etc.;
	GERUND_P	Path participles/gerunds, such as *verlassend*; *en traversant* etc.;

Table 106 (continued)

Category	Specific annotation	Example
Motion verb construction [VCONST]	VM_P	A Manner verb construction with Path device, such as *Sie rennt rein*; *Elle court après lui*; *Aşağı doğru koştu* etc.;
	VP_P	A Path verb construction with Path device, such as *Er verschwindet in das Haus*; *Elle entre dans la maison*; *iceriye girdi* etc.
	VMP_P	A Manner-Path verb construction with Path device, such as *Er klettert hoch*, *Elle grimpe jusqu'à la fenêtre*, *aşağıya tırmanıyor* etc.;
	VGEN_P	A Generic verb construction with Path device, such as *Sie geht in das Haus*, *Elle va chez lui*, *Eve gitti* etc.;
	VM_M	A Manner verb construction with Manner device, such as *Sie rennt schnell in das Haus*; *Elle marche lentement*, *Zıplaya zıplaya yuvarlanıyor*;
	VP_M	A Path verb construction with Manner device, such as *Sie verlässt schnell das Haus*; *Elle entre en courant*; *Koşarak eve girdi* etc.;
	VGEN_M	A Generic verb construction with Manner device, such as *Sie geht schnell*, *Elle va à quatre pied*, *Çabuk gitti*;
	VM_0	A bare Manner verb construction w/o Manner/Path device, such as *Sie rennt*, *Elle court*, *koştu* etc.;
	VP_0	A bare Path verb construction w/o Manner/Path device, such as *Sie verschwindet*, *Elle entre*, *Girdi* etc.;
	VMP_0	A bare Manner-Path verb construction w/o Manner/Path device, such as *Sie klettert*, *Elle grimpe*, *Tırmanıyor* etc.;
	VGEN_0	A bare Generic verb construction w/o Manner/Path device, such as *Sie kommt*; *Elle vient*; *Geliyor*;
	VM_P_M	A Manner verb construction with Path and Manner device, such as *Sie ist ganz schnell herum gelaufen*;
	VP_P_P	A Path verb construction with directional Path device and Path converb, such as *Inerek aşağı ordan suya indi*;
	VGEN_P_M	A Generic verb construction with directional Path and Manner device, such as *Sie ist auf Zehenspitzen über die Hunde gegangen*; *Içeriye uçarak gidiyor*;
	VAUX_P	An (non-motion verb) auxiliary verb construction with Path device, such as *Er ist rein*;

(continued)

Table 106 (continued)

Category	Specific annotation		Example
	VAUX_P_M		A (non-motion verb) auxiliary verb construction with directional Path and Manner device, such as *Der kater ist ganz schnell hinterher*;
	VMOD_P		A (non-motion verb) modal verb construction with directional Path device, such as *Er will rein*;
	VMOD_	VM VM_P VP VP_P etc.	A modal verb construction with, for instance, a bare Manner verb (such as *Sie will klettern*), a Manner verb+directional Path device (such as *Sie will reinrennen; Elle veut courir en bas; Duvara kadar sallanmak istiyor*) etc. (see description of construction types above);
	VSC_	VM_P VGEN VM etc.	A subordinate construction with, for instance, a Manner verb+directional Path device, such as *Sie sieht wie er hin und her läuft*, a bare Generic verb, such as *Gördü geldiğini*, a bare Manner verb, such as *Il ya un oiseau qui se balance* etc. (see description of construction types above);
	VCONV_	(V)P_P (V)M_0 (V)M_P (V)GEN_0 etc.	A converb construction with, for instance, a Path converb+directional Path device, such as *silvester aşağa inip*;
	VLV_M		A motion construction with semantically weak verbs which encodes Manner, such as *Sie spielt Tarzan; Elle a fait de la balançoire*;
Path elaboration [ELAB]	GROUND_0		A motion verb construction with a Path, Manner or Generic verb and no directional Path device, such as *Sie fällt; Elle tombe; Düşüyor*;
	GROUND_1		A motion verb construction with a Path, Manner or Generic verb and one directional Path device, such as *Sie fällt runter; Elle tombe en bas; Pencereden düşüyor*;
	GROUND_2+		A motion verb construction with a Path, Manner or Generic verb and two (or more) directional Path devices, such as *Sie fällt von dem Fenster herunter; Elle s'envole de la cage; Pencereden aşağı düşüyor.*

Note: The table only provides information about the annotation specifics of linguistic devices and constructions which at least were found once in the corpus. Whenever an example in a respective language is not indicated, this means that this device or construction was not used by speakers of that language.

III. Coding method of questionnaires

a. Parental questionnaires (child bilinguals)

Table 107: Coding method of questionnaires for parents of bilingual participants.

Questionnaire no.	Coding	Category
QBILPAR2	1=Germany/France; 2=Turkey; 3=other country	Biography child
QBILPAR3.2	0=no; 1=Turkey; 2=other country	Biography child
QBILPAR3.3	1=<1 year; 2=1–2 years; 3=2–3 years; 4=3–4 years; 5=>4 years	Biography child
QBILPAR7.1	0=no; 1=yes	Language acquisition
QBILPAR7.2	1=German/French; 2=both; 3=Turkish; 4=other	Language acquisition
QBILPAR7.3	1=German/French; 2=both; 3=Turkish; 4=other	Language acquisition
QBILPAR8	1=German/French; 2=both; 3=Turkish; 4=other	Language acquisition
QBILPAR9.2	0=nobody; 1=one; 2=two; 3=three; 4= four; 5 =all	Language acquisition
QBILPAR10.2	0=no; 1=yes; 2=yes, with specialist; 3=yes, without specialist	Language acquisition
QBILPAR11.2	0=no; 1=no, learned with someone else; 2=yes in GER/FR/other country; 3=yes in Turkey	Language acquisition
QBILPAR11.3	0=no; 1=1 year; 2=2 years; 3=3 years; 4= 4years; 5=5+ years	Language acquisition
QBILPAR11.4	0=no; 1=private; 2=mosque/school; 3=bilingual education in school	Language acquisition
QBILPAR11.5	1=one; 2=two;3=three;4=four	Language acquisition
QBILPAR12.2	0=no; 1=English; 2=other	Language acquisition
QBILPAR12.3	0=none;1= < one year; 2=1–2 years; 3=2–3 years; 4=3–4 years	Language acquisition
QBILPAR12.4	0=none; 1=school; 2= language class	Language acquisition
QBILPAR12.5	0=none;1=1–2 hours per week;2=2–3 hours per week; 3=3–4 hours per week	Language acquisition
QBILPAR14.1	1=Germany/France; 2=Turkey; 3=other country	Biography parents
QBILPAR14.2	1=Germany/France; 2=Turkey; 3=other country	Biography parents
QBILPAR15.1	0=no;1=<5 years; 2=5–10 years;3=>10–15 years;4= 15–20 years; 5=>20 years	Biography parents
QBILPAR15.2	0=no;1=<5 years; 2=5–10 years;3=>10–15 years;4= 15–20 years; 5=>20 years	Biography parents
QBILPAR16.1	0=level 0; 1=level 1; 2= level 2; 3=level 3	Education parents
QBILPAR16.2	0=level 0; 1=level 1; 2= level 2; 3=level 3	Education parents
QBILPAR17.1	1=Germany/France; 2=Turkey; 3=other country	Education parents
QBILPAR17.2	1=Germany/France; 2=Turkey; 3=other country	Education parents
QBILPAR18.1	0=no; 4=level 4; 5=level 5; 6=level 6; 7=level 7; 8=level 8	Education parents

(continued)

Table 107 (continued)

Questionnaire no.	Coding	Category
QBILPAR18.2	0=no; 4=level 4; 5=level 5; 6=level 6; 7=level 7; 8=level 8	Education parents
QBILPAR19.1	1=Germany/France; 2=Turkey; 3=other country	Education parents
QBILPAR19.2	1=Germany/France; 2=Turkey; 3=other country	Education parents

b. Parental questionnaires (minimal bilinguals)

Questionnaire no.	Coding	Category
QMONOPAR2	1=Germany/France/Turkey; 2=other country	Biography child
QMONOPAR3.1	0=no; 1=yes	Biography child
QMONOPAR3.2	1=<1 year; 2=1-2 years; 3=2-3 years; 4=3-4 years; 5=>4 years	Biography child
QMONOPAR6.1	0=no; 1=yes	Language acquisition
QMONOPAR6.2	1=German/French/Turkish; 2=other	Language acquisition
QMONOPAR6.3	1=German/French/Turkish; 2=other	Language acquisition
QMONOPAR7	1=German/French/Turkish; 2=other	Language acquisition
QMONOPAR8	0=no; 1=yes; 2=yes, with specialist; 3=yes, without specialist	Language acquisition
QMONOPAR9.1	0=no; 1=English; 2=other	Language acquisition
QMONOPAR9.2	0=none; 1= < one year; 2=1-2 years; 3=2-3 years; 4=3-4 years	Language acquisition
QMONOPAR9.3	0=none; 1=school; 2= language class	Language acquisition
QMONOPAR9.4	0=none; 1=1-2 hours per week; 2=2-3 hours per week; 3=3-4 hours per week	Language acquisition
QMONOPAR10.1	1=Germany/France/Turkey; 2=other country	Biography parents
QMONOPAR10.2	1=Germany/France/Turkey; 2=other country	Biography parents
QMONOPAR11.1	0=no; 1=<5 years; 2=5-10 years; 3=>10-15 years; 4= 15-20 years; 5=>20 years	Biography parents
QMONOPAR11.2	0=no; 1=<5 years; 2=5-10 years; 3=>10-15 years; 4= 15-20 years; 5=>20 years	Biography parents
QMONOPAR12.1	0=level 0; 1=level 1; 2= level 2; 3=level 3	Education parents
QMONOPAR12.2	0=level 0; 1=level 1; 2= level 2; 3=level 3	Education parents
QMONOPAR13.1	1=Germany/France/Turkey; 2=other country	Education parents
QMONOPAR13.2	1=Germany/France/Turkey; 2=other country	Education parents
QMONOPAR14.1	0=no; 4=level 4; 5=level 5; 6=level 6; 7=level 7; 8=level 8	Education parents
QMONOPAR14.2	0=no; 4=level 4; 5=level 5; 6=level 6; 7=level 7; 8=level 8	Education parents
QMONOPAR15.1	1=Germany/France/Turkey; 2=other country	Education parents
QMONOPAR15.2	1=Germany/France/Turkey; 2=other country	Education parents

c. Child bilingual questionnaires

Questionnaire no.	Coding	Variable
QBIL4.1.1	1=German/French;2=both;3=Turkish;4=other	Domain language use with parents
QBIL4.1.2	1=German/French;2=both;3=Turkish;4=other	Domain language use with parents
QBIL4.1.3	1=German/French;2=both;3=Turkish;4=other	Domain language use with parents
QBIL4.1.4	1=German/French;2=both;3=Turkish;4=other	Domain language use with parents
QBIL4.1.5	1=German/French;2=both;3=Turkish;4=other	Domain language use with siblings/peers
QBIL4.1.6	1=German/French;2=both;3=Turkish;4=other	Domain language use with siblings/peers
QBIL4.1.7	1=German/French;2=both;3=Turkish;4=other	Domain language use with siblings/peers
QBIL4.1.8	1=German/French;2=both;3=Turkish;4=other	Domain language use with siblings/peers
QBIL4.1.9	1=German/French;2=both;3=Turkish;4=other	Domain language use with siblings/peers
QBIL4.1.10	1=German/French;2=both;3=Turkish;4=other	Domain language use with siblings/peers
QBIL4.2.1	1=German/French;2=both;3=Turkish;4=other	Domain language use with parents
QBIL4.2.2	1=German/French;2=both;3=Turkish;4=other	Domain language use with parents
QBIL4.2.3	1=German/French;2=both;3=Turkish;4=other	Domain language use with parents
QBIL4.2.4	1=German/French;2=both;3=Turkish;4=other	Domain language use with parents
QBIL4.2.5	1=German/French;2=both;3=Turkish;4=other	Domain language use with siblings/peers
QBIL4.2.6	1=German/French;2=both;3=Turkish;4=other	Domain language use with siblings/peers
QBIL4.2.7	1=German/French;2=both;3=Turkish;4=other	Domain language use with siblings/peers
QBIL4.2.8	1=German/French;2=both;3=Turkish;4=other	Domain language use with siblings/peers
QBIL4.2.9	1=German/French;2=both;3=Turkish;4=other	Domain language use with siblings/peers
QBIL4.2.10	1=German/French;2=both;3=Turkish;4=other	Domain language use with siblings/peers
QBIL9.1	0=never; 1=sometimes; 2=often	Domain reading activities/media

(continued)

(continued)

Questionnaire no.	Coding	Variable
QBIL9.2	0=never; 1=sometimes; 2=often	Domain reading activities/media
QBIL11.1	0=never; 1=sometimes; 2=often	Domain reading activities/media
QBIL11.2	0=never; 1=sometimes; 2=often	Domain reading activities/media
QBIL15.2.1	0=never; 1=sometimes; 2=often	Domain reading activities/media
QBIL15.2.2	0=never; 1=sometimes; 2=often	Domain reading activities/media
QBIL16.2.1	0=never; 1=sometimes; 2=often	Domain reading activities/media
QBIL16.2.2	0=never; 1=sometimes; 2=often	Domain reading activities/media

C. Results

I. Language dominance

Table 108: Summary of combinations of fine "L1-dominance" (3), "L2-dominance" (1), "no dominance" (2) patterns in domain and dimension of Turkish-German (TURGER) and Turkish-French (TURFRE) bilinguals.

Speaker	Group	Domain			Dimension		
		parents	siblings/ peers	media/ reading	TpL	Verbal fluency	Code Mixing
Alisa	TURGER	3	1	2	3	1	1
Beren	TURGER	1	1	1	1	1	1
Dana	TURGER	3	2	2	2	1	2
Eda	TURGER	3	1	1	1	3	1
Ela	TURGER	3	1	2	2	1	2
Esna	TURGER	3	2	3	2	2	1
Gamze	TURGER	3	1	1	3	1	1
Kurt	TURGER	3	2	1	2	2	2
Melis	TURGER	3	2	3	3	3	3
Ozan	TURGER	2	1	1	2	1	1
Sefar	TURGER	3	2	2	2	3	2
Serkan	TURGER	3	2	3	2	2	1
Taylan	TURGER	3	2	3	1	2	2
Tuba	TURGER	3	1	1	2	2	3
Yigit	TURGER	1	2	2	1	1	1
Adile	TURFRE	3	2	2	2	1	2
Arda	TURFRE	2	2	1	1	1	2
Bircan	TURFRE	2	1	3	2	2	2
Devin	TURFRE	1	1	1	1	1	2
Dilşah	TURFRE	3	1	1	1	3	1
Emre	TURFRE	2	1	1	2	2	2
Geza	TURFRE	3	1	1	1	2	1
Gözde	TURFRE	3	2	1	2	3	2
Maide	TURFRE	3	2	1	1	2	2
Mert	TURFRE	2	1	1	2	2	2
Nezihe	TURFRE	2	1	1	1	1	2

(continued)

Table 108 (continued)

Speaker	Group	Domain			Dimension		
		parents	siblings/peers	media/reading	TpL	Verbal fluency	Code Mixing
Nihal	TURFRE	2	2	2	1	2	2
Özgür	TURFRE	1	1	1	1	2	2
Seçkin	TURFRE	2	1	1	2	2	2
Shirin	TURFRE	2	2	2	2	3	1

Table 109: Summary of combinations of global "L1-dominance" (L1), "L2-dominance" (L2), "no dominance" (no) and mixed dominance (mixed) patterns in domain and dimension of Turkish-German (TURGER) and Turkish-French (TURFRE) bilinguals.

Dominance		TURGER	TURFRE
Domain	Dimension		
L1	L1	1 (Melis)	/
L1	no	2 (Esna, Serkan, Taylan)	/
no	no	2 (Dana, Sefar)	2 (Adile, Nihal)
no	L2	1 (Yiğit)	1 (Arda)
L2	L2	4 (Beren, Eda, Gamze, Ozan)	4 (Dilşah, Geza, Nezihe, Devin)
L2	no	1 (Tuba)	4 (Mert, Emre, Seçkin, Özgür)
no	mixed	/	1 (Shirin)
mixed	no	2 (Ela, Kurt)	3 (Gözde, Maide, Bircan)
mixed	L2	1 (Alisa)	/

II. Manner Verb Control Task

Table 110: Proportion of Turkish motion verb lemmas in Manner Verb Control Task of Turkish-German (TURGER), Turkish-French (TURFRE) bilinguals and Turkish minimal bilinguals (TUR) (in %).

LEMMA	Turkish		
	TURGER	TURFRE	TUR
atlamak	11.56	8.16	15.23
yürümek	11.56	9.52	8.61
koşmak	9.52	10.20	9.27

(continued)

Table 110 (continued)

LEMMA	Turkish		
	TURGER	TURFRE	TUR
düşmek	10.20	8.84	9.27
uçmak	8.84	8.84	9.27
zıplamak	9.52	10.88	6.62
tırmanmak	6.12	6.12	8.61
yuvarlanmak	6.80	5.44	8.61
girmek	2.72	4.08	7.28
hoplamak	6.80	7.48	0.00
gitmek	6.12	2.72	3.97
binmek	4.08	0.68	1.32
çıkmak	1.36	4.08	0.66
dönmek	0.68	4.76	0.00
geçmek	0.68	2.04	2.65
sallanmak	2.04	0.68	1.99
inmek	0.00	0.00	3.31
emeklemek	0.68	0.68	0.66
gezmek	0.00	2.04	0.00
sürünmek	0.68	0.68	0.00
takla atmak	0.00	0.00	1.32
dalmak	0.00	0.68	0.00
denge durmak	0.00	0.00	0.66
denge sağlamak	0.00	0.00	0.66
denge tutmak	0.00	0.68	0.00
tarzan yapmak	0.00	0.68	0.00
TOTAL (in numbers)	147	147	151

Table 111: Proportion of German motion verb lemmas in Manner Verb Control Task of Turkish-German (TURGER) and German minimal bilinguals (GER) (in %).

LEMMA	German	
	TURGER	GER
springen	21.60	17.79
klettern	9.26	9.82
fliegen	9.26	8.59

(continued)

Table 111 (continued)

LEMMA	German	
	TURGER	GER
rennen	9.88	7.98
rollen	8.64	8.59
schleichen	8.64	7.98
balancieren	7.41	8.59
fallen	8.02	6.13
schwingen	3.70	6.75
krabbeln	4.32	3.68
kriechen	2.47	2.45
gehen	3.70	0.61
laufen	1.85	2.45
rutschen	0.62	1.84
Salto machen	0.00	1.84
hüpfen	0.00	1.23
auf allen Vieren gehen	0.00	0.61
fahren	0.00	0.61
gleiten	0.00	0.61
kullern	0.00	0.61
schaukeln	0.00	0.61
steigen	0.00	0.61
wälzen	0.62	0.00
TOTAL (in numbers)	163	162

Table 112: Proportion of French motion verb lemmas in Manner Verb Control Task of Turkish-French (TURFRE) and French minimal bilinguals (FRE) (in %).

LEMMA	French	
	TURFRE	FRE
sauter	24.50	17.93
marcher	10.60	12.41
courir	9.93	9.66
tomber	9.93	9.66
rouler	8.61	8.97
voler	9.27	7.59

(continued)

Table 112 (continued)

LEMMA	French	
	TURFRE	FRE
grimper	5.96	9.66
faire X	5.30	6.90
monter	4.64	0.00
se mettre X	1.99	2.76
aller	1.32	2.76
descendre	0.66	2.76
passer	1.32	2.07
plonger	2.65	0.69
se balancer	0.00	3.45
entrer	0.00	1.38
rentrer	1.32	0.00
tenir l'équilibre	0.00	1.38
avancer	0.66	0.00
partir	0.66	0.00
rester en équilibre	0.66	0.00
TOTAL (in numbers)	151	145

III. Voluntary Motion Task

Table 113: Proportion of Turkish motion verb lemmas in Voluntary Motion Task of Turkish-German (TURGER), Turkish-French (TURFRE) bilinguals and Turkish minimal bilinguals (TUR) (in %).

LEMMA	Turkish		
	TURGER	TURFRE	TUR
girmek	17.54	17.42	14.24
gitmek	16.02	17.28	12.59
çıkmak	12.72	5.37	7.18
düşmek	5.32	9.00	9.86
binmek	2.45	12.35	3.65
gelmek	7.76	5.48	5.12
sallanmak	4.44	5.50	5.01
geçmek	4.19	2.63	6.24

(continued)

Table 113 (continued)

LEMMA	Turkish		
	TURGER	TURFRE	TUR
yakalamak	1.21	5.93	4.80
kaçmak	3.36	2.61	5.76
tırmanmak	1.90	3.78	5.49
yürümek	4.48	1.91	3.40
inmek	1.51	1.59	4.51
yuvarlanmak	3.45	0.83	1.71
koşmak	3.72	1.07	1.21
sürmek	2.83	1.17	1.34
kovalamak	0.33	0.44	3.59
uçmak	1.75	0.37	0.29
atlamak	0.81	0.66	0.74
dönmek	0.29	0.96	0.83
yüzmek	1.55		0.26
yapmak X		1.53	
fırlamak	0.83		0.39
kaymak	0.37	0.79	
kovmak		0.62	0.35
hoplamak	0.87		
takip etmek		0.37	0.42
ulaşmak			0.70
sürünmek	0.29	0.33	
dolaşmak			0.32
TOTAL (in numbers)	282	252	293

Table 114: Proportion of German motion verb lemmas in Voluntary Motion Task of Turkish-German (TURGER) and German minimal bilinguals (GER) (in %).

LEMMA	German	
	TURGER	GER
gehen	33.27	11.11
klettern	7.76	11.40
rennen	10.66	6.94

(continued)

Table 114 (continued)

LEMMA	German	
	TURGER	GER
kommen	9.78	6.89
rollen	5.11	7.69
laufen	3.35	9.19
fliegen	5.02	5.70
fallen	4.13	4.63
schaukeln	3.17	4.01
schwingen	2.50	3.79
sein	0.71	4.68
fahren	1.53	3.05
balancieren	2.03	2.52
wollen	1.29	2.91
schleichen	1.89	2.31
springen	1.58	1.29
landen	0.55	2.25
steigen	1.03	0.85
rudern		1.48
paddeln	0.76	0.53
rutschen	0.49	0.58
tauchen	0.71	0.32
kriechen	0.55	0.48
abhauen	0.51	0.39
jagen	0.32	0.26
schlüpfen		0.52
schnappen		0.52
hechten		0.48
fangen		0.39
kugeln		0.39
Tarzan spielen		0.39
verschwinden		0.39
schwimmen	0.37	
verfolgen		0.33
rasen		0.32
murmeln	0.30	
flitzen		0.27
tanzen		0.26

(continued)

Table 114 (continued)

LEMMA	German	
	TURGER	GER
flattern		0.25
hüpfen	0.25	
zwängen		0.25
flüchten	0.23	
krabbeln	0.17	
TOTAL (in numbers)	383	330

Table 115: Proportion of French motion verb lemmas in Voluntary Motion Task of Turkish-French (TURFRE) and French minimal bilinguals (FRE) (in %).

LEMMA	French	
	TURFRE	FRE
monter	14.96	11.32
rentrer	17.55	8.45
partir	10.51	8.92
aller	5.75	7.46
tomber	5.65	6.19
attraper	5.38	5.53
rouler	3.94	5.09
balancer	3.25	5.30
venir	4.52	3.64
passer	2.41	3.71
sortir	2.84	3.05
conduire	0.86	4.58
entrer	1.38	3.36
courir	2.94	1.73
descendre	1.31	3.08
arriver	2.38	1.95
faire X	1.93	2.00
sauter	1.80	1.86
grimper	3.14	
atterrir		2.84

(continued)

Table 115 (continued)

LEMMA	French	
	TURFRE	FRE
poursuivre	1.31	0.91
enfuir	0.67	1.24
marcher		1.78
avancer		1.11
voler	1.09	
glisser	0.56	0.51
tourner		0.84
chasser		0.84
nager	0.78	
échapper	0.75	
traverser		0.71
faufiler		0.65
tenir l'équilibre		0.60
lancer	0.51	
suivre		0.45
escalader	0.44	
se fonçer	0.39	
accrocher	0.35	
promener	0.35	
reculer		0.31
danser	0.28	
TOTAL (in numbers)	241	205

Table 116: Turkish motion verb constructions (VCONST) and the syntactic patterns (SYNPAT) in Voluntary Motion Task of Turkish-German (TURGER), Turkish-French (TURFRE) bilinguals and Turkish minimal bilinguals (TUR) (in %).

VCONST	SYNPAT	Turkish		
		TURGER	TURFRE	TUR
VP_P	VCONV	0.33	0.59	3.67
	VMOD	3.95	4.69	3.73
	VSC			0.48
	MC	31.08	26.76	24.03
	TOT	**35.37**	**32.05**	**31.91**

(continued)

Table 116 (continued)

VCONST	SYNPAT	Turkish		
		TURGER	TURFRE	TUR
VM_O	VCONV	0.42	0.32	1.57
	VMOD	2.47	3.80	3.27
	VSC	0.42		0.39
	MC	16.03	13.84	17.41
	TOT	**19.34**	**17.96**	**22.65**
VGEN_P	VMOD	2.43	1.03	2.30
	VSC			0.49
	MC	12.83	12.73	7.46
	TOT	**15.26**	**13.75**	**10.25**
VM_P	VCONV	0.42	1.03	2.05
	VMOD	0.93	0.67	0.98
	MC	9.17	3.90	6.64
	TOT	**10.51**	**5.59**	**9.67**
VMP_P	VMOD		0.29	0.63
	MC	5.84	6.71	9.51
	TOT	**5.84**	**7.00**	**10.14**
VGEN_O	VCONV			1.20
	VMOD		1.04	0.72
	VSC	0.39	0.74	0.35
	MC	6.67	5.61	4.11
	TOT	**7.06**	**7.38**	**6.39**
VP_O	VMOD	1.16	1.03	0.56
	VSC	0.33	0.65	0.26
	MC		4.07	0.67
	TOT	**1.49**	**5.75**	**1.48**
VMP_O	MC	0.96	4.75	2.89
	TOT	**0.96**	**4.75**	**2.89**
VP_P_M	VCONV			0.30
	VMOD		0.44	0.24
	MC	1.85		1.56
	TOT	**1.85**	**0.44**	**2.10**
VM_M	VMOD	0.33	0.74	
	MC	0.82	0.29	
	TOT	**1.16**	**1.03**	**0.00**

(continued)

Table 116 (continued)

VCONST	SYNPAT	Turkish		
		TURGER	TURFRE	TUR
VLV_M	VMOD		1.53	
	MC			0.42
	TOT	**0.00**	**1.53**	**0.42**
VGEN_P_M	VMOD	0.32		
	MC	0.29	0.44	0.57
	TOT	**0.61**	**0.44**	**0.57**
VGEN_M	VMOD		0.74	
	MC	0.56		0.26
	TOT	**0.56**	**0.74**	**0.26**
VP_M	VMOD		1.12	
	MC			0.32
	TOT	**0.00**	**1.12**	**0.32**
VP_P_P	MC			0.95
	TOT			**0.95**
VGEN_0	VCONV		0.44	
	TOT		**0.44**	
TOTAL (in numbers)		282	252	293

VCONF = converb construction; VMOD = infinitive construction with modal or other non motion verbs; VSC = subordinate verb construction; MC = main verb construction; TOT = total constructions.

Table 117: German motion verb constructions (VCONST) and the syntactic patterns (SYNPAT) in Voluntary Motion Task of Turkish-German (TURGER) and German minimal bilinguals (GER) (in %).

VCONST	SYNPAT	German	
		GERTUR	GER
VM_P	VMOD	2.72	4.49
	VSC	0.32	0.74
	VSC_VMOD	0.32	
	MC	23.89	33.87
	TOT	**27.24**	**39.10**

(continued)

Table 117 (continued)

VCONST	SYNPAT	German	
		GERTUR	GER
VGEN_P	VMOD	2.96	2.42
	VSC	2.05	1.25
	VSC_VMOD	0.30	
	MC	32.86	10.03
	TOT	**38.17**	**13.70**
VM_0	VMOD	0.32	2.19
	VSC	0.55	1.13
	MC	13.61	8.98
	TOT	**14.48**	**12.30**
VMP_P	VMOD		1.68
	VSC	0.69	0.92
	MC	9.76	13.37
	TOT	**10.45**	**15.96**
VGEN_0	VSC		0.39
	VSC_VMOD	0.32	
	MC	3.79	2.92
	TOT	**4.11**	**3.31**
VM_P_M	VMOD		0.60
	VSC_VMOD		0.25
	MC	1.35	3.16
	TOT	**1.35**	**4.00**
VAUX_P	MC	0.71	4.35
	TOT	**0.71**	**4.35**
VMOD_P	VSC	0.23	
	MC	1.06	2.52
	TOT	**1.29**	**2.52**
VGEN_P_M	MC	1.06	0.98
	TOT	**1.06**	**0.98**
VM_M	MC		1.92
	TOT		**1.92**
VMP_0	MC	0.74	0.33
	TOT	**0.74**	**0.33**
VGEN_M	MC	0.42	
	TOT	**0.42**	
VLV_M	VMOD		0.39
	TOT		**0.39**

(continued)

Table 117 (continued)

VCONST	SYNPAT	German	
		GERTUR	GER
VP_P	MC		0.39
	TOT		**0.39**
VAUX_P_M	MC		0.33
	TOT		**0.33**
TOTAL (in numbers)		338	330

VMOD= infinitive construction with modal or other non motion verbs; VSC= subordinate verb construction; MC= main verb construction; VSC_VMOD= infinitive construction with modal or other non motion verbs in a subordinate construction; TOT= total constructions.

Table 118: French motion verb constructions (VCONST) and the syntactic patterns (SYNPAT) in Voluntary Motion Task of Turkish-French (TURFRE) and French minimal bilinguals (FRE) (in %).

VCONST	SYNPAT	French	
		FRE	TURFRE
VP_P	VMOD	5.01	2.33
	VSC	0.40	3.31
	MC	26.28	30.82
	TOT	**31.68**	**36.46**
VM_O	VMOD	4.14	4.57
	VSC	4.17	0.44
	MC	18.48	13.55
	TOT	**26.79**	**18.57**
VP_O	VMOD	1.52	2.50
	VSC	0.40	2.27
	VSC_VMOD		0.35
	MC	11.77	9.28
	TOT	**13.70**	**14.40**
VGEN_P	VMOD	1.19	0.89
	VSC	0.40	
	VSC_VMOD		0.35
	MC	6.78	5.56
	TOT	**8.37**	**6.80**

(continued)

Table 118 (continued)

VCONST	SYNPAT	French	
		FRE	TURFRE
VM_P	VMOD		0.44
	VSC	0.65	
	MC	6.91	5.75
	TOT	**7.56**	**6.20**
VMP_P	VMOD		0.96
	VSC	0.51	0.44
	MC	2.34	3.98
	TOT	**2.85**	**5.38**
VMP_O	VMOD		0.51
	VSC		0.44
	MC	3.34	2.90
	TOT	**3.34**	**3.86**
VGEN_O	VMOD		0.48
	VSC		0.51
	MC	1.82	2.54
	TOT	**1.82**	**3.53**
VLV_M	VMOD	1.24	1.33
	MC	0.75	0.61
	TOT	**2.00**	**1.93**
VP_M	MC	0.60	1.53
	TOT	**0.60**	**1.53**
VM_M	VMOD		0.44
	MC	0.40	
	TOT	**0.40**	**0.44**
VGEN_M	MC	0.51	0.28
	TOT	**0.51**	**0.28**
VP_P_M	MC		0.61
	TOT		**0.61**
VGEN_P_M	MC	0.40	
	TOT	**0.40**	
TOTAL (in numbers)		205	241

VMOD = infinitive construction with modal or other non motion verbs; VSC = subordinate verb construction; MC = main verb construction; VSC_VMOD = infinitive construction with modal or other non motion verbs in a subordinate construction; TOT = total constructions.

References

Abraham, Werner. 2010. Types of transitivity, intransitive objects, and untransitivity – and the logic of their structural designs: Ways to keep apart derivation in syntax and in the lexicon. In Patrick Brandt & Marco García García (eds.), *Transivity*, 15–68 (Linguistik Aktuell/ Linguistics Today 166). Amsterdam: John Benjamins.

Ahrenholz, Bernt. 2006. Wortstellung in mündlichen Erzählungen von Kindern mit Migrationshintergrund. In Bernt Ahrenholz (ed.), *Kinder mit Migrationshintergrund. Spracherwerb und Fördermöglichkeiten*, 221–240. Freiburg im Breisgau: Fillibach.

Akıncı, Mehmet-Ali. 1996. Pratiques langagières des immigrés Turcs en France. *Ecarts d'Identité* 76. 14–17.

Akıncı, Mehmet-Ali. 2001. *Développement des compétences narratives des enfants bilingues turc-français en France âges de 5 à 10 ans* (Lincom Studies in Language Acquisition 3). München: Lincom Europa.

Akıncı, Mehmet-Ali. 2002. Errors and repairs in French language use of Turkish-French bilingual children and teenagers. In Anxo Lorenzo Suarez, Fernado Ramallo & Xoan Rodriguez-Yanez (eds.), *Bilingual socialization and bilingual language acquisition. Proceedings from the second International Symposium on Bilingualism*, 167–182. Vigo: Servizo de Publicacions da Universidade de Vigo.

Akıncı, Mehmet-Ali. 2006. Du bilinguisme à la bilittéracie. Comparaison entre élèves bilingues turc-français et élèves monolingues français. *Langage et Société* 116. 93–110.

Akıncı, Mehmet-Ali. 2008. De l'apprentissage des langues aux pratiques langagières des jeunes bilingues turcs en France. *Cahiers de l'observatoire des pratiques linguistiques* 2. 64–72.

Akıncı, Mehmet-Ali & Ad Backus. 2004. The structure and the role of code-switching in Turkish-French conversations. In Jens Jørgensen & Christine Dabelsteen (eds.), *Languaging and language practices*, 150–160 (Copenhagen Studies in Bilingualism 36). Copenhagen: University of Copenhagen, Faculty of the Humanities.

Akıncı, Mehmet-Ali, Harriet Jisa & Sophie Kern. 2001. Influence of L1 Turkish on L2 French narratives. In Ludo Verhoeven & Sven Strömqvist (eds.), *Narrative development in a multilingual context*, 189–208 (Studies in Bilingualism 23). Amsterdam: John Benjamins.

Akıncı, Mehmet-Ali & Jan Jaap de Ruiter. 2004. Multilingualism in Lyon. In Guus Extra & Kutlay Yağmur (eds.), *Urban multilingualism in Europe: Immigrant minority languages at home and school*, 251–274 (Multilingual Matters 130). Clevedon, UK: Multilingual Matters.

Aksan, Yeşim, Mustafa Aksan, Ahmet Koltuksuz, Taner Sezer, Ümit Mersinli, Umut Ufuk Demirhan, Hakan Yılmazer, et al. 2012. Construction of the Turkish National Corpus (TNC). In Nicoletta Calzolari, Khalid Choukri, Thierry Declerck, Mehmet Uğur Doğan, Bente Maegaard, Joseph Mariani, Asuncion Moreno, Jan Odijk & Stelios Piperidis (eds.), *Proceedings of the eight International Conference on Language Resources and Evaluation (LREC'12)*, 3223–3227. İstanbul: European Language Resources Association (ELRA).

Aksu-Koç, Ayhan. 1994. Development of linguistic forms: Turkish. In Ruth Berman & Dan Slobin (eds.), *Relating events in narrative: A crosslinguistic developmental study*, 339–392. Hillsdale, NJ: Lawrence Erlbaum.

Allen, Shanley. 2007. The future of Inuktitut in the face of majority languages: Bilingualism or language shift? *Applied Psycholinguistics* 28(3). 515–536. doi:10.1017/ S0142716407070282.

Allen, Shanley, Aslı Özyürek, Sotaro Kita, Amanda Brown, Reyhan Furman, Tomoko Ishizuka & Mihoko Fujii. 2007. Language-specific and universal influences in children's syntactic packaging of manner and path: A comparison of English, Japanese, and Turkish. *Cognition* 102(1). 16–48. doi:10.1016/j.cognition.2005.12.006.

Altmann, Hans & Silke Kemmerling. 2005. *Wortbildung fürs Examen*. Göttingen: Vandenhoeck & Ruprecht.

Ammerlaan, Tom. 1996. *"You get a bit wobbly...": exploring bilingual lexical retrieval processes in the context of first language attrition*. Enschede: CopyPrint 2000.

Appel, René & Pieter Muysken. 2005. *Language contact and bilingualism*. Amsterdam: Amsterdam University Press.

Arias Oliveira, Roberto. 2012. *Boundary-crossing: Eine Untersuchung zum Deutschen, Französischen und Spanischen*. München: Ludwig-Maximilians-University (Doctoral dissertation).

Aske, Jon. 1989. Path predicates in English and Spanish: A closer look. In Kira Hall, Michael Meacham & Richard Shapiro (eds.), *Proceedings of the annual meeting of the Berkeley Linguistics Society*, vol. 15, 1–14. Berkeley, CA: Berkeley Linguistics Society.

Aurnague, Michel. 1995. Orientation in French spatial expressions: Formal representations and inferences. *Journal of Semantics* 12(3). 239–267. doi:10.1093/jos/12.3.239.

Aurnague, Michel. 1996. Les noms de localisation interne: Tentative de caractérisation sémantique à partir de données du basque et du français. *Cahiers de Lexicologie* 69. 159–192.

Autorengruppe Bildungsberichterstattung. 2014. *Bildung in Deutschland 2014: Ein indikatorengestützter Bericht mit einer Analyse zur Bildung von Menschen mit Behinderungen*. Bielefeld: Bertelsmann.

Backus, Ad. 2006. Turkish as an immigrant language in Europe. In Tej Bhatia & William Ritchie (eds.), *The handbook of bilingualism*, 689–724 (Blackwell Handbooks in Linguistics 15). Malden, MA: Blackwell.

Backus, Ad & Hendrik Boeschoten. 1998. Language change in immigrant Turkish. In Guus Extra & Jeanne Maartens (eds.), *Multilingualism in a multicultural context: Case studies on South Africa and Western Europe*, 221–237. Tilburg: Tilburg University Press.

Balthasar, Lukas & Michel Bert. 2005. La plateforme "Corpus de langues parlées en interaction" (CLAPI). Historique, état des lieux, perspectives. *Lidil* 31. 13–33.

Bamberg, Michael. 1979. The notion of space, time and overextension in child language acquisition. *Linguistische Berichte* 59. 27–50.

Bamberg, Michael. 1994. Development of linguistic forms: German. In Ruth Berman & Dan Slobin (eds.), *Relating events in narrative: A crosslinguistic developmental study*, 189–238. Hillsdale, NJ: Lawrence Erlbaum.

Beavers, John, Beth Levin & Shiao Wei Tham. 2010. The typology of motion expressions revisited. *Journal of Linguistics* 46(2). 331–377. doi:10.1017/S0022226709990272.

Berman, Ruth & Dan Slobin (eds.), 1994. *Relating events in narrative: A crosslinguistic developmental study*. Hillsdale, NJ: Lawrence Erlbaum.

Bernini, Giuliano, Lorenzo Spreafico & Ada Valentini. 2006. Acquiring motion verbs in a second language: The case of Italian L2. *Linguistica e filologia* 23. 7–26.

Berthele, Raphael. 2004. The typology of motion and posture verbs: A variationist account. In Bernd Kortmann (ed.), *Dialectology meets typology: Dialect grammar from a cross-linguistic perspective*, 93–126. Berlin: de Gruyter Mouton.

Berthele, Raphael. 2006. *Ort und Weg: Die sprachliche Raumreferenz in Varietäten des Deutschen, Rätoromanischen und Französischen*. Berlin: de Gruyter.

Berthele, Raphael. 2007. Sein+Direktionalergänzung: Bewegung ohne Bewegungsverb. In Ljudmila Geist & Björn Rothstein (eds.), *Kopulaverben und Kopulasätze. Intersprachliche und intrasprachliche Aspekte*, 229–252 (Linguistische Arbeiten 512). Tübingen: Niemeyer.

Berthele, Raphael. 2009. The many ways to search for a frog: On a fieldworker's trouble collecting spatial language data. In Jiansheng Guo, Elena Lieven, Nancy Budwig, Susan Ervin-Tripp, Keiko Nakamura & Şeyda Özçalışkan (eds.), *Crosslinguistic approaches to the psychology of language: Research in the tradition of Dan Isaac Slobin*, 163–174. New York: Taylor & Francis.

Berthele, Raphael. 2013. The encoding of motion events: Building typology bottom-up from text data in many languages. In Juliana Goschler & Anatol Stefanowitsch (eds.), *Variation and change in the encoding of motion events*, 55–76 (Human Cognitive Processing 41). Amsterdam: John Benjamins.

Berthele, Raphael. 2017. When bilinguals forget their manners. Language dominance and motion event descriptions in French and German. *Vigo International Journal of Applied Linguistics* 14. 39–70.

Berthele, Raphael & Ladina Stocker. 2017. The effect of language mode on motion event descriptions in German-French bilinguals. *Language and Cognition* 9(4). 648–676. doi:10.1017/langcog. 2016.34.

Bialystok, Ellen. 2009. Bilingualism: The good, the bad, and the indifferent. *Bilingualism: Language and Cognition* 12(1). 3–11. doi:10.1017/S1366728908003477.

Birdsong, David. 2014. Dominance and age in bilingualism. *Applied Linguistics* 35(4). 374–392. doi:10.1093/applin/amu031.

Birdsong, David. 2016. Dominance in bilingualism: Foundations of measurement, with insights from the study of handedness. In Carmen Silva-Corvalan & Jeanine Treffers-Daller (eds.), *Language dominance in bilinguals: Issues of measurement and operationalization*, 85–105. Cambridge, UK: Cambridge University Press.

Boeschoten, Hendrik. 1994. Second language influence on first language acquisition: Turkish children in Germany. In Guus Extra & Ludo Verhoeven (eds.), *The cross-linguistic study of bilingual development*, 253–263. Amsterdam: North-Holland.

Boeschoten, Hendrik. 1998. Codeswitching, codemixing, and codealternation: What a difference. In Rodolfo Jacobson (ed.), *Codeswitching worldwide*, vol. 1, 15–24. Berlin: de Gruyter Mouton.

Bohnemeyer, Jürgen, Sonja Eisenbeiss & Bhuvana Narasimhan. 2006. Ways to go: Methodological consid erations in Whorfian studies on motion events. *Essex Research Reports in Linguistics*, vol. 50, 1–19. Colchester: University of Essex.

Bommes, Michael, Müge Ayan Ceyhan, Anja Boneß, Dilara Koçbas, Ulrich Mehlem, Helena Olfert, John Peterson, et al. 2011. *Literacy acquisition in schools. Preliminary project report*. Potsdam: University of Potsdam (Unpublished manuscript).

Borillo, Andrée. 1998. *L'espace et son expression en français*. Paris: Ophrys.

Bot, Kees de, Paul Gommans & Carola Rossing. 1991. L1 loss in an L2 environment: Dutch immigrants in France. In Herbert Seliger & Robert Vago (eds.), *First language attrition*, 87–98. Cambridge, UK: Cambridge University Press. http://ebooks.cambridge.org/ref/id/CBO9780511620720A017.

Bot, Kees de, Wander Lowie & Marjolijn Verspoor. 2007. A dynamic systems theory approach to second language acquisition. *Bilingualism: Language and Cognition* 10(1). 7–21. doi:10.1017/S1366728906002732.

Brennan, Susan & Maurice Williams. 1995. The feeling of another's knowing: Prosody and filled pauses as cues to listeners about the metacognitive states of speakers. *Journal of Memory and Language* 34(3). 383–398. doi:10.1006/jmla.1995.1017.

Brizić, Katharina. 2006. The secret life of languages. Origin-specific differences in L1/L2 acquisition by immigrant children. *International Journal of Applied Linguistics* 16(3). 339–362. doi:10.1111/j.1473-4192.2006.00122.x.

Brown, Amanda & Marianne Gullberg. 2008. Bidirectional crosslinguistic influence in L1-L2 encoding of manner in speech and gesture: A study of Japanese speakers of English. *Studies in Second Language Acquisition* 30(2). 225–251. doi:10.1017/S0272263108080327.

Brown, Amanda & Marianne Gullberg. 2010. Changes in encoding of path of motion in a first language during acquisition of a second language. *Cognitive Linguistics* 21(2). 263–286. doi:10.1515/COGL.2010.010.

Brown, Amanda & Marianne Gullberg. 2012. L1–L2 convergence in clausal packaging in Japanese and English. *Bilingualism: Language and Cognition* 16(3). 1–18. doi:10.1017/S1366728912000491.

Bryant, Doreen. 2011. Der Erwerb von Positionsverben – Warum Kinder so an hängen hängen? *Linguistische Berichte* 226. 199–242.

Bryant, Doreen. 2012. *Lokalisierungsausdrücke im Erst- und Zweitspracherwerb.* Baltmannsweiler: Schneider Verlag Hohengehren.

Bylund, Emanuel & Scott Jarvis. 2011. L2 effects on L1 event conceptualization. *Bilingualism: Language and Cognition* 14(1). 47–59. doi:10.1017/S1366728910000180.

Cadierno, Teresa. 2004. Expressing motion events in a second language: A cognitive typological approach. In Michel Achard & Susanne Niemeier (eds.), *Cognitive linguistics, second language acquisition, and foreign language teaching*, 13–39. 2004th ed (Studies on Language Acquisition 18). Berlin: de Gruyter Mouton. http://www.reference-global.com/doi/book/10.1515/9783110199857.

Cadierno, Teresa. 2008. Learning to talk about motion in a foreign language. In Peter Robinson & Nick Ellis (eds.), *Handbook of cognitive linguistics and second language acquisition*, 239–275. New York: Routledge.

Cadierno, Teresa. 2010. Motion in Danish as a second language: Does the learner's L1 make a difference? In Zhaohong Han & Teresa Cadierno (eds.), *Linguistic relativity in SLA: Thinking for speaking*, 1–33 (Second Language Acquisition). Bristol, UK: Multilingual Matters.

Cadierno, Teresa & Peter Robinson. 2009. Language typology, task complexity and the development of L2 lexicalization patterns for describing motion events. *Annual Review of Cognitive Linguistics* 7. 245–276. doi:10.1075/arcl.7.10cad.

Cadierno, Teresa & Lucas Ruiz. 2006. Motion events in Spanish L2 acquisition. *Annual Review of Cognitive Linguistics* 4. 183–216. doi:10.1075/arcl.4.08cad.

Cantone, Katja, Tanja Kupisch, Natascha Müller & Katrin Schmitz. 2008. Rethinking language dominance in bilingual children. *Linguistische Berichte* 215. 307–343.

Cardini, Filippo-Enrico. 2010. Evidence against Whorfian effects in motion conceptualisation. *Journal of Pragmatics* 42(5). 1442–1459. doi:10.1016/j.pragma.2009.09.017.

Carroll, Mary. 2000. Representing path in language production in English and German: Alternative perspectives on figure and ground. In Christopher Habel & Christiane von Stutterheim (eds.), *Räumliche Konzepte und sprachliche Strukturen*, 97–118. Tübingen: Niemeyer.

Choi, Soonja & Melissa Bowerman. 1991. Learning to express motion events in English and Korean: The influence of language-specific lexicalization patterns. *Cognition* 41. 83–121. doi:10.1016/0010-0277(91)90033-Z.

Cindark, Ibrahim & Sema Aslan. 2004. Deutschlandtürkisch? Mannheim: Institut für Deutsche Sprache. http://www1.ids-mannheim.de/fileadmin/prag/soziostilistik/Deutschlandtuerkisch.pdf.
Conover, William. 1999. *Practical nonparametric statistics*. New York: Wiley.
Cook, Vivian. 1991. The poverty-of-the-stimulus argument and multicompetence. *Second Language Research* 7(2). 103–117. doi:10.1177/026765839100700203.
Cook, Vivian. 1992. Evidence for multicompetence. *Language Learning* 42(4). 557–591. doi:10.1111/j.1467-1770.1992.tb01044.x.
Cook, Vivian. 1997. Monolingual bias in second language acquisition research. *Revista Canaria de Estudios Ingleses* 34. 35–50.
Cook, Vivian. 2002. Background to the L2 User. In Vivian Cook (ed.), *Portraits of the L2 user*, 1–28. Clevedon, UK: Multilingual Matters.
Cook, Vivian. 2003. Introduction: The changing L1 in the L2 user's mind. In Vivian Cook (ed.), *Effects of the second language on the first*, 1–18. Clevedon, UK: Multilingual Matters.
Crawley, Michael. 2014. *Statistics: An introduction using R*. Chichester, West Sussex: Wiley.
Croft, William, Jóhanna Barðdal, Willem Hollmann, Violeta Sotirova & Chiaki Taoka. 2010. Revising Talmy's typological classification of complex event constructions. In Hans Boas (ed.), *Contrastive studies in construction grammar*, 201–236 (Constructional Approaches to Language 10). Amsterdam: John Benjamins.
Crutzen, Danièle & Altay Manço. 2003. *Compétences linguistiques et sociocognitives des enfants de migrants*. Paris: L'Harmattan.
Czinglar, Christine, Katharina Korecky-Kröll, Kumru Uzunkaya-Sharma & Wolfgang Dressler. 2015. Wie beeinflusst der sozioökonomische Status den Erwerb der Erst- und Zweitsprache? In Arne Ziegler & Klaus-Michael Köpcke (eds.), *Deutsche Grammatik in Kontakt*, 207–240. Berlin: de Gruyter.
Dąbrowska, Ewa. 2014. Recycling utterances: A speaker's guide to sentence processing. *Cognitive Linguistics* 25(4). 617–653. doi:10.1515/cog-2014-0057.
Dąbrowska, Ewa & Elena Lieven. 2005. Towards a lexically specific grammar of children's question constructions. *Cognitive Linguistics* 16(3). 437–474. doi:10.1515/cogl.2005.16.3.437.
Daller, Michael, Jeanine Treffers-Daller & Reyhan Furman. 2011. Transfer of conceptualization patterns in bilinguals: The construal of motion events in Turkish and German. *Bilingualism: Language and Cognition* 14(1). 95–119. doi:10.1017/S1366728910000106.
Daller, Michael, Cemal Yıldız, Nivia de Jong, Seda Kan & Ragıp Başbağı. 2011. Language dominance in Turkish-German bilinguals: Methodological aspects of measurements in structurally different languages. *International Journal of Bilingualism* 15(2). 215–236. doi:10.1177/1367006910381197.
Deny, Jean. 1921. *Grammaire de la langue turque (dialecte osmanli)*. Paris: Leroux.
DeReKo. 2012. DEUTSCHES REFERENZKORPUS, http://www.ids-mannheim.de/kl/projekte/korpora/ [2014-12-01] (1 December, 2014).
DeReWo. 2012. *Korpusbasierte Wortformenliste (bzw. Wortgrundformenliste) DeReWo, derewo-v-ww-bll-320000g-2012-12-31-1.0, mit Benutzerdokumentation*. Mannheim: Institut für Deutsche Sprache, Programmbereich Korpuslinguistik. http://www.ids-mannheim.de/derewo.
DESI-Konsortium. 2008. *Unterricht und Kompetenzerwerb in Deutsch und Englisch: Ergebnisse der DESI-Studie*. Weinheim: Beltz.
Dijkstra, Ton & Walter van Heuven. 2002. The architecture of the bilingual word recognition system: From identification to decision. *Bilingualism: Language and Cognition* 5(3). 175–197. doi:10.1017/S1366728902003012.

Dirim, İnci & Peter Auer. 2004. *Türkisch sprechen nicht nur die Türken: Über die Unschärfebeziehung zwischen Sprache und Ethnie in Deutschland.* Berlin: de Gruyter.
Dirim, Inci, Kathrin Hauenschild & Birgit Lütje-Klose. 2008. Einführung: Ethnische Vielfalt und Mehrsprachigkeit an Schulen. In Inci Dirim, Kathrin Hauenschild, Birgit Lütje-Klose, Jessica Löser & Isabell Sievers (eds.), *Ethnische Vielfalt und Mehrsprachigkeit an Schulen. Beispiele aus verschiedenen nationalen Kontexten,* 1–21. Frankfurt am Main: Brandes & Apsel.
Edwards, John. 2006. Foundations of bilingualism. In Tej Bhatia & William Ritchie (eds.), *The handbook of bilingualism,* 7–31 (Blackwell Handbooks in Linguistics 15). Malden, MA: Blackwell.
Eisenberg, Peter. 2006. *Das Wort* (Grundriss der deutschen Grammatik 1). Stuttgart: Metzler.
Ellis, Nick & Fernando Ferreira–Junior. 2009. Construction learning as a function of frequency, frequency distribution, and function. *The Modern Language Journal* 93(3). 370–385. doi:10.1111/j.1540-4781.2009.00896.x.
Engberg-Pedersen, Elisabeth & Naja Trondhjem. 2004. Focus on action in motion descriptions. The case of West-Greenlandic. In Sven Strömqvist & Ludo Verhoeven (eds.), *Relating events in narrative: Typological and contextual perspectives,* vol. 2, 59–88. Mahwah, NJ: Lawrence Erlbaum.
Engemann, Helen, Anne-Katharina Harr & Maya Hickmann. 2012. Caused motion events across languages and learner types: A comparison of bilingual first and adult second language acquisition. In Luna Filipović & Katarzyna Jaszczolt (eds.), *Space and time in languages and cultures: Linguistic diversity,* 263–288 (Human Cognitive Processing 36). Amsterdam: John Benjamins.
Filipović, Luna. 2007. *Talking about motion: A crosslinguistic investigation of lexicalization patterns* (Studies in Language Companion Series 91). Amsterdam: John Benjamins.
Filipović, Luna. 2010. The importance of being a prefix: Prefixal morphology and the lexicalization of motion events in Serbo-Croatian. In Victoria Hasko & Renee Perelmutter (eds.), *New approaches to Slavic verbs of motion,* 247–266 (Studies in Language Companion Series 115). Amsterdam: John Benjamins.
Filipović, Luna. 2011. Speaking and remembering in one or two languages: Bilingual vs. monolingual lexicalization and memory for motion events. *International Journal of Bilingualism* 15(4). 466–485. doi:10.1177/1367006911403062.
Filipović, Luna & Iraide Ibarretxe-Antuñano. 2015. Motion. In Ewa Dabrowska & Dagmar Divjak (eds.), *Handbook of cognitive linguistics,* 526–545 (HSK 39). Berlin: de Gruyter.
Finkbeiner, Matthew, Janet Nicol, Delia Greth & Kumiko Nakamura. 2002. The role of language in memory for actions. *Journal of Psycholinguistic Research* 31(5). 447–457.
Flecken, Monique, Mary Carroll, Katja Weimar & Christiane von Stutterheim. 2015. Driving along the road or heading for the village? Conceptual differences underlying motion event encoding in French, German, and French–German L2 users. *The Modern Language Journal* 99, supplement issue. 100–122. doi:10.1111/j.1540-4781.2015.12181.x.
Flecken, Monique, Christiane von Stutterheim & Mary Carroll. 2014. Grammatical aspect influences motion event perception: Findings from a cross-linguistic non-verbal recognition task. *Language and Cognition* 6(1). 45–78. doi:10.1017/langcog.2013.2.
Fortis, Jean-Michel & Benjamin Fagard. 2010. Space in language: The typology of motion events. Part III. Workshop hold at the Leipzig Summer School on linguistic typology (August 14–28, 2010). http://www.eva.mpg.de/lingua/conference/2010_summerschool/pdf/course_materials/Fortis_3.MOTION%20EVENTS.pdf.

Gagneux, Charlotte. 2013. *Les difficultés lexicales en français des enfants bilingues francoturcs de Grande Section de Maternelle: Problème de signifiant ou de signifié?* Besançon: Université de Franche-Comté UFR SMP - Orthophonie (Unpublished MA thesis).

Gass, Susan & Larry Selinker (eds.). 1992. *Language transfer in language learning: Revised edition* (Language Acquisition and Language Disorders 5). Amsterdam: John Benjamins.

Gathercole, Virginia & Erika Hoff. 2007. Input and the acquisition of language: Three questions. In Erika Hoff & Marilyn Shatz (eds.), *Blackwell handbook of language development*, 107–127. Malden, MA: Blackwell.

Genesee, Fred. 2010. Dual language development in preschool children. In Eugene Garcia & Ellen Frede (eds.), *Young English language learners: Current research and emerging directions for practice and policy*, 59–79. New York: Teachers College Press.

Genesee, Fred, Elena Nicoladis & Johanne Paradis. 1995. Language differentiation in early bilingual development. *Journal of Child Language* 22(3). 611–631. doi:10.1017/S0305000900009971.

Gennari, Silvia, Steven Sloman, Barbara Malt & Tecumseh Fitch. 2002. Motion events in language and cognition. *Cognition* 83(1). 49–79. doi:10.1016/S0010-0277(01)00166-4.

Gogolin, Ingrid & Hans Reich. 2001. Immigrant languages in federal Germany. In Guus Extra & Durk Gorter (eds.), *The other languages of Europe: Demographic, sociolinguistic and educational perspectives*, 193–214. Clevedon, UK: Multilingual Matters.

Göksel, Aslı & Celia Kerslake. 2005. *Turkish: A comprehensive grammar*. London: Routledge.

Goldberg, Adele. 1995. *Constructions: A construction grammar approach to argument structure*. Chicago: University of Chicago Press.

Goldberg, Adele. 2006. *Constructions at work: The nature of generalization in language*. Oxford: Oxford University Press.

Goldberg, Adele, Devin Casenhiser & Nitya Sethuraman. 2004. Learning argument structure generalizations. *Cognitive Linguistics* 15(3). 289–316.

Goldstein, Bruce. 2010. *Sensation and perception*. Belmont, CA: Wadsworth, Cengage Learning.

Gor, Kira, Svetlana Cook, Vera Malyushenkova & Tatyana Vdovina. 2009. Verbs of motion in highly proficient learners and heritage speakers of Russian. *Slavic & East European Journal* 53(3). 386–408.

Goschler, Juliana. 2009. Typologische und konstruktionelle Einflüsse bei der Kodierung von Bewegungsereignissen in der Zweitsprache. In Said Sahel & Ralf Vogel (eds.), *Proceedings of the tenth Norddeutsches Linguistisches Kolloquium*, 40–65. Bielefeld eCollections.

Goschler, Juliana. 2013. Motion events in Turkish-German contact varieties. In Juliana Goschler & Anatol Stefanowitsch (eds.), *Variation and change in the encoding of motion events*, 115–132 (Human Cognitive Processing 41). Amsterdam: John Benjamins.

Goschler, Juliana & Anatol Stefanowitsch (eds.), 2013a. *Variation and change in the encoding of motion events* (Human Cognitive Processing 41). Amsterdam: John Benjamins.

Goschler, Juliana & Anatol Stefanowitsch. 2013b. Introduction. Beyond typology: The encoding of motion events across time and varieties. In Juliana Goschler & Anatol Stefanowitsch (eds.), *Variation and change in the encoding of motion events*, 1–14 (Human Cognitive Processing 41). Amsterdam: John Benjamins.

Goschler, Juliana, Till Woerfel, Anatol Stefanowitsch, Heike Wiese & Christoph Schroeder. 2013. Beyond conflation patterns: The encoding of motion events in Kiezdeutsch. In Anatol Stefanowitsch (ed.), *Yearbook of the German Cognitive Linguistics Association*, vol. 1, 237–252. Berlin: de Gruyter Mouton.

Gries, Stefan. 2013. *Statistics for linguistics with R: A practical introduction*. Berlin: de Gruyter Mouton.
Grosjean, François. 1985. The bilingual as a competent but specific speaker-hearer. *Journal of Multilingual and Multicultural Development* 6(6). 467–477. doi:10.1080/01434632.1985.9994221.
Grosjean, François. 1989. Neurolinguists, beware! The bilingual is not two monolinguals in one person. *Brain and Language* 36(1). 3–15. doi:10.1016/0093-934X(89)90048-5.
Grosjean, François. 1998. Studying bilinguals: Methodological and conceptual issues. *Bilingualism: Language and Cognition* 1(2). 131–149. doi:10.1017/S136672899800025X.
Grosjean, François. 2016. The complementarity principle and its impact on processing, acquisition, and dominance. In Carmen Silva-Corvalan & Jeanine Treffers-Daller (eds.), *Language dominance in bilinguals: Issues of measurement and operationalization*, 66–84. Cambridge, UK: Cambridge University Press.
Haberzettl, Stefanie. 2005. *Der Erwerb der Verbstellungsregeln in der Zweitsprache Deutsch durch Kinder mit russischer und türkischer Muttersprache*. Tübingen: Niemeyer.
Haggblade, Elisabeth. 1995. *Die Lexikalisierung von semantischen Komponenten in den Bewegungsverben: Vergleichende Untersuchungen zur Semantik von Partikelverben im Englischen und Deutschen*. Berlin: Microfiche edition.
Hamurcu, Büşra. 2014. Gestualité et développement lexical chez les enfants bilingues franco-turcs de 3 à 5 ans. In Aurélia Confais, Camille Couvry, Roxane Joannidès, Emilie Lebreton & Maulde Urbain-Mathis (eds.), *Actes du colloque: Sociologie et sciences du langage: Quel dialogue, quelles interactions?*, 104–118. Rouen: Laboratoire Dysola.
Harr, Anne-Katharina. 2012. *Language-specific factors in first language acquisition: The expression of motion events in French and German*. Boston: de Gruyter Mouton.
Hart, Betty & Todd Risley. 1995. *Meaningful differences in the everyday experience of young American children*. Baltimore: Paul H. Brookes.
Hasko, Victoria. 2010. The role of thinking for speaking in adult L2 speech: The case of (non) unidirectionality encoding by American learners of Russian. In Zhaohong Han & Teresa Cadierno (eds.), *Linguistic relativity in SLA: thinking for speaking*, 34–58 (Second Language Acquisition 50). Bristol, UK: Multilingual Matters.
Heijden, Hanneke van der & Ludo Verhoeven. 1994. Early bilingual development of Turkish children in the Netherlands. In Guus Extra & Ludo Verhoeven (eds.), *The cross-linguistic study of bilingual development*, 51–73. Amsterdam: North-Holland.
Hendriks, Henriëtte & Maya Hickmann. 2010. Space in second language acquisition. In Vivian Cook & Benedetta Bassetti (eds.), *Language and bilingual cognition*, 315–339. New York: Taylor & Francis.
Hendriks, Henriëtte, Maya Hickmann & Katrin Lindner. 2010. Space, language, and cognition: New advances in acquisition research. *Cognitive Linguistics* 21(2). 181–188. doi:10.1515/COGL.2010.006.
Herdina, Philip & Ulrike Jessner. 2002. *A dynamic model of multilingualism: Perspectives of change in psycholinguistics* (Multilingual Matters 121). Clevedon, UK: Multilingual Matters.
Herskovits, Annette. 1986. *Language and spatial cognition: An interdisciplinary study of the prepositions in English*. Cambridge, UK: Cambridge University Press.
Hickmann, Maya. 2006. The relativity of motion in first language acquisition. In Maya Hickmann & Stéphane Robert (eds.), *Space in languages: Linguistic systems and cognitive categories*, 281–308. Amsterdam: John Benjamins.

Hickmann, Maya. 2007. Static and dynamic location in French: Developmental and cross-linguistic perspectives. In Michel Aurnague, Maya Hickmann & Laure Vieu (eds.), *The categorization of spatial entities in language and cognition*, 205–231. Amsterdam: John Benjamins.

Hickmann, Maya & Henriëtte Hendriks. 2006. Static and dynamic location in French and in English. *First Language* 26(1). 103–135. doi:10.1177/0142723706060743.

Hickmann, Maya, Henriëtte Hendriks & Christian Champaud. 2009. Typological contraints on motion in French and English child language. In Jiansheng Guo, Elena Lieven, Nancy Budwig, Susan Ervin-Tripp, Keiko Nakamura & Şeyda Özçalışkan (eds.), *Crosslinguistic approaches to the psychology of language: Research in the tradition of Dan Isaac Slobin*, 209–224. New York: Taylor & Francis.

Hickmann, Maya, Pierre Taranne & Philippe Bonnet. 2009. Motion in first language acquisition: Manner and path in French and English child language. *Journal of Child Language* 36(4). 705–741. doi:10.1017/S0305000908009215.

Hijazo-Gascón, Alberto. 2011. *La expresión de eventos de movimiento y su adquisición en segundas lenguas*. Zaragoza. University of Zaragoza (Unpublished doctoral dissertation).

Hijazo-Gascón, Alberto. 2018. Acquisition of motion events in L2 Spanish by German, French and Italian speakers. *The Language Learning Journal* 46(3). 241–262. doi:10.1080/09571736.2015.1046085.

Hijazo-Gascón, Alberto & Iraide Ibarretxe-Antuñano. 2010. Tipología, lexicalización y dialectología aragonesa. *Archivo de filología aragonesa* 66. 245–279.

Hijazo-Gascón, Alberto & Iraide Ibarretxe-Antuñano. 2013. Same family, different paths: Intratypological differences in three Romance languages. In Juliana Goschler & Anatol Stefanowitsch (eds.), *Variation and change in the encoding of motion events*, 39–54 (Human Cognitive Processing 41). Amsterdam: John Benjamins.

Hlavac, Jim. 2011. Hesitation and monitoring phenomena in bilingual speech: A consequence of code-switching or a strategy to facilitate its incorporation? *Journal of Pragmatics* 43(15). 3793–3806. doi:10.1016/j.pragma.2011.09.008.

Hoff, Erika. 2006. How social contexts support and shape language development. *Developmental Review* 26(1). 55–88. doi:10.1016/j.dr.2005.11.002.

Hoff, Erika, Cynthia Core, Silvia Place, Rosario Rumiche, Melissa Señor & Marisol Parra. 2012. Dual language exposure and early bilingual development. *Journal of Child Language* 39(1). 1–27. doi:10.1017/S0305000910000759.

Hoff, Erika, Brett Laursen & Twila Tardif. 2002. Socioeconomic status and parenting. In Marc Bornstein (ed.), *Handbook of parenting*, 231–252. Mahwah, NJ: Lawrence Erlbaum.

Hoff-Ginsberg, Erika. 1991. Mother-child conversation in different social classes and communicative settings. *Child Development* 62(4). 782–796. doi:10.2307/1131177.

Hoff-Ginsberg, Erika. 1998. The relation of birth order and socioeconomic status to children's language experience and language development. *Applied Psycholinguistics* 19(4). 603–629. doi:10.1017/S0142716400010389.

Hohenstein, Jill, Ann Eisenberg & Letitia Naigles. 2006. Is he floating across or crossing afloat? Cross-influence of L1 and L2 in Spanish–English bilingual adults. *Bilingualism: Language and Cognition* 9(3). 249–261. doi:10.1017/S1366728906002616.

Houwer, Annick de. 1990. *The acquisition of two languages from birth: A case study*. Cambridge, UK: Cambridge University Press.

Houwer, Annick de. 2007. Parental language input patterns and children's bilingual use. *Applied Psycholinguistics* 28(3). 411–424. doi:10.1017/S0142716407070221.

Houwer, Annick de. 2014. The absolute frequency of maternal input to bilingual and monolingual children: A first comparison. In Theres Grüter & Johanne Paradis (eds.), *Input and experience in bilingual development*, 37–58 (Trends in Language Acquisition Research 13). Amsterdam: John Benjamins.

Ibarretxe-Antuñano, Iraide. 2004. Motion events in Basque narratives. In Sven Strömqvist & Ludo Verhoeven (eds.), *Relating events in narrative: Typological and contextual perspectives*, vol. 2, 89–112. Mahwah, NJ: Lawrence Erlbaum.

Ibarretxe-Antuñano, Iraide. 2009. Path salience in motion events. In Jiansheng Guo, Elena Lieven, Nancy Budwig, Susan Ervin-Tripp, Keiko Nakamura & Şeyda Özçalışkan (eds.), *Crosslinguistic approaches to the psychology of language: Research in the tradition of Dan Isaac Slobin*, 403–414. New York: Taylor & Francis.

Ibarretxe-Antuñano, Iraide & Alberto Hijazo-Gascón. 2012. Variation in motion events: Theory and applications. In Luna Filipović & Katarzyna Jaszczolt (eds.), *Space and time in languages and cultures: Linguistic diversity*, 349–372 (Studies in Language Companion Series 36). Amsterdam: John Benjamins.

Institut für deutsche Sprache. 2014. Datenbank für Gesprochenes Deutsch (DGD-2). dgd.ids-mannheim.de.

Jarvis, Scott. 2000. Semantic and conceptual transfer. *Bilingualism: Language and Cognition* 3(1). 19–21.

Jarvis, Scott. 2007. Theoretical and methodological issues in the investigation of conceptual transfer. *Vigo International Journal of Applied Linguistics* 4. 43–71.

Jarvis, Scott. 2009. Lexical transfer. In Aneta Pavlenko (ed.), *The bilingual mental lexicon: Interdisciplinary approaches*, 99–124 (Bilingual Education & Bilingualism 70). Bristol, UK: Multilingual Matters.

Jarvis, Scott & Terence Odlin. 2000. Morphological type, spatial reference, and language transfer. *Studies in Second Language Acquisition* 22(4). 535–556.

Jarvis, Scott & Aneta Pavlenko. 2010. *Crosslinguistic influence in language and cognition*. London: Routledge.

Jessen, Moiken. 2013. Semantic categories in the domain of motion verbs by adult speakers of Danish, German, and Turkish. *Linguistik online* 61(4). 57–78.

Jessen, Moiken. 2014. The expression of Path in L2 Danish by German and Turkish learners. *Vigo International Journal of Applied Linguistics* 11. 81–110.

Jessen, Moiken & Teresa Cadierno. 2013. Variation in the categorization of motion events by Danish, German, Turkish, and L2 Danish speakers. In Juliana Goschler & Anatol Stefanowitsch (eds.), *Variation and change in the encoding of motion events*, 133–160 (Human Cognitive Processing 41). Amsterdam: John Benjamins.

Jessner, Ulrike. 2003. A dynamic approach to language attrition in multilingual systems. In Vivian Cook (ed.), *Effects of the second language on the first*, 234–246. Clevedon, UK: Multilingual Matters.

Jeuk, Stefan. 2011. *Erste Schritte in der Zweitsprache Deutsch: Eine empirische Untersuchung zum Zweitspracherwerb türkischer Migrantenkinder in Kindertageseinrichtungen*. Freiburg im Breisgau: Fillibach.

Johanson, Lars. 1991. Zur Sprachentwicklung der Turcia Germanica. In Ingeborg Baldauf, Klaus Kreiser & Semih Teczan (eds.), *Türkische Sprachen und Literaturen: Materialien der ersten deutschen Turkologen-Konferenz Bamberg, 3.-6. Juli 1987*, 199–212. Wiesbaden: Harrassowitz.

Johanson, Lars. 1998. The structure of Turkic. In Lars Johansson & Éva Csató (eds.), *The Turkic Languages*, 30–66. London: Routledge.

Jovanovic, Jelena & Aida Martinovic-Zic. 2004. Why manner matters: Contrasting English and Serbo-Croatian typology in motion description. In Carol Lynn Moder & Aida Martinovic-Zic (eds.), *Discourse across languages and cultures*, 211–226 (Studies in Language Companion Series 68). Amsterdam: John Benjamins.

Karasu, Ibrahim. 1995. *Bilinguale Wortschatzentwicklung türkischer Migrantenkinder vom Vor- bis ins Grundschulalter in der Bundesrepublik Deutschland*. Frankfurt am Main: Peter Lang.

Keim, Inken. 2004. Linguistic variation and communicative practices in migrant children and youth groups. Languaging and language practices. In Jens Jørgensen & Christine Dabelsteen (eds.), *Languaging and language practices*, 75–91 (Copenhagen Studies in Bilingualism 36). Copenhagen: University of Copenhagen, Faculty of the Humanities.

Keim, Inken. 2012. *Mehrsprachige Lebenswelten*. Tübingen: Narr.

Koch, Nikolas. in prep. Gebrauchsbasierte Grammatik: Der Erwerb von Schemata im Erstspracherwerb. Eine Traceback-Studie für das Deutsche. (Linguistik – Impulse & Tendenzen). Berlin: de Gruyter.

Koch, Nikolas & Till Woerfel. 2018. Der Einfluss konstruktioneller Gebrauchsmuster in L1 und L2 auf die Verbalisierung intransitiver Bewegung bilingualer türkisch- deutscher Sprecher(innen). In Anja Ballis & Nazlı Hodaie (eds.), *Perspektiven auf Mehrsprachigkeit. Individuum, Bildung, Gesellschaft* (DaZ-Forschung 16) 61–83. Berlin: de Gruyter Mouton.

Kopecka, Aneta. to appear. From a satellite- to a verb-framed pattern: A typological shift in French. In Hubert Cuyckens, Walter de Mulder & Tanja Mortelmans (eds.), *Variation and change in adpositions of movement*. Amsterdam: John Benjamins.

Kopecka, Aneta. 2004. *Étude typologique de l'expression de l'espace: localisation et déplacement en français et en polonais*. Lyon: Université Lumière Lyon 2 (Doctoral dissertation).

Kopecka, Aneta. 2006. The semantic structure of motion verbs in French: Typological perspectives. In Maya Hickmann & Stéphane Robert (eds.), *Space in languages: Linguistic systems and cognitive categories*, 83–101. Amsterdam: John Benjamins.

Kopecka, Aneta. 2009. Continuity and change in the representation of motion events in French. In Jiansheng Guo, Elena Lieven, Nancy Budwig, Susan Ervin-Tripp, Keiko Nakamura & Şeyda Özçalışkan (eds.), *Crosslinguistic approaches to the psychology of language: Research in the tradition of Dan Isaac Slobin*, 415–426. New York: Taylor & Francis.

Kopecka, Aneta. 2013. Describing motion events in Old and Modern French: Discourse effects of a typological change. In Juliana Goschler & Anatol Stefanowitsch (eds.), *Variation and change in the encoding of motion events*, 163–184 (Human Cognitive Processing 41). Amsterdam: John Benjamins.

Köpke, Barbara. 1999. *Attrition de la première langue chez le bilingue tardif: implications pour l'étude psycholinguistique du bilinguisme*. Toulouse: Université de Toulouse-Le Mirail. (Unpublished doctoral dissertation).

Köpke, Barbara & Monika Schmid. 2004. Language attrition: The next phase. In Monika Schmid, Barbara Köpke, Merel Keijzer & Lina Weilemar (eds.), *First language attrition: Interdisciplinary perspectives on methodological issues*, 1–43 (Studies in Bilingualism 28). Amsterdam: John Benjamins.

Köpke, Barbara, Monika Schmid, Merel Keijzer & Susan Dostert (eds.), 2007. *Language attrition: Theoretical perspectives* (Studies in Bilingualism 33). Amsterdam: John Benjamins.

Kroffke, Solveig & Monika Rothweiler. 2006. Variation im frühen Zweitspracherwerb des Deutschen durch Kinder mit türkischer Erstsprache. In Maurice Vliegen (ed.), *Variation in*

Sprachtheorie und Spracherwerb, 145–153 (Linguistik International 16). Frankfurt am Main: Peter Lang.

Kroll, Judith & Erika Stewart. 1994. Category interference in translation and picture naming: Evidence for asymmetric connections between bilingual memory representations. *Journal of Memory and Language* 33(2). 149–174. doi:10.1006/jmla.1994.1008.

Küntay, Aylin & Dan Slobin. 1999. The acquisition of Turkish as a native language: A research review. *Turcic language* 3(2). 151–188.

Kupisch, Tanja. 2006. *The acquisition of determiners in bilingual German-Italian and German-French children*. München: Lincom Europa.

Küppers, Almut, Christoph Schroeder & Esin Gülbeyaz. 2014. Languages in transition. The situation of Turkish in formal education in Germany. Policy Brief. İstanbul Policy Center.

Lane, David. n.d. Introduction to normal distributions. In David Lane (ed.), *Online statistics education: A multimedia course of study*, 250–252. Houston, TX: Rice University. http://onlinestatbook.com/Online_Statistics_Education.pdf.

Larrañaga, Pilar, Jeanine Treffers-Daller, Françoise Tidball & Maricarmen Gil Ortega. 2012. L1 transfer in the acquisition of manner and path in Spanish by native speakers of English. *International Journal of Bilingualism* 16(2). 117–138. doi:10.1177/1367006911405577.

Le Coz, Audrey & Alice Lhoste-Lassus. 2011. *Competences lexicales et morphosyntaxiques des enfants bilingues Franco-Turcs de Grande Section de Maternelle: Comparaison avec leurs pairs monolingues français*. Lyon: Institut des Sciences et Techniques de la Réadaptation - Université Claude Bernard Lyon 1 (Unpublished MA thesis).

Lenneberg, Eric. 1967. *Biological foundations of language*. New York: Wiley.

Levelt, Willem. 1989. *Speaking: From intention to articulation*. Cambridge, MA: MIT Press.

Lieven, Elena, Dorothé Salomo & Michael Tomasello. 2009. Two-year-old children's production of multiword utterances: A usage-based analysis. *Cognitive Linguistics* 20(3). 481–507. doi:10.1515/COGL.2009.022.

Löser, Jessica & Till Woerfel. 2017. Herkunftssprachenunterricht in Deutschland, Österreich und der Schweiz. In Bernt Ahrenholz & Ingelore Oomen-Welke (eds.), *Deutsch als Zweitsprache*., 577–589 (Deutschunterricht in Theorie Und Praxis 9). Baltmannsweiler: Schneider Verlag Hohengehren.

Matras, Yaron. 2007. Contact, connectivity and language evolution. In Jochen Rehbein, Christiane Hohenstein & Lukas Pietsch (eds.), *Hamburg Studies on Multilingualism*, vol. 5, 51–74. Amsterdam: John Benjamins Publishing Company. doi:10.1075/hsm.5.05mat.

McNeill, David. 2001. Analogic/analytic representations and cross-linguistic differences in thinking for speaking. *Cognitive Linguistics* 11(1–2). 43–60. doi:10.1515/cogl.2001.010.

Meisel, Jürgen. 2009. Second language acquisition in early childhood. *Zeitschrift für Sprachwissenschaft* 28(1). 5–34. doi:10.1515/ZFSW.2009.002.

Miller, George & Philip Johnson-Laird. 1976. *Language and perception*. Cambridge, MA: Belknap Press of Harvard University Press.

Muysken, Pieter. 2000. *Bilingual speech: A typology of code-mixing*. Cambridge, UK: Cambridge University Press.

Naigles, Letitia, Ann Eisenberg, Edward Kako, Melissa Highter & Nancy McGraw. 1998. Speaking of motion: Verb use in English and Spanish. *Language and Cognitive Processes* 13(5). 521–549. doi:10.1080/016909698386429.

New, Boris, Christophe Pallier, Ludovic Ferrand & Marc Brysbaert. 2001. Une base de données lexicales du français contemporain sur internet: LEXIQUE. *L'Année Psychologique* 101. 447–462.

Nicoladis, Elena & Howard Grabois. 2002. Learning English and losing Chinese: A case study of a child adopted from China. *International Journal of Bilingualism* 8(4). 441–454.

Noble, Kimberly, Michael Wolmetz, Lisa Ochs, Martha Farah & Bruce McCandliss. 2006. Brain-behavior relationships in reading acquisition are modulated by socioeconomic factors. *Developmental Science* 9(6). 642–654. doi:10.1111/j.1467-7687.2006.00542.x.

Noonan, Michael. 2003. Motion events in Chantyal. In Erin Shay & Uwe Seibert (eds.), *Motion, direction and location in languages*, 211–234 (Typological Studies in Language 56). Amsterdam: John Benjamins.

Oakley, Todd. 2007. Image schemas. In Dirk Geeraerts & Hubert Cuyckens (eds.), *The Oxford handbook of cognitive linguistics*, 214–235. Oxford: Oxford University Press.

Ochsenbauer, Anne-Katharina & Helen Engemann. 2011. The impact of typological factors in monolingual and bilingual first language acquisition: Caused motion expressions in English and French. *Language, Interaction and Acquisition / Langage, Interaction et Acquisition* 2(1). 101–128.

Ochsenbauer, Anne-Katharina & Maya Hickmann. 2010. Children's verbalizations of motion events in German. *Cognitive Linguistics* 21(2). 217–238.

O'Connell, Daniel & Sabine Kowal. 2005. Uh and um revisited: Are they interjections for signaling delay? *Journal of Psycholinguistic Research* 34(6). 555–576. doi:10.1007/s10936-005-9164-3.

Odlin, Terence. 1989. *Language transfer: Cross-linguistic influence in language learning*. Cambridge, UK: Cambridge University Press.

Odlin, Terence. 2011. Cross-linguistic influence. In Catherine Doughty & Michael Long (eds.), *The handbook of second language acquisition*, 436–486 (Blackwell Handbooks in Linguistics 14). Malden, MA: Blackwell.

Oller, David & Rebecca Eilers. 2002. *Language and literacy in bilingual children*. Clevedon, UK: Multilingual Matters.

Özçalışkan, Şeyda. 2013. Ways of crossing a spatial boundary in typologically distinct languages. *Applied Psycholinguistics* 36(2). 1–24. doi:10.1017/S0142716413000325.

Özçalışkan, Şeyda & Dan Slobin. 1999. Learning how to search for the frog: Expression of manner of motion in English, Spanish, and Turkish. In Annabel Greenhill, Heather Littlefield & Cheryl Tano (eds.), *Proceedings of the 23rd Annual Boston University Conference on Language Development*, 541–552. Somerville, MA: Cascadilla Press.

Özçalışkan, Şeyda & Dan Slobin. 2000a. Climb up vs. ascend climbing: Lexicalization choices in expressing motion events with manner and path components. In Catherine Howell, Sarah Fish & Thea Keith-Lucas (eds.), *Proceedings of the 24th Annual Boston University Conference on Language Development.*, 558–570. Somerville, Mass.: Cascadilla Press.

Özçalışkan, Şeyda & Dan Slobin. 2000b. Expression of manner of movement of monolingual and bilingual adult narratives: Turkish vs. English. In Aslı Göksel & Celia Kerslake (eds.), *Studies on Turkish and Turkic languages: Proceedings of the ninth International Conference on Turkish Linguistics, Lincoln College, Oxford, August 12–14, 1998*, 253–262. Wiesbaden: Harrassowitz.

Özyürek, Aslı & Sotaro Kita. 1999. Expressing manner and path in English and Turkish: Differences in speech, gesture, and conceptualization. In Martin Hahn & Scott Stoness (eds.), *Proceedings of the twenty-first Annual Conference of the Cognitive Science Society*, 507–512. Mahwah, NJ: Lawrence Erlbaum.

Özyürek, Aslı, Sotaro Kita, Shanley Allen, Reyhan Furman & Amanda Brown. 2005. How does linguistic framing of events influence co-speech gestures? Insights from crosslinguistic variations and similarities. *Gesture* 5(1). 219–240. doi:10.1075/gest.5.1.15ozy.

Pallier, Christophe, Stanislas Dehaene, Jean-Baptiste Poline, Denis LeBihan, Anne-Marie Argenti, Emmanuel Dupoux & Jacques Mehler. 2003. Brain imaging of language plasticity in adopted adults: Can a second language replace the first? *Cerebral Cortex* 13(2). 155–161. doi:10.1093/cercor/13.2.155.

Papafragou, Anna, Justin Hulbert & John Trueswell. 2008. Does language guide event perception? Evidence from eye movements. *Cognition* 108(1). 155–184. doi:10.1016/j.cognition.2008.02.007.

Papafragou, Anna, Christine Massey & Lila Gleitman. 2002. Shake, rattle, 'n' roll: the representation of motion in language and cognition. *Cognition* 84(2). 189–219. doi:10.1016/S0010-0277(02)00046-X.

Paradis, Johanne. 2007. Second language acquisition in childhood. In Erika Hoff & Marilyn Shatz (eds.), *Blackwell handbook of language development*, 387–405. Malden, MA: Blackwell.

Pavlenko, Aneta. 2000. L2 Influence on L1 in late bilingualism. *Issues in Applied Linguistics* 11(2). 175–205.

Pavlenko, Aneta. 2004. L2 influence and L1 attrition in adult bilingualism. In Monika Schmid, Barbara Köpke, Merel Keijzer & Lina Weilemar (eds.), *First language attrition: Interdisciplinary perspectives on methodological issues*, 47–59 (Studies in Bilingualism 28). Amsterdam: John Benjamins.

Pavlenko, Aneta. 2010. Verbs of motion in L1 Russian of Russian–English bilinguals. *Bilingualism: Language and Cognition* 13(1). 49–62. doi:10.1017/S1366728909990198.

Pavlenko, Aneta. 2014. *The bilingual mind: And what it tells us about language and thought*. Cambridge, UK: Cambridge University Press.

Pavlenko, Aneta & Scott Jarvis. 2002. Bidirectional transfer. *Applied Linguistics* 23(2). 190–214. doi:10.1093/applin/23.2.190.

Pearson, Barbara. 2009. Children with two languages. In Edith Bavin (ed.), *Cambridge handbook of child language*, 379–398. Cambridge, UK: Cambridge University Press.

Pelc, Linda. 2001. *L1 lexical, morphological and morphosyntactic attrition in Greek-English bilinguals*. New York: City University of New York (Unpublished doctoral dissertation).

Pfaff, Carol. 1991. Turkish in contact with German: Language maintenance and loss among immigrant children in Berlin (West). *International Journal of the Sociology of Language* 90(1). 97–130.

Pfaff, Carol. 1994. Early bilingual development of Turkish children in Berlin. In Guus Extra & Ludo Verhoeven (eds.), *The cross-linguistic study of bilingual development*, 75–97. Amsterdam: North-Holland.

Pfaff, Carol. 1999. Changing patterns of language mixing in a bilingual child. In Guus Extra & Ludo Verhoeven (eds.), *Bilingualism and migration*, 97–121. Berlin: de Gruyter Mouton.

Porquier, Rémy. 2001. "Il m'a sauté dessus", "je lui ai couru après": Un cas de postposition en français. *Journal of French Language Studies* 11(01). 123–134. doi:10.1017/S0959269501000163.

Porquier, Rémy. 2003. "Gli corro dietro" / "Je lui cours après" : À propos d'une construction verbale spécifique en italien et en français. In Mathee Giacomo-Marcellesi & Alvaro Rocchetti (eds.), *Il verbo italiano. Studi diacronici, sincronici, contrastivi, didattici*, 491–500. Roma: Bulzoni.

Pourcel, Stéphanie. 2004. *Relativism in the linguistic representation and cognitive representation of motion events across verb-framed and satellite-framed languages*. Durham, UK: University of Durham (Doctoral dissertation).

Pourcel, Stéphanie & Aneta Kopecka. 2005. Motion expression in French: Typological diversity. *Durham and Newcastle Working Papers in Linguistics* 11. 139–153.
Pulverman, Rachel, Lulu Song, Kathy Hirsh-Pasek, Shannon Pruden & Roberta Golinkoff. 2013. Preverbal infants' attention to manner and path: Foundations for learning relational terms. *Child Development* 84(1). 241–252. doi:10.1111/cdev.12030.
Queen, Robin. 2001. Bilingual intonation patterns: Evidence of language change from Turkish-German bilingual children. *Language in Society* 30(1). 55–80. doi:10.1017/S0047404501001038.
Queen, Robin. 2006. Phrase-final intonation in narratives told by Turkish-German bilinguals. *International Journal of Bilingualism* 10(2). 153–178. doi:10.1177/13670069060100020301.
R Core Team. 2013. *R: A language and environment for statistical computing*. Vienna, Austria: R Foundation for Statistical Computing. http://www.R-project.org/.
Rehbein, Jochen, Wilhelm Griesshaber, Petra Löning, Monika Hartung & Kristin Bührig. 1993. *Manual für das computergestützte Transkribieren mit dem Programm syncWRITER nach dem Verfahren der Halbinterpretativen Arbeitstranskriptionen (HIAT)*. Hamburg: University of Hamburg, Germanisches Seminar.
Rehbein, Jochen, Annette Herkenrath & Birsel Karakoç. 2009. Turkish in Germany - On contact-induced language change of an immigrant language in the multilingual landscape of Europe. *Language Typology and Universals* 62(3). 171–204. doi:10.1524/stuf.2009.0011.
Rehbein, Jochen & Birsel Karakoç. 2004. On contact-induced language change of Turkish aspects: Languaging in bilingual discourse. In Jens Normann Jørgensen & Christine Dabelsteen (eds.), *Languaging and language practices*, vol. 36, 125–149 (Copenhagen Studies in Bilingualism). Copenhagen: University of Copenhagen, Faculty of the Humanities.
Rehbein, Jochen, Thomas Schmidt, Bernd Meyer, Franziska Watzke & Annette Herkenrath. 2004. Handbuch für das computergestützte Transkribieren nach HIAT (Arbeiten Zur Mehrsprachigkeit B 561).
Reich, Hans. 2009a. Entwicklungswege türkisch-deutscher Zweisprachigkeit. In Ursula Neumann & Hans Reich (eds.), *Erwerb des Türkischen in einsprachigen und mehrsprachigen Situationen*, 63–91 (FörMig-Edition 6). Münster: Waxmann.
Reich, Hans. 2009b. *Zweisprachige Kinder: Sprachenaneignung und sprachliche Fortschritte im Kindergartenalter*. Münster: Waxmann.
Reshöft, Nina. 2011. Converging evidence in the typology of motion events: A corpus-based approach to interlanguage. In Doris Schönefeld (ed.), *Converging evidence. Methodological and theoretical issues for linguistic research*, 293–316 (Human Cognitive Processing 33). Amsterdam: John Benjamins.
Riehl, Claudia. 2013. Multilingual discourse competence in minority children: Exploring the factors of transfer and variation. *European Journal of Applied Linguistics* 1(2). 254–292. doi:10.1515/eujal-2013-0012.
Riehl, Claudia. 2014. *Sprachkontaktforschung*. Tübingen: Narr.
Riehl, Claudia. 2015. Language attrition, language contact and the concept of relic variety: The case of Barossa German. *International Journal of the Sociology of Language* 236. 261–293. doi:10.1515/ijsl-2015-0028.
Romaine, Suzanne. 1995. *Bilingualism*. Oxford: Blackwell.
Rothweiler, Monika. 2006. The acquisition of V2 and subordinate clauses in early successive acquisition of German. In Conxita Lleó (ed.), *Interfaces in multilingualism: Acquisition and representation*, 91–113. Amsterdam: John Benjamins.

Ruberg, Tobias. 2013. Problembereiche im kindlichen Zweitspracherwerb. *Sprache Stimme Gehör* 37(4). 181–185. doi:10.1055/s-0033-1358698.

Schaufeli, Anneli. 1994. First language text cohesion in a Turkish-Dutch bilingual setting. In Guus Extra & Ludo Verhoeven (eds.), *The cross-linguistic study of bilingual development*, 199–218. Amsterdam: North-Holland.

Schmid, Monika. 2002. *First language attrition, use and maintenance: The case of German Jews in anglophone countries* (Studies in Bilingualism 24). Amsterdam: John Benjamins. http://www.jbe-platform.com/content/books/9789027296870.

Schmid, Monika. 2007. The role of L1 use for L1 attrition. In Barbara Köpke, Monika Schmid, Merel Keijzer & Susan Dostert (eds.), *Language attrition theoretical perspectives*, 135–153 (Studies in Bilingualism 33). Amsterdam: John Benjamins.

Schmid, Monika. 2011. *Language attrition*. Cambridge, UK: Cambridge University Press.

Schmid, Monika, Barbara Köpke, Merel Keijzer & Lina Weilemar (eds.), 2004. *First language attrition: Interdisciplinary perspectives on methodological issues* (Studies in Bilingualism 28). Amsterdam: John Benjamins.

Schmidt, Thomas & Kai Wörner. 2009. EXMARaLDA – Creating, analysing and sharing spoken language corpora for pragmatic research. *Pragmatics* 19. 565–582.

Schönenberger, Manuela, Monika Rothweiler & Franziska Sterner. 2012. Case marking in child L1 and early child L2 German. In Kurt Braunmüller & Christoph Gabriel (eds.), *Multilingual individuals and multilingual societies*, 3–22 (Hamburg Studies on Multilingualism 13). Amsterdam: John Benjamins. https://benjamins.com/catalog/hsm.13.03sch.

Schroeder, Christoph. 2001. Markierungsvariation von Dativ und Null bei nicht-deiktischen Lokalangaben im Türkischen: Eine exemplarische Fallstudie. In Winfried Boeder & Gerd Hentschel (eds.), *Variierende Markierung von Nominalgruppen in Sprachen unterschiedlichen Typs*, 325–344. Oldenburg: BIS Verlag.

Schroeder, Christoph. 2004. *Depiktive im Sprachvergleich Deutsch-Türkisch. Eine kontrastivtypologische Analyse*. Osnabrück: University of Osnabrück (Unpublished habilitation).

Schroeder, Christoph. 2008. Adverbial modification and secondary predicates in Turkish: A typological perspective. In Christoph Schroeder, Gerd Hentschel & Winfried Boeder (eds.), *Secondary predicates in Eastern European languages and beyond*, 339–358. BIS Verlag.

Schroeder, Christoph. 2009. Gehen, laufen, torkeln: Eine typologisch gegründete Hypothese für den Schriftspracherwerb in der Zweitsprache Deutsch mit Erstsprache Türkisch. In Karen Schramm & Christoph Schroeder (eds.), *Empirische Zugänge zu Sprachförderung und Spracherwerb in Deutsch als Zweitsprache*, 185–201. Münster: Waxmann.

Schroeder, Christoph & Yazgül Şimşek. 2010. Die Entwicklung der Kategorie Wort im Türkisch-Deutsch bilingualen Schrifterwerb in Deutschland. *IMIS-Beiträge* 37. 55–79.

Schulze, Wolfgang. 2015. The emergence of diathesis markers from MOTION concepts. In Javier Díaz-Vera (ed.), *Metaphor and metonymy across time and cultures*, 171–223. Berlin: de Gruyter Mouton.

Selinker, Larry. 1972. Interlanguage. *International Review of Applied Linguistics in Language Teaching* 10(3). 209–231.

Selting, Margret, Peter Auer, Dagmar Barth-Weingarten, Jörg Bergmann, Pia Bergmann, Karin Birkner, Elizabeth Couper-Kuhlen, et al. 2009. Gesprächsanalytisches Transkriptionssystem 2 (GAT 2). *Gesprächsforschung - Online-Zeitschrift zur verbalen Interaktion* 10. 353–402.

Shiffler, Ronald. 1988. Maximum z scores and outliers. *The American Statistician* 42(1). 79–80.

Şimşek, Yazgül & Christoph Schroeder. 2011. Migration und Sprache in Deutschland - am Beispiel der Migranten aus der Türkei und ihrer Kinder und Kindeskinder. In Şeyda Ozil,

Michael Hofmann & Yasemin Dayıoğlu-Yücel (eds.), *50 Jahre türkische Arbeitsmigration in Deutschland*, 205–228 (Türkisch-Deutsche Studien 2011). Göttingen: V&R unipress.
Sincich, Terry. 1986. *Business statistics by example*. San Francisco: Dellen.
Slobin, Dan. 1991. Learning to think for speaking: Native language, cognition, and rhetorical style. *Pragmatics* 1(1). 7–25.
Slobin, Dan. 1993. Adult language acquisition: A view from child language study. In Clive Perdue (ed.), *Adult language acquisition: Cross-linguistic perspectives*, vol. 2, 239–252. Cambridge, UK: Cambridge University Press.
Slobin, Dan. 1995. Converbs in Turkish child language: The grammaticalization of event coherence. In Martin Haspelmath & Ekkehard König (eds.), *Converbs in cross-linguistic perspective: Structure and meaning of adverbial verb forms - adverbial participles, gerunds* (Empirical Approaches to Language Typology 13). Berlin: de Gruyter Mouton.
Slobin, Dan. 1996a. From "thought and language" to "thinking for speaking." In John Gumperz & Stephen Levinson (eds.), *Rethinking linguistic relativity*, 70–96 (Studies in the Social and Cultural Foundations of Language 17). Cambridge, UK: Cambridge University Press.
Slobin, Dan. 1996b. Two ways to travel: Verbs of Motion in English and Spanish. In Masayoshi Shibatani & Sandra Thompson (eds.), *Grammatical constructions*, 195–219. Oxford: Clarendon Press.
Slobin, Dan. 1997. Mind, code, and text. In Talmy Givón, Joan Bybee, John Haiman & Sandra Thompson (eds.), *Essays on language function and language type dedicated to T. Givón*, 437–467. Amsterdam: John Benjamins.
Slobin, Dan. 2000. Verbalized events: A dynamic approach to linguistic relativity and determinism. In Susanne Niemeier & René Dirven (eds.), *Evidence for linguistic relativity*, 107–138. Amsterdam: John Benjamins.
Slobin, Dan. 2003. Language and thought online: Cognitive consequences of linguistic relativity. In Dedre Gentner & Susan Goldin-Meadow (eds.), *Language in mind: Advances in the study of language and thought*, 157–191. Cambridge, MA: MIT Press.
Slobin, Dan. 2004a. How people move: Discourse effects of linguistic typology. In Carol Moder & Aida Martinovic-Zic (eds.), *Discourse across languages and cultures*, 195– 210 (Studies in Language Companion Series 68). Amsterdam: John Benjamins.
Slobin, Dan. 2004b. The many ways to search for a frog: Linguistic typology and the expression of motion events. In Sven Strömqvist & Ludo Verhoeven (eds.), *Relating events in narrative: Typological and contextual perspectives*, vol. 2, 219–257. Mahwah, NJ: Lawrence Erlbaum.
Slobin, Dan. 2006. What makes manner of motion salient? Explorations in linguistic typology, discourse, and cognition. In Maya Hickmann & Stéphane Robert (eds.), *Space in languages: Linguistic systems and cognitive categories*, 59–81 (Typological Studies in Language 66). Amsterdam: John Benjamins.
Slobin, Dan & Nini Hoiting. 1994. Reference to movement in spoken and signed languages: Typological considerations. In Susanne Gahl, Christopher Johnson & Andy Dolby (eds.), *Proceedings of the twentieth annual meeting of the Berkeley Linguistics Society: February 18–21, 1994. General session dedicated to the contributions of Charles J. Fillmore*, 487–504. Berkeley, CA: Berkeley Linguistics Society.
Song, Lulu, Elizabeth Spier & Catherine Tamis-Lemonda. 2014. Reciprocal influences between maternal language and children's language and cognitive development in low-income families. *Journal of Child Language* 41(2). 305–326. doi:10.1017/S0305000912000700.
Soroli, Efstathia & Maya Hickmann. 2010. Language and spatial representations in French and in English: Evidence from eye-movements. In Giovanna Marotta, Alessandro Lenzi, Linda

Meini & Francesco Rovai (eds.), *Space in language: Proceedings of the Pisa International Conference*, 581–597. Pisa: Edizioni ETS.

Stam, Gale. 2006. Thinking for speaking about motion: L1 and L2 speech and gesture. *International Review of Applied Linguistics in Language Teaching* 44(2). 145–171. doi:10.1515/IRAL.2006.006.

Statistisches Bundesamt. 2015. *Bevölkerung und Erwerbstätigkeit. Bevölkerung mit Migrationshintergrund – Ergebnisse des Mikrozensus 2012* (Fachserie 1 2.2). Wiesbaden: Statistisches Bundesamt

Stutterheim, Christiane von, Martin Andermann, Mary Carroll, Monique Flecken & Barbara Schmiedtová. 2012. How grammaticized concepts shape event conceptualization in language production: Insights from linguistic analysis, eye tracking data, and memory performance. *Linguistics* 50(4). 833–867. doi:10.1515/ling-2012-0026.

Stutterheim, Christiane von & Ralf Nüse. 2003. Processes of conceptualization in language production: language-specific perspectives and event construal. *Linguistics* 41(5). 851–881.

Talmy, Leonard. 1985. Lexicalization patterns: Semantic structure in lexical forms. In Timothy Shopen (ed.), *Language typology and syntactic description: Grammatical categories and the lexicon.*, 57–149. Cambridge, UK: Cambridge University Press.

Talmy, Leonard. 2003. *Toward a cognitive semantics: Typology and process in concept structuring*. Cambridge, MA: MIT Press.

Talmy, Leonard. 2008. Lexical typology. In Timothy Shopen (ed.), *Language typology and syntactic description: Grammatical categories and the lexicon*, 66–168. Cambridge, UK: Cambridge University Press.

Talmy, Leonard. 2009. Main verb properties and equipollent framing. In Jiansheng Guo, Elena Lieven, Nancy Budwig, Susan Ervin-Tripp, Keiko Nakamura & Şeyda Özçalışkan (eds.), *Crosslinguistic approaches to the psychology of language: Research in the tradition of Dan Isaac Slobin*, 389–402. New York: Taylor & Francis.

Tesnière, Lucien. 1959. *Éléments de syntaxe structurale*. Paris: Klincksieck.

Thoma, Dieter & Rosemarie Tracy. 2006. Deutsch als frühe Zweitsprache: Zweite Erstsprache? In Bernt Ahrenholz (ed.), *Kinder mit Migrationshintergrund. Spracherwerb und Fördermöglichkeiten.*, 58–79. Freiburg im Breisgau: Fillibach.

Thomason, Sarah. 2001. *Language contact*. Edinburgh: Edinburgh University Press.

Thordardottir, Elin. 2011. The relationship between bilingual exposure and vocabulary development. *International Journal of Bilingualism* 15(4). 426–445. doi:10.1177/1367006911403202.

Thordardottir, Elin. 2014. The typical development of simultaneous bilinguals: Vocabulary, morphosyntax and language processing in two age groups of Montreal preschoolers. In Theres Grüter & Johanne Paradis (eds.), *Input and experience in bilingual development*, 141–160 (Trends in Language Acquisition Research 13). Amsterdam: John Benjamins.

Tracy, Rosemarie & Vytautas Lemke. 2012. Young L2 and L1 learners: More alike than different. In Marzena Watorek, Sandra Benazzo & Maya Hickmann (eds.), *Comparative perspectives on language acquisition: A tribute to Clive Perdue*, 303–323 (Second Language Acquisition 61). Bristol, UK: Multilingual Matters.

Treffers-Daller, Jeanine & Tomasz Korybski. 2016. Using lexical diversity measures to operationalize language dominance in bilinguals. In Carmen Silva-Corvalan & Jeanine Treffers-Daller (eds.), *Language dominance in bilinguals: Issues of measurement and operationalization*, 106–133. Cambridge, UK: Cambridge University Press.

Treffers-Daller, Jeanine & Jeanette Sakel. 2012. Why transfer is a key aspect of language use and processing in bilinguals and L2-users. *International Journal of Bilingualism* 16(1). 3–10. doi:10.1177/1367006911403206.
Tribalat, Michèle. 1998. Populations originaires de Turquie en France. In Laurent Gervereau, Pierre Milza & Emile Temime (eds.), *Toute la France. Histoire de l'immigration en France au XXème siècle*. 161–163, Paris: Somogy.
Tschander, Ladina. 1999. Bewegung und Bewegungsverben. In Ipke Wachsmuth & Bernhard Jung (eds.), *KogWis99: Proceedings der 4. Fachtagung der Gesellschaft für Kognitionswissenschaft, Bielefeld, 28. September-1. Oktober 1999*, 25–30. Sankt Augustin: Infix.
Tunç, Seda. 2012. *Der Einfluss der Erstsprache auf den Erwerb der Zweitsprache: Eine empirische Untersuchung zum Einfluss erstsprachlicher Strukturen bei zweisprachig türkisch-deutschen, kroatisch-deutschen und griechisch-deutschen Hauptschülern und Gymnasiasten*. Münster: Waxmann.
Tyler, Andrea. 2012. *Cognitive linguistics and second language Learning: Theoretical basics and experimental evidence*. New York: Routledge.
Vandeloise, Claude. 1991. *Spatial prepositions: A case study from French*. Chicago: University of Chicago Press.
Verspoor, Marjolyn, Kees de Bot & Wander Lowie (eds.), 2011. *A dynamic approach to second language development: Methods and techniques* (Language Learning & Language Teaching 29). Amsterdam: John Benjamins.
Volynsky, Maria. 2012. *Encoding of motion events in the two languages of Russian-English bilinguals*. Pennsylvania: Temple University (Doctoral dissertation).
Wälchli, Bernhard. 2001. A typology of displacement (with special reference to Latvian). *Language Typology and Universals* 54(3). 298–323. doi:10.1524/stuf.2001.54.3.298.
Wälchli, Bernhard. 2009. *Motion Events in Parallel Texts* (Unpublished Habilitation). Bern: University of Bern.
Wälchli, Bernhard & Fernando Zúñiga. 2006. Source-Goal (in)difference and the typology of motion events in the clause. *Language Typology and Universals* 59(3). 284–303. doi:10.1524/stuf.2006.59.3.284.
Wandruszka, Mario. 1979. *Die Mehrsprachigkeit des Menschen*. München: Piper.
Weber, Gerhard. 1983. *Untersuchungen zur mentalen Repräsentation von Bewegungsverben: Merkmale, Dimensionen und Vorstellungsbilder*. Braunschweig: University of Braunschweig (Unpublished doctoral dissertation).
Weinert, Sabine, Susanne Ebert & Minja Dubowy. 2010. Kompetenzen und soziale Disparitäten im Vorschulalter. *Zeitschrift für Grundschulforschung* 3. 32–45.
Weinreich, Uriel. 1953. *Languages in contact. Findings and problems*. New York: Linguistic Circle of New York.
Wiese, Heike. 2009. Grammatical innovation in multiethnic urban Europe: New linguistic practices among adolescents. *Lingua* 119(5). 782–806. doi:10.1016/j.lingua.2008.11.002.
Wiese, Heike. 2012. *Kiezdeutsch ein neuer Dialekt entsteht*. München: Beck.
Woerfel, Till. 2014. Früher Zweitspracherwerb und Herkunftssprachenunterricht in Bayern: Fluch oder Segen? *Bavarian Working Papers in Linguistics* 3. 135–152.
Woerfel, Till & Seda Yılmaz. 2011. Lexical development of German-Turkish bilinguals: A comparative study in written discourse. In Chris Cummins, Chi-Hé Elder, Thomas Godard, Morgan Macleod, Elaine Schmidt & George Walkden (eds.), *Proceedings of the sixth Cambridge Postgraduate Conference in Language Research*, 240–251. Cambridge, UK: Cambridge Institute of Language Research.

Yağmur, Kutlay. 2004. Language maintenance patterns of Turkish immigrant communities in Australia and western Europe: The impact of majority attitudes on ethnolinguistic vitality perceptions. *International Journal of the Sociology of Language* 165. 121–142. doi:10.1515/ijsl.2004.001.

Yağmur, Kutlay. 2011. Does ethnolinguistic vitality theory account for the actual vitality of ethnic groups? A critical evaluation. *Journal of Multilingual and Multicultural Development* 32(2). 111–120. doi:10.1080/01434632.2010.541914.

Yağmur, Kutlay & Mehmet-Ali Akıncı. 2003. Language use, choice, maintenance, and ethnolinguistic vitality of Turkish speakers in France: Intergenerational differences. *International Journal of the Sociology of Language* 164. 107–128. doi:10.1515/ijsl.2003.050.

Younger, Mary. 1979. *Handbook for linear regression*. North Scituate, MA: Duxbury Press.

Zlatev, Jordan, Johan Blomberg & Caroline David. 2010. Translocation: Language and the categorization of experience. In Vyvyan Evans & Paul Chilton (eds.), *Language, cognition and space: The state of the art and new directions*, 389–418. London: Equinox.

Index

Adnominal encoding 60, 61, 73, 75, 97, 111, 220, 312
Adverbal encoding 60, 71, 97, 98, 99, 220
Age of onset (AoO) 10, 11, 14, 15, 34, 35, 106, 120, 125
AoO. *See* Age of onset (AoO)
Attrition. *See* Language attrition
Avoidance 3, 28, 29, 36, 37, 104, 107, 110, 112, 122, 175, 180, 191, 227, 252, 265, 271, 282, 301, 302, 305, 311, 312

Bidirectional influence 15, 23–29, 40, 112, 176, 207, 233, 296, 297, 305, 306
Bilingualism
– age of onset of 15, 34
– balanced 11, 24
– child 10–41, 95, 111, 120, 207
– minimal vs. maximal 22
Borrowing 25, 26, 28, 29, 161
Boundary crossing constraint 83, 85, 87, 88, 98, 106, 108, 176, 191, 273, 274, 277, 279, 285, 287, 290, 291, 292, 302, 303
Bounded space 46, 71, 82, 84, 85, 87, 181, 183, 186, 188, 189, 190, 191, 264, 265, 271, 272, 275, 276, 277, 288, 289, 303, 312

Co-event 47, 48, 53, 55, 56, 91
Code-mixing 114, 128, 130–131, 144, 153, 159–165, 167, 169, 173, 174
Code-switching 38, 39
Cognition 9, 23, 42–100, 310, 317, 318
Cognitive capacity 101, 238
Conceptual knowledge 43, 95
Conceptualisation of a motion event. *See* Motion event conceptualisation
Conflation pattern. *See* Lexicalisation patterns
Construction Grammar 27, 50
Convergence 25, 27, 28, 29, 37, 107, 108, 114, 252, 294, 301, 305, 309
Corpus analysis 61, 65, 67, 70, 79, 98, 181, 186, 189, 211, 215, 216, 218, 276, 290, 292

Correlation 142, 168–170, 173, 200, 202, 206, 232, 234, 246, 250, 261, 262, 268, 269, 282
– negative 142, 169, 200, 202, 206, 261, 282
– Pearson's 142, 200, 202, 206, 232, 234, 246, 261, 262, 268, 269, 282
– positive 142, 169, 206, 232, 234, 246, 261
– Spearman's 142, 168, 169
Cross-linguistic influence 8, 9, 21, 23, 25, 28, 29, 36, 37, 94, 95, 100, 107, 114–116, 175, 177, 178, 192, 202, 203, 206, 207, 232, 233, 235, 237, 238, 246, 250, 261–263, 269, 282, 294–297, 301, 304–306, 308, 312

Diaspora 8, 30, 31, 33, 35, 108, 143, 174, 308
Domain and dimension 16, 111–114, 116, 144, 167, 168–173, 175, 177, 204, 209, 223, 236, 247, 251, 252, 264, 270–272, 284, 285, 291, 292, 295, 296, 305–309, 314
Dominance shift 11, 14–16, 21, 33, 35, 113, 143, 144, 167, 170, 172, 174, 308

Education 1, 8, 16–20, 31–34, 40, 112, 121–122, 125, 137, 138, 196–198, 200–202, 208, 209, 310
– educational background 16, 18, 19, 20, 34, 112, 121–122, 126, 137, 196–198, 201, 202, 208, 209
– educational disadvantage 16, 34
– educational level 17, 40, 121, 137
Encoding of motion events. *See* Motion encoding
Ethno-linguistic vitality 32, 35
Exposure 17, 18, 19, 22, 36, 39, 106, 111, 117, 121, 316

Hesitation 13, 127, 129, 130, 314

Immigration background 1, 30, 34
Input 6, 16–21, 35, 37, 38, 45, 96, 102, 106, 125, 128, 173, 174, 200, 316
International Standard Classification of Education (ISCED-2011) 137, 138

Intra-typological difference 103, 109, 110, 176, 192, 218, 237, 299, 302, 303, 309, 310
Intra-typological variation 8, 59, 111, 238, 304, 307, 312–314
ISCED. *See* International Standard Classification of Education (ISCED-2011)

L1-instruction 33, 118, 121, 174
Language
– knowledge 6, 8, 9, 15, 18, 19, 20, 23, 45, 113, 143, 167, 172, 173, 174, 175, 308, 309, 314, 317
– maintenance 1, 32, 33, 143, 307, 308
– shift 1, 27–28, 34–36
– skills 6, 8, 9, 11, 16, 18, 20, 40, 95, 113, 143, 167, 169, 172, 173, 175, 308, 310, 314
Language attrition 1, 11, 14–16, 21, 25, 26, 28, 29, 34–37, 316
Lexical development 36, 38, 103, 174, 197, 198, 200
Lexical repertoire 13, 16, 152, 153–159, 173, 174, 178, 197, 198, 200, 202, 209, 218, 219, 293, 300, 314
Lexicalisation patterns 42, 55–62, 90, 91, 97, 100, 110, 121, 131, 192, 193, 207, 219, 237, 313, 318

Majority language 1, 10, 15, 18, 31, 32, 35, 117, 143
Minority language 1, 8, 10, 18, 31, 40
Mother tongue education. *See* L1-instruction
Mother tongue instruction. *See* L1-instruction
Motion construction 50–53, 64, 107, 110, 131–133, 179, 185, 186, 188, 189, 190, 195, 200, 205–207, 213, 214, 229, 230, 237, 244, 247, 250, 258, 265, 267, 282, 283, 305
Motion encoding 5, 7, 8, 9, 41, 73, 81, 97, 101, 111, 115, 116, 122, 143–306, 309–313, 315–318
Motion event conceptualisation 26, 45, 47–48, 67, 92, 95, 131, 309
Motion event situation 43–46, 48, 53, 90, 123, 124, 135

Motion image 44–46, 53, 79, 83, 93, 100, 102, 104, 105, 191, 276, 304
Multicompetence 6, 10–41, 91, 95, 96, 100, 111, 176, 294, 308

Paratactic organisation 107, 302–304
Perception 28, 32, 43, 44, 94, 318
Proficiency 5, 11, 13, 14, 15, 16, 20, 23, 24, 32, 36, 45
Reading activities 138, 144, 146, 168, 169, 172, 173

Restructuring 25, 26–29, 95, 110, 204, 299, 303, 309, 310

S-language. *See* Satellite-framed language (S-language)
Salience
– manner 59, 276, 313
– path 9, 55, 59–61, 220, 313
Satellite-framed language (S-language) 5, 56, 57, 59–63, 71, 75–77, 79, 81, 85, 86, 91–94, 98, 99, 106, 109, 110, 111, 116, 192, 237, 272, 304, 309, 311, 317
Satellites 5, 7, 8, 33, 55–56, 58–59, 69–70, 74, 76, 77, 79–81, 83, 86, 87, 91–92, 97, 101, 106–108, 239, 276, 282, 307, 312
Second language acquisition 1–11, 14, 18, 20, 21, 23, 37, 40, 105, 106, 115, 200, 307–311, 315–316
SES. *See* Socio-economic status (SES)
Socio-economic status (SES) 16–21, 34, 196, 208
Spatial boundary 81, 83, 84, 191, 261, 274, 277, 293
Strategies
– alternative 28, 29, 36, 292, 303, 312
– encoding 7, 99, 116, 123, 190, 220, 222, 225, 227, 261, 264, 269, 285, 304
Subordinate clause(s) 26, 53, 85, 88, 89, 105, 131–133, 238, 245, 249, 252
Syntax
– syntactic construction 39, 104, 241, 245, 249

– syntactic mapping 48, 49, 50
– syntactic organisation 5, 61, 75–81, 97, 104

T-test 140, 141, 142, 153, 154, 156, 157, 195, 199, 205
Thinking for speaking 6, 9, 92, 94, 95, 111
Transfer
– conceptual 95–96, 100, 109, 111, 112, 176, 193, 200, 272, 281, 293, 298, 299, 300, 301, 309
– conceptualisation 9, 95, 96
– lexical 26
Turkish minority 1, 29–32, 34, 35, 117, 118, 307
Typological difference 5, 23, 103, 109, 110, 176, 192, 218, 220, 237, 299, 301, 302, 303, 309, 310
Typology 4, 7, 9, 39, 40, 54, 56, 57, 59, 60, 80, 91, 99, 225, 312, 318

Usage-based 20, 61, 80, 99, 111, 114, 313

Usage preferences 5, 9, 80, 139, 178, 195, 202, 232, 235, 241, 246, 250, 256, 262, 269, 278, 282, 290, 301, 304, 310, 315, 316

V-language. *See* Verb-framed language (V-language)
Verbal fluency 13, 15, 37, 114, 129, 144, 150–152, 158, 165, 167, 169, 173, 295, 314
Verb-framed language (V-language) 7, 8, 56, 58–62, 65, 75–78, 80–83, 86, 87, 91–94, 97–99, 104, 106, 109, 110, 111, 114, 116, 190, 191, 219, 227, 228, 272–276, 287–289, 304, 309, 311, 312, 317, 318
Verbal slot 178, 225, 226

Wilcoxon rank sum test. *See* Wilcoxon test
Wilcoxon Sign Rank Test. *See* Wilcoxon test
Wilcoxon test 141, 142, 158, 199
Working memory 44, 45, 95, 96, 101

www.ingramcontent.com/pod-product-compliance
Lightning Source LLC
Chambersburg PA
CBHW031413230426
43668CB00007B/293